A treatise on Christian Banking

A treatise on Christian Banking

Morten Bøsterud

WIPF & STOCK · Eugene, Oregon

A TREATISE ON CHRISTIAN BANKING

Copyright © 2022 Morten Bøsterud. All rights reserved. Except for brief quotations in critical publications or reviews, no part of this book may be reproduced in any manner without prior written permission from the publisher. Write: Permissions, Wipf and Stock Publishers, 199 W. 8th Ave., Suite 3, Eugene, OR 97401.

Wipf & Stock
An Imprint of Wipf and Stock Publishers
199 W. 8th Ave., Suite 3
Eugene, OR 97401

www.wipfandstock.com

PAPERBACK ISBN: 978-1-6667-5400-1
HARDCOVER ISBN: 978-1-6667-5401-8
EBOOK ISBN: 978-1-6667-5402-5

Originally published by AOSIS Publishing, 2021

Cover image: Original design created with the use of provided image. The image is https://www.pexels.com/photo/person-holding-black-ceramic-pig-coin-bank-3943723/, released under Pexels License.

Religious Studies domain editorial board at AOSIS

Commissioning Editor
Andries G. van Aarde MA, DD, PhD, D Litt, South Africa

Board Members
Warren Carter, Professor of New Testament, Brite Divinity School, Fort Worth, United States of America
Christian Danz, Dekan der Evangelisch-Theologischen Fakultät der Universität Wien and Ordentlicher Universität professor für Systematische Theologie und Religionswissenschaft, University of Vienna, Austria
Pieter G.R. de Villiers, Associate Editor, Extraordinary Professor in Biblical Spirituality, Faculty of Theology, University of the Free State, South Africa
Musa W. Dube, Department of Theology & Religious Studies, Faculty of Humanities, University of Botswana, Botswana
David D. Grafton, Professor of Islamic Studies and Christian-Muslim Relations, Duncan Black Macdonald Center for the Study of Islam and Christian-Muslim Relations, Hartford Seminary, Hartford, Connecticut, United States of America
Jens Herzer, Theologische Fakultät der Universität Leipzig, Germany
Jeanne Hoeft, Dean of Students and Associate Professor of Pastoral Theology and Pastoral Care, Saint Paul School of Theology, United States of America
Dirk J. Human, Associate Editor, Deputy Dean and Professor of Old Testament Studies, Faculty of Theology, University of Pretoria, South Africa
D. Andrew Kille, Former Chair of the SBL Psychology and Bible Section, and Editor of the Bible Workbench, San Jose, United States of America
William R.G. Loader, Emeritus Professor Murdoch University, Perth, Western Australia
Isabel A. Phiri, Associate General Secretary for Public Witness and Diakonia, World Council of Churches, Geneva, Switzerland
Marcel Sarot, Emeritus, Professor of Fundamental Theology, Tilburg School of Catholic Theology, Tilburg University, the Netherlands
Corneliu C. Simut, Professor of Historical and Dogmatic Theology, Emanuel University, Oradea, Bihor, Romania
Rothney S. Tshaka, Professor and Head of Department of Philosophy, Practical and Systematic Theology, University of South Africa, Pretoria, South Africa
Elaine M. Wainwright, Emeritus Professor School of Theology, University of Auckland, New Zealand; Executive Leader, Mission and Ministry, McAuley Centre, Australia
Gerald West, Associate Editor, School of Religion, Philosophy and Classics in the College of Humanities, University of KwaZulu-Natal, South Africa

Peer review declaration

The publisher (AOSIS) endorses the South African 'National Scholarly Book Publishers Forum Best Practice for Peer Review of Scholarly Books'. The manuscript was subjected to rigorous two-step peer review prior to publication, with the identities of the reviewers not revealed to the author(s). The reviewers were independent of the publisher and/or authors in question. The reviewers commented positively on the scholarly merits of the manuscript and recommended that the manuscript be published. Where the reviewers recommended revision and/or improvements to the manuscript, the authors responded adequately to such recommendations.

Research Justification

The main thesis of this book is: As all banking practice and theory can be seen as value driven, there will be no such thing as value neutral banking activities, and thus, the application of Christian ethical and pastoral principles adds insights to the field of banking for all its participating stakeholders.

Practical theology is a broad field of research, and the results presented in this book are original and have been developed over several years, all while partaking in the academic discourse particularly connected to business life in general, and banking and finance in particular. The book represents a comprehensive elaboration of research, with attendant theories that are generated as a result of this book project, and which will be found to be original by the specific academic community connected to practical theology. It is challenging to outline the utility of the present theories for other academics, but the expectation is that they will be found to be of interest as they highlight an academic area of great interest and societal importance. By way of connecting practical theology directly to a field of practice (banking and finance) this study contributes to the originality of the research results prevalent in this book. The originality of this academic book is that it elaborates the connected subject matter in both the detail found here and in the broad scope as herein presented.

This book contributes to the specific scientific discourse of practical theology, as this typically appears with the subfields of ethics and pastoral studies. Christian ethics and pastoral principles as applied in banking is a largely neglected area in the wider academic discourse found within practical theology, and as the research presented in this book contributes new knowledge to the field with particular emphasis on banking practice, it is expected that the theories presented herein will be of interest for other scholars, both within the realm of practical theology and also in a cross-domain perspective where scholars in a broad field of disciplines will find the research and academic positions of interest. Such academic fields would include economics, finance, business administration, sociology, history, anthropology and perhaps more.

The methodology applied in this book is that of textual studies, and a commonly accepted mode of hermeneutics has been applied. The research for this book has not included any interaction with research subjects of any kind.

The book is based on a substantial reworking of my two PhD dissertations as written in Ethics and Pastoral Studies. There are clear overlaps between the two academic fields, but oftentimes they deal with separate aspects. In the book I rectify this difference, and put the two fields together in a comprehensive manner. Thus, by further developing and adding to them I have introduced a complete and new whole.

It is hereby declared that there is no plagiarism present in this book.

It is hereby declared that this book represents a scholarly discourse, and that it is written by a scholar and for scholars. In other words, this book will be of interest mainly for the scholarly academic community.

Morten Bøsterud, Unit for Reformational Theology and the Development of the South African Society, Faculty of Theology, North-West University, Potchefstroom, South Africa.

Contents

Abbreviations Appearing in the Text	xv
List of Abbreviations	xv
Glossary	xvii
Biographical Note	xix
Acknowledgements	xxi
Preface	xxiii

Chapter 1: Setting the stage — 1
Introduction — 1
Scope of interest — 2
   Credit, moneylending and interest — 2
   Investment management/advisory — 3
   Core problem area — 5
Theological location — 6
   Systematic terminology — 6
   Reformed paradigm — 6

Chapter 2: Economic-philosophical backdrop — 7
Introduction — 7
Scarcity paradigm – Finite resources — 8
   Antiquity — 8
   Medieval era — 11
   Renaissance – Reformation — 12
   Towards industrialism — 14
   Colonialism — 16
   Scarcity accepted — 17
Sufficiency paradigm – Unlimited potential — 18
   Industrial revolution — 18
   Marx and production — 19
   Keynes and the Cambridge School — 20
   Friedrich Hayek — 21
   Milton Friedman — 22
   Sufficiency affirmed — 23
Governmental participation — 24

Traditional government	24
Budding welfare state	25
Active state	26
Governmental investment funds	26
Current state – Globalisation	27
Post-World War II	27
Globalised economy	28
Current situation	30
Statistics	30
The political-economic discourse	30

Chapter 3: The phenomenon of money — 33

Introduction	33
Emergence of money	34
Antiquity	34
The barter myth	34
Mesopotamia	35
Homeric age	36
Greek city-states	36
The Romans	37
The medieval era	38
Modern era	40
The gold standard	42
Fiat money	43
Crypto and independent currency	44
Money as social technology	45

Chapter 4: The event of banking — 47

Introduction	47
The evolution of banking	48
Antiquity	48
Mesopotamia and Babylonia	48
Greek city-states	50
The Romans	50
The medieval era	52
Modern era	54
The 20th century and beyond	56
Modes of banking	58
Societal functions of banking	58
Borrower and lender	58

The maturity gap	59
Stakeholders and society	60
The stakeholder construct	60
The CSR movement	61
Prevailing Western model	61
Islamic/sharia banking	62
Predetermined loan repayments are prohibited	64
Profit and loss sharing	64
Unacceptable to make money from money	64
Uncertainty is forbidden	65
Sanctity of contract	65
Investment must be sharia-approved	65
The sharia board	66
Ethical banking	67
Christian banking	68
Chapter 5: Philosophical and theological schemata	**71**
Introduction	71
Terminology	72
Virtue formats	73
A broad church	73
Antiquity	74
Medieval era	75
Modern era	75
The futility of virtue ethics	76
Consequentialist extractions	76
Utilitarianism	76
Forerunners in antiquity	77
Proto-utilitarianism	77
Classical utilitarianism	78
Ideal utilitarianism	80
Act Utilitarianism	81
Rule Utilitarianism	82
The paucity of consequentialism	83
Deontological dispensations	84
Different vantage points	84
Situation ethics	85
Unqualified absolutism	86
Conflicting absolutism	87
Graded absolutism	89

Reformed position	91
Revelation	91
Constructive ethical attitude	93
The plenitude of deontology	95
Pastoral trajectories	96
Old Testament	96
God's ministry	96
Moses	98
Other leadership figures	99
The family	100
New Testament	100
Different literary strands	100
Synoptic gospels	101
John	103
Paul	103
Pastoral epistles	104
Historical development	105
A post-Christ focus	105
The early centuries	105
Medieval era	107
The reformation	109
Modern era	111
Twentieth century and onwards	113
Contemporary praxis model	114
Espoused pastoral-ethical model	116
Introduction	116
Inclusive and constructive model	117
Praxis and context oriented	117

Chapter 6: Scriptural foundations	**119**
Introduction	119
Moneylending	120
Context	120
Lending or giving – To the needy only?	120
Borrowing – A moral act?	121
Duration and security	123
Charging interest	125
Risk and stability	129
Context	129
Scriptural stance	130

Truthfulness	134
Context	134
Scriptural stance	134
Greed	136
Context	136
Scriptural stance	136
Covetousness	138
Context	138
Scriptural stance	139
Sanctity of life	140
Context	140
Imago Dei	141
Sixth commandment	143
Consequences of transgression	145
Value of life	146
Capital punishment	147
Context	147
Prescribed, allowed or prohibited?	147
War	149
Context	149
Pacifism	149
Activism	150
Selectivism – Just war	151
Acceptable moral position on war	154
Health and disease	154
Context	154
Caring for the sick	155
Abortion	157
Euthanasia	159
Biomedical challenges	161
Context	161
Manipulating life	161
Human rights	163
Context	163
The human rights construct	163
Education	164
Freedom of speech	166
Freedom of belief	167
Equal opportunities	169
Working conditions	171
Child labour	172

Senior constituency	174
Private property ownership	175
Government – Civil disobedience	179
Nature and ecology	182
Context	182
Animal welfare	182
The natural environment	185
Bioethical challenges	186
Societal morality	187
Context	187
Family	187
Pornography	189
Gambling	190
Drugs, alcohol and tobacco	192
Consumerism	193

Chapter 7: Banking praxis — 195

Introduction	195
Moneylending	196
Unacceptable practices	196
Lending	196
Borrowing and deposits	197
Duration and security	199
Acceptable practices	201
Lending	201
Borrowing and deposits	202
Duration and security	203
Charging interest	204
Unacceptable practices	204
Acceptable practices	206
Risk and stability	207
Unacceptable practises	207
Acceptable practices	211
Truthfulness	212
Unacceptable practices	212
Acceptable practices	213
Greed	214
Unacceptable practices	214
Acceptable practices	214
Covetousness	215

Unacceptable practices	215
Acceptable practices	216
Sanctity of life	217
Unacceptable practices	217
Prisons	217
Weapons production and sales	218
Medical service providers	220
Medical products	220
Biomedical science and products	221
Acceptable practices	222
Women and family	222
Promoting peace – Trade and technology	224
Medical service providers	224
Pharmaceuticals and medical equipment	225
Health-promoting assets	226
Human rights	226
Unacceptable practices	226
Unjust regimes	226
Child labour	227
Labour rights, gender and racism	228
Acceptable practices	228
Educational service providers	228
Emerging nations	229
Information technology and media	230
Technology manufacturing and distribution	231
Equal opportunities	232
Dignified work life	233
Nature and ecology	234
Unacceptable practices	234
Animal welfare	234
Pollution – Harmful products and practices	236
Bioethical considerations	237
Acceptable practices	238
Food and animals	238
Sustainable production and technology	239
Ecotourism	241
Societal morality	241
Unacceptable practices	241
Family	241
Pornography	242
Gambling	243

Drugs, alcohol and tobacco 243
Mass consumption 244
Acceptable practices 245
Family 245
Law and order 246
Retail consumer sector 246

Chapter 8: Operationalisation **249**
Introduction 249
Organisation 250
The organisational technology 250
The establishment 250
The personnel 251
Supervisory board 252
Organisational location 252
Composition 253
Tasks 254
Formulating guidelines 254
Product development 254
Partaking in training programs 255
Supervising practicing guidelines 255
Deliberating specific cases 255
Guidelines 256
Strategising 257
Balance sheet 258
Product types – Financial instruments 259
Indexing 259
Learning initiatives 260
Knowledge generation 261
Recommendation 261

References **263**
Index **287**

Abbreviations Appearing in the Text

List of Abbreviations

CDO	Collateralised Debt Obligation
CSR	Corporate Social Responsibility
DBA	Doctor of Business Administration
DPI	Disposable Personal Income
EPC	Engineering, Procurement and Construction
ESG	Environmental Social and Governance
GARP	Gender Appreciative Recruitment Practice
GDP	Gross Domestic Product
GBP	British Pound
GM	Gene Modification
IHL	International Humanitarian Law
IMF	International Monetary Fund
IOR	Istituto per le Opere di Religione
IT	Information Technology
IVF	In Vitro Fertilisation
LGBT	Lesbian, Gay, Bisexual and Transgender
LTV	Loan-to-value
MBS	Mortgage-backed Securities
NGO	Non-governmental Organisation
PBP	Pastoral Banking Practice
PPP	Public–Private Partnerships
RIP	Reoriented Investment Protocol
TBL	Triple Bottom Line
UCITS	Undertakings for Collective Investment in Transferable Securities
UNFAO	United Nations Food and Agriculture Organization
UK	United Kingdom
US	United States

Glossary

The clarification of my general use of central concepts will be included in this section. I have drawn on conventional thinking when defining the concepts for my purposes, and have used Investopedia (n.d.), Downes & Goodman (2014) and Merriam-Webster's online dictionary (n.d.) for inspiration:

- **Acceptable banking practices:** Banking practices aligned with the constructive ethical-pastoral norms of the Reformed paradigm as defined in this treatise.
- **Banking:** Payment services, origination of various banking products and financial instruments, capital management, investment advisory, financial advisory, investment banking, proprietary trading and any other activity related to the obtainment of capital for individuals, companies, governments and other entities, whether by debt or equity in any form, or any other activity performed by the banking profession.
- **Borrowing:** The act in which an individual, a public group, a private group or a financial institution receives money made available from others with the obligation to repay the money.
- **Capitalism:** An economic and political system in which trade and industry are controlled by private owners, rather than by the state, and where typically, aggregates of capital provide income for its owners.
- **Christian Banking:** The application of the banking methodology as described in this treatise.
- **Credit:** The act in which one party receives something of value from another party and agrees to pay for it at some date in the future.
- **Command Economy:** An economic and political system in which the government controls the capital, and where the government and not the market actors decides what and how much goods and services should be produced, and at what price.
- **Debt:** The situation whereby an amount of money is owed by one party to another.
- **EPC:** Engineering, Procurement and Construction.
- **Equity:** Any representation of ownership interest.
- **Financial Instruments:** Tradable financial assets such as cash, shares, bonds, options and derivatives.
- **Financing:** The act of providing money for business activities, making purchases or investments or for satisfying any other human need or activity, either by equity or by debt.
- **Free Market:** An economic and political system in which decisions on allocation of resources and the creation of prices are determined by the forces of supply and demand as acted out among the participating market actors.

Typically, the interference of government in the market mechanisms will be absent or minimal.
- **Gambling:** An activity that involves betting something of material value, where the outcome is not certain and based on chance, and where the transaction leads to the gain of one party and a loss of another party.
- **Interest:** The act of charging for the privilege of borrowing money or receiving credit, typically expressed as an annual or monthly percentage rate.
- **Investment:** The acquisition or ownership of any kind of asset, for the purpose of financial gain by way of capital yield, increase, use or maintenance. The insertion of funds to non-governmental organisations (NGOs) or other eleemosynary organisations will fall outside the use of the term 'investment' in this dissertation, as will any capital use that does not have financial gain or practical utilisation as its purpose.
- **Investment management:** The act of advising on or managing investments on behalf of third parties, or where the banking organisations manage assets for themselves, as posited on their balance sheet.
- **Laissez-faire capitalism:** The purest form of capitalism, in which the private owners can pursue their economic interests unrestricted by any governmental or other regulatory restrictions.
- **Lending/Moneylending:** The act in which an individual, a public group, a private group or a financial institution makes money available to another with the expectation that the money will be repaid.
- **Scarcity Paradigm:** The philosophical position that resources available for human use, goods and services, are finite, and that thus, inequality and poverty will exist in perpetuity.
- **Sufficiency Paradigm:** The philosophical position that resources available for human use, goods and services, can be infinitely increased, and that thus, inequality and poverty exist due only to the incompetency of political systems, or by societal design.
- **Unacceptable banking practices:** Banking practices conflicting with the constructive ethical-pastoral norms of the Reformed paradigm as defined in this treatise.
- **Usury:** The lending of money at exorbitant interest rates.

Biographical Note

Morten Bøsterud
Unit for Reformational Theology and the Development of the South African Society,
Faculty of Theology, North-West University,
Potchefstroom, South Africa
Email: mortenbosterud@gmail.com
ORCID: http://orcid.org/0000-0001-5305-0501

My first education was in law, at the University of Oslo, where in 1990 I earned a Cand. Jur. (BA and MA), *cum laude*, after passing the compulsory Ex. Phil., *cum laude*. In 2013, I embarked on a Doctor of Business Administration (DBA) program at the University of Liverpool, from which I graduated in 2017. Along with the DBA I pursued research in theology with the main emphasis on ethics and pastoral studies, and I earned two PhDs at North-West University, Potchefstroom, SA. The first was obtained in 2016 (ethics), and the second in 2018 (pastoral studies). In addition, I have earned a Certificate in Advanced Graduate Study (CAGS) in theology from St. Joseph's College, Maine, USA. I started as Extraordinary Senior Lecturer at North-West University, Faculty of Theology in 2016, and since 2019, my title there is that of Extraordinary Researcher. I serve as a member of the Editorial Council of *Christianity in the Middle East*, and have published a few articles on ethics and pastoral theology. This is my second published book. My main research interests are Christian ethics and pastoral theology, with particular emphasis on banking, government and animal welfare.

Acknowledgements

This book, entitled *A Treatise on Christian Banking*, presents research findings from Dr Morten Bøsterud's PhD theses, 'Public ownership and morality: Proposed investment guidelines of the Norwegian Sovereign Wealth Fund: A Christian ethical perspective' (2016) and 'Financing, credit, moneylending and charging of interest. A Christian-ethical and pastoral perspective' (2018) which was submitted to North-West University. A majority of the references cited in the chapter(s) are also drawn from Dr Morten Bøsterud's PhD theses. The book represents a reworking of more than 55% of the original theses to meet the standards of the publisher and the Department of Higher Education and Training (DHET). It is his own work in conception and execution, and all the relevant sources that he has used or quoted have been indicated and acknowledged by means of complete references.

Preface

The advent of this treatise has been a long time in the coming. The ideas underpinning the theories presented herein are a result of my personal experiences through active business participation for almost three decades. My professional background spans various fields with the starting point being practising corporate law where I was subjected to a great variety of commercial clients who covered business operations both national and international, small corporations as well as large, and I was also involved in arranging transactions of all sizes. In the late 1990s, I changed the scope of my professional life from practising law, as a pure advisor, to becoming an active participant in the field of investment management. Thus, since the late 1990s, I have managed private equity-type investments both for third-party investors as well as for myself, and also founded and co-founded several companies in various sectors. The investments I managed and partook in included a wide range of investment opportunities and industries, mainly focusing on the area of Scandinavia and the Nordics including Russia, and the wider northern European region.

A common denominator that I recognised with myself and among those I interacted with at this stage of my career, was the thirst for profit and a low awareness of moral aspects connected to the businesses we were involved in, as well as our own roles in these commercial enterprises. Aspects of corporate social responsibility (CSR) and/or Environmental Social and Governance issues (ESG) and the like were emerging in the wider business realm, but within the narrower world of investments, finance and banking, I noticed little interest in such aspects of our day-to-day activities. During my years in investment management and investments, I was nonetheless often confronted with moral dilemmas, such as environmental issues, labour law and arms production, among others. These conflicts developed my understanding and expanded my thinking to reach outside the immediate and intrinsic events of my business practice, and, through this, my awareness of moral and ethical considerations gradually emerged regarding decisions that were taken or should have been taken. At times, I raised ethical questions with my partners and/or the salaried corporate management involved in the companies I dealt with, but rarely did I find any true resonance with my ethical concerns.

In concert with my career development and active participation in the corporate world, the CSR/ESG movement gained traction in the broader business community. Also, while my career developed, Norway, my country of origin, was becoming increasingly wealthy from its petroleum revenues. In fact, Norway was becoming wealthy to such a degree that it could not spend

---

How to cite: Bøsterud, M., 2021, 'Preface', in *A treatise on Christian banking*, pp. xxiii–xxvii, AOSIS, Cape Town. https://doi.org/10.4102/aosis.2021.BK263.00

its wealth domestically, impacted by fear of domestic inflation and overspending among its citizens. As a result of this, in 1995, the Norwegian government established the Norwegian Sovereign Wealth Fund, which was to develop into one of the largest investors in the world. At the time of writing, this fund manages more than $1 trillion. The Norwegian Sovereign Wealth Fund was not immune to the increasing ethical demands stemming from the CSR/ESG movement, and thus, the fund established ethical guidelines to be followed in its investment strategy management. My personal budding interest for ethical concerns connected to investments and corporate activities led me to investigate the Norwegian Sovereign Wealth Fund and its ethical rules, searching for its moral underpinnings as well as for how its rules were formulated and implemented. As Norway is a traditionally Christian country, where the Christian foundation is well-represented even in its constitution, I was surprised to find that the fund's ethical rules were solely informed by secular consequentialist philosophy. This surprising realisation correlated with my personal career planning, and, at this time, I was considering returning to academia, which I had not been a formal part of since leaving law school in 1990.

Around 2010, I began orientating myself towards embarking on a PhD research track, and I was making initial enquiries at different universities at this time. As exciting as such orientations may be, I found a good programme at the University of Liverpool for a Doctor of Business Administration (DBA), which I could pursue while continuing to work. In 2013, I started this programme and graduated in 2017. During my research on the DBA, the CSR/ESG movement was one of many areas that I researched, and I found, to my bewilderment, that the moral underpinnings of this movement solely seemed to be secular and consequentialist, something I found concerning as such an important movement, in my view, should not be untouched by Christian values and deontological moral philosophy. Upon this realisation, I again experienced the need to orientate myself further into the academic world, hoping to find answers based on deontological moral philosophy. I came to realise that instead of searching deeper into institutions of a traditional business school type, and its adjacent production of literature, I should rather look at the moral questions that have been at the core of doing business for centuries.

With this conclusion, I started contacting theological schools and universities and soon found that within this academic realm I could expect to have my questions highlighted in the deep tradition that is theology, and that I would most likely find my answers here. This brought me into contact with the UK-based Greenwich School of Theology and North-West University, Potchefstroom, South Africa, where I found a home for my ideas on combining Christian ethical philosophy with modern-day Western business life and investment practice. At North-West University, I was fortunate to come into contact with Professor J.M. Vorster, whom I consider a towering figure within the academic field of practical theology and ethics. Professor Vorster responded well to my initial ideas and concerns – what I brought to him was primarily my bewilderment on how a major global investor such as the Norwegian Sovereign Wealth Fund established in a traditionally Christian country could let its investment strategies and practices be guided by secular thought.

At North-West University, in 2014, I embarked on a PhD research programme in theology (ethics), which I pursued along with the DBA, where I focused on the ethical guidelines of the Norwegian Sovereign Wealth Fund and how these aligned with Christian moral norms, and indeed how such Christian norms could inform the investment practices of the fund in particular, and the wider investment community in general. During this PhD research, I developed a comprehensive system for investments where investment practices are guided in accordance with Christian moral norms. I named my academic invention the Reoriented Investment Protocol with the attendant acronym, RIP. It must be admitted that the acronym is not coincidental and that its semiotic connotations are intended. In my theological PhD work, I had the advantage of my past educational and professional experience, ranging from legal aspects to practical investment decisions and ownership considerations concerning real-life business practice. This useful combination of practical and theoretical experience led to the PhD being finalised in 2016, a year ahead of the DBA.

After having defined the RIP methodology, I found that determining the ethical aspects of investments and ownership only covered one side of the coin, and left out a vast area of the banking field, namely, practical banking and finance. Thus, in 2016, I continued my research into banking, moneylending and financing, and embarked on another theological PhD, this time in pastoral studies. Through this PhD research, I developed a comprehensive methodology for performing banking and financing activities in accordance with applicable Christian ethical and pastoral norms. From this research, I developed what I termed the Pastoral Banking Practice (PBP) which together with RIP represent what I perceive as a foundation for Christian banking. I graduated with my third doctoral degree in 2018, and, with doctorates, there is no such thing as 'three is a crowd'. In tandem with my three doctorate programmes, I deepened my appreciation of Christian thought and philosophy, not least through the Certificate in Advanced Graduate Study in theology that I completed in 2019 at Saint Joseph's College, Maine.

It is the result of immersing myself in research and theological studies that I am able to present this reworked version of my PhD work, DBA research and published articles as a comprehensive repositioned presentation partly based on substantial new research of what would constitute a paradigm for Christian banking and finance (Bøsterud 2016, 2017, 2018, 2019b; Bøsterud & Vorster 2017, 2019). Although these former research results are of great importance, they represent only a fragmented version based on my initial conclusions from my previous research where notably, equity investments and practical banking are treated separately, and where few lines are drawn between the two domains. What is presented in this treatise is beyond a mere synthesis of the RIP and PBP paradigms, as here is outlined a new comprehensive and integrated proposal pertaining to a Christian banking systematic exhibiting ample new research and knowledge generation, which covers investments activity and practical banking as a whole, as merely 'banking', as aligned with the general nomenclature of the banking profession. My hope is that this will represent a fuller answer to the Christian calls for moral practice that I assume are given by any concerned constituent of the banking community, and/or any person involved in any mode of financing activity, whether it be in a professional or non-professional capacity.

I appreciate that this treatise is merely the start of what, in the future, may become a comprehensive Christian alternative to conventional and traditional banking as we see it in the West, and in most of the world for that matter. It is my vision that perhaps this treatise could represent a building block in what may become a Christian banking alternative that may offer the concerned Christian an alternative banking mode that would mirror what the Islamic banking paradigm represents for Muslims.

Even though the banking sector develops quickly and in concert with wider society, staying with Christian ethical and pastoral norms as foundational guidance for banking practice is a steadfast and certain way to safeguard banking practice for the benefit of all societal stakeholders. Further, even though the norms for what is acceptable may change over time in different societies, the ethical and pastoral principles, as given in Scripture, remain unchanged, and should be binding on banking practitioners and investors at all times.

Because of the practice-led makeup of the philosophical field relevant to banking and financing, I will outline tendencies connected to the banking realm from a historical, philosophical and political vantage point. From this starting point, I elaborate on the main currents of ethics, and in particular Christian ethics, which will further show how banking, philosophy and religious thought have evolved alongside each other throughout history. When the philosophical and theological aspects that could be applicable to banking have been covered, how these could be used in a pastoral capacity is addressed, as applied in a real-life practical setting, where theology is used to inform leadership and direction-giving. I aim to demonstrate how aspects of Christian ethics connected to banking would be of use both in pastoral leadership and counselling of participants in the banking industry, as well as among concerned non-professionals. In addition, pastoral activities could be based on the principles developed in this treatise, particularly when coming into contact with individuals who see themselves as victims of harmful banking practices. As always, to the individual, whether in a strong or weak position in a banking relationship, the matter of subjective sensemaking as a means to assessing and interpreting human experience could benefit from scripturally based pastoral guidance.

Albeit that the Christian banking paradigm as will be presented in this treatise is in its early inceptions, it is assumed here that it has a future among banking practitioners, not least as what the CSR/ESG discourse over the last decades has shown, is an emergent interest in ethical matters related to all manner of commercial activity. Also, as the Islamic banking paradigm in its modern mode has existed for decades now, and is in a rapid growth mode, there is reason to hope, if not believe, that the Christian ethical and pastoral norms that underpin the Christian banking paradigm as expressed here may experience a similar development among the Western banking community, which will still be expected to cater to a community of actors from a dominantly Christian-cultural background. If so, the Christian banking paradigm may have a promising future ahead, and this treatise, will then hopefully be replaced by new and practice-based representations of the paradigm. It is at least possible to hope!

In addition to being applied in practice, it is also hoped that the Christian banking paradigm will be given increased academic interest, something that may result in further research into its foundations and practical applications. As an extension of such academic effort, it is expected that the tertiary educational institutions will create degree programmes related to the Christian banking paradigm, at par with those of the Islamic banking paradigm. If so, the interest in – and prestige of – Christian banking will be expected to grow further, and its practical utilisation to increase.

Chapter 1

Setting the stage

Keywords: moneylending; interest; investment management; practical theology; ethics; pastoral principles.

■ Introduction

Economic activities for individuals and societies need to be financed, whether they are business projects and enterprises, or expenditures of a private nature, such as purchasing a home or paying for education. Financing human activity can be conducted in two principally different ways: by using equity belonging to the initiator, or by receiving loans, credit or equity from a third party. At a basic level, it may be assumed that there is a defined line between moneylending and equity financing, but these methods may also coexist in an equity–loan mix. When both are in use, it could be of interest to examine the sustainable and moral degree of loan as seen against the applied loan to equity ratio. This is a question that has different solutions under different moral, legal and religious paradigms.

In this treatise, both third-party financing and equity financing (investments) are covered contrary to expectations of some of the readers. For readers from outside the world of finance, the use of the term 'banking' will give rise to connotations of third-party financing more than investments, whereas among seasoned banking professionals, banking and equity investments are typically perceived as two sides of the same coin. As seen from the side of the one in

How to cite: Bøsterud, M., 2021, 'Setting the stage', in *A treatise on Christian banking*, pp. 1–6, AOSIS, Cape Town. https://doi.org/10.4102/aosis.2021.BK263.01

need of financing, equity may be the preferred mode of financing a said activity, but in lacking sufficient equity, or perhaps in search of alleviating risk, third-party financing may be preferred, in whole or as part of their financing mix. This is the case even when the financier is required to get an activity started, as the choice to initiate has to be taken by the borrower. However, from the lender's perspective, usage of the lent equity remains a concern, and as explained in this treatise, the two main forms of financing will be equal when seen from a moral perspective.

∎ Scope of interest
Credit, moneylending and interest

Views on financing and interest vary among different cultural and religious affiliations and are subject to rules and regulations that vary in strictness and often involve limits protecting the debtor against the power of the creditor. From historical sources for India and China in the medieval era for example, it appears that there were governmental concerns to protect the (perceived) weaker debtor against the creditor, and that rules were introduced stating maximum interest rates as well as the principle that interest could not exceed the principal (Graeber 2012). From sources within Christendom, we know of similar impulses for regulating credit, ranging from the Old Testament (NIV 2011) law of debt cancellation every 7 years (Dt 15:1–3), and the release of those held in debt bondage every 49 years (Lv 25:39), to Calvin's moderate scepticism of letting capitalism exist unchecked (Graafland 2009).

Interestingly, within the Islamic world, the matter of debt, interest and capital hoarding has been subjected to closer scrutiny when compared to the predominantly Christian West. Within Islam, a tradition of banking based on Islamic moral rules has been developed, and a paradigm of capital use has evolved covering most aspects of third-party financing and the application of capital. This financial model is often referred to as sharia banking or Islamic banking, and was developed in the 1970s (Abdul-Rahman 2010; Jamaldeen 2012).

Looking at other cultures, a pertinent question that arises is whether such a moral position on financing and credit can be matched in Christian pastoral philosophy, or is the free market and unbridled capitalism the acceptable norm for Christian individuals and their societies? Also, if we accept that credit and financing are to be perceived as a 'good' (in the economic sense), should they be evenly distributed among all societal constituents, or only provided to a select few? If loans and credit are morally neutral, why is it then that we seldom use interest in close relationships such as within families and among friends, and the line between loan and credit on the one side and gifts on the other is blurred? The concept of such 'soft financing' is also found in the practice of microfinancing, which has become fashionable and is perhaps even perceived as a morally acceptable practice among actors in the West. However, does that mean it is morally viable from a Christian pastoral perspective (Mayoux 2001)?

In the West, all types of financial instruments, including loans, leveraged investment structures and products, bonds and interest are regarded as acceptable from a mercantile perspective, but the moral aspects are seldom considered. It would seem that to be in debt has become commonplace in the West, and that debtors and creditors alike accept this state of affairs as natural and useful, both for the individual and society. It seems that the ramifications of this practice of debt creation are seldom considered, whether from the perspective of morality, society, the economy, political stability or the environment. In addition to the debt levels that exist within the Western world, there is the matter of debt for states, where the creditors are either other states, private organisations such as privately owned banks, or international financers such as the World Bank or the International Monetary Fund (IMF). The events that occurred in Greece in 2015 would alone serve as an example of how governmental debt can be seminal in destabilising a society, where all citizens bear the burden of governmental (over-) spending and newborns come into this world with a high level of debt to be paid – debt which the weakest of the citizens had no intention in taking (Varoufakis 2016). Added moral dilemmas can be found when so-called developing countries are under debt of Western states or private organisations, and where there could be only a miniscule possibility of paying back the loans. A valid question then could be whether such structures represent a modern-day revival of old-style political colonialism. The possibility of credit giving destabilising whole societies is well known in history, with the great crash that occurred in the late 1920s in the Western financial markets being a prime example (Galbraith 2009).

Investment management/advisory

A core area of banking is investment management, which is a field where banking practitioners act as advisors and caretakers for third parties, or where the banking organisations manage assets for themselves, as posited on their balance sheet. Such management activity can take on different forms, including long-term index funds, UCITS structures, private equity, proprietary trading et cetera. When we turn from third-party financing to investments, the matter of what kind of activity to be involved in not only from an ethical, but also from a financial perspective, has risen to the surface in public and corporate perceptions, and has increasingly been highlighted as a core question connected to equity investments. Here, investment management will be seen from the perspective of the banker, and it will be the banker who is subject to moral and ethical evaluation. However, the banker's customer, the investor, will be subjected to the same accountability as the advisor/manager, and thus, any non-professional seeking to invest according to Christian norms would be well-advised to follow the principles outlined in this treatise. The highlight of this treatise is that no matter in what banking service or area of life banking is involved, the activity and involved actors should be held accountable against the same standards. It will never be acceptable for any banking professional to hide behind the customers/clients and their autonomous choices, or vice versa for that matter.

The influence exerted through investment activity is perceived by some as value-free, and by others as an indication of how the involved view the purpose of their capital, from an individualistic, societal or political perspective. The mere investment from one actor, could, depending on their relative societal influence, be expected to influence the perceptions others have toward the target assets; for example, ownership can be perceived as an endorsement of the company or sector in question. This can be of importance with regard to controversial companies operating within business sectors or countries with questionable moral legitimacy.

At times, investment activity is seen as controversial, and the purpose and aim of such choices are sometimes contentious. To evaluate the merits of investment activity, it is first necessary to assess what value assumptions and drivers may be present among the ultimate owners and/or their managers. The rationales for equity engagement may be diverse, ranging from profit maximisation, securing future earnings for the ultimate owners, securing the future of the living and unborn in the involved actors' families, influencing industry or creating a more just and benign world. The assumption here is that most equity investors and their managers such as traditional banking professionals, will be following a conventional investment purpose of maintaining or increasing the capital, and ensuring an annual financial yield in accordance with market expectations. Thus, despite the increasing focus on Corporate Social Responsibility (CSR) and Environmental Social and Governance (ESG), considerations of a charitable nature on the part of an equity investor cannot be taken for granted. However, the advent and continuous discussions on paradigms such as ESG and CSR have placed increased emphasis on the effect economic activities may have on a wide array of stakeholders, both on those who are directly involved in the activity as such, as well as those in the wider societal sphere. Such increased interest in non-financial and indirect consequences has no doubt heightened the awareness on how to invest. No matter what the underlying aims are, investment activities will have an impact on a large number of corporate and societal stakeholders (Burnes & By 2012).

The emergence of moral awareness in equity investments has resulted in some prominent examples of setting ethical guidelines for some major investors. One example here could be the Norwegian Sovereign Wealth Fund, which, in 2004, established an ethical board, in theory independent of the fund's management, to advise the owner's representative, the Norwegian Ministry of Finance, whether to withdraw or continue investments in accordance with certain set ethical rules (Norwegian Government n.d.). The ethical guidelines are not comprehensive, and it could be argued that the philosophical foundations of the rules are unclear at best. This is a particularly pertinent example, as at the time of writing, the fund manages more than $1 trillion, and that because of its enormity, it may be expected that its system of ethical consideration could serve as an influencing yardstick for other investors. Here, the focus is on the societal usefulness of banking practices and attendant topics from a Christian perspective, wherein different stakeholder categories are described and considered, as well as questions pertaining to the morality of the underlying activity, for example, arms production or the promotion of financial speculation or consumerism.

Core problem area

In this treatise, professional activities connected to the areas of credit, moneylending, interest, origination of financial instruments, financial advisory, investment products and investment management, proprietary trading or any other activity performed by the banking profession are collectively termed as 'banking' or 'banking practice', which will be in line with the general nomenclature among constituents of the international banking community. When the term banking used in this wide manner is evaluated against Christian ethical and pastoral norms, the main problem to be addressed is: How should banking be guided from a Christian perspective?

This then gives rise to questions such as:

1. Can banking practices be morally neutral?
2. What Christian ethical and pastoral principles are applicable to banking?
3. What banking practices should be avoided as counteracting Christian ethical and pastoral norms?
4. What banking practices should be encouraged as promoting Christian ethical and pastoral norms?
5. How can banking practices be operationalised to correlate with the Christian banking principles formulated herein?

The aim of this treatise is to evaluate different modes of banking practices from a theological perspective, and to indicate how Christian ethical and pastoral norms can add value to and guide current and future banking activities.

This treatise does not include a detailed set of recommended ready-to-use guidelines for banking activities but aims to determine the main relevant Christian ethical and pastoral considerations that could collectively qualify as a comprehensive description of Christian banking.

■ Theological location

Systematic terminology

Within the academic realm of theology, there is a conventionally recognised systematic divide between the fields of ethics and pastoral theology although both areas are included under the umbrella term 'practical theology'. In this treatise, the term 'Christian ethical and pastoral' will frequently be in use, as it is recognised that ethical and pastoral norms are adjacent and partly overlapping, and that for any exegete who attempts to mine out practical guidelines for living, it will be with great (and unnecessary) difficulty that these two fields are strictly demarcated. For the author, scriptural norms typically express how it is right to act as well as how it is right and best to treat others, in a pastoral sense. Rarely, if ever, will there be a case of something being prudent from a strictly ethical or pastoral perspective, where one of these perspectives will rule out the other. Consequently, the central theological argument in this treatise is that Christian ethical and pastoral norms can add value to guiding banking and equity investment practices.

Reformed paradigm

The treatise is based on a Reformed biblical-theological approach, as this approach is evident in the work of, for example, Calvin (2012) and Grudem (1994). At times, the author is described by his critics as neo-Calvinist, something to which no response will be given. A detailed description of the epistemological stance and hermetical position that undergirds the scriptural interpretations demonstrated in this treatise will not be formulated, but they will be based on generally accepted hermeneutical principles as found within the Reformed paradigm (Bøsterud 2020). It is assumed here that even though other traditions would adhere to different authorities to evaluate in an interpretive study such as this, the ethical and pastoral outcome would not differ greatly (Gustafson 1989; Kerkhofs 1994).

Chapter 2

Economic-philosophical backdrop

Keywords: scarcity paradigm; sufficiency paradigm; globalisation; government investors; welfare state.

■ Introduction

In this chapter, economic history is viewed from an occidental, Christian-cultural perspective at a general level and from a broad vantage point, and on distribution of material resources and opportunities on a global scale. The focus here is on the material output of production and will encompass physical goods and services alike; covering all non-spiritual needs of humanity. I discuss whether ruling economic conditions determine the understanding and philosophies of economics and vice versa and investigate how these theories influence the actual state of economic conditions at given times in history. The contention here is that descriptions of economic history reflect the real economy, and the perceived possibilities it entails at any time. As in other sciences, the economist acts in a descriptive and reactive manner towards his perceptions of reality and does not invent economic reality any more than Sir Isaac Newton invented gravity. The perceived lawfulness of any scientific observation, within natural or social sciences, remains a reflection of the observer's limited tools for perceiving the real nature of his surroundings (Calàs & Smircich 1999; Derrida 1997). Thus, in the following explanation, I use

How to cite: Bøsterud, M., 2021, 'Economic-philosophical backdrop', in *A treatise on Christian banking*, pp. 7-32, AOSIS, Cape Town. https://doi.org/10.4102/aosis.2021.BK263.02

various sources of economic thought and philosophy as a basis for describing the historical and current state of occidental economy.

I follow two main economic thought trajectories of overarching importance and influence – those of scarcity and sufficiency – and show how the real economy and attendant theory have been guided by these principles. The principle of scarcity, 'the Scarcity Paradigm' is defined by the notion that resources available for human use, goods and services, are finite, and that thus, inequality and poverty will exist in perpetuity. The principle of sufficiency, 'the Sufficiency Paradigm' is defined by the notion that resources available for human use, goods and services, can be infinitely increased, and that thus, inequality and poverty exist only because of the incompetency of political systems, or by societal design. Both paradigms are discussed and constitute important scaffolding for the theoretical development of the topics of the treatise.

■ Scarcity paradigm – Finite resources
Antiquity

Within the central tradition of occidental economic thought, the overarching assumption has been that of inevitable resource scarcity, and this powerful image still resides in large parts of the current political society in the West. The idea and reality of scarcity, and thus, inevitable inequalities and impossible distributive ameliorations of poverty, has traditionally held pride of place in human cognition, and is for example scripturally expressed in the Eden narrative (Gn 3), leading to the subsequent economic theorising and societal acceptance of inequality and material suffering. In the story of Adam and Eve being cast out of Eden, the transition from abundance in Paradise to hardship and resource scarcity is powerfully demonstrated. In this image, humans have forsaken for good the ability to obtain a sense of material fulfilment, and only through hardship 'with painful labour you will give birth to your children' (Gn 3:16) and by strenuous work 'By the sweat of your brow …' (Gn 3:19), would human life thereafter persist (Lowry 2003).

The notion of inevitable and compulsory material insufficiency commands strong power over human thought, and is represented in Scripture in several places, at least if read superficially and in isolation, as for instance through the immorality of idleness (2 Th 3:10), and subsequent economic theory has had this premise as a condition at par with any physical law of the natural sciences. Even though economic realities and possibilities have developed, the fear of experiencing scarcity or outright poverty is a strong motivator in societal projections of work, labour and production, to such a degree that the acceptance of unbridled amassing of wealth often passes unchecked even in affluent societies (Veblen 2007). As with Newton and gravity, the Eden narrative does not invent or impose scarcity, but rather describes the perceived economic realities in a basically agricultural society where land and limited resources established boundaries on human subsistence. For the purposes of this treatise, I will refer to this main direction in economic thought as the 'Scarcity Paradigm'.

There is no substantial heritage by way of economic theorising, at least in the available sources we have. From the earliest times of the ancient Greeks, we know that the focus of economic thought was the household and how to run the economy it contained. This hands-on approach to philosophy is typical of the ancient Greeks, who connected their theorising to the human life and the concrete problems it involved. It would be Plato and Aristotle who did some theorising on economic life which we can consider as economic analyses in the modern-day sense (Schumpeter 2009). Plato, in his *The Republic*, is mostly concerned with superficial economic structures visible to him, and his theorising does not go much deeper than explaining the different phenomena observed from an etiological perspective. His ideas on the perfect economy were based on a stale social stratification, much like the Greece of his time, and his ideal could best be seen as a command economic model, with strict control on private lives, which included limitation of the wealth of individuals (Plato 1977).

Aristotle's economic analysing went further and deeper than that of Plato, and his works *The Politics* (1992) and *The Nicomachean Ethics* (2009), can together be considered as the first-known systematic depiction of social science (Schumpeter 2009). In Aristotle's thinking, the aim of the perfect state was still present, but he analysed economic phenomena beyond merely accepting what he observed. For instance, Aristotle was concerned with explaining the concepts of slavery, economic development, barter and money, interest, division of labour, the concept of value and the concept of wealth (Aristotle 1992, 2009). Judging from the modern perspective, Aristotle's theories and sociological explanations may contain several non-sequiturs, but nonetheless, he gave us valuable insights from the economic life and theorising of time, from which we may glean useful learning (Schumpeter 2009). As an overall comment to the context here, Aristotle was a proponent of scepticism towards trade and commerce, considering moneylending as usury, in line with Judaic tradition, and hence, profit from lending should not be permitted (Aristotle 2009; Lowry 2003). We know this scepticism as further represented in scriptural sources as well, for instance when Jesus cleanses the temple of moneychangers (Jn 2:13–16; Mk 11:15–19).

Aristotle's contribution is noteworthy in that he established a principle of reciprocity, which would be used by later thinkers to justify scepticism against charging interest, and to justify fairness of contracts through the principle of equal considerations given and received by the involved parties (Aristotle

2009; Wykes 2003). Not only did Aristotle develop this justice-in-exchange principle, but he also expressed derision for usury and moneylenders. It is worth noting how Aristotle distinguished between 'economics' and 'chrematistics'. By economics, he referred to the activities of acquiring household goods and satisfying basic needs, and by chrematistics, he referred to the activity of acquiring wealth for wealth's own sake. As part of chrematistics, Aristotle particularly derided the charging of interest, as this went against the true nature and use of money as he saw it – money was to be used only as a means of exchanging goods. The idea that money should yield money from itself, as interest, was against his view of nature and the concept of obtaining offsprings by natural processes, such as the birth of the calf from the cow (Aristotle 1992). The central element in Aristotle's criticism of usury was that money could not in itself create more than its principal, and this argument may have been due to his perception of money as coins, and as coins were not a part of the natural world, they could not yield any offspring (Langholm 1984).

Roman society was based on labour of slaves and the free citizens relied on slaves to perform necessary tasks; thus the society did not involve any substantial level of private consumer economy. Less than 1% of the inhabitants of the Roman Empire had a 'paying job' in the modern sense of the expression (Treggiari 1979). A wider distribution would not have been possible because of evident limitations in the extant capital, and in antiquity, the common person was not free, and did not possess any personal economy with which to create a wider demand for goods and services. This economic system clearly influenced the contemporary thinkers, so that Seneca (2010), relating to the relatively affluent and free citizens, advises a moderate level of affluence as the correct character-building amount of wealth. In his elaborations on wealth and happiness for free, Seneca (2008) also warns that prosperity may be more deceitful than misfortune. Such thinking reflects the affluence awarded to the few residing in the higher echelons of Roman society, and in conjunction with the prevalent slave economy, did not promote thoughts of just distribution of extant societal resources.

Perhaps the most important legacy left by the Romans connected to economics was the concept of private property and legislation regarding private treaties. Prior to the Romans, the concept of private property was not practical, as any right held by the individual was granted by the ruler. The introduction of individual ownership rights by the Romans which were not connected to the ruler(s), in combination with a well-developed legal and physical infrastructure within the empire, stemmed from exchange among tradesmen of different nationalities and customs. The development of civil law respecting the individual's right to ownership spearheaded the economic development of the Romans, and greatly influenced the theories developed in medieval and modern times (Baldwin 1959).

In Roman society, regulations pertaining to maximum allowed interest on loans were in force, and the fact that occasional state initiatives were established to stave off the worst effects of credit crisis is an example of how even in the Roman society credit and debt were not left completely to be regulated among the involved parties. It would appear, then, that even in the Roman society, which placed such a strong emphasis on private property rights and freedom of contract, credit giving and debt creation were too important for the state not to contribute regulation, at least occasionally (Homer & Sylla 1996; Niczyporuk 2011).

Overall, the historical perceptions related to economy and ethical acceptance of commerce were influenced by the low level of civil liberties provided to the population, and the prevalence of slave economy held back the real economy and attendant philosophical theorising.

Medieval era

In medieval times, ecclesiastical thinkers took an ambiguous stance on trade and commerce, as the perception was that to partake in commerce, either by selling merchandise or rendering services, it was necessary to lie and suppress the truth, which was sinful. The focus of the medievals was on interpretations of sinfulness connected to covetousness and usury, building on anti-usury and just price doctrines. However, the church thinkers were not all negatively disposed towards trade and commerce, for the social necessity of trade and tradesmen was acknowledged by some (Walsh 2004). San Antonino of Florence (1389–1459) (cited in Walsh 2004), for example, expresses this attitude in *Summa Theologica*:

> The notion of business implies nothing vicious in its nature or contrary to reason. Therefore, it should be ordered to any honest and necessary purpose and is so rendered lawful, as for example, when a businessman orders his moderate gain which he seeks to the end that he and his family may be decently provided for according to their condition, and that he may also assist the poor. Nor is condemnation possible when he undertakes a business as a public service lest necessary things be wanting to the state and seeks gain therefrom, not as an end, but in remuneration for his labour observing all other due considerations which we mention. But if he places his final purpose in gain, seeking only to increase wealth enormously and to keep it for himself, his attitude is to be condemned. (p. 246)

With the basic understanding that trade and commerce was, at best, bordering on sin, combined with the lauding of poverty as a pure lifestyle, the ecclesiastical thinkers of medieval times did not move economic thought beyond the systematic confines of the Scarcity Paradigm. On the contrary, in the medieval era, the sceptical attitude towards commerce and trade, paired with scriptural statements on sinful idleness (1 Tm 5:13) and questionable wealth (Mk 10:23–27), could be seen as theoretical scaffolding for the poverty pledges taken by Francis of Assisi and other influential medieval Christian role models (Cataldo 2007).

An important church philosopher of the medieval era was Thomas Aquinas (1225–1274), who contributed to matters of morality and also to the realm of societal economy and trade. To Aquinas, the root of human happiness does not lie in accumulating riches, and the pursuit of wealth accumulation is, therefore, not the road to happiness. On the contrary, to Aquinas (1998), the purpose of physical wealth is its distribution and use. Aquinas, who fully accepted the premise of private property, addressed matters of trade and commerce from a perspective of justice and fairness, evaluating the moral aspects of society's economic activity. Aquinas envisaged that it was possible to determine a correct price on any good or service, and from this he established the doctrine of 'just price'. To Aquinas, a just price was not only fair and just as the basis for exchange between consenting parties, but also moral and good (Friedman 1980).

In the medieval era, the church was particularly concerned with credit and debt, especially with the question of whether the charging of interest was moral or should be considered usury and thus immoral and consequently unlawful. For most of the medieval era, the church's stance on interest was that the charging of interest was considered usury, and should be deemed unlawful, and this was also explained by Aquinas, who among the scholastics was a prominent voice advocating the immorality of charging interest (Aquinas 2003; Wykes 2003). Aquinas followed the approach of Aristotle by viewing interest and usury through the lens of justice and perceived charging payment in the form of interest as immoral, as it could only be morally acceptable to charge for losses incurred. To Aquinas, to charge interest as compensation for not making a profit on the money he lent would represent immoral usury, as this indicate charging for something he had not already earned, and which he could be prevented from earning in numerous ways (Aquinas 2010).

The medieval era held a sceptical attitude towards trade, commerce and wealth, but adjusted the ruling theories to accept what would be perceived as a necessary level of economic activity.

Renaissance – Reformation

With the end of the medieval era, in the Renaissance, came the Reformation with its theological schisms, which included differences of views on trade, commerce and not the least on human industriousness. Max Weber (1864–1920) in *The Protestant Ethic and the Spirit of Capitalism* elaborates on the development of Christian Reformed thought and its implications on the advent of modern capitalism (Weber 2012). Weber connects the new acceptance of work and industriousness to Luther's Bible translation and the use of the German word *Beruf* or the English 'calling', which gives the notion of mundane vocational calling a new scriptural acceptance; the fulfilment of one's personal duty was deemed a highly moral, worldly activity. He indicates that this originated in the apocryphal Sirach. He claims that this sense of 'calling' is typical for Protestants, and until the Reformation was unknown in the Catholic world. He describes the development of Protestant thought from the pietistic Calvinism onwards to modernity, via other Reformed societies, like Baptists and Methodists to whom he ascribes ideals of industriousness and thrift, with doctrines against wastefulness and idleness.

The acceptance of wealth as not sinful, but even moral, developed under the Reformed paradigm. Weber (2012) describes the Protestant ethic of the era that wealth is only unethical if it elicits idleness and wasteful carefree enjoyment of life. He further explains that the view held was that individuals were obligated to utilise all their talents and abilities, and that to refrain from such use was seen as sinful. In contrast with the earlier ideals of poverty, the new era included a perception that to choose poverty could be equal to wishing to be unhealthy. Weber finally posits that the focus on asceticism and vocational calling could be seen as an ethical platform for the modern approach of work specialisation and division of labour.

Another effect of the Reformed acceptance of commerce and industry was the increased use of Arabic numerals. Until the Reformation, Roman numerals were most widely used in Europe. The Roman numerals are adequate for counting and keeping tally, much like the Chinese numerals, but are inappropriate for the complicated calculations necessary for mathematics, engineering and modern industry. With Roman numerals, it is not possible to calculate decimals, and thus, interest, which of course can easily be performed with Arabic numerals, and which, in turn, may have given added support to the development of credit and banking, both useful tools in the modern capitalist society (Lieber 1968). Although the Reformed theologians adopted a different, more accepting view on interest compared to the medievals, this did not mean that society at large unanimously came to accept interest as moral, and usury was nonetheless deemed an unacceptable banking practice (Galbraith 1989).

Whether the different views on wealth, moneylending, trade, work and industry in the Catholic and Reformed paradigms can solely explain the differences in economic development between Southern Europe and South America as compared to Northern Europe and North America cannot be easily concluded. For this, there are too many societal and historical variables involved in the economic development and current state of these two major global regions to identify substantial differences based on only one trajectory of argumentation (Goody 2003). It is, however, compelling that the difference in belief systems could in some way be involved in the quite substantial economic differences between the regions, such as the Southern European inclination to the welfare state and socialism and the Northern European route of a free market and limited state control. Whether one set of economic cognition is to be preferred over the other is another matter.

The attitudes towards a civil society involving trade, commerce and manufacturing activities became more accepting from the time of the European Renaissance and Reformation. The grounds for this development may be numerous, and the new power structures following the religious and political upheaval of the Reformation could have played a central part.

Towards industrialism

In the wake of the Great Discoveries in the 15th and 16th centuries, such as new territories and navigable sea routes to Asia and the Americas, came the need for spreading risk and risk capital generation, as the opportunities in the New World were plentiful but risk-laden. The traditional manner in which capital was raised and risked was on an individual basis by businessmen or in partnerships among several people. This method had its clear disadvantages, one being the limitations on how much capital could be raised, and another being the risk and responsibility placed on individual investors and their families. To alleviate such difficulties, and to further business activity in areas prone to disaster and risk, with the corresponding possibility of great rewards, the modern limited company came into existence. The creation of the limited company came through several charters in the colonial states, and several companies were established for the exploitation of the newfound opportunities. For example, there was both a British and Dutch 'East India Company'. The construction of a limited capital structure like the limited company entailed that each individual investor risked only his deposited capital, and, by participating in more than one company, the risk was dispersed across a range of sources of risk, thus counterbalancing a high risk (and reward) on one aspect with a lower risk (and potentially fewer rewards) with another. Thus, the limited company with its ability to take on ever greater risk, through the garnering of ever greater capital amounts, played a central role in the advent of modern Western capitalism (Micklethwait & Woolridge 2005).

Approaching the end of the pre-industrial period, and still bound by the cognitive schemata of scarcity, new economic knowledge and philosophy emerged. Adam Smith (1723–1790), central to the Scottish Enlightenment movement, developed theories of division of labour and principles of free trade. Smith, later mainly connected to free trade principles, was a proponent of the greater good with emphatic recognition of the interests and sentiments of others, and not purely an advocate of the promotion of self-interest for the few, as often assumed. These thoughts were developed in his first major work, *The Theory of Moral Sentiments* (Smith 2009), first published in 1759, a work that has often been seen by several later scholars in contradiction to his more famous work: *An Inquiry into the Nature and Causes of the Wealth of Nations* (Smith 2012), first published in 1776. The reason for this is the apparent focus in the latter work on efficiency, division of labour and profitability, with no evident concern for the actors involved. As Smith wrote from a religious perspective, Ekelund, Hébert and Tollison (2005) posit that the apparent contradictions in Smith's philosophies relate to later misinterpretations that did not take Smith's holistic view of society, religion and economy into consideration, and that when correctly interpreted the inconsistencies disappear, revealing Smith's perceptions of the multi-layered human condition. When describing the philosophical movement of liberalism, it is common to attribute its inception to the theories set forth by Adam Smith (2012) who advocated letting the market itself decide prices, wages and other terms, without any state interference, and famously, he used the metaphor of the 'invisible hand', which would create order in the seemingly order-less social institution that is the free market.

During the period of *c.* 1500 to *c.* 1800, following the Great Discoveries, the main Western system of economic practice was that of mercantilism. Mercantilism may not have been an economic philosophy as such, but more of a practical system, where the state was at the helm of much of the societal economic activity, not the least international trade and finance, and where free market activity was not sought (Heckscher 2013). It was not until Adam Smith issued his *Wealth of Nations* in 1776 that ideas of free market and liberal economic thought were introduced as alternatives to the regulated markets of the mercantilist era (Galbraith 1989; Smith 2012). Indeed, it was Smith himself who coined the term 'mercantilism'. However, there was no clean break with mercantilism just because of the publication of Smith's theories, as governmental control of economic life, hereunder banking, remained the mainstay of the Western societies throughout the period. In the German states of the 17th and 18th centuries, cameralism (an economic theory which advocated a strong public administration managing a centralised economy primarily for the benefit of the state) was an espoused variant of mercantilism, which after the Thirty Years War (1618-1648) was utilised in rebuilding societal infrastructure and cities after the destruction caused by warfare (Kurz 2016).

Thomas Robert Malthus (1766-1834) is known for his theories of population control connected to scarcity and material limitation (Malthus 2013). For Malthus, the poor classes existed on the minimal material subsistence level, the population would increase and decrease in accordance with the material possibilities in their society, and the poor should not be allowed to overpopulate by way of any benevolent exogenous assistance (Piketty 2014). According to Malthus (2013), the poor should be left to self-regulate their numbers by means of food supply and emigration, the latter an unfortunate and happiness-reducing but necessary consequence of overpopulation. Compared with 21st century standards, Malthus' glum view on humanity and the value of life seems uncharitable and without consideration of the individual, but within the Scarcity Paradigm, this would be perceived as a law of nature, and not by societal design. In my opinion, his thinking clearly demonstrates the way the real economy was understood, even at the onset of the modern industrial age.

A political thinker and a contemporary of Smith and Malthus was David Ricardo (1772–1823). Ricardo's main contribution to economic thought was related to rents, wages and theories on comparative advantages among trading partners (Ruffin 2002). Ricardo was a wealthy businessman from a privileged background, basing his ideas on practical experience of rising land prices on the assumption of real scarcity (Piketty 2014). His view on the place of the poor is represented in his assertion that their wages are 'that price which is necessary to enable the labourers, one with another, to subsist and perpetuate their race, without either increase or diminution' (Ricardo 1891:n.p.). This was later referred to as the 'Iron Law of Wages', and it could be argued that it cemented the further understanding of universal scarcity as a natural law, as recognised from the Eden narrative, and society's experiential knowledge of economy, which still had a hold on thinkers like Ricardo and several subsequent thinkers (Baumol 1983). Ricardo was inspired by the free trade theories of Smith, and further developed the liberal economic model, and his liberal ideas extended beyond the realm of economics, and he was an avid critic of slavery (King 2013; Ricardo 2001).

In the 18th and 19th centuries, with a development in which the masses came into the focus of the philosophers as visible in the societal political landscape, matters pertaining to the well-being of the 'common man' became worthy of interest for the elite. Even though the thoughts were still at an early stage of development, and often religiously based, the presented theories were seminal in the later development of the civil liberal societies that came to be in the West.

Colonialism

The overly practical and stark perceptions of societal utility related to people, land, raw materials and resources in general represented by the 18th and 19th century thinkers, also reflect the development of Western colonialism, which took place in parallel with the economic development and activities leading up to the Industrial Revolution and beyond. The Western colonies in the New World opened up new trade, and in conjunction with organisational developments like the limited company, it was possible to minimise risk and maximise resource utilisation. It became possible to retrieve inexpensive raw materials from the colonies, sometimes through slave labour or ruthless taxation, and later, to sell finished products, made in the 'master' nation, back to the colonial inhabitants often at inflated, monopolistic prices (Habib 1985; Trapido 1978). The colonial system, which continued up to World War II and beyond, greatly augmented the wealth of the Western nations at the expense of the colonial populations, establishing a lasting difference in affluence levels, not yet equalised. Remnants of the British Empire, for example, still exist in many forms, of which the Commonwealth is but one (Bridge & Fedorowich 2003; Cain & Hopkins 1987).

The colonial system may have been a decisive element in the development of the Western economic system and thought, as it provided an outlet for excess population in the colonising countries and represented an ever-growing consumer market demand for Western finished products.

Scarcity accepted

The above elaboration of economic thought leading up to the Industrial Revolution, via the Enlightenment period, is but a miniscule outline of the total body of knowledge connected to the economic state of the West as experienced by a few select thinkers. The presented philosophies are, however, representative of the development of economic learning following medieval times, and a result of the advances in technology and travels following the Great Discoveries of the 15th century and beyond.

That the Scarcity Paradigm has not only represented economic theory up until modernity, but has also been a fair representation of reality for the masses, is expressed by John Maynard Keynes (1933):

> From the earliest times of which we have record – back, say, to two thousand years before Christ – down to the beginning of the 18th century, there was no very great change in the standard of living of the average man living in the civilized centers of the earth. Ups and downs certainly. Visitations of plague, famine and war. Golden intervals. But no progressive violent change. (p. 360)

The quote eloquently shows how subsistence and mere survival most likely dominated human economic life until the advent of industrialisation during the Industrial Revolution as experienced in the West during the late 18th and early 19th centuries. However, although the Keynes quote seems absolute and unconditional, there have been a few pockets of wealth among some craftsmen and citizens, in addition to that of leading nobles and clergy, for instance in the Roman period (Kieser 1989). The definition of capital under the Scarcity Paradigm is one of limitation, and subsequent theorising mainly pertained to different elaborate models explaining why and how affluence could reside with the few and not the many.

The Scarcity Paradigm has been an 'iron claw' on human perception, and has arguably been the resort of many an oppressive ruler and their minions. Even in the 21st century, this philosophy holds a firm grip on Western thinking, and as is demonstrated later, the notion of inevitable scarcity is still alive and actively used to serve several different political and economic agendas. The paradigm gives comfort to some powerful individuals and nations, as when adhering to this philosophy, there is not enough for everyone anyway, and so real change in the economic state of the world is not possible, rendering them without responsibility. It seems better then, to leave it as it is it, and not to disconfirm the perceptions of the status quo (Schein 1999). Perception becomes reality. Furthermore, for these reasons, the Scarcity Paradigm may also induce complacency in the affluent and the poor alike, so that instead of engaging in ridding the world of poverty, the extant situation is accepted, and patronising the poor through different kinds of glorifying their dignity in poverty may arise. Such glorification may be seen in certain Catholic circles, as for example in the liberation theology movement, and such misunderstandings of the socio-economic state that is poverty well illustrates the flaws of this paradigm (Gutiérrez & Muller 2015).

■ Sufficiency paradigm – Unlimited potential
Industrial revolution

The process of industrial innovations referred to as the Industrial Revolution initiated a move away from the subsistence agriculture and crafts-based society. This was an innovative process, which took place in England and Scotland during the late 18th and early 19th centuries, and entailed a number of improvements to production, which had been stagnant for centuries (Baumol 1990). The new regimen of factories took over from the earlier, and often well-organised, cottage production, leading to a mass exodus from the countryside to towns and cities (De Vries 1994; Galbraith 1989). In its turn, this mass movement of people changed the social makeup of society, creating new social conditions, the advent of the urban working class and the modern industrial city (Hall & Barrett 2012; Kim & Short 2008). It has been a common perception among economic historians that the Industrial Revolution resulted in an increased number of poor, who earlier had lived in relative comfort in the countryside. Friedrich Hayek (1899–1992) opposed this view, and posited that the advent of industrialism with its increased production output gave opportunities to many previously poor people to live under improved material conditions, with augmented survival opportunities (Hayek 1967):

> The very increase of wealth and well-being which had been achieved raised standards and aspirations. What for ages had seemed a natural and inevitable situation, or even as an improvement upon the past, came to be regarded as incongruous with the opportunities which the new age appeared to offer. Economic suffering both became more conspicuous and seemed less justified, because general wealth was increasing faster than ever before. (p. 209)

Although the new brand of industrialism would give the individual newfound opportunities and freedoms, the mass migration of the poor to the cities involved the creation of new societal strata, which gave rise to hitherto unknown social strains and conflicts among the classes, with lasting consequences (Banerjee & Duflo 2012).

Marx and production

Karl Marx (1818–1883) conceptualised a philosophy of potential, and his theories on production and society established a new perception related to capital formation and aggregation. A pivotal point of Marx's (2013) theorising was that in the industrial society, land and finite resources did not represent the totality of capital, as it would also include machinery, technology and labour. From this analysis, Marx introduced the perception of an economy that is capable of producing goods of any kind in sufficient quantities as to allow all societal members to exist in a state of material sufficiency.

In a sense, as explained by Piketty (2014), Marx introduced a philosophy of potential for unlimited material growth both as a possibility and as a purpose driven by the accumulation instincts of the ruling capitalist (Zou 1994). The consequence of such a philosophy is that all members of society may enjoy material sufficiency, given that the production outcome, the created wealth, is justly and effectively distributed. Following this, there is no need for extracting wealth from the rich and redistributing it to the poor, because the means of production may be duplicated without practical limits, allowing the potential for production sufficient to meet the needs of all.

For the purposes of this treatise, I will refer to this main direction in economic thought as the 'Sufficiency Paradigm'. Marx, who, with his publications *The Capital*, and the *Communist Manifesto* with Friedrich Engels, inspired what perhaps is the strongest societal control on economic life, hereunder banking, which has touched the occidental modern societal and economic development in the modern era (Marx 2013; Marx & Engels 2002). It is worth noting that Marx, in his publications, sought mainly to present scientific theories on capitalism and the economy, covering topics such as production, monopolies and diminishing returns, and that his writings did not represent a template for developing socialist political or economic models for political governance. Nevertheless, during the 20th century, numerous socialist movements took Marx's teachings to heart, or at least, their interpretations of them, and attempted to form societies built on these ideas. Typically, this led to different versions of strong command economic systems. Most notable here, of course, would be the Soviet Union, but the idea of controlling vast tracts of social and economic life also took hold outside the strictly communist/socialist circles (Kurz 2016).

Marx' seminal thoughts on unlimited potential for production as a root of limitless material growth is explained by Galbraith (1998:102) as principles of potential never-ending growth of capital, and thus affluence. He (Galbraith 1998) posited that 'production – the output of the economic system' can be increased in the following ways:

1. The productive resources that are available, in particular the labour and capital (including available raw materials), can be more fully employed. In other words, idleness can be eliminated.
2. Given the technical state of the arts, these resources can be more efficiently utilised. Labour and capital can be used in the most advantageous combination, one with the other, and the two can be distributed to the greatest advantage, consumer tastes considered, between the production of various things and the rendering of various services.
3. The supply of labour can be increased.
4. The supply of capital, which also serves as a substitute for labour, can be increased.
5. The state of the arts can be improved by technological innovations. As a result, more output can be obtained from a given supply of labour and capital, and the capital will be of better quality. (p. 102)

As the quote shows, the contemporary theoretical understanding of capital and affluence is that it in principle can be perpetually expanded without practical human limitations. The potential for distribution, or redistribution for that matter, is therefore theoretically present, blocked only by societal and political processes of inequality and marginalisation (Bottero 2005; Hughes, Sharrock & Martin 2010).

It is the position here that because of the political and social unfairness that permeated Western society at the time of Marx and Friedrich Engels (1820–1895), contemporary and later readers and political commentators have viewed their theories mainly as a path to material and ideological fairness through redistribution as seen through the lens of the Scarcity Paradigm. Rather than perceiving the theories in this limiting manner, the Marxian understanding of economic laws should be seen to involve the possibility of well-distributed affluence, without mainly focusing on the agonistic aspects of redistributing already scarce resources; in other words, accepting the Sufficiency Paradigm.

Keynes and the Cambridge School

As the evolving understanding of societal economics was being developed by the above thinkers, and notably by Marx, the pressures for public partaking in the economic output from the production in which they participated were increasing. John Maynard Keynes, creator of the so-called Cambridge School, is commonly seen as the creator of theories pertaining to democratic governmental intervention in the free market economy of a nation. Keynes further developed the ideas of earlier thinkers and is regarded as the creator of modern macroeconomic philosophies (Harcourt & Kerr 2003). He focused on the idea that through market interventions, unemployment would be avoided, and such interventions were necessary to counteract tendencies of boom-and-bust phases permeating traditional free market systems. The main theory was that if the government took short-term action, the long term would take care of itself (Smithies 1951). He was also an avid proponent of governmental fiscal interventions in the economy for the amelioration of the negative effects of periods of economic depression (Galbraith 1989).

Acceptance of added political control with markets took hold after the great Depression in the 1930s, where the theories of Keynes represented a compromise between the free market ideologies of unchecked capitalism and the command-and-control aspects of socialism. A key element in his theories picked up by policy-makers was to allow public spending to increase demand in the economy, when the market forces alone did not create sufficient demand (Galbraith 1989). Keynes' (2012) *The General Theory of Employment, Interest and Money*, which was published in 1936, became his most influential work, where his main theories on societal economy were outlined. The importance of *The General Theory* cannot be overestimated in the history of economics, and Galbraith (1989), for example, likens it to the importance of Smith's *Wealth of Nations* in 1776, and Marx's *Capital* in 1867. Under the Keynesian philosophy, governmental intervention, not least by the central bank, is a useful measure for creating growth, fostering financial stability and increasing production output (Keynes 2012). Keynes' theories on economic governance in a blended model of capitalism and government control would prove highly influential in the post-war era, not least in Europe, where several countries espoused his theories, sometimes referred to as public demand theories, and used them as justification for different levels of limiting the freedom of the markets. This was the case in the social democracies of Scandinavia (Crouch 2008).

It is fair to state that Keynes is one of the most influential economic thinkers of the mid-20th century, substantially contributing to the development of the modern liberal state, and that the popularity of his theories only waned with the advent of liberalism in the 1980s (Galbraith 1989; Skidelsky 2010).

Friedrich Hayek

Friedrich Hayek espoused the concept of spontaneous order appearing in a market, himself being a strong advocate of free markets and anti-protectionist trade practices (Hayek 2001). Hayek was the 20th-century inspiration for the liberalist movement, and although the liberalist ideas had not been in full effect in any Western country since its inception, after the two World Wars, the West was left in a state where control and state governance were deemed necessary to restructure the Western world politically, socially and economically. The post-war system of financial controls and regulations, not least promoted through the Bretton Woods convention, was coming to an end when the gold standard was abolished in the early 1970s, and soon after, the international exchange controls were lifted (Galbraith 1989; Neal 2015).

Because of this, liberalist ideas gained new traction and, spurred on by thinkers like Hayek and Milton Friedman, influential politicians like Ronald Reagan (1911–2004) and Margaret Thatcher (1925–2013) used these ideas as their basis for modernising the economic systems of the West during the late 1970s and 1980s, in what is sometimes referred to as neoliberalism (Peck 2008). The relative success of the Western economies at this time may have played a role in the collapse of the Eastern Bloc, where command economic principles had reigned since World War II, and with this disintegration, liberalist ideas gained support in the former Eastern Bloc areas. Coming into the 21st century, then, the occidental world had reunited around liberalist ideas, and with them, the rise of liberal democracies in the erstwhile dictatorships of the eastern realm (Peck & Tickell 2002).

Milton Friedman

The final economic thinker to be discussed under the Sufficiency Paradigm is Milton Friedman (1912–2006), to whom many have attributed the negative stigma of proposing the introduction of an almost unbridled free market economic system. Friedman was an avid opponent of the governmental interventions of the Keynesian school, and advocated maximum freedom for the market actors, trusting their free choices to be optimal for both the individual and society (Friedman 1970). Friedman's theories gained momentum in the late 20th century and have influenced several modern states in creating liberal democracies. Typically, in countries where the norm has been suppressive, as in the former Eastern bloc, the transition towards a free, liberal economic system has been supported by representations of market-directed economic systems, and Friedman's seemingly unbridled freedom of the individual market actor seems to fit the bill. However, even though Friedman's (2002) views pertain to topics such as monopoly, government and the educational system, monetary control and trade agreements, the notion that his ideas are merely serving the rich and powerful on behalf of the poor and weak may be a misrepresentation of the fuller scope of his idea of the ideal society.

The perception of Friedman's theories as brutal and liberal for the benefit of the few has, at times, permeated Western political discourse, but could not be more mistaken. For Friedman, the theory was that if all people were left to choose their best option for earning a living, maximum affluence for all would be generated. It would probably be surprising to those understanding Friedman only from media and political discourse, that he was an advocate for a kind of citizens' salary for the least fortunate. His proposal was that the tax system would include a 'negative tax' for those earning the least or nothing, so that this group would be able to meet their minimum needs (Friedman 2002; Moffitt 2003). Without making a political point, the ideas of Friedman on negative income tax can be seen as progressive, and perhaps ahead of their time, as to the best of my knowledge, any real form of citizens' basic salary has not materialised in any Western democratic country (Galbraith 1989). To my knowledge, to receive something from any Western state, the recipient needs to demonstrate and declare some sort of personal failure or embarrassment, pleading to the benevolence of the state for the satisfaction of material needs, even when economic theory and practice, as described above, allows for the fairly distributed satisfaction of needs, given a systemic minimum competence.

Friedman's theories share the predicament of many other original thinkers, in that the more ground-breaking and original his thoughts were, the greater focus these often-controversial aspects have received in the sensationalised political discourse. The possibilities for the poor and the disadvantaged, which Friedman sought to improve, have received scarce attention when presented to the wider public.

Sufficiency affirmed

As discussed in the preceding text, following the Great Discoveries and the emergence of modern industrialism, the notion of sufficient resources for all to enjoy full material needs satisfaction gradually took hold. Surely, the combination of abundant supply of raw materials from the New World and the newfound manufacturing capabilities of the Industrial Revolution must have made it difficult to continue the belief in scarcity as a natural law. As is pointed out elsewhere in this chapter, the notion of material sufficiency may be difficult to accept for individuals, groups and states for a number of reasons, one being that it challenges the acceptance of status quo. This both for themselves and on behalf of others, whether in a state of affluence and ample needs satisfaction or not. When the Sufficiency Paradigm is affirmed, core questions relating to local and global fairness of distribution and just access to material goods and societal opportunities will become more pressing, not least as it will then become clear that the current situation where many suffer scarcity must be due to the poor state of the human family and how we accept treating each other.

Despite the uncomfortable aspects of accepting the Sufficiency Paradigm, the seminal thinkers mentioned in this section are but just a few among practitioners and theorisers in the modern era who accepted and promoted the idea of sufficient material resources for all to enjoy. As with the philosophy of scarcity, the Sufficiency Paradigm is also rooted in scriptural interpretations (*tota Scriptura*), and under the Reformed paradigm the position is that God in creation has provided for complete and total needs satisfaction for the entire human family (e.g. Gn 1:28; Ec 5:19; Ps 23:1–6). Thus, affirming the Sufficiency Paradigm will be the only acceptable position for any Christian exegete.

Economic-philosophical backdrop

■ Governmental participation
▪ Traditional government

The traditional place of government in the occidental culture has been that of the strong ruling the weak, channelling most if not all of the surplus wealth in society upwards through the social strata. A striking example from Scripture is in the Nativity narrative (Lk 2:1–4) where Augustus calls for a general census. A census may be seen as the ultimate expression of power and supremacy, and at the same time act as a useful tool for taxation and keeping control, as several later similar examples would indicate, for example William the Conqueror's Doomsday Book in England.

Matthew's Nativity narrative (Mt 2:2), with its introduction of the new king threatening the existing rule, could also indicate a seminal forewarning event of the decline and subsequent fall of the Roman Empire, built on worldly power and relying on material wealth. When the Western empire fell in 476 AD, organised government and influence previously exerted in Western Europe fell with it. The early medieval era was dominated by societal decline and Arabic influences, and the next real step in establishing proper indigenous rule in Western Europe came with Charlemagne (c. 742 AD – 814 AD), who was crowned Roman Emperor by the Pope in 800 AD. This empire was some 300 years later to be called the Holy Roman Empire, exerting great influence on most societal levels and areas of life (Haaugaard 1979; Mayr-Harting 1996).

Notwithstanding Charlemagne and his attempts at ruling, the place of government in societal economics remained rudimentary and weak, still revolving around modes of taxation and warfare. The church was to a certain degree the only remaining organisational infrastructure of the Roman Empire in the West, and did perform some important societal tasks related to marriage, family law, land ownership, caring for the sick and education for the few (Woods 2012). Further contributions to society's economy came through monasticism, agricultural innovation, architecture and construction (Hitchcock 2012; MacCulloch 2010).

With the Great Discoveries, governments took a greater interest in managing their newfound foreign wealth but did not take any deeper interest in the economics of society, other than securing the spoils for the highest echelons of society. As discussed earlier, the advent of industrialism commenced with increased societal division, and the state took little interest in the industrial practices, other than perhaps to rectify some of its starkest excesses, like the eventual abolishment of the notorious and widely-condemned practice of using 'chimney-children' (Jordanova 1987).

The weak position of the state in society's economic life can probably be attributed to several factors, but with the prevalence of the Scarcity Paradigm and its clasp on human cognition, it could also be said that there was not much a government believed it could do, even if it wanted to. On the other hand, the churches and attendant organisations did contribute toward some redistribution of wealth by helping the poor, but even for the churches, it is assumed here that the Scarcity Paradigm did not allow for any large-scale growth theorising on a societal level, where all could participate and improve their material conditions in concert.

Budding welfare state

In the late 19th century, early indicators of increased governmental participation became evident. Otto von Bismarck (1815–1898) can arguably be recognised as the inventor of the modern welfare state, or at least an early version of it. Through legislation initiated by him, the harsher aspects of capitalism were alleviated, and in 1884 and 1887, the Reichstag passed laws securing worker insurance schemes for sickness, accidents, old age and disability. In Britain, some 25 years later, the modern welfare state became a reality through legislation under Lloyd George (1863–1945), introducing a non-contributory old age pension system and unemployment benefits beyond those of Germany (Galbraith 1989). The idea of a welfare state has been introduced throughout the Western world to different degrees, and thinkers like Marx and Keynes have offered seminal influences. However, some societies have not adopted the nomenclature of the welfare state, yet have similar structures in place, safeguarding a minimum satisfaction of material needs and welfare, including education and basic health services (Woods 2005). Even though the ideological language in use may differ, say between that of the United States (US) and France, the basic outline of society is not that different in relation to caring for the poor and protecting the rich (Alesina & Glaeser 2004; Alesina, Glaeser & Sacerdote 2001).

On the basis of the theories of Marx and Engels, some states have gone beyond that of the modern benevolent liberal welfare state and experimented with what has been termed socialist states, without the liberal democratic structures of the West. In these states, notably Soviet Union, China and their affiliates, the state played an all-encompassing role in the citizens' life, including control of professional activity and material needs satisfaction, securing on the surface the common person from the cradle to the grave (Marx & Engels 2002). As is well-documented elsewhere, these states have failed both formally and in real terms, and today only a couple of such systems exist (e.g. Cuba and North Korea), and these exist only by way of hard-line political suppression that keeps the common people in a state of deep poverty. Attempts at planning the real economy and simulating the free market and its mechanisms have proved not to be feasible in the real economic life of any nation, with all the different pushes and pulls of the citizens' needs and expectations (King 2003). It seems that it has been impossible to convince any free population that the state should have all power in a democratic structure, and none of the unfree states have been able to increase production output through their all-consuming ideological superstructures.

Another political movement that grasped onto anti-capitalist philosophies and espoused public spending and control was the National Socialism of Adolf Hitler (1898–1945). The National Socialist economic policies of Hitler after taking office in 1933 included substantial public infrastructure projects, such as the building of the autobahns, and later the production of arms. By 1936, German unemployment was substantially reduced (Galbraith 1989). For well-known historical reasons, the German National Socialist economic policies would not last.

Although the government has been accepted as a valid participant in the economic sphere in the West, governmental influence is not uncontroversial, and the full acceptance of the Sufficiency Paradigm has not been achieved. Societal economic discourse in the West is still influenced by the notion that if some actors are to receive more than they have, someone else will have to get less. The more progressive ideas of Milton Friedman, allowing all citizens a minimum wage, or negative income tax for the poor, have not taken root in the public political discourse in any Western liberal democracy. In the current Western society, the influence of the state in the economy, education and health services is still surprisingly contentious, and has been for centuries (Hayek 2001).

Active state

In addition to the welfare aspect of the citizens, the state has also participated in the creation of infrastructure, such as roads or bridges, and in particular in Europe, also in establishing some capital-intensive industries, such as mines, smelters, railway systems, telecommunication and banking. This has led to a situation in which the state has taken the place of the investor in some countries; such influence has been controversial in the public discourse, and in most liberal Western democracies this participation is waning and is generally being discontinued (Mazzucato 2014).

Governmental investment funds

Another level of state capitalism can be found in the financial management of pensions for the citizens, and such structures are mainly managed according to capitalist profit maximisation principles. A few select countries, among them Norway and Abu Dhabi, have arrived at such high levels of public wealth that they are beyond merely looking after the material needs of their existing population, and the managing of surplus wealth is to be utilised for future generations (Piketty 2014). Others, like China and Hong Kong, maintain investment funds based on industrial income, and partake in the investment community even though the satisfaction of the citizens' needs may not yet have reached a satisfactory level.

The activities of the governmentally operated investment funds are followed closely by other countries and outside economists, as the political control that is exerted over the capital in these funds is frowned upon and met with suspicion. It seems that the traditional profit maximisation of the well-known capitalist is easier to stomach than that of the governmentally-salaried investment manager, even though the wealth managed by the sovereign wealth funds does not amount to more than the aggregate of the Forbes billionaires, approximately 1.5% of the world's total private wealth (Piketty 2014). The reason for this scepticism may lie in the possibility of tacit political agendas that could be part of a diplomatic strategy outlined by the funds' owners, in reality, a foreign government. That this contention even exists is an example of the comfort with which the global community coexists with traditional Western-style capitalism and the so-called free market. It is conceivable that the situation could be opposite, and that the global community would welcome state influence on investment activity.

■ Current state – Globalisation
Post-World War II

The capitalist free market of the West was up until the 1950s and 1960s a political structure almost solely benefitting the wealth levels of occidental states and their populations. These nations controlled most of the industrial production output, and the rest of the world remained suppliers of raw materials to the West and represented demand for the finished products through Western exports. This situation was unquestioned in the West and most, if not all, of Western economic teachings, and the knowledge generation accepted the premise of Western economic supremacy. The main argument of this unequal economic state was the lauding of the free market. This was particularly prevalent in the US and British tradition, including that of German theory. After World War II, the Japanese economy was based on the rebuilding of its industrial equipment to modern standards. The Japanese, however, had a different take on the free market, as Marxist leanings were more prevalent than in the West, and the state permeated capital ownership, allowing for a different breed of industrial capitalism to evolve. This system of cooperation between private and governmental capital also had an augmented focus on human capital, long before this was considered significant in the West (Galbraith 1989).

The growth of the Japanese economy through successful exports, not least to the West, with development of multilateral trade agreements and organisations, opened the door for other countries to partake in the 'free market' of the West. Gradually, this led to an increasingly globalised economy, directing resources to where the returns were highest, and cost lowest, and this has increased global production output and productive efficiency. Nonetheless, globalisation has not come without cost to those involved. In its earlier stages, environmental destruction and labour exploitation were localised away from the Western consumer, resulting in ever-falling prices on consumer goods. However, this led to the dismantling of major Western industrial hubs, such as the European shipbuilding industries, and the European and US auto manufacturers, resulting in falling employment levels in the West with subsequent political resistance (Van Aelst & Walgrave 2002).

The post-World War II period has been a time of great change in the world economy, and the Western hegemony has become substantially weakened. The remnants of the colonial system have been almost completely removed on the formal level, with some exceptions such as the Commonwealth, but the West still enjoys a relatively strong economic position in the global arena.

Globalised economy

After the stock market failure in the late 1980s, and the subsequent perceived austerity in the West, the anti-globalisation proponents became more visible in the public discourse, warning against the effects of a globalised economy. The rationale for the adversarial globalisation position varied from that of trade unions protecting their members, nationalistic chauvinism, ecology and fear of losing the Western hegemonic position (Klein 2001). The general tendency in the anti-globalisation argumentation was to spread fear in the West, and the matter of economic equalisation and wealth sharing was seldom mentioned. A main tendency in the discourse, and in particular with those involved in ecologic argumentation, was that globalisation diminishes our common finite resources (Dietz & O'Neill 2013). Thus, the Scarcity Paradigm has been given a renewed impetus, and the fear of perceived inevitable poverty and ecological devastation has become a line of argumentation (Daly & Farley 2011).

Piketty (2014) demonstrates how the distribution of global wealth and opportunities has shifted in the post-World War II era, through the global shift in production. He explains (Piketty 2014:59) that in the years between 1900 and 1980, 70%–80% of world goods and services production were concentrated in the US and Europe, and that this share fell to approximately 50% by 2010. He predicts that this development will continue and may end at around 20%–30%, a level comparable to the US–European share of the world population. This would show that globalisation has a participatory universal effect, and that the free market the world currently experiences involves redistribution of opportunities as well as increased industrial output. If everyone were to be given their share of the opportunities, and this could happen without decline in the Western standards of living, then the standard of living would improve for most, if not all.

In Western political life, a feeling of inadequacy has gradually set in, and the public discourse is increasingly concentrating on the taxation of international corporations, as these have now become objects of sceptical criticism, much unlike the celebrated companies of previous times, such as the Dutch East India Company, to mention just one. The notion is that the international corporations cannot be democratically controlled, and so they are viewed as problematic societal actors, threatening the very existence of Western democracy and standards of living (Hertz 2002).

The speed of globalisation is probably increasing, and with trade and new technology, new possibilities follow. In addition to continuously improving the logistics of physical goods, the Internet and attendant web-based technologies make it possible today to distribute information and to offer services across the globe, at high speed and at relatively low cost. These opportunities will most likely be further utilised in the future, leading to increased unemployment in the established markets of the West, and increasing the opportunities for partakers in the markets of Asia, Africa and South America, who previously were left outside, with scarce possibilities of enjoying the wealth creation of the West (Stiglitz & Charlton 2005). The tendency of falling relative wealth in the West, with rising unemployment in its wake, is already creating some social unrest, and the anti-globalisation movement has not yet burned out (Ayres 2004).

In keeping with the modern version of the liberalist economic philosophy, the 'invisible hand' could be seen as the highest, and perhaps wisest, moderator of human economic interaction, and with it, a globalised economy has appeared. This new, globalised economy now exists at a scale never before seen, where the individual has been presented with a myriad of economic choices, with attendant consequences for the individual and the environment. This new globalised and liberalist economic world order has been met with substantial criticism, not least from Western political and academic thinkers; their arguments are varied, and point to unwanted environmental consequences and social injustice (Klein 2001; Piketty 2014). The globalised economy may have had its seminal beginnings in the necessity for selling Western products, and thus, initially served as a tool for the maintenance of the established Western beneficial economic position. However, as the demands of trade reciprocity have been met, the West is now experiencing a situation where when the door is open, products and services flow in both directions, perhaps signifying a fairer distribution of global opportunities.

Current situation
Statistics

Finally, to assess the state of global wealth and its distribution is a discouraging task, as statistics abound, and affluence and poverty have different definitions, both in relative and absolute terms. The United Nations Food and Agriculture Organization (UNFAO) stated that, in 2011, there were at least 850 million undernourished people globally, which may have grown over the intervening years to 925 million at the time of writing. The UNFAO further explains that because of growth in the global population, the prevalence of undernourishment has declined in relative terms. The countries accounting for 98% of the world's hungry, they explain, demonstrate a prevalence of the undernourished at 15% of the population. According to UN statistics, even as substantial progress has been achieved during the last three decades, approximately 10% of the global population lived on less than $1.90 per day in 2015 (736 million people), and in 2018, 8% were living under this threshold, which is the UN's current poverty definition. Furthermore, 55% of the global population has no access to any social cash benefit protection. The UNFAO further explains that poverty is geographically distributed unevenly worldwide, and that in the sub-Saharan region of Africa, for example, the drop in poverty levels has been marginal at best in relative terms, and in absolute terms, the number of poor in the region has almost doubled (UN n.d.; UNFAO 2012).

It would be possible to demonstrate global inequality through several markers other than absolute poverty and hunger. However, for this treatise, these items are sufficient to underscore the extant global inequalities, and to point towards areas of improvement, which can be deemed feasible within the scope of international banking and financial investment activity. The division of wealth is still geographically skewed, and it is the contention here that, even though global economic development is generally moving in an equalising and thus fairer direction through the wider economic participation of all global regions, there are steps that need to be taken for all to participate. It is probably fair to say that the so-called 'free' market has most likely never been as 'free' as today, and thus the activities of the powerful market actors, have an unprecedented opportunity to exert a positive influence on global fairness and equalisation through the application of morally constructive capitalism.

The political-economic discourse

The perceptions of accessibility of resources for human use have varied over time and place. The Scarcity Paradigm has been the dominant influence on ideas regarding the possible subsistence of humanity. It is perfectly understandable that the Scarcity Paradigm has been prevalent, as it fits a particular societal perception of reality. On the individual level, the sense of scarcity is simple to accept, and it is easy to doubt the possibility of abundance which is not readily available to observe or enjoy.

The emergence of the Sufficiency Paradigm has been slow in the making and has yet to permeate the global political discourse and individual cognition. With the Sufficiency Paradigm, some uncomfortable conclusions pertaining to the state of the global political system arise, namely, the individual's responsibility and the setting of common human goals. To accept the Scarcity Paradigm is probably less demanding for most, as this philosophy explains the current unjust economic state, and relieves the individual and society of responsibility for their fellows. After all, if there are not enough resources for all, why should we then have to share? No one would have a greater claim to enjoy the resources than others would, and thus, the unjust situation of today will not be any worse than any other unjust distribution of the scarce finite resources available for human use. Under the Sufficiency Paradigm, this changes dramatically, as all partakers will have to question how and why today's situation has been created and whether it is acceptable, and how to adjust and ameliorate the distribution of opportunities for all. If there is enough for everyone, then the inevitable conclusion is that the global political system is incompetent on most, if not on all, levels.

Even though the Sufficiency Paradigm is well-documented and somewhat accepted, several societal actors, such as Western ecologists and anti-globalisation proponents, tenaciously hold on to the Scarcity Paradigm in their agitation. This is perhaps with good intentions, but leaves the audience with perceptions of hopelessness, and accepts large tracts of the global population as servile, helpless beggars. In the occidental countries, the population perceives the relative economic decline, and the focus is on retaining wealth. Even though the ecologists in principle may be correct in stating that the world's resources are finite, this does not mean that they are in a practical sense, since the material needs of humanity are limited and need not be met excessively. The matter of global fairness is only marginally touched on in Western public discourse, and influential thinkers like Piketty (2014) place greater emphasis on the perils of social unrest in the West resulting from relative wealth differences, than on absolute global poverty and desired global wealth distribution. At this stage in history, the West is mostly concerned with relative wealth, often masked as issues of relative poverty, but these Western societies have populations living far above the UN's absolute poverty definition of $1.90 per day. By maintaining a public debate pertaining to taxation of wealthy Western citizens and global corporations for its use in the Western liberal democratic nations, the Western middle classes divert attention from the real global issues of fairness and poverty, and free themselves from responsibility as stakeholders in the global inequality. If the Sufficiency Paradigm were duly trusted, this line of thinking would not be viable, and perceptions of scarcity are most likely used rhetorically to support the unjust agenda of the Western middle classes. To stay with the notion of inevitable scarcity can only lead to a perpetuation of perceived lawfulness of global inequality and suffering, but a move towards the Sufficiency Paradigm would leave the current powerful societies, including those of the West, with a responsibility to act morally when partaking in the global economy as investors and political actors.

The era of neoliberalist policies instigated at the end of the 20th century, with Margaret Thatcher and Ronald Reagan as figureheads that flowed over the Western political landscape with its substantial deregulations of the banking sector may prove to be short lived (Peck 2004; Peck & Tickell 2002). This newfound view on the advantages of free market forces has been under constant criticism, and since the market crash of 2007/2008, influential political voices in the West are yet again calling for increased market regulations and limitations on the freedom of international trade (Piketty 2014). Notably, the presidency of Donald Trump (1946–) and the 'Brexit' focused premierships of Theresa May (1956–) and Boris Johnson (1964–), can all be said to represent a clear regression to former models of economic public governance, such as mercantilism and nationalism, through their expressed isolationist policies connected to trade and international cooperation. It is evident that, throughout history, there has been a constant societal acceptance, if not urge, to impose controls on the free market, and also on the banking sector. These governance impulses have been motivated by political, religious and pragmatic reasoning, in isolation and in combination, and in the current Western political climate there seems to be a growing tendency to increase the level of control on banking activities. This control philosophy is supported both by exponents on the political left, like the 'Occupy Wall Street' movement and the like, as well as by the apparently right-wing present-day world leaders mentioned above.

Chapter 3

The phenomenon of money

Keywords: money; social technology; gold standard; fiat money; crypto currency; independent currency.

■ Introduction

In this chapter, the development of money as a social technology is explored, and a historical and philosophical account will be given. Different societal and academic perceptions on the emergence of money will receive particular treatment. The main focus here is on sources of financial and economic life connected to the development of the occidental monetary system in societal economy.

When attempting to understand the development of banking, the typical author takes money for granted, seeing moneylending and debt as something made possible by the pre-existence of money (e.g. Investopedia n.d.). Typically, the position is that in primitive, primeval society, human beings resorted to bartering with each other if they could not themselves produce the physical objects they needed for their subsistence (e.g. Smith 2012). After all, using money as a medium for acquiring needs satisfaction can easily be perceived as more advanced than interchanging physical objects through bartering, such as one pig for two goats. For the purposes here, in order not to resort to circular argumentation where debt is created by borrowing money and where money is necessary to create debt, it is necessary to delve deeper into the

How to cite: Bøsterud, M., 2021, 'The phenomenon of money', in *A treatise on Christian banking*, pp. 33–46, AOSIS, Cape Town. https://doi.org/10.4102/aosis.2021.BK263.03

origin of money, which typically is seen as the object of debt and credit. Only if we understand how money originated as a measurement for debt and/or credit can we understand how banking has come about in society, and how it may be useful and/or problematic from societal, religious and philosophical vantage points.

The concept of money as a social technology and/or as an inter-human value measurement is of seminal importance in this treatise, as it is foundational for the views and assumptions related to both the origin of financing and the usefulness of banking for developing societal economy.

■ Emergence of money
Antiquity

Our knowledge about money and debt and the financial system in the earlier stages of occidental society is rudimentary, and evidence is scarce, because of the limited existence of written sources, and physical evidence like coins will have to suffice as evidence of monetary systems. However, the absence of physical evidence such as coins cannot in itself illustrate how ancient society managed economic affairs, exchange of goods and trade.

The barter myth

Graeber (2012) addresses the topic of money from the aspect of debt, and explains how economists typically view money as a means of keeping count, payment and debt (e.g. Case et al. 1999), and promotes the view that this has typically been the main perception of economic thought and study. He further posits that it is from the academic realm of sociology and anthropology that interest for money has been taken with a non-orthodox perspective, allowing for a deeper understanding of the actual origin of money in society from a user-driven vantage point where measurement of obligations was at the core. This view is opposed to the traditional economists' perceptions, where a top-down perspective is typically taken, and where money is seen as originated and controlled by institutions of authority. The orthodox thinking among economists has been that bartering first existed as a means of material exchange before the invention of money, and then, with the increased use of money, a banking and credit system has developed over time resulting from the monetary system as we now know it (e.g. Maunder et al. 1991). This idea of initial interpersonal bartering to satisfy human needs is compelling, as it places primitive humanity and society in a linear historical context, which is perceived as inferior to later historical periods, including our own. Graeber (2012) further explains how the idea of an antecedent bartering system, representing an earlier primitive version of the way money is used today, has never been proven to exist in any known society either in historical times or contemporary society. His conclusion, then, is that a pre-money state of inter-human bartering is a figment of economists' imagination, and is based on, and perpetuates, the mere myth of money taking the place of a more primitive preceding bartering system. This stance is supported by Dalton (1982) who posits that although bartering has occurred among people at all times it has never had any more than a marginal place in the economic system and has not functioned in the place of a monetary exchange system. However, the myth of bartering as a societal financial system is persistent for a reason: after all, when Adam Smith (2012) invented the academic field of economics, he represented the story of the linear development from bartering to the modern monetary systems including that of credit and finance. Nonetheless, this was not the academic origination of the bartering myth, as, in 330 BC, Aristotle in his *Politics* (1992) speculated on such a phyletic development starting with primitive bartering between individuals and gradually developing into a system where money was necessary leading to the ascension of debt as a means of financing. By whatever means the barter myth may have been initiated and perpetuated, the premise in this treatise is that the barter myth is just that – a myth – and that the conclusions of Dalton (1982) and Graeber (2012) should be accepted as valid.

Mesopotamia

The Eastern ancient civilisations in Mesopotamia had developed their own systems of reckoning and goods distribution, including accounting for debts, already in the third millennium BC at Uruk and later Ur, which were the headquarters of these relatively advanced civilisations. With their thousands of hectares of land being cultivated, in addition to breweries and fish farms and substantial trading operations, it was necessary to create a bureaucracy and systems to organise economic activity. From these advanced societies, and not least from their complex and organised modes of operating their societies, some of the most important human inventions for developing society were created, including literacy, numeracy and accounting (Van de Mieroop 1992). A part of the Mesopotamian accounting system included the use of clay tablets with inscriptions in cuneiform, and from findings dating back to 2500 BC it can be noted that silver was used as a form of payment. Pieces of gold and silver were called shekels, or talents, and they would typically represent corresponding values of oil, beer or wheat; this system was highly useful for merchants when transferring goods from one party to another and this use of metals could be seen as a kind of proto-money (Weatherford 1997).

☐ Homeric age

Societies in the Homeric age used gift exchange, booty distribution and division of sacrifice as means of economic exchange and had not yet developed a system for debt reckoning like that of the Mesopotamians. From the occidental cultural realm, the epic poems of the *Iliad* (Homer 1991) and the *Odyssey* (Homer 2003) contribute important learning about how early and possibly pre-monetary societies organised their financial affairs. From the *Iliad* and *Odyssey*, which were composed in the 8th century BC, we learn how the Greek societies organised themselves during the 'dark ages' of Hellenistic culture, approximately 1100 BC to 900 BC, also known as the 'Homeric age' (Donlan 1985). It is important to note that the society in the Homeric age was based mainly on self-sufficiency within small groups of families, hamlets and towns, and that such self-sufficiency did not give rise to the need for a monetary system. In the absence of economic goods to be exchanged among individuals and groups, money would not be useful within this type of society (Martin 2014). From these early sources, and in particular the *Iliad*, we find that when ancient Greece was in a state of warfare, distribution of war booty among the partakers was done according to a non-democratic structure with the nobility on top deciding the division. In addition, as part of the religious sacrifice of oxen, the roasted meat was distributed among societal partakers according to set rules of division. Finally, and, in particular from the *Odyssey*, we learn that when society was in a more peaceful state, there were reciprocal gift exchanges between aristocrats (Homer 1991). The ongoing distribution of sacrificial meat could be seen as the long-term transactional order in society, and the division of war booty and reciprocal gift exchange could be seen as a short-term transactional order, which would serve to ensure that all members of society had their basic needs for food and drink met (Seaford 1994).

☐ Greek city-states

Although the Mesopotamians invented the above-mentioned important technologies, the concept of money was not created or discovered by them. What was lacking among the Mesopotamians was the concept of a universally accepted value measurement. When the Phoenicians of the Levant started to trade with the Greeks, the concepts of accounting and literacy from the Mesopotamian culture were introduced to the Greeks, and from this exchange, the concept of money may have been born. This could be due to the primitive systems of the Greeks connected to distribution of booty, sacrifice and gifts, wherein a concept of universal value was embedded; when this was connected to the bureaucratic abilities and literacy of the Mesopotamians, money could be created, as we know from later usage. In other words, when the concepts of literacy, numeracy, accounting and universal value were all combined, money came into being (Martin 2014; Neal 2015). The first-known Greek coins were made by the Lydians, who, between 640 BC and 630 BC, minted coins from electrum, a naturally existing alloy of gold and silver. The Lydian kings made the coins of uniform weight, to discontinue the need for time-consuming weighing up of the metals by the merchants when trading. For preventing coins from easily being counterfeited, the Lydian kings imprinted a lion's head on each coin. This imprinting, or minting, would also make the pieces of electrum flatter, as to resemble, however vaguely, what today are considered coins. In addition, as the advent of these early coins made it possible to participate in trade without the use of scales, now, counting was sufficient to measure the correct number of coins, which also led to a more rapid advancement of trade (Weatherford 1997). The use of coins and minting spread over the Hellenistic world, and around 480 BC nearly 100 mints were operating in the Greek world (Van de Mieroop 1992; Von Reden 2010).

The invention of money rapidly led to a widespread monetisation of what had traditionally been reciprocal social obligations. For example, traditional sharecroppers became tenants with money to pay rent, and military contributions, private and public obligations, could now all be settled in cash money (Von Reden 2010). The advent of money would also lead to substantial changes in society, not least in the established hierarchical power structures, because money may be acquired by anyone; however, as this falls outside the scope of this treatise, it will not be discussed further here. It suffices to say, that with the advent of money, a central question arose: namely, who could issue money? Initially this was performed by minting coins, a practice that was appropriated by the Greek city-states, who were in a position of power, allowing them to lay claim to this important societal task (Kim 2011).

☐ The Romans

The opportunities that money provided for creating a free market went well with the Roman invention of absolute private property, *dominium*, as this concept lends itself to further increasing monetisation, and the minting of coins was performed in Roman society by the state. The first Roman coinage was made in the 4th century BC and coincided with the abolition of the traditional debt bondage (Scheidel 2008).

The Roman monetary system originated with the use of bronze coins of different denominations. Even though vast quantities of bronze coins were issued during the first half of the 2nd century BC, this did not meet the increasing demand caused by the developing monetisation of the Roman society and its economy. This led to increasing use of silver coins, and these were frequently cut into smaller pieces to compensate for the lack of smaller denominations to be used as change. Periodically, the Romans also used gold for their coinage, especially when engaged in warfare, when the need for transportation of high-value money was greater than during peacetime. In the early stages, Roman minting was decentralised allowing for minting in different areas of the Empire. However, in the 1st century AD, Rome gradually managed to centralise the mint, and thus was able to gain control of the issuance of coins, as it was able to issue sufficient denominations in both the lower valued copper as well as the standard silver coins (Scheidel 2008).

The Roman monetary system was not restricted solely to using money as a means for payment in transactions, but also allowed for extending credit and issuance of bonds, and the use of personal cheques also came into existence (Harris 2008). Within the Roman economy, there were bankers who were able to make and settle international payments and transactions among private investors, and the monetary system allowed for investors to stay solely financially invested without being connected to real assets, as had been necessary prior to the advent of the monetised Roman economy (Andreau 1999; Harris 2006). However, the monetary advancement of the Roman economy did not provide shelter from the kind of financial mayhem we know from later time periods. Consequently, the Roman economy suffered from periods of hyperinflation, booms, busts and financial collapse, and in its later stages, the Roman economy rapidly declined. The economic system eroded to such a degree that after the fall of the Western Empire in 476, the use of money mostly fell out of use in Western Europe (Harris 2008).

The medieval era

Following the fall of the Western Empire, almost 1000 years of the history of using money in Western Europe mostly fell by the wayside, and it would be almost another 1000 years until the restoration of a monetary economy in Western Europe. Although the monetary economy mostly fell apart in Western Europe, it was in use in the Eastern Empire. From the fall of the Western Empire until the Italian Renaissance, the European economy developed into feudalism, where the manor estate was the economic centre. This was a virtually moneyless economy, where debts were settled in terms of crops and labour (Weatherford 1997). The Western European economy was, however, not completely void of attempts to be remonetised, and there was occasional use of money and minting. For example, under the rule of Charlemagne (742–814), there was an attempt to reintroduce money into the economy in a systematic manner, and coins were minted in different denominations such as pounds, shillings and pence. However, when the Holy Roman Empire collapsed, this money structure collapsed with it (Martin 2014).

Following the collapse of the Holy Roman Empire, it was in the second half of the 12th century that Western Europe's serious re-monetisation started to gain real traction. This renaissance of the money economy was based on the two-millennia-old paradigm created by the Aegean societies. The initial point of this new monetisation was connected to the obligations created under the feudalistic economy, where now the previously personal and/or in-kind obligations of the landholders towards their overlords were converted to obligations to be paid in money (Spufford 2002). Typical of post-Charlemagne Europe was the lack of political unification, and except for England, it was only in a few major cities and their surrounding areas where political rule could be found. In this fragmented political landscape, with a large number of small kingdoms, fiefdoms and principalities, the new monetisation came in the form of a large variety of coinages, with local use, and without uniform perceptions of value. Even though the Charlemagne system of pounds, shillings and pence was utilised throughout Europe during the late medieval era, monetary standardisation did not exist, and the result was somewhat chaotic. An interesting aspect is that even though the main technology was the minting of coins, under the new European monetisation system, the norm was that the coins did not have fixed values. It was up to the ruler, such as the local prince, to decide what the value of the issue and money was. This discretion meant that the ruler could decide the value of the money at his leisure, and if devalued this would allow the ruler to withdraw value from the subjects; this was a practice known as 'crying down' the value of money unilaterally from the side of the ruler. After such a devaluation of the currency, the ruler could re-issue new coins, and therefore he created more monetary wealth in his own hands. If the currency was 'cried down', in reality, this meant that the ruler had appropriated value from the holders of the currency. As we understand from modern societies, 'crying down' the value of the currency in reality represents a taxation on the holders of this currency. However, as this debasement practice inevitably led to both old and new coins circulating alongside each other, difficulties arose among the users in interpreting value, and at times, this led the users to value coins by weight. In a sense, then, the 'crying down' of the currencies could in reality involve a regression to a non-monetised economic system (Rolnick, Velde & Weber 1996).

From this early monetisation of the European economy, the concept of seigniorage was born. Seigniorage refers to the net profit that remains when currency is issued, which appears by subtracting the cost of minting from the decided value of the coins. For example, if it costs $90 to mint $100, the seigniorage is $10 (Bordo 1986). Through such seigniorage, the ruler was given the right to impose tax on the subjects by way of earning money by issuing money. In other words, when the ruler took his payments for things such as rents, he made the tenant pay more than the cost of the money, which is what would constitute taxation in modern terminology. As we understand from this second monetisation of Europe, much like the first 2000 years, the re-introduction of money into society meant that traditional social and societal relations became uprooted, because now citizens could pay for obligations with money instead of settling their societal and economic debts through labour, in-kind payments or whatever mode was previously required. As to be expected, the advent of money was followed by the advent of a class focusing on money, the 'money interest'. For the rulers, this was a useful situation, as the more money that was needed in circulation to satisfy trade and the money classes, the more the money that could be issued to earn the ruler his seigniorage (Gandal & Sussman 1997). As this possibility was not limitless for the rulers, it is briefly touched upon in the next section, 'Modern era'.

The new monetisation of the European economy in the late medieval era gave rise to extensive international trade throughout Europe and beyond. This new trade activity benefitted from the use of money, but the use of coins as payment was cumbersome and included risk for the holders. If money were to be transported from one part of Europe to another, it took time because of volume and weight constraints, and the money transfer needed to be guarded from thieves and other perils on the way. From these impracticalities connected to the minted coin-based money, new financial instruments were created in lieu of money. Most important here is the Italian bankers' invention of the so-called bills of exchange. A bill of exchange is a document that prescribes payment of a certain amount of money to another person at a given time and place (De Roover 1944). The bills of exchange were much more practical in international trade compared to coins, and could be used at higher speeds, again inducing growth in European international trade (Weatherford 1997). More details on how banking evolved in the late medieval era and the early Renaissance are provided in Chapter 4.

Modern era

The tension created in the late medieval era between the money interest and the sovereign powers continued to develop and created unease in the monetised society well into the Renaissance and the Enlightenment. On the one hand, there was the practical financial interest of the money interest, who used money as a tool for trade, and on the other hand, the interests of the sovereign to perform seigniority as a means for governmental moneymaking. In England, this tension developed further, leading into what could be termed 'the great monetary settlement' (Martin 2014:109). The great monetary settlement sought to alleviate the tensions between the rulers and the practitioners using money and was a politically contested topic to such a degree that, in 1665, Sir Charles Downing (1623–1684) proposed that the English Treasury should be transformed into a bank backed by the government. This was dismissed by the king with the formal political motivation that it would not be suitable in a monarchy like England (Roseveare 2014). However, a year before, the Bank of England had been established as a means of raising funds through loans for rebuilding the English Navy after suffering substantial defeats by France. To ensure subscription of these loans, it was important that the Bank of England was accepted as a legitimate representative of the English state, and the bank was therefore given exclusivity to issue bank notes (Quinn 2001). This exclusivity to issue banknotes indicated an endorsement from the government and secured the success of the Bank of England and the notes (Barkai 1989). In the midst of the discussions about whether it was beneficial to have public or private ownership of the Bank of England, the views varied, but Adam Smith, who took a broader view, expressed the view that the Bank of England and the British government were equally stable (Smith 2012).

Adam Smith's view originated in 1776, almost a century after the formation of the Bank of England in 1694, which played a crucial role in the great monetary settlement where both the state and the mercantile practitioners' interests were taken into consideration. During the period from its inception until Smith's conclusion, the Bank of England's role in society had developed on several fronts. In 1709, it was awarded the monopoly (at least in practice) of banknote issuance within England, and in 1710, it was appointed as a receiver of public money for lotteries (Quinn 2001). In the late 18th century, the uncertainties of the Bank of England's place in the political constitution of England had diminished, and in 1781, Prime Minister Lord North described the bank as being the real public Exchequer in practice (Roberts & Kynaston 1995).

That the Bank of England now had been accepted as the de facto central bank of England did not mean that the intervening period since its inception had gone by without monetary difficulty. At the turn of the 18th century, there was a major debate about silver coinage, as the coins had been devalued by clipping, filing and shearing, and because of the new form of money issued as banknotes by the Bank of England, the Exchequer decided to attend to the difficulties by using the original form of money, the silver coins. What happened to the original silver coins was a result of inflation, the silver value of each coin being higher than the denomination of the coin itself, which often led the holders to melt the coins down and sell them as bullion. From the minting performed in 1663, almost all the coins had disappeared and had been melted down as bullion by 1690. Further, the remaining coins were in a poor state due to being cut to pieces, as merchants, aware of the rising silver prices, clipped the coins to make them fit with the denominated value in silver. By the end of the 17th century, the English Exchequer evaluated the extant coins to be worth around 25% more in the form of silver bullion than as coins (Mayhew 1999). How to alleviate the problem with the silver price rising was intensely debated, and John Locke, who was central in this debate, took a stance in the matter, claiming that silver itself was the true yardstick when measuring value in trade, and that a pound was an objective reference to a certain rate of silver (Locke 1695). On account of the political prestige of Locke, his views won the day, and the Exchequer minted new silver coins according to the absolutist value paradigm of Locke. However, because of inflation, these coins were instantly worth more than their stated denominations, and large quantities were exported from England as bullion (Mayhew 1999). It is clear from the example that Locke's ideas on the intrinsic value of money suffered from lack of practical understanding of the nature and use of money. It is worth noting here that Locke's perspective on money was at odds with the original use of money among the ancients, as previously presented above, who had used money as a social technology and as a practical value measure for determining debts and redemptions. The perception of the ancients had also been prevalent among Locke's opponents in debating the re-coinage; they had long understood that as inflation happened, coins had lost their value against silver and that the pound was just a socially agreed measuring tool for trade. Locke, on the other hand, contrasted this traditional view and perceived that, while silver had maintained its value, it was money that had lost its value (Martin 2014).

Although the Bank of England may not have been the first central bank, as the Bank of Amsterdam (Amsterdam Wisselbank 1609) and Bank of Sweden (Sveriges Riksbank 1668) preceded it, it would become the template national bank on which other nations would base their central banks (Crowe & Meade 2007; Quinn & Roberds 2006). The concept of central banks developed from the Bank of England's example. All these banks gradually developed their monetary functions, and the banks are often associated with the issues of so-called fiat money, although many of the extant central banks were created during the realm of the international gold standard (1944–1971). Typical tasks for central banks connected to monetary politics, would be to finance the government, regulate its currency, issue banknotes and serve as a lender of last resort to other banks and financial institutions (Goodhart 1999).

The gold standard

The initial issue of banknotes by the Bank of England was not without backing from precious metals, as, at this stage, the concept of fiat money (see below) had not yet been accepted by the markets. The idea of issuing banknotes against a promise to be redeemed in set quantities of precious metals was a practice already ongoing in both England and the Dutch areas (Quinn 1996). In England, the practice was carried out by the so-called Goldsmith bankers, who had created a system where bills were issued against the right for redemption in gold (Kim 2011; Neal & Quinn 2001). The Bank of England, which at the early stages was a privately owned bank, not nationalised until 1946, was in many ways in the same position as other private issuers of bonds, as it was still only the Exchequer that could mint coins. The Bank of England operated on a set ratio between the value of silver and gold, where gold was the more valuable of the two metals and used this ratio as a promise against the banknotes issued. Because of the relative increase in price of gold and silver, the Bank of England was, from its inception, de facto operating on a gold standard (Neal 2015).

The issuing of banknotes under a gold standard means that, as with traditional ancient coinage, any denomination has its equal in the weight of gold, for example $40 for one ounce of gold (Flandreau 2002). As this system was further developed by the Bank of England, it spread throughout the occidental world, where the norm among the central banks in issuing banknotes was to tie the denominations to the fixed price of gold. In reality, then, the banknotes were perceived as representations of the precious metals, gold and silver. The theoretical understanding of money still resided within the paradigm of Locke, where it was the precious metal that held a true and lasting monetary value, and not that money was a social institution used in economic exchange (Locke 1695). Tying the value of money to the value of precious metals would have its advantages, not least in international trade, where precious metals in a sense could be seen as the financial 'Esperanto' of the economic realm. However, as most occidental economists still operated within a bimetallic system, where the gold price was fixed against silver, fluctuations in gold price could still be experienced. To alleviate such a problem, it was necessary to abolish the bimetallic standard and concentrate on one uniform global system, and in 1870, both France and USA agreed to introduce a one-metal gold standard and discontinue the bimetallic system; by 1880, the Germans did the same (Flandreau 1996; Velde & Weber 2000).

The relative success of the gold standard for international financial transactions was reinforced during the Bretton Woods conference in 1944, when the Allied Nations met to restore the financial system after World War II (Gavin & Rodrik 1995). During this conference, the system was developed for international currency, where different currencies were pegged onto a fixed gold value, allowing the floatation of the relative value of the international currencies only to move within 1% of the gold value standard (Bordo 1993). However, such a system based on a gold standard had some disadvantages, one of which was that the US dollar kept falling in real terms, something which led the US to terminate the gold standard for US dollars in 1971 (Neal 2015).

Fiat money

The termination of the gold standard in the US left the US dollar as a so-called fiat currency. When money is termed fiat currency, it indicates that the monies are declared by a government as so-called legal tender, and that it is not convertible into any other goods like a precious metal, nor fixed to any other set standard (Keynes 1930). The breakdown of the gold standard led several other currencies to also become so-called 'free-floating', of which some pegged their value to the US dollar, and in a sense made the US dollar the new gold (Neal 2015). With the introduction of fiat currency, money had again come full circle back to Aegean times, where it was seen as a mere social construct, a universally accepted value measurement used in exchange of goods and services. This perception of money, where money is not backed by anything but a governmental promise, has rendered certain groups uncomfortable. Gold coins such as Krugerrand, Maple Leaf and the like, are still being minted, and although they are not being used as currency, they still represent value today as bullion (Jaffe 1989).

Crypto and independent currency

Scepticism towards fiat currency has led some groups to introduce their own currencies, of which the Bitcoin is currently the most well-known. The idea of Bitcoin is that it is not backed by any government and consists of a fixed number of Bitcoins in circulation, a number not to be increased (Barber et al. 2012). Such a concept of a set amount of currency is thought by its proponents to give it real value, and to prevent the boom-and-bust excesses of the financial markets (Fein 2013; Scott 2015). However, as the number of available Bitcoins is limited, its value has increased substantially since the introduction, something that could indicate that it could stymie financial activity if not adapted by dividing each Bitcoin into fractions. If so, this would then be similar to introducing fractional Bitcoins, just like the former 'clipping' of metal-based currencies, when the metal prices were raised to levels beyond what was most practical in trade (Mayhew 1999).

Some proponents of anti-government ideologies have introduced their own money, often used locally in tightknit communities, for example the 'Brixton Pound' and the 'Bristol Pound'. These currencies are used locally (in Brixton in London and in Bristol, United Kingdom [UK]), and it is issued by way of depositing against the British pound (GBP). Again, the idea behind such monies is to attain a real and practical value to the currency, and to be left outside the grip of the government and the banking industry, both often vilified by the currency users (Ferreira, Perry & Subramanian 2015; Taylor 2014).

What can be said of both the electronic cryptocurrencies like Bitcoin and the idealistically motivated local currencies, is that both systems represent a harking back to the money paradigm of Locke (1695), and thus, that their proponents fail to understand money as a social institution for value measure. A part of this is connected to the belief that it is the government who controls all aspects of money, and by this, its issue and quantity. This would be a misconception, as if seen as a value measure, money is issued by the users by way of production and debt creation. To create an easy example: person A performs a job for his neighbour B, for example mows his lawn, and the price is set at $100. If the payment is given by credit, then the parties themselves in reality have 'issued' $100. The point here, of course, is that the money in use in this example has not been issued by any government but exists only as a measure of value between the parties. Maybe later, B does work for A, at the value of $100, and the debt is settled, and then, $200 has been created, but physically has never seen the light of day. Furthermore, in the example, there has been no involvement by any governmental or other extra-party authority or organisation. As the example shows, the concept of money is an abstract social construct that works as value measurement among its users as long as they agree to a uniform reciprocal value attributed to the monies in use.

Money as social technology

The understanding that money is an abstract value measure, as understood by the Aegean societies described above, was rediscovered in the 20th century during the reign of the international gold standard. This understanding was brought forth from the academic realm of anthropology, from studies on the small island of Yap in the Pacific Ocean, where the inhabitants were living a basic agricultural and hunter-gatherer existence, and where the conventional economic assumption would be that bartering would fully satisfy the need for exchange of goods among societal participants. However, the anthropologist W.H. Furness (1866–1920) discovered during his journey to Yap during 1903 that the islanders had a monetary system, where the currency was named *fei*. The *fei* in use, however, consisted of large circular stone ornaments, much greater than it was possible to carry around, and this would indicate that the islanders would use the *fei* as an abstract method of measurement for exchanging economic goods. In fact, there was even an example of a family who was considered rich because of owning a *fei* that was considered very valuable, but which had not been seen in generations, as it had been lost in a shipwreck. That it was possible to trade with money (*fei*) residing at the bottom of the ocean, and which had never been seen by a living person, was taken as an example that money did not need to be physical, nor that intrinsic value needed be attributed to it (Furness 1910). This was a 'primitive' society then, where currency was in full use when trading, and where the currency was based on trust and, in reality, credit giving.

Furness' travel account from Yap was picked up by John Maynard Keynes, who understood the significance of the Yap people's use of *fei* as currency and as a measurement of abstract value. To Keynes, the use of currency as abstract account-keeping of inter-actor obligations was understood and appreciated as a higher level of philosophical thinking about money as a financial construct compared to his contemporary thinkers (Keynes 1915). Interestingly, this theory was not widely discussed during the 20th century but was accepted by Friedman (1991) who realised the importance of the philosophy underpinning the *fei* system. To him this was juxtaposed against the contemporary understanding of money and currency, where the idea of money being attributed intrinsic value had been widely believed by use of the gold standard long into the 20th century.

As the studies of the Yap people demonstrated, money does not need to be physically manifested in order to be useful as a means value measurement concerning debt or economic trade and financial activity, and, as picked up by Keynes and Friedman, the findings let the occidental understanding of money return to its Aegean origins. This perception of money has gained increased traction among contemporary academic thinkers, and not least through the theories of Graeber (2012), who problematises how we as humans perceive debt and reciprocal social obligations. Graeber (2012) convincingly posits that, contrary to the traditional view, debt did not come as a result of a monetary economy, but rather that debt pre-dates the existence of money, and that money has been created as means to pay debts, and not the other way around. Thus, the conceptual understanding of money has then come full circle, and again is seen as social technology. The contention is that money has developed into a societal technology by way of practical use among independent actors, rather than by governmental influence and edict. This explanation of money as a social technology is likely at odds with conventional thinking, as money often is perceived as developed by the ruler/government, such that controlling money is the privilege of the state rather than representing a useful measurement of social interaction and reciprocity developed by and among the actual users thereof. Summing this up, money will always represent a debt, either to be repaid as money, or to be settled with physical goods or services that are seen as equal in value as measured on a common value scale, such as money. However, the notion that money always represents debt, actual or latent, does not automatically indicate that all debt is money. For debt to become money, it will have to be expressed in the measurement that is money, and all involved parties must recognise money as a means to settle the debt. Thus, the construct of money allows exchange of goods and services, as well as lending and borrowing without any interventions of governments or (their) banks.

This treatise is built on the premise that money is a social technology, void of intrinsic value, and thus, only in existence and use as far as it is practical for measuring and settling inter-actor obligations.

Chapter 4

The event of banking

Keywords: maturity gap; stakeholder construct; CSR; sharia banking; ethical banking; Christian banking.

■ Introduction

This chapter deals with how banking has contributed to society at different historical stages, and how the banking sector has originated from such practice-driven societal utility.

As with the invention of money, the development of banking and financing has sprung out of human interaction and the need for tools regulating the stipulation and redemption of inter-actor obligations, and as technology when societal complexity increased through escalated commercial activity and long-distance trading. How such augmented complexity enhanced the need for formalised banking practices, and later, banking organisations will be explained. As banking practice has been a forerunner of philosophy in this area, much of the available thought on banking and financing would be expected to be closely intertwined with the practical real-life fields wherein they appear. As this treatise aims to elucidate matters of Christian ethical conduct and pastoral care concerned with moneylending and banking practices, I discuss how different modes of banking may answer calls for increased moral focus in banking from banking professionals and their customers.

How to cite: Bøsterud, M., 2021, 'The event of banking', in *A treatise on Christian banking*, pp. 47–70, AOSIS, Cape Town. https://doi.org/10.4102/aosis.2021.BK263.04

The evolution of banking
Antiquity
Mesopotamia and Babylonia

Archaeological study of the ancient Mesopotamians has indicated that their economic activity included production and trading at quite advanced levels without the use of money. It is therefore not surprising that financing and banking may also have preceded the invention of money. In the ancient Mesopotamian cities of Uruk and Ur such economic activity was taken to particularly advanced levels, including trade with several different nations, over substantial distances, with alien counterparties, and included economic ventures covering substantial time periods.

The Mesopotamian trading culture as known to exist from the beginning of the 3rd millennium BC was based on a system of literacy, where the different business interests were noted down on clay tablets in the cuneiform language, which was suitable for imprinting on wet clay. The business ventures of Babylonians could include several traders, and evidence shows that up to 30 parties may have been involved in a single venture, and each business partner noted down what the originally invested stake was. This system was advanced in that the liability of each partner was proportional to his original investment. In this financial activity, prior to monetary invention, debts were carefully recorded and accounted and when expressed not in kind, different silver rate equivalents were used as currency (Keister 1963; Powell 1996). The growth of the business and trade activity in ancient times, as today, created booms and busts, and in 1788 BC, King Rim-Sin declared all debts void, leading to substantial havoc among the business community. Subsequent to this universal debt moratorium, there were numerous lawsuits and general turmoil existed among traders and partners in business ventures, rendering this to be the first financial crisis recorded in financial history (Van de Mieroop 1992). The practice of declaring universal debt moratoriums is known in later history, and from Babylonian sources, we know the system of Jubilee as given at certain intervals (Alexander 1938). The Jubilee system is also known from biblical sources, such as for instance in Leviticus 25:10, 'Consecrate the fiftieth year and proclaim liberty throughout the land to all its inhabitants'. This principle is also reflected in earlier scriptural passages, such as in Exodus 21:2, where it is said about bonded servants that 'he is to serve you for six years. But in the seventh year, he shall go free, without paying anything' and in Deuteronomy 15:1, 'At the end of every seven years you must cancel debts'. The connection between the Babylonian laws and the scriptural expressions of aligned norms may stem from a wider and not directly identifiable oral tradition that existed in the Middle East at the time, where scriptural and governmental law-making resulted from codifications of extant practice rather than ground-breaking social innovations (Wright 2009a). However, it is a fact that, in the law code of Hammurabi, there were several quite detailed regulations on credit and debt, and these would indicate a governmental influence that was seen as necessary to uphold societal values in banking activities (Horne & Johns 2007).

The ability to keep accounts, and record all credits and debts, led to substantial development in international trade. In the 2nd millennium BC, the appearance of long-distance trade on the Levant and in the Middle East led to the establishment of advanced trade organisations similar to the later concept of societies. These trading societies were regulated and systemised the division of profits and liabilities/losses (Foster 1977). There were examples of Assyrian traders who established societies for financing caravan-based trading ventures, where the participants paid their stakes to a central individual, holding what was known as the *naraqqum* (money-bag), and such enterprises could last for as long as 10 years. Other aspects of this intricate trading system were that in Mesopotamia traders were given free passage in wartime and were allowed exemptions for certain obligations imposed on the non-trading citizens (Veenhof 2010). In the Babylonian trading arrangement, the main value measure was different units of silver weights, and the *shekel* was the defined accepted unit. By means of this uniform shekel measure, scribes could note prices for core commodities and follow the fluctuations in prices over time. From the starting point of silver weights as payment for goods, the Babylonians through their literacy and accounting were able to create and issue promissory notes that alleviated problems in long-term long-distance trade, where the prices were represented in the given shekel weight-denominations (Neal 2015).

The advanced financial system that was created in Bronze Age Mesopotamia (Babylonia) did not last into later eras but was disrupted for reasons not completely clear today. One known adverse effect on the Eastern Mediterranean societies occurred around 1628 BC as a result of the volcanic explosions on the island of Thera, which substantially disturbed the development of the Minoan civilisations, and could have disrupted and diminished the existing trade routes and trading arrangements to both the east and north. In addition, we know of increased military activity in the region, by the Hittites with their superior iron arms, as well as by other seagoing people who attacked Mediterranean and Near Eastern societies during this era (Jursa 2010). As the dark age of the Aegean civilisations ended around the 6th century BC, this coincided with the innovation of money in the Aegean culture, and, in addition to money in the form of coins with their ability to serve in impersonal payment transactions, military innovations may also have spurred the further development of financing and proto-banking technologies (Cohen 1997; Economou, Kyriazis & Metaxas 2015). For example, King Darius II achieved substantial military successes in the Persian region in the 4th century BC by financing his warfare through borrowing, and thus financing his subsequent ascension to power (Neal 2015).

Greek city-states

The innovation of coins in the post-Greek Dark Age led to substantial advances in banking and financing. Coins allowed for impersonal modes of payment, and the merchants were no longer required to trust each other on their word or through contract, as it was sufficient to present a claim and demand settlement in the form of coins. Coins were now an asset anyone could acquire, no questions asked, and unlike before, coins represented a democratisation of the economic sphere of society. The advent of coins produced the first banking professionals whose job was to weigh and measure the different kinds of coins in their various denominations, and to determine the value and metal quality, allowing merchants to use them for efficient settlements. There were also systems for long-distance trade, where coins could be deposited in sealed containers that were not to be opened until delivery was performed, and then the skill of the banker was trusted on both sides of the transaction (Goitein 1967). The advent of the money market gave rise to redevelopment and the reestablishment of long-distance trading, which was central to the substantial increase in prosperity of the era (Millett 2002). The Greeks further used the money markets to raise money for warfare; this activity is an early recorded example of governments using the markets for providing finance for performing public tasks. War was financed by way of taxing the wealthy, in addition to voluntary public subscription open for all, where all participants were party to the spoils of war and could share in them according to the degree of their taxation or subscription (Neal 2015).

The Romans

Roman banking had its inception in the temples of religious worship. In Roman temples, typically, valuables and monies of the citizens were kept in the basement for safekeeping. Because the temples were populated by priests and guards enjoying high societal esteem, the early Roman citizens felt comfortable in keeping their treasures in the temple basements, and trusted these institutions, something which proved to be a useful starting point for the later banking activities the temples themselves were involved in, such as lending and taking deposits. The Roman temples did not charge interest on deposits, but charged interest on loans (Bromberg 1957).

As with other societal innovations, the Romans continued the use of financing known from the Greek city-states, and were also accustomed to the issuance of a variety of promissory notes, something which was crucial for developing some of the bigger projects within the Roman Empire.

Coins were useful for the smaller transactions, but financing by way of banking technology was needed for major projects, which, during the Roman era, increased manifold. In Rome, by law, interest rates were capped at 12% per annum, but several examples are known from historical sources when this maximum was not used (Homer & Sylla 1996). For example, in long-distance trading using sea voyages, formalised sea loans were in use, where interest rates could exceed 20% per annum, and particularly if the venture was to last more than one year, indicating that the dreaded autumn storms would be a risk factor (Neal 2015; Ziskind 1974). In the Roman period, banking was developed to an advanced standard, and banking professionals included moneychangers handling international currency transactions and public bankers, who were appointed by the government for special occasions such as wartime, times of grave poverty or financial crisis. These public bankers were not much different from what we today would consider 'bad bankers', as their role often included solving problems caused by financial collapse followed by stark poverty and social unrest (Martin 2014; Niczyporuk 2011). The concept of credit crisis is not a recently invented phenomenon, for as far back as AD 33, under Tiberius, the situation got so out of hand that regulations for tightening credit were imposed on society to halt the excessive lending activity that had led to the crisis (Frank 1935; Thornton & Thornton 1990).

In addition to the public functions that could be addressed by financing and banking, Rome also had numerous private banks distributed across the Roman Empire. It is of interest to note that although these private banks were advanced in the use of financial instruments such as mortgage bonds and long-term private bonds and securities, the Roman system did not entail any traded public debt bonds, which would be expected in modern banking (Temin 2004).

At the pinnacle of Roman society, the Romans utilised a wide spectrum of the different financial tools that had been developed in the Mediterranean and the Near Orient in the preceding historical periods. These different financial technologies included formalised sea contracts, mortgages, collateralisation, certain public treasury functions and aspects of central banking. However, it is important to note that these financial tools were all used in a specific Roman context, with a prevalence of slavery, and consequently the lack of a mass consumer market as we know from later history. Nonetheless, these financial capabilities were utilised for trading both within the Roman Empire and with other areas such as China over the Silk Road, and for financing public projects and warfare, to mention but a few functions (Goetzmann 2016).

As the Roman Empire declined, so did the level and sophistication of the Roman financial and banking system. With the fall of the Western Empire in 476 went the use of money, and the European financial system all but disappeared. Again, Europe entered a dark age with regard to the use of finance, which would last for centuries, and its redevelopment would not be commenced in the West until the 11th century. Meanwhile, in the Byzantine East, banking and financing continued based on the Roman system, but interest rates oscillated in tune with the increasing Christian scepticism towards charging of interest (Homer & Sylla 1996).

The medieval era

Subsequent to the inception of the Crusades in the 11th century, often attributed to a sermon given by Urban II in 1095, Europe again engaged in long-distance ventures with the outside world, something that spurred on the need for financial and economic innovations (Cowdrey 1970). Following the first Crusade and its recapture of Jerusalem in 1099, a European 'industry' of pilgrimage back and forth to the Holy Land was created. Formed in 1119, the Knights Templar, a military religious order, had as its main objective protecting and safeguarding the travels of these pilgrims against the perils that such a journey would entail (Martin 2011). One such peril for a pilgrim would be to be robbed of his valuables, and the Templars created a solution for alleviating this. The Templars introduced a system whereby a pilgrim could deposit his valuables such as money, gold or otherwise, at his point of origin in Europe, and the Templars would then issue him a letter of credit against the valuables deposited with them. This letter of credit could be brought with the pilgrim to Jerusalem, where the Templars, less their transactional cost, would pay him the monies due under the letter (Buckley & Nixon 2009). As the Templars' wealth and power grew, so did the number of castles and fortifications belonging to them, and at the height of their powers they possessed more than 800 castles around Europe and the Mediterranean region, reaching from Jerusalem all the way to England. These castles were ideal points for storing valuables and performing exchange and payments under the letters of credit, so that the castles developed into banking outlets as we would see them in modern times (Weatherford 1997). In addition to safeguarding the pilgrims' valuables, the Templars managed funds for religious organisations and private individuals, and also for extending loans to kings and other secular powers, and not least, to knights before setting out on crusades themselves (De la Torre 2008). The Templars provided a broad spectrum of financial services to the nobility and kings of Europe and acted in certain treasury functions for both the English and the French kings. The fact that kings elected to deposit their valuables with the Templars gives a good indication of the level of their influence and might at the height of their power, and, at one time, the English crown jewels were deposited in the London Temple, instead of the customary Tower of London (Goetzmann 2016).

Over the roughly 200 years of the existence of the Templars, they evolved into the most powerful financial institution of the medieval era, something which subjected them to jealousy and animosity. Subsequently, this would lead to persecution by the French king, who had the Templar order finally disbanded in 1312. With it was brought down the most advanced, efficient and powerful financial institution in Europe (Read 2001). Following the dismantling of the Templar order, a void was created in European financial history, one that could be filled neither by secular nor ecclesiastical powers of the time (Weatherford 1997).

Entrepreneurial financial actors from the Italian city-states would, however, soon fill the vacuum in European financial life left by the fall of the Knights Templar. These financial entrepreneurs came in the form of Italian families from the city-states of Verona, Venice, Genoa, Florence and Pisa, and they supplied to the financial markets services previously rendered by the Templars. These Italian bankers created a banking and financial system outside the control of the church and the government, and this freedom made it possible for them to trade with ease with Christians, Muslims, Jews and pagans alike. The success of the Italian banking families created a pan-European banking network, which also held trading stations across the known world from Africa to China and from Scandinavia to the Indian continent (Weatherford 1997). As opposed to the Templars, the Italian bankers did not only serve nobility, but traded with all societal strata, and had their core operations in the European marketplaces, where merchants met to trade. While the Knights Templar had practised banking under the church limitation on usury, which forbade the charging of interest, the Italian banking families, however, found a way to overcome this limitation, in that they meticulously avoided issuing loans. What they offered instead of loans was the trade in bills of exchange. A bill of exchange is a document in which it is promised that a certain amount of money will be paid to a certain person, at a given place and time, perhaps in a different currency. As it will appear, then, a transaction involving a bill of exchange was in reality the sale of one type of money in exchange for another type of money, but the church prohibition against usury and interest specifically referred to loans only, so this method of earning money from money was not included in the ban (Munro 2003). This circumvention of the usury prohibition worked well within the Christian world, but in meetings with Muslim traders the European-style bills of exchange were not acceptable, as the Koran contained a stricter usury prohibition than did the Bible, and within the Islamic trading tradition it was the letter of credit that was in use (Labib 1969; Weatherford 1997).

A substantial financial innovation of the medieval era occurred in the late 12th century, when the Doge of Venice issued public debt. The issuance of this debt came in the form of a forced loan, which was issued in the format of bonds, and was necessary for financing warfare against the Byzantines for control of the Adriatic Sea. These Venetian public bonds carried an interest of 5% until redemption, something that was problematic with the church ban on usury (Munro 2003). A new development connected to the Venetian bonds was that they were subjected to secondary trading among financers. From this appeared a new era of financing, as now the relationship between the creditor and debtor became impersonal, something which would indicate the possibility of raising far larger amounts of capital as opposed to the traditional personal creditor/debtor relationship (Goetzmann 2016). This impersonal and secondary relationship also gave rise to useful societal dynamics, in that now the state was dependent on its reputation for raising loans, and, seen from the creditor's side, the given credit was dependent on the success of the state to secure his repayments and interests under the bond stipulations (Goetzmann 2016). These new impersonal aspects of finance gave rise to increased influence and political power among the citizenry outside the circle of the landed nobility, something that was a new development in the later medieval era. This would also give rise to the creation of powerful banking families, who would yield influence within both secular and ecclesiastical societal strata. The Medicis serve as a useful example here as, from their banking beginnings in 15th-century Florence, they made their mark on European history for several centuries (Strathern 2005).

Modern era

As the example of the Venetian practice of public war financing illustrates, governments gradually discovered their ability to raise money through issuance of debt to the public. The debt bonds issued by states may be seen as a variation of the letters of credit or letters of exchange, and, in the late medieval era and the modern era, European states increasingly used this opportunity to raise capital for financing their activities (Neal 2015). Examples of this could be found among the Dutch republics during the 16th and 17th centuries, when capital was raised through debt by issuing life annuities to citizens. A life annuity was something that was known already from antiquity, which solved the challenge of individuals exploiting their savings during their lifetime. By purchasing a state-guaranteed annuity, the holder of such a bond would be sure to have a steady income stream during his lifetime or for a set number of years (Fritschy 2003). The rise of governmental debt bonds, with their guaranteed income streams, also gave rise to an increasing secondary market for trading in such instruments. Such trade could typically be motivated by differences in perceptions of the duration of the state (in uncertain times), its ability to repay on the bonds or needs among the bond holders to receive payments before the guaranteed time. This ability to raise money by the state would be instrumental in developing the secular state in Europe and allowed these budding modern states to take advantage of and exploit the opportunities that the state had at hand. At the turn of the 16th century, such substantial opportunities were to be found in the discoveries of the 'New World', and this gave the secular governments a welcome opportunity to increase their earnings, in a time of religious and political upheaval in Europe, not least expressed during the Reformation with all its consequences (Goetzmann 2016).

For the governments of northern Europe, the New World explorations also gave rise to their own modes of raising cash for the governments, initially by way of selling charters to individuals with time-limited exclusive rights to exploit these overseas opportunities. These charters were a necessary means of financing the Great Discoveries and their subsequent explorations, as, under them, the holder had a monopoly to exploit certain rights with the protection of the issuing state (MacMillan 2006). This symbiotic relationship between the secular state and private financial interests would have a lasting impact on the subsequent political and financial development of the West (Neal 2015). The possibilities connected to the New World discoveries also spurred on the development of the mercantile structure that is the corporation, with the financial instrument that is the share/stock (Geljon & De Graf 2013). Corporations had been known in more primitive forms already in ancient times, and in south-western Europe under the Visigoth ruler Alaric II, a Roman law codification had been established in AD 506, which gave rise to corporate structures lasting well into the medieval era, centred round Toulouse and southwest France (Barnwell 2000). These corporate structures were rediscovered in the modern era, and with the discovery of the New World, they were central in raising large amounts of risk capital needed for initiating these ventures. A closer description of the advent of the corporation falls outside the scope of this treatise, but it should be pointed out that the charter-giving states gradually took advantage by themselves of the rights previously granted to the charter holders, and corporations were assimilated into the formal structures of the different states. Cases in point here could be the Dutch and English East India companies (Goetzmann 2016).

With the propagation of corporations, there followed an increasing activity in second-hand trading of shares in these companies, aligned with the above-described rationale of second-hand trading in debt bonds. During the 17th century, this trade developed both in Amsterdam and in London, developing from basic interparty transactions into more professional second-hand share (equity) brokerage. In the City of London, the existing Royal Exchange, which was founded in 1577, initially only allowed the trade of physical goods, and in the early days of stockbrokerage, financial instruments could not be traded on the Exchange, as the brokers were not allowed in, and consequently, set up business in the surrounding coffee houses. Such trading started out in a systematised way in the different areas of the City of London, and similar developments took place in the European continent, where Amsterdam was in its early stages of development of the equity trading market (Goetzmann 2016). However, in the late 17th century, the English Parliament regulated the stockbrokerage, and as this coincided with the building of a new

Royal Exchange after the Great Fire of London, the share traders were allowed onto the trading floor. This represented the budding start of a regulated stock market in the modern sense (Stringham 2002). At the turn of the 18th century, then, northern European states had developed central banking functions, a market for trading in shares and other financial securities, as well as the states' own treasury functions. In the early stages of the modern era, the latter were mostly concerned with raising debt for financing the states' different activities, such as warfare (Neal 2015).

The financial innovations of the modern era, where it was possible both for the state and for private individuals to raise capital through debt, by way of issuing debt bonds and shares in private corporations, increased societies' opportunities for further developing economic life. One such major economic development was the Industrial Revolution, which most historians particularly attribute to the northwest of England in the mid-18th century (Galbraith 1989). The British Industrial Revolution was largely based on the advancement of the iron and coal industry, which had been developed through the financial tools described above. The fact that the British financial system was more advanced than its surrounding competing nations at this stage made it possible for the Industrial Revolution to develop in England, and it gained traction through the relative ease with which these financial tools were available. The massive build-up of government debt during the Napoleonic Wars made it possible for private bondholders to raise new capital in the private market by using their government bonds as collateral for the fresh private credit (Neal 2015).

The 20th century and beyond

Following the Industrial Revolution, a new class of salaried workers arose throughout northern Europe in particular, leading to the creation of a consumer market that was more substantial than ever before, and that in itself drove further industrial and financial development. During the 19th and 20th centuries, the results of the Industrial Revolution furthered an increasing democratisation of the Western societies, and new modes of finance and credit would gradually evolve during the 20th century to meet the demands of the new, free and salaried classes (Galbraith 1998). However, banking and financing were severely disrupted in the first part of the 20th century as a result of the two World Wars. These World Wars were financed as before, through the issuance of war bonds and other debt instruments, and after World War II, the Western societies entered a new and liberal democratic era, based not least on the wartime participation of all societal classes. This development included a furthered interest in consumerism and financing through different modes of sellers' credits, and banking innovations spurred consumerism further (Ryan, Trumbull & Tufano 2011).

As World War II came to an end, the Western powers realised a need for re-establishing a functional international monetary system, not least on account of disruptions during the war. What could be expected coming out of the war was a largely dysfunctional international financial system, where many individuals and institutions would be holders of war bonds issued by states no longer in practical existence, such as Japan and Germany. At the Bretton Woods conference in 1944, the IMF and the World Bank were established, and their practical inception came just after the war, in 1945. From its inception, the main objective of the IMF was to maintain a stable international financial system, including stability in currency movements (Boughton 2004). Whether this was actually achieved may be debated, especially considering different booms and busts of the world financial markets after the creation of the IMF, and not least, the Great Crash of 2007–2008 (Adrian & Shin 2010; Reinhart & Rogoff 2002). The fall of the gold standard in 1971 marked the end of the Bretton Woods era in international monetary state cooperation, and a new era of increased financial freedom commenced. The post-Bretton Woods era is typified by increasingly letting the free market forces work, and the dismantling of governmental influence on key financial indicators like currency and interest rates (Ravenhill 2014).

One particularly visible aspect of the new democratic post-war era was the increasing growth of the markets for consumer finance. Consumers could as before readily make small purchases, but for handling the larger purchases, such as cars, TV sets, refrigerators, washing machines and the like – the so-called durable goods – consumer financing was necessary. In the early 20th century, producers of durable goods had already instituted a practice of financing the purchases for their customers by way of seller credits, and this practice was later converted into the producers offering vendor finance, and creating their own consumer financing banks, such as General Electric's GE Capital (Boczar 1978). The GE example is just one of many, and during the second half of the 20th century, Western consumerism led to the development of several innovations that put the consumer into debt for financing their consumption (Hyman 2008). Among such innovations were credit cards, debit cards, payday loans and more, which at the end of the 20th century, had reached such prevalence among Western consumers that it virtually permeated consumer society (Ryan et al. 2011).

The different financial innovations backed by the increasing consumerism in the occidental societies, including real estate purchases by individuals, led to an increasingly expanding array of financial products ready for the global financial markets to securitise and utilise as investment objects, something that was exported throughout the world, led by the Western banking community. From this development, different versions of securitised investment products based on consumer debt can be mentioned, perhaps the most famous being the instrument issued against US consumers, the mortgage-backed securities, or the MBS, which was the industry-attributed acronym (Brown 2007). When the global financial market experienced its severe meltdown in 2007/2008, the wider sentiment was that the collapse of the global financial system could be directly attributable to this aggressive financial engineering (Mian & Sufi 2015).

Going into the 21st century, there can be no doubt that the banking sector is a major global industry, whose tentacles are spread over almost all aspects of human activity, financing infrastructure, housing, education, travel, durable goods and more. The financial tools in use can be beneficial for many by creating a useful societal infrastructure, and also be extremely profitable for the few, and thus contribute to perpetuation of differences in human needs satisfaction (Piketty 2014). Piketty (2014) casts interesting light on banking as he describes the global economic development over the last centuries from a perspective of human equality or the lack thereof. He examines how uneven capital build-up among individuals, organisations and states may have contributed to an uneven, and perhaps unjust, growth of the global economy in the modern era. Following this line of thought is Kay (2016), who questions whether extant Western banking institutions and their practices perform the kind of beneficial financing of commercial ventures and societal needs as often purported, or whether they are principally self-serving entities focusing on their own profitability.

■ Modes of banking
Societal functions of banking
Borrower and lender

In today's society, we still build on the banking technology that was developed in the ancient and medieval eras; however, we package it in modern-day disguises and innovative acronyms. As demonstrated in previous chapters, banking has had great importance for societal developments in the West, and it has been shown how, from its early beginnings, debt has been a factor in society, with the invention of money as a later addition for settling debts. It is also of importance to recognise that the ancient cultures of the occidental world and the near Orient were more akin to command economies than market economies as we know them now, and thus, that innovations in social technology would have developed at a slower pace than in the later eras, where individual freedoms and attendant practical expressions became a factor in societal evolution, not least within the commercial sector.

The core role of banks in modern Western society, then, is to act as deposit-takers, as any other borrower, and to act as lenders, and thus to supply liquidity to other actors who will have use of this for their own goals. Following this, banks have a central role in influencing the use of financial risk and capital allocation in the Western societies, and through this, their role in developing the societal economies in beneficial directions is of paramount importance. The advanced and often complex variants of financial structured instruments that are involved in contemporary banking will in reality only serve as tools created to support these core and useful banking tasks.

☐ The maturity gap

The construct of money allows for lending and borrowing without any interventions of governments or banks, and this must have been the original state of moneylending. Notwithstanding this apparent independence of governmental authority, as the financial system has become more complex, the state has attained certain functions in order to stabilise and smoothen some of the difficulties such complexity may impose on the financial markets. For example, a core task for the central banks in an economic society is to alleviate what may be termed the 'maturity gap' for the banks (Martin 2014:230). The maturity gap occurs when there is a mismatch between what and when one party can claim outstanding debt settled and what and when this party has to pay out money to another party. The picture may vary, but this is a typical situation for banks, as depositors can regularly withdraw their monies at any time, but the deposits will be covered by the banks' assets, not all of which will be liquid, such as for example loans to customers that will mature in the future.

For illustration: typically, a bank will use its liquidity, for example raised by deposits or issuance of bonds, to lend money to third parties, who will be obligated to pay back the loans with interest at certain times in the future. This is a way for the bank to earn money so the bank can also pay the depositors the interest they expect. However, as it will then appear, the bank has on the one hand short-term creditors, that is the depositors who can demand immediate repayment through withdrawal at any time, and on the other side of the equation, the bank has become a creditor for debt with longer-term payment obligations (Casu, Girardone & Molyneux 2015). This situation will represent the maturity gap, where the bank in principle is not able to cover its debt to the depositors from the assets it owns (e.g. bonds) and that have not come to maturation. For the bank, this poses a delicate balance to maintain, and in practical terms, it will be expressed by way of creating a weighted average of the time to maturity for its financial assets minus the weighted average of the time to maturity of its liabilities. Through such an average maturity-weighted expression of assets less liabilities, the bank can assess the market value of both sides of its balance sheet, and thus, estimate its liquidity risk (Investopedia n.d.). As often happens, if there is a run on the bank, this maturity gap on the side of the bank can have dire consequences indeed if banks do not have sufficient capitalisation and liquid reserves (Galbraith 2009). A key role of the central banks is to alleviate the strains that the maturity gap places on the commercial banks, and this is mainly done by supplying the commercial banks with sufficient liquidity (Neal 2015). Such liquidity loans may then be secured against the bank assets that mature in the future.

Stakeholders and society
The stakeholder construct

To fully understand the following exploration of banking and its societal implications, it is important to appreciate the creation and use of the stakeholder construct, as this is in use among academics and banking practitioners alike. In the discourse relating to corporate stakeholders concerned with banking, the positions vary from those stating that the only task of businesses and commercial activity is to generate profit for its owners and direct participants, to those who claim that corporations have fiduciary obligations to consider the interests of extra-organisational actors as part of their core activities (McManus 2011; Parmar et al. 2010). Among such other stakeholders to be considered are the communities where the business is conducted, vocational organisations, regulatory bodies, sub-contractors and many more (Goodpaster 1991).

The topic of extra-organisational actors and their interests was discussed with some intensity from the 1970s to the early 1990s, when Carroll (1991) established what have later become the accepted taxonomic divisions of different levels of corporate stakeholder constituency, flowing from the primary direct insiders, like owners and employees, to the secondary indirect extra-corporate actors with tangible yet more distant interests in the organisational activity, including those of special interest activist groups. A central division of his taxonomy deals with the essence of stakeholder interests, ranging from the purely formal to the purely altruistic. Dividing organisational stakeholders according to their corporate proximity is not the entire picture, however, as the corporations also need to consider the extent of the legitimacy of interests claimed. Santana (2012) presents a useful taxonomy in positing that the so-called definitive stakeholders be included in corporate concerns are those with legitimate claims on the corporation, based on characteristics related to claim presentation, social perceptions and stakeholder behaviour. She further contends that the definitive stakeholders are those with bona fide organisational claims that need to be considered in corporate strategising, and all others she defines as 'dangerous stakeholders', a self-explanatory term related to her views on the value of their interests.

The CSR movement

As an extension of the stakeholder construct, within the academic realm of organisational theory and among the broader business community, a discourse on CSR and ESG has arisen, pertaining to how this could be constructed, how far this should reach and whether and/or to what degree this should be a salient aim for corporations to report on and to adhere to. The CSR theories that have been espoused, particularly in the occidental business realm, pertain to recognising the wider group of corporate stakeholders other than the owners and the staff. Sub-terminology and related nomenclature would include 'sustainability', 'corporate citizenship', 'triple bottom line' (TBL) and 'social impact assessment' (Dhiman 2008; Schwab 2008; Vanclay 2004). As with the stakeholder debate, within the adjacent CSR discourse, widely different positions are held. On one side of the debate are the ideas of Milton Friedman, who posited that the only responsibility of a corporation is to create profits for its owners, and that all other societal matters were to be dealt with by other actors, who presumably were better suited to do so (Friedman 1970). Opposite to that vantage point are several modern theorists, who claim that CSR in itself will render different levels of intrinsic values for the corporations, and that as such, CSR is not just a charitable activity, but also works for the benefit of all corporate stakeholders (McManus 2011; Pava 2008). At the extreme end of the spectrum are those who advocate that sustainability and CSR are the core of corporate activity, and should be integrated in corporate strategising (Hadders 2009; Wikström 2010).

Although the terms 'stakeholder', 'CSR' and 'ESG' would indicate usefulness for the concerned banking practitioner, without a foundation like that of the Christian ethical and pastoral norms explained in this treatise, the theories may well lead to a kind of ethical window-dressing applied mainly for profit-seeking marketing purposes (Galbreath 2009). The above-described discourse, which resides within the academic realm of management sciences, is of interest in this treatise as it pertains to possible societal improvement through business activity, hereunder banking, but it should be emphasised that its main paradigmatic adherence is to secular consequentialist ethical philosophy (Freeman & Hasnaoui 2011).

Prevailing Western model

This liberalist Western philosophy of the free economic actors has taken hold on societal actors and has become the mainstay within the banking sector too, which the post-Bretton Woods, free-flowing international currency regimen allowed for credit to be left increasingly unregulated from the 1980s and onwards. In the Western banking industry, the advent of ever-increasing free and unregulated credit available to individuals has developed into an ever more specialised banking world where consumer credit in different versions is being issued and traded in a growing global market (Neal 2015). As discussed further, this unregulated and free system of credit does not exist without critical political and religious counterarguments.

As with any philosophy on societal organisation, the liberalist ideas on a completely free and ungoverned economic society as the highest ideal, sometimes referred to as the laissez-faire economic model, has never been used to full effect in any society (Peck 2008). At the different times and places where the liberalist ideas have been espoused, the market has still been in need of regulations – to protect the state against losing its power, to protect the other market actors through antitrust legalisation and to protect the consumer against unfair terms and practices. Despite this, the ideas on free markets and minimal government intervention have gained influence in the occidental world since the demise of Bretton Woods, to a degree where the Western consumer is presented with purchasing proposals and attendant financing on a daily basis. It would be a fair assessment that, in the West, it is widely accepted that individuals, viewed as equal market participants, may make their own financial decisions and live with all the consequences under the fair rule of the 'invisible hand'. However, the pendulum may have swung somewhat regarding the acceptance of free market forces, and with the stock market crash in 2007–2008 and the subsequent economic meltdown, the voices that advocate increased control are again heeded with more care.

Islamic/sharia banking

Among Western economic thinkers there has been a perception that the medieval era was mostly devoid of economic theorising, and that in reality there was a 500-year gap in economic theorising in Western Europe stretching from the final fall of Greek-Roman culture, which then will be connected to the end of Charlemagne's reign, to the scholastic period, when Aquinas was considered to be at the pinnacle. Such views on the economic thought and academic developments in the West were firmly established by Joseph Schumpeter (1883–1950), who, in his *History of Economic Analysis,* claimed that several hundred years of philosophical silence pertaining to economic theory were ended by the authorship of Aquinas (Schumpeter 2009). Later, historical theory has refuted Schumpeter's view, and pointed to the seminal importance of the influence that Islamic authors have had on Western thinking. With the 500-year gap theory, it was thought that Islamic sources have provided some transferral of Greek philosophers such as Aristotle through translations in medieval libraries, but this acceptance of Islamic writers handing us back only what is 'ours' and Western has not stood the test of time. In fact, from the 9th century and onwards, Muslim theologians and jurists rendered substantial scholarly and philosophical contributions to the field of economic academia, which would also become influential among Western thinkers (Hosseini 2008).

The medieval Islamic view on economic activity and the market was based on the economic reality of that society, with its developed trade and adjacent credit systems (Kavus 1951). Opposite their medieval counterparts in Europe, Muslim theorists despised poverty and hailed the accumulation of affluence. Further, their grasp of division of labour was advanced even long before the Industrial Revolution, and the market outlook was one of free markets, where prices were set freely between the market actors (Hosseini 2008).

Without going into further historical detail on Islamic banking, it should be noted that from the 13th century, this approach to banking, while still in use in the Islamic world, fell into a less expressed state because of various factors, such as governmental decline, intermixing with secular banking practices and Western colonialism (Chachi 2005). What is of particular interest here is the resurrection of Islamic banking in the second half of the 20th century, and its development from there to become a vibrant and growing paradigm for banking practice based on religious beliefs and deontological ethics. The development of what today is considered Islamic or sharia banking only started to develop in earnest in the 1970s, with the Dubai Islamic Bank established as the first modern-style Islamic bank in 1979, and the first sharia-compliant investment fund established as late as 1986, with the establishment of the Amana Income Fund. Interestingly, the Amana Fund structure was established in the US state of Indiana (Jamaldeen 2012).

The main basis for the Islamic banking ethos is the notion that everything in the world belongs to Allah, and that all human dealings with material goods need to be compliant with God's plan as expressed by the Prophet Muhammad (Abdul-Rahman 2010). With God as the lawgiver, sharia is expressed as the path to be followed to avoid servitude to others than God, and this path, sharia, regulates human relationships with God and each other. The Quran is the main source document of sharia, and its main principles are:

- The interest of the larger society will precede the interest of individuals.
- Relieving suffering and furthering welfare are both core values under sharia, but relieving suffering precedes furthering welfare.
- A larger loss cannot be inflicted to alleviate a lesser loss, and a larger benefit may not be ceded to create a smaller. Conversely, a smaller loss may be exacted to avoid a larger loss, and a lesser benefit may be ceded for a larger.

In addition to the Quran, the so-called Sunnah is an important secondary source of sharia, as the Sunnah reveals how to live where the Quran is quiet and is based on the life practices of the Prophet Muhammad (Kettell 2011).

From the above ethical pillars, a modern system of banking practice has been developed, after which most modern-day banking needs are met. These practices do, however, deviate from several of the similar Western practices, not least because within Islamic law, charging of interest is prohibited (Abdul-Rahman 2010). It would fall outside the scope of this treatise to render a detailed description of all aspects of the sharia banking practices, but in the following, I will describe some of the main principles in use, both concerning practical commercial and private needs, as well as investment practices under the sharia paradigm.

Predetermined loan repayments are prohibited

According to sharia, it is not permitted to predetermine loan repayments that exceed the loan principal. This relates to the sharia principle that charging or taking interest, so-called *riba*, is prohibited for Muslims (Ariff 1988). Under sharia banking practices, the prohibition of *riba* has led to a number of leasing-type financial constructions, which allow the financially less endowed to obtain financing for their purchases of substantial goods, such as cars and houses (Jamaldeen 2012).

Profit and loss sharing

At the heart of sharia banking is the concept of profit and loss sharing among the parties participating in a financial arrangement. The principle is based on the Islamic encouragement to invest money, as opposed to hoarding and keeping capital idle, and this is met by the lender and the borrower creating partnerships rather than conventional Western-style loan relationships. Through such partnership structures the lender can be rewarded for letting the borrower use his capital, and this can take place without the use of interest. It is of importance to note that, under sharia, the lender can only partake in the fruits of a financial venture if such a venture carries risk (Kettell 2011).

Unacceptable to make money from money

Under Islamic thought, resonating with Aristotelian philosophy, money is just a medium for payment and exchange, and has no intrinsic value. Money then is viewed as potential capital, and not as capital in itself, as it is only when it is in practical use that money may represent capital for the owner. This is again linked to the hoarding ban under sharia, and could instil a will to invest actively, which otherwise – by allowing interest-based financial transactions – would not be encouraged (Ahmad & Hassan 2007).

☐ Uncertainty is forbidden

Under sharia, to speculate or take risks involving financial uncertainty, *gharar*, is prohibited. The principle here is that parties in a financial arrangement should have full insight into the counter value involved in any transacted exchange (Kettell 2011). The main aim in the *gharar* prohibition is the protection of the weak party, and this leads to banning various futures and options contracts that would be the mainstay of Western-style speculative banking practices (Chong & Liu 2009).

☐ Sanctity of contract

Under Islamic banking principles, all contracts need be entered into under the sharia code of ethics, and the concept of honesty and symmetrical information is central. For example, creating monopolies and fixing prices are prohibited, and the concept of volunteering and disclosing proper and sufficient information pertains to both sides of a financial arrangement, whether it be lending, security, pledge or surety (Jamaldeen 2012; Kettell 2011).

☐ Investment must be sharia-approved

In contrast to secular Western-style banking practices, the Islamic banking practices are founded on the value system of Islam. Therefore, any investment entered, needs to be sharia-compliant. This points to the rules for which investments are considered sharia acceptable (see more further), and the notion is that sharia-compliant investments and contracts are not harmful to society, but rather, promote good societal values (Kettell 2011). In addition to the main principles listed above, the sharia rules prescribe that certain types of industries and assets may not be involved in investment and banking activity for Muslims. In short, the prohibited areas of involvement would be:

- conventional non-sharia financial activities
- alcohol production and any activities connected thereto
- pork production, and any related products
- production connected to dead animals not slaughtered according to sharia law
- any products and activities connected to gambling
- production of tobacco and recreational drugs, and activities connected thereto
- any activities related to pornography, prostitution and adult entertainment industry
- arms and weapons of mass destruction
- certain biomedical activities, such as cloning.

The above list is not complete, but outlines the important parameters under the Islamic banking paradigm, which would further assist in keeping within the sharia principles (Jamaldeen 2012; Kettell 2011).

The above principles and categorisations have been used to develop numerous financial products pertaining to banking and investments, hereunder a specific mode of insurance coverage, as well as to avoid certain Western-style activities, such as day trading, margin trading and options trading (Ariff 1988; Jamaldeen 2012). Typical tenets of such banking practice are that the lender and borrower both participate in any risk taken, and that there is a spirit (and reality) of partnership rather than an interplay of weaker and more powerful parties.

The sharia board

To safeguard the necessity to be sharia-compliant, Islamic banking has developed the institution of the sharia board, which oversees the ongoing banking activities in the Islamic financial institutions. A sharia board comprises individuals knowledgeable of Islam and sharia and will typically comprise Islamic scholars with knowledge of the financial industries (Maali, Casson & Napier 2006). The sharia board will act as a supervisory board to the management of the Islamic financial institution, and will typically advise on a continuous basis, as well as conduct sharia audits at intervals it finds prudent (Kettell 2011). Because of the rapid growth in the Islamic banking sector over the last decades, there is a shortage of candidates to fill the positions on the sharia boards, something that may give rise to certain aspects of conflict of interest and confidentiality challenges. Some Muslim-dominated countries such as Malaysia and Pakistan have established national level sharia boards, to set out broader sharia banking policies, and to aid the institutionally-based sharia boards of the individual financial operators (Jamaldeen 2012).

To bolster the development and growth of Islamic banking, educational programs have been developed related to sharia-compliant financial activity at several universities around the world. Not surprisingly, this is most prevalent in typically Muslim-dominated countries, such as Malaysia and Indonesia, but such programs are today offering full degrees at masters and doctoral levels also at universities in the West, for example in the UK (University of Malaya n.d.; University of Salford n.d.).

The current state of Islamic banking shows global growth. The Islamic banking institutions, referred to by some as 'participation banks', managed more than $2.6 trillion in 2019, and are expected to reach a staggering $3.5 trillion by 2021 (Global Islamic Finance Report 2019; International Finance n.d.). The main hubs for these institutions are found in Asia and the Middle East, where the Persian Gulf area is a major contributor, but these institutions are also found in Europe, and in the UK alone, there are several banks operating on the sharia basis (EY 2016; Islamic Finance n.d.).

Ethical banking

Since the 1990s, there has been an added focus on charitable works and ethics in banking in the West through specialised banking products such as microfinancing and impact investment, alongside the development of modern stakeholder and CSR theories (Galbreath 2009; Schwab 2008). As part of the CSR movement, the UN has created frameworks for so-called responsible investments and banking, where the focus is on environmental, social and governance issues within corporations (typically referred to as ESG), and the frameworks have several international signatories who are mainly large institutional investors and banks. The values of the UN frameworks seem to be based on the typically secular values of the CSR movement, and highlight transparency as a means to improve their engagement in environmental, social and governance issues with regard to their investment targets (UNEP Finance Initiative n.d.). Extending from the emergent CSR focus are different modes of investment rationales purported to support CSR values, which come with different names, such as 'green investment' and 'impact investment'. The common characteristics of these types of investment methodologies are that they cater to the CSR-minded investor, and provide alternatives to the conventional investment classes, without becoming completely based on charity (Mulgan et al. 2011; Saltuk, Bouri & Leung 2011). Such banking products are now widely distributed, either by conventional banks who add such offerings to their product mix, or by banks that present their entire operation and product range as ethical (e.g. Triodos Bank n.d.).

On the back of the CSR debate there has been the offshoot that typically is referred to as 'microfinance'. Microfinance is part of a movement where corporate for-profit actors offer finance (loans) to the poor of developing nations, so that they are able to lift themselves out of the deepest levels of poverty. Typically, the objects that are financed are basic production means, such as sewing machines and other technical equipment, and the idea is that this will lead to a ripple effect in the community where the finance is extended (Zeller & Sharma 2000). Such finance answers call for creating a fairer world, through application of more fairly distributed finance, but is not without its critical voices, who warn that uncritically applying such capital in the so-called underdeveloped societies may disturb established social structures and could lead to uncontrolled social side effects (Mayoux 2001; Rogaly 1996).

The scope for ethical finance is expanding, but the CSR movement is not uniform, and its ethical foundations seem merely secular, and most likely based on consequentialist philosophies, often sharing the perspective that all others aspire to the Western way of life. As such, the movement calls for some form of voluntary self-constraint on the side of the stronger actors, typically Western institutions and individuals, and an underlying ethos seems to be that this is sufficient, and that legislative regulation is not needed (Gick 2003; McDonald 2010).

Christian banking

With the different modes of banking philosophies as described above, one might think that Christian groups in society would have developed a Christian-style banking methodology, perhaps at par with that of Islamic banking. This is not the case, and research into how Christian ethics and moral values guide Western banking practices reveals that only a few attempts at applying Christian moral norms to banking have been made, and indeed, are actively in practice.

In the Christian realm in the modern era, once interest became acceptable after the Reformation, the churches and Christian society have been only scantily involved directly in banking, and then mostly for purposes of their own financial needs. A classic example would be the Institute for Religious Works (IOR, the *Istituto per le Opere di Religione*) often referred to as the Vatican Bank. The IOR was established in 1942 and has as its main goal the management of the assets of the Catholic Church (IOR n.d.). Although the IOR was established by the Catholic Church, its financial dealings have historically not been based on any real and recognisable Christian moral code, and the IOR has been involved in a number of financial scandals (Posner 2015).

There have been a few banks claiming to uphold Christian values, and some continue to exist, but they would mostly have been aimed at attracting customers who are confessing and/or practising Christians, and the expressed Christian element seems mostly to be for marketing purposes. An example here could be the UK-based Reliance Bank, which is the bank of the Salvation Army, and was originally established in 1890 by William Booth for financing buildings vital to the activities of the Salvation Army. When looking at Reliance Bank's own statements on ethics, it is clear that the main positions are close to those of the secular CSR movement, although the bank will not take deposits based on earnings from pornography, tobacco or other vices. Further, as part of the ethical statement, it is specified that the staff will not earn large bonuses, and that, as the bank does not place funds in equities, there is no need for screening companies as investment targets (Reliance Bank n.d.). Although the Reliance Bank has its origins in a religious movement, like the IOR, its banking practices do not constitute what could be seen as 'Christian' banking if compared to the integrated version that has developed within the Islamic world. The use of Christianity as a means of marketing will not necessarily imply a 'Christian' mode of banking, and the mentioned banks are just stated as examples. Other examples could be the US-based Ave Maria Mutual Funds, the Evangelical Christian Credit Union, or the UK-based Kingdom Bank, all of which use the Christian aspect in their marketing (Ave Maria Mutual Funds n.d.; Evangelical Christian Credit Union n.d.; Kingdom Bank n.d.).

The fact that the above-mentioned banking institutions may not represent a fully-fledged Christian banking paradigm as compared to that of Islamic banking does not mean that there are no movements on the matter. For example, in 2015 a Paris-based non-profit organisation called Christian Finance Observatory formed a charter aiming at promoting Christian values within the banking sector. What is of specific interest with this charter is that it not only seeks to avoid immoral financial activities, called 'negative objectives' but it also seeks to promote morally beneficial activities, termed 'positive objectives'. Among the positive objectives mentioned in the charter are core Christian values such as protecting the weak and the environment, and among the negative objectives financial activities contrary to Christian ethics, such as pornography and genetic bio-manipulation of humans are mentioned. What is of further interest in the charter is how it also details specific financial practices as immoral and 'negative' and this could be seen as a step towards a mode of Christian banking that is practically oriented and operational in real-life banking (Christian Finance Observatory n.d.).

There are also other budding examples from academic theory pointing towards the development of a Christian banking paradigm. For example, Bøsterud and Vorster (2017) outline a set protocol for equity investment activity, which is wholly based on scripturally founded Christian ethics, and is termed the Reoriented Investment Protocol (RIP), based on my first PhD dissertation and DBA research (Bøsterud 2016, 2017). According to the RIP paradigm, the investors are required to invest in a manner that actively promotes Christian values. The aim of the RIP is to incite investors to act in a constructive ethical manner, where core scriptural principles are adhered to. The RIP framework can be seen as a seminal step in developing financial products that are compliant with Christian values. This is a break with much of the former ethical framework developed within CSR and Christian investment motivation, which has focused mainly on what not to invest in, and which has not offered the scripturally based constructive perspective of RIP.

Building on the RIP ethos, is Bøsterud and Vorster (2019), where a Christian pastoral banking paradigm termed Pastoral Banking Practice (PBP) is introduced. The PBP presents a broad method of banking, which goes beyond the equity investment focus of RIP, and where most areas of practical banking are discussed through a lens of Christian cognition. This practice-based methodology is based on my second PhD dissertation and DBA research (Bøsterud 2017, 2018).

The concept of Christian banking is in its very seminal beginning, if in existence at all. The examples listed above represent the state of affairs well, and within academia there are scant activities ongoing in the field, where the RIP, PBP and the Christian Finance Observatory are merely budding examples of what would need to be followed if the Islamic banking is to be given a Christian counterpart. From this, it follows that currently there is no systematic education programme on offer in Christian banking.

Chapter 5

Philosophical and theological schemata

Keywords: virtue ethics; utilitarianism; deontology; pastoral praxis; constructive ethics.

■ Introduction

In this chapter, the main philosophical schools of thought pertaining to ethics and pastoral care will be discussed. This will include descriptions of virtue ethics, secular relativist or consequentialist persuasions, some deontological ethical dispensations and their scriptural anchoring, if any, as well as an outline of a viable pastoral praxis model as based on biblical and historical sources. I will explain some trends in the perception of what constitutes pastoral norms, how they have been developed and point to sources whence such norms originate. In pulling the ethical and pastoral strands of thought together, the hereto espoused ethical-pastoral model will be exhibited. Although the aim of this treatise is to lay out a viable Christian ethical-pastoral trajectory to be followed in banking practice, it is of interest to describe some ethical schools of thought residing in the secular philosophical realm, both for purposes of delineation and to demonstrate outside societal influences to which banking actors may be subjected. The boundaries between Christian and secular philosophy have historically not been completely clear and remain blurred to this day (Bøsterud 2020).

How to cite: Bøsterud, M., 2021, 'Philosophical and theological schemata', in *A treatise on Christian banking*, pp. 71–118, AOSIS, Cape Town. https://doi.org/10.4102/aosis.2021.BK263.05

■ Terminology

In this treatise, a nomenclature pertaining to philosophy of ethics and pastoral care is in use, and it is prudent to explain how the different terms are applied, so as to clarify the positions taken here when applied towards banking practice.

The term 'consequentialism' will be used as a wider term denoting philosophical positions on ethics where an act is deemed ethically viable due to the (wanted) consequences of such acts. Among the different brands of consequentialism will be various sub-branches, such as that of utilitarianism. What will typically be connected to utilitarianism, is that it is a brand of consequentialism where any sought consequence of an act will be deemed good, and the precondition in this line of thinking will be that humans always seek what is good. This is in contrast to the wider use of the term consequentialism, where a consequence of a sought act does not necessarily need to be good. In other words, any ethical philosophy that is guided by consequences will be reckoned among the consequentialist, no matter what kind of consequence is attached. A watered-down version of utilitarian consequentialism is that of 'pragmatism', which is a school of thought where the focus is on seeking consequences that may work satisfactorily in the sense that its consequences are practically acceptable, all considered. For the purposes of this treatise, any consequentialist brand of ethics that will not be seeking beneficial outcomes will be deemed to fall outside the scope, not least as it will be expected that such philosophies will be far out of the field of interest for the professional setting of banking.

The term 'relativism' will be used to describe an ethical position where morality is relative to the norms of one's culture, or where an action is assessed by the relative value of its consequences. That is, whether an action is morally acceptable will depend on the moral norms of the society or group in which it is practised. Thus, an action may be considered morally right in one social or practical context, and be considered morally wrong in another.

The term 'virtue ethics' is used to explain ethical philosophies where the emphasis is placed on individual character and virtue in pursuit of happiness, instead of on following duty or seeking beneficial consequences. Typical virtues that will be considered can be those of individual honesty, compassion, self-control and prudence to mention but a few examples.

The term 'deontology' will be used to denote ethical philosophies where the focus is on the action itself, and whether it is right or wrong, rather than on the consequences of an action. Under this paradigm, the individual has a duty to perform acts that are considered good, or morally right, according to whichever rules are adhered to as determining the acceptability of an action. The terms 'duty ethics' and 'legalism' may also be applied to describe this paradigm.

To contrast consequentialism and deontology, it can be said that consequentialism directs how to act because of the consequences, whereas deontology informs how to act despite the consequences. For the purposes of this treatise the term 'consequentialism' will be used in its different senses and forms when describing the different modes of utilitarian philosophies collectively. Only if it is deemed useful to separate out certain versions of the theories will they be named in accordance with the presentation above. Generally, the consequentialist term is used when contrasting the deontological Christian theories as rooted in Scripture.

To define pastoral theology, or norms for that matter, could be challenging, as the vantage points are many, but in short, pastoral theology pertains to how Christians guide and care for others in practice; in other words, how Christians exert love as Christ first loved them. To some authors, pastoral theology and attendant norms are typically related to how to carry out ministry, in a stricter or wider sense, but as is emphasised further, pastoral norms pertain to all Christians, in all aspects of their lives and practical activities (Whipp 2013).

The theological field of pastoral theology is found adjacent to that of ethics, both of which could be described as versions of practical theology. There is a certain overlap between practical and pastoral theology, but the use of the term 'pastoral theology' precedes that of practical theology, as it goes back to the earliest Christian times, whereas the term 'practical theology' came into use among German Protestant academics in the late 18th century (Pattison & Woodward 2000). Seminal in this development was Friedrich Schleiermacher (1768–1834), who developed a scientific method towards exegesis and theological development, and who is widely considered the creator of the categorisation of theological academics as we know it today, and who contributed widely to the fields of hermeneutics and dogmatics (Graham 2002; Schleiermacher 1998, 2011). A useful contemporary definition of the wider term 'practical theology' where both ethics and pastoral norms may be fitted in is found in the work of Heitink (1999:6), who explains it as 'the empirically oriented theological theory of the mediation of the Christian faith in the praxis of modern society'.

■ Virtue formats
A broad church

A brand of ethical philosophy pertains to human virtues and seeking happiness, generally referred to as 'virtue ethics', and this line of thinking focuses on human qualities as a basis for human actions. The overall idea is that if humans are morally good, their actions will be good. Virtue ethics as a philosophy has had a following ranging from the ancient Greek philosophers, most notably Plato and Aristotle, and onwards via medieval thinkers such as Aquinas to a revival in the 20th century. The modern revival of virtue ethics may have come about as a reaction to the main discourse on moral philosophy in modernity, namely between the positions of utilitarianism and deontology, whether this be based in Christian moral theory or Kantianism. The main criticism posited by the proponents of contemporary virtue ethicists has been that deontology and utilitarianism places too little emphasis on the individual human agent and its well-being, and because in the deontological dispensations the focus is too much on duty, and the utilitarian theories are too demanding for the individual. The criticism highlights the fact that these philosophies disregard core human aspects such as interpersonal relationships, family, emotions and more. Thus, the modern virtue ethics movement may be seen more as a counter philosophy than as a clarified path onto specific moral results. The virtue ethics movement hosts a broad array of moral directions, and at this stage it is not obvious that this movement has gathered around a coherent moral consensus (Bennett 2010; Hursthouse & Glen Pettigrove 2018).

Antiquity

In his *The Republic* (1977), Plato establishes what he sees as the four cardinal virtues; wisdom, justice, fortitude and temperance. These virtues were in Plato's thinking foundational for a virtuous individual, and through cultivating these individual virtues the person would act according to his virtues and his actions would be happiness-inducing. In other words, by being a carrier of these virtues the individual would interact with his surroundings in a benign manner.

Another early proponent of virtue ethics was Aristotle who expanded on Plato's foundational ideas on virtues, most notably in his *The Nicomachean Ethics* (2009). Similar to Plato, Aristotle perceived the fact that the purpose of human life was happiness, *eudaimonia*, and that this state can be reached through individual moral and intellectual virtues. To Aristotle, *eudaimonia* is a sense of personal well-being in virtue, and this sense of happiness-seeking may not directly be considered hedonism, although the aim of his ethics pertains to seeking well-being at a personal level. In his theorising, Aristotle created an expanded taxonomy of human virtues that included: courage, magnificence, temperance, magnanimity, truthfulness, friendless and more. A core point in Aristotle's thinking is that such human virtues may be chosen by the individual, so that the path of acting virtuously would be open for all. As the individual needs to choose his virtues, and also what constitutes happiness, this would imply a teleological aspect in Aristotelian moral philosophy, and it should be noted that as with most of the philosophical theories of antiquity when it pertains to society and morality, this thinking will be coloured by societal values of the day. These values readily accepted slavery and many other forms of suppressions as the norm for the acceptable in mainstream society. In other words, in the roots of virtue ethical thought, we can already observe traces of moral relativism.

Medieval era

With the medieval rediscovery of philosophical texts from antiquity came a renewed interest for studying Greek philosophy in the West. Among the scholastics, Thomas Aquinas rendered the most comprehensive evaluation of classical virtue ethics in his *Summa Theologica* (2010) and *Commentaries on the Nicomachean Ethics* (1993). Aquinas cannot be said to be a virtue ethicist, but he accepts the Aristotelian premise of determining actions on whether they contribute to or hinder us in reaching happiness. However, to Aquinas, humans cannot obtain complete happiness in their worldly life, as such a state can only be reached in supernatural communion with God, something which is beyond our natural human capacities. Therefore, he posits, as much as we need virtues, they will not be sufficient as God is also needed to perfect our nature, so as to be fitted for participation in divine beatitude. Even though Aquinas accepts the teleological aspects of classical virtue ethics, he does not see happiness as something that may be achieved in this life, as true happiness may only be found in union with God in a state of divine beatitude, and as such he synthesises Christian moral philosophy and Aristotelian virtue ethics.

Modern era

In the post-World War II Western discourse, the ethical schools of deontology and utilitarianism were awarded lessened interest and moved towards the margins of the ethical debate, something which established a philosophical space for a revival of virtue ethics. The modern versions of virtue ethics are not uniform, but an early proponent is found in G.E.M. Anscombe's (1919-2001) article *Modern Moral Philosophy* (1958), where it is argued that duty-oriented moral theories are incoherent, as they are founded on law, or duties, without a legitimate law-giving source. From there it is argued that an answer to such incoherence would be to return to the ideals of the ancient Greek philosophers, in particular Aristotle and his brand of happiness-seeking virtue ethics. She further contends that philosophy and psychology should replace moral philosophy and that philosophers should react back and feed into moral philosophical thought by way of virtue ethics. Since this article was published, vast literature has come to existence, wherein several schools of thought are advocated and albeit they share a virtue ethical nomenclature; the impression left from this body of literature is one of disunity and fragmentation. A central tenet of virtue ethics remains to be the fact that actions will be measured against how a virtuous person would act under certain circumstances, regardless of whether the agent himself is a virtuous person. Modern versions of virtue ethics focus not only on concrete actions, but also on the character of the person performing the act (Crisp 1998; Trianosky 1990).

The futility of virtue ethics

As a practical guideline for human life, virtue ethics poses several problems and carries unsolvable logical challenges. For instance, the idea that certain personal qualities are to be considered 'good', whether innate, chosen or developed, is difficult to accept as virtue ethical theories do not provide any convincing guidance as to how the 'goodness' of such qualities will be decided. Furthermore, even though the value of purported good qualities may be decided individually or in groups, this paradigm has not revealed any uniform or collective yardstick against which to measure human qualities, nor can the general consensus on acceptable virtues be observed. This points to a root problem with the virtue ethical paradigm, as if to accept the existence of virtues, one also has to presuppose an *a priori* knowledge of what is good, and this without the contribution of a source for such a knowledge. Furthermore, even if the virtues could be decided, this theory still points towards the human goal of happiness which again is open for interpretation. After all, can happiness be universally decided? And what about deciding good virtues: can this be universally agreed upon? Without answers to these questions, virtue ethics cannot be practised convincingly, and as it will appear, this paradigm quickly collapses into situational relativism.

Consequentialist extractions

Utilitarianism

Utilitarianism can briefly be introduced as a normative ethical school of philosophy, where the aim is to maximise human utility, sometimes seen as happiness or total benefit, in an anthropocentric perspective, and likewise to minimise human suffering and negative influences. The measure of utilitarianism lies in the consequences of actions, and this would by its proponents be seen in a reductionist perspective, where the good of the many will be preferred over the negatives of the fewer. The most recognised proponents of utilitarianism are Jeremy Bentham (1748-1832) and John Stuart Mill (1806-1873), who both defined the modern version of the theory, and are described in some detail further, again inspiring contemporary consequentialist theorists such as Peter Singer (1946-), Laurence M. Krauss (1957-) and Timothy Sprigge (1932-2007).

▫ Forerunners in antiquity

The pursuit of happiness as a human goal was not introduced by Bentham and Mill but has been the topic of philosophical ponderings in the West from the time of Socrates onwards, often seen as theories of hedonism. A well-known example is that of Plato's Ring of Gyges problem in his *The Republic*, where the topic of discussion is related to what humans would do if they could possess a ring giving them absolute powers, including that of invisibility (Plato 1977). In the example, Socrates argues that seeking the best for all is embedded in good humans, but his opponents posit that if given the opportunity, the powerful will seek their own pleasure regardless of the unhappiness caused to others. The discussions that Plato describes could be seen as a version of motivational hedonism, and already at this stage, proponents of the search for unbridled happiness were warned about the ethical and societal pitfalls connected to this teleology.

For Aristotle, the aim of all things and humans is to seek what is good. It could be said that this is a hedonistic paradox, because if all seek their own personal good, the naturalist philosophies would imply that there may not be enough good to go around, so that, inevitably, the good for some may be the worse for others. Further, Aristotle extends the argument to the individual, pointing out that all actions have consequences, also for the individual performing them; eventually, pleasure will turn to misery. An example here would be to point to the different lifestyle problems typically found in the West, pertaining to obesity and cancer, which could be connected to antecedent exaggerated pleasure-seeking by the affected individuals (Aristotle 2009).

Not to over-elaborate the ancients and their views of happiness-seeking, as this also has been expounded on in relation to virtue ethics above, it would be pertinent to move towards the classical utilitarianism of Bentham and Mills. Some theological and secular thinkers such as Thomas Hobbes, Richard Cumberland and John Gay preceded their models, leading up to the utilitarianism that today contrasts the different deontological formats.

▫ Proto-utilitarianism

It would be of interest briefly to mention the proto-utilitarian writers, Thomas Hobbes (1588–1679), Richard Cumberland (1631–1718) and John Gay (1699–1745).

Thomas Hobbes can be considered a precursor to classical utilitarianism, through his political authorship, and in particular with his *Leviathan*, wherein he outlines his theories of what motivates human activity (Hardin 1991; Hobbes 2008). To him, humans are mainly, if not solely, motivated by the pursuit of self-interest and happiness-seeking. His main idea, as presented in *Leviathan*, is that the correct human behaviour is that of self-promotional welfare-seeking, and that any moral justification pertains to the social code connected to the well-being served by the observer. In other words, all societal constituents participate in a social order where the optimal welfare of the individual is sought, not considering the effects it may have on others (Hobbes 2008). It is worth noting that the theories of Hobbes as presented in *Leviathan* were designed as a political commentary at the era of the early Enlightenment, and thus the interpretation of his theories as ethically oriented may not lend sufficient justice to his authorship. He is, however, important in the understanding of utilitarianism, as later thinkers, both supporters and dissenters, refer to him.

Richard Cumberland, in his *Treatise of the Laws of Nature*, addresses what he believes to be the mistaken focus of Hobbes on an acceptance of individual egoism, and proposes an opposing argument through his ethical program of universal benevolence. To Cumberland, in all humans resides an impulse to seek what is good and reject what is detrimental and harmful, and that indeed, without such an impulse, there would be no merit for the existence of the human race at all. Because of this, he maintains that the common good is the highest aim, and that this collective aim cannot be separated from the individual. In a sense, he is opposed to the hedonists or the overly reductionist utilitarians, as he includes the self-interest of the individual wholly in the interest of the collective (Cumberland 2005).

John Gay extends the perception of humans seeking what is good and adds the value of benevolence and the consequent public esteem following good deeds (Lawrence 1948). He further sees humanity as under obligation to be virtuous, and to adhere to civil obligations following societal laws, as these and any other obligations follow from the authority of God. He continues that it is only God who can instil happiness or unhappiness in humans, and thus, humanity is continuously obligated to conform to virtue, and God's supreme authority directs this. In an extension of this, if followed in a soteriological perspective, if humanity is to obtain salvation, conformity to God and virtue is the caveat, and furthering benevolence and happiness for oneself and others is in accordance with God's design, and not coincidental (Gay 1731). As will be evident, this is not fully aligned with what is defined above as utilitarianism, and what is further explained in the following, since the will of God, and his influence on the good deeds and happiness of people, subtract from the naturalist reductionist characteristics of the theory.

☐ Classical utilitarianism

With Jeremy Bentham (1748–1832) came the further development of the utilitarian ethical paradigm, as the ideas were taken out of the religious context and pragmatically assessed as a prudent ethical position for the best of society and its partakers. In his *An Introduction to the Principles of Morals and Legislation* (Bentham 1907), he famously introduces the axiom that the two 'masters' of pain and pleasure rule humans, and that these masters motivate all human activities. He continues that these sole main influences direct all our activities and what we say, both as we perform and also our planning. He sees this as a state of nature, coins the term 'principle of utility' and refutes any criticism of this principle as futile and capricious. To Bentham, the measure of happiness, or pleasure, is subjective and rests with the perception of the individual; moral conduct will therefore be that which increases the total amount of subjective pleasure the most. He does not distinguish between different pleasures on a qualitative basis, and because of this, it could be argued that not only the pleasure of humans is relevant, and also that of other sentient beings. The core of Bentham's philosophy allows for an egoistic pleasure-seeking and does not recognise the possibility that individuals can sometimes act with the best interest of the collective in mind. The act-oriented utilitarianism of Bentham would impose on the individual a constant activity of weighing the good against the worse, but Bentham advises this to be solved through the experience of the individual, so that a person would be increasingly trained in determining which actions lead to the desired goal of pleasure (Bentham 1907).

John Stuart Mill (1806–1873) was an admirer of Bentham and redirected classical utilitarianism toward increasingly evaluating the quality of the sought pleasure, but not only on the individual level. The concept Bentham had introduced was seen by Mill as too egalitarian, as all and any pleasure or perception of happiness was of equal value according to this thinking. While maintaining that pleasure was a psychological condition resting within the individual, he divided different pleasures into different categories and attached different values to them, not fully accepting Bentham's strictly quantitative approach to measuring happiness. For example, intellectual pleasures would have a higher value compared to the lower and sensual ones, like the ones we all can share, even with the animals. He contended that it was possible to prove what was good in a naturalist manner, that it is possible to prove different levels of happiness in kind and that the best proof of happiness is to consider what is sought to render happiness among the seekers. He further posited that all people seek happiness and that the utilitarian goal is to create the maximum aggregate societal pleasure for all people (Mill 2001).

The contention put forward by Mill, that it is possible to present objective proof of what constitutes happiness, can be refuted on several grounds. It can be said that he falls into the trap of naturalistic fallacy, as he argues that what people do represents proof of what they ought to do, in their attempt to reach the end goal of utilitarianism – happiness. Further, he can be seen as falling into the fallacy of equivocation, in that he deduces that if someone desires something, it in itself is desirable. Finally, Mill can be criticised for committing the fallacy of composition, in that he seems to believe that because individuals seek their own personal happiness, it will follow that all people will desire the happiness of the collective (Popkin 1950).

Mill's theories should be read in light of his participation in the public academic discourse of his time concerning societal rule versus the individual, and to him, the idea of the free will of the individual is central to the understanding of his version of utilitarianism. In a sense, the emphasis on the individual and one's right to seek what is good on an individual level is juxtaposed and contrasted with the interests of the ruling state. Despite his eagerness to promote the free will and right of expression of the individual, he admits that a person can cause harm to others, both by action and omission, and that the individual should be held responsible for such damage inflicted (Mill 2005).

Henry Sidgwick (1838-1900), in his *The Methods of Ethics*, presents a strong defence of utilitarianism, and his writing can be seen as an entry to contemporary academic discourse, relating to Bentham, Mill, and their supporters and critics. For Sidgwick, central themes are those of truth and justice, and how these may conflict and subsequently be solved. To him, the utilitarian theories could be seen as the basic tenet of any moral philosophy, because, however considered, mere intuition would not outweigh the utilitarian principles of pleasure-seeking. He contended that beyond immediate human experience we need a higher principle for our decisions between good and bad, right and wrong, and he found this elevated principle in utilitarianism. Interestingly, he raised controversy in stating that moral philosophy should be kept away from the general public, and that through an esoteric existence, utilitarianism would best be adapted and practised in society. His belief in the advantages of seeking pleasure was so strong that he advocated increasing the population for the purpose of maximising the aggregate average, and thus, total societal happiness (Sidgwick 1874).

☐ Ideal utilitarianism

Moore (1873-1958), in his *Principia Ethica*, repudiated the hedonistic approach of classical utilitarianism, although he commended the advancement of good. To him, good was not limited to perceived pleasure or experienced happiness but included intrinsic values such as beauty. If something was beautiful, he posited, this was a value independent of the onlooker and the emotions it could evoke. Moore did not accept that pleasure in itself would represent an intrinsic good, as the concept of pleasure could not pass what he proposed as an objective, isolation test of pleasure. Opposing Bentham, Moore could not include the pleasure found in harming others, like that of a sadist, in his brand of utilitarianism as good or as happiness-inducing; it should rather be discounted. Moore further contributed an idea of organic unity as a measure of value.

The term is somewhat unclear but entails the fact that the sum of the whole will not reveal true value, but in conjunction, the parts in organic unity will have greater value. For example, the intrinsic value of beauty and the pleasure of experiencing it will, if individually summed, be less than the value of conjoined beauty and its experience. Further, believing in the true reality of an object enhances the value of the whole, and knowledge-based informed happiness is superior to that of deluded ignorance (Moore 1903).

Act Utilitarianism

The classical theory of Bentham, as described above, is often referred to as 'Act Utilitarianism', as the perceived goal of increased pleasure on a psychological level will need to be evaluated with regard to each separate contemplated or performed act. The measure will then be whether a specific act has increased pleasure in a quantitative manner, no matter whether it is right or wrong by any metaphysical or intrinsic measure. The best of others, or society as a whole, short- or long-term, will not be assessed according to this brand of utilitarianism; this will happen only if the quantity of happiness relatively increases.

The application of Act Utilitarianism poses several problems, both for societal interests and for the individual attempting to use it as a measure of what is good and moral conduct. The individual will be left with the near impossible task of calculating all effects of an action, and neither Bentham nor anyone else has so far presented evidence that this would be even nearly possible. Under Act Utilitarianism, the consequence is the only point of measure, and concepts like loyalty and friendship would easily suffer. Such social constructions are difficult to defend under Act Utilitarianism, as often, more happiness may be created in the quantitative sense of Bentham if normal and expected rules of conduct may be broken. For example, if an individual lends a book to a friend, she will expect the friend to return it. On the other hand, under an Act Utilitarian regime, the friend will return it only if he finds that returning it is beneficial for him, and the lender will not be able to expect it to be handed back. Other examples can be connected to crime and punishment. One aspect of punishing crimes is widely accepted to be that of public deterrence. However, under generally accepted Western rules of justice, members of society would expect that the punished are indeed guilty of the crime. Under an Act Utilitarian paradigm, the matter of guilt may not be central, as the aim of deterrence for the wider public may equally be served by punishing the innocent, which by other ethical philosophies would be deemed immoral (Bennett 2010).

As demonstrated above, Act Utilitarianism disconnects what is right from what is practical, and it would be a reasonable position to take that Act Utilitarianism cannot be seen as a viable theory of ethics. In a societal perspective, it will entail added manipulation and perhaps even suppression of large groups for the benefit of control and effective rule (Machiavelli 2009). In an ethos of 'the end justifies the means', there will be no intrinsic good or moral acts, such as saving a life or helping the poor. The horrors of World War II, and the practical approach to an efficient society, pure race and ethnic homogeneity as measures of happiness known from the Third Reich, should be sufficient to rule out Act Utilitarianism as a viable ethical theory, or a theory of morality at all.

Rule Utilitarianism

Mill's brand of utilitarianism dampens some of the more problematic effects of the pure Act Utilitarianism, as he advises that the general principle of utility be observed when assessing the moral value of actions. His restated version of utilitarianism is often referred to as Rule Utilitarianism, as he recognises the need for a higher overruling principle of utility, guiding lower-ranging rules of general conduct. The actions of humans are according to this measured by rules which imply what is good or bad for humans to adhere to, under the overruling principle of utility, which will lead the rules. This position is challenging, as it is difficult to assess, both for the individual and for the collective, what would explain the obligation to act in a way that defines the aim of the general good, and instead lead to performing a sub-optimal action. This will position Rule Utilitarianism in a grey area between pure models of utilitarianism and deontological philosophies. It is easy to raise the point that this would represent poor versions of both utilitarianism and deontology, as the individual is left with the obligation of choice outside the realm of his cognition.

As Rule Utilitarianism presupposes the existence of general rules that are beneficial beyond the good of the individual act, it is pertinent to ask whence such rules derive and draw authority. The answer, according to Mill, would be that they emanate from the principle of utility itself, as this implies that the greater good is served. For example, if an individual finds a purse on the street and that contains a large sum of money belonging to a rich person, the Act Utilitarian morality would indicate that it is better to donate the money to charity than to give it back to someone not in need of it. However, if a general rule would imply that to give the money back to its owner complies with rules of conduct according to Rule Utilitarianism, the right thing would be to give back the money no matter what might lead to the best individual result. It would be natural to deduce from this that following the rule would indicate a promotion of the rule as the right course of action. However, if this were the case, it would defy the purpose, as the greater good is better served by breaking the rule and donating to charity. This raises the question: Why follow the rules in such a circumstance? And if not following them is the right action, how then can rules be derived from the higher principle of utility? (Deigh 2010).

The above questions are not answered within the realm of Rule Utilitarianism as the rules are presented as auto-defining, draw all authority from themselves and are not based on logic. For this reason, it is difficult to accept Rule Utilitarianism as a viable compromise between strict Benthamian utilitarianism and deontology, and if the purpose is to build on pure logic, the theory fails as an ethical guideline on this point alone.

The paucity of consequentialism

Drawing on all the above versions of utilitarianism with its hedonistic roots, a prudent summing up of the theories will see them as consequentialist, as their main goal is to elect actions with consequences leading to added happiness and utility, and the least amount of suffering and unhappiness. As has been described above, the utilitarian theories fail on several levels, including those of logic and reason. Despite this, as Western society has become increasingly secularised in the 20th century, consequentialist thinking stands strong and is in opposition to the deontological theories, which, to the reductionist consequentialists, appear mystical and based on the authority of metaphysical forces. This aspect is at the very core of this treatise, as it is unclear what the authority of the consequentialist adherents will be, and how and who can alter and adjust the applicable rules when the desired consequences change.

The consequentialist ethic has received notable criticism as an applied model in society. For example, Popper (1902–1994) posited that the seeking of the best for the many would inevitably lead to totalitarianism, as it would impose solutions desired by the majority on to the minority against their will. He further proposed that instead of seeking to maximise pleasure, the aim should be to minimise pain because, as he saw it, one man's pleasure cannot justify the pain of another (Popper 1947).

Marx criticised the consequentialist theories for not being dynamic, and for assuming that human character does not change over time, and with it, what is perceived as good and harmful (Marx 2013).

Even though utilitarianism with its professed good-seeking may appear with some immediate and superficial appeal to the untrained eye, it has severe defects typical of any brand of consequentialism. For instance, what is a good, how can it be decided and by whom? It will be to expect, that one of the many failings of utilitarianism is that it will be impossible to agree on what is good, not least as this may vary among individuals and groups. As with any other consequentialist ethical theory, when utilitarianism is the moral undergird for making choices, relativism will always be lurking in the background.

■ Deontological dispensations
Different vantage points

Opposed to the different versions of consequentialism described above are the deontological ethical models. A main distinguishing feature between the two lines of ethical thinking is that for the consequentialists, the value of an action lies in its perceived outcome, or consequence, and for the deontological, the action itself is in focus. To state it simply; consequentialism informs how to act because of the consequences, whereas deontology informs how to act regardless of the consequences. Deontological ethical models are sometimes referred to as legalism, as the rules of conduct are given priority over the evaluation of the consequences of conduct. God is the 'law giver' for the Christian, and the rules are revealed from Scripture through hermeneutical and exegetical activities. Consequentialism is often referred to as teleological or branded as relativism, as it assesses the goodness of an action by the relative value of its consequences, and because an action is chosen on the merit of the relative advantage of the result of one action compared to that of another (Driver 2007). For deontological ethics, such evaluation is not relevant, as the action is either good or not, irrespective of its consequences (Norman 1998). This starting point of inherently good or bad actions as discussed further is subject to some modifications. The deontological dispensations contrast against the virtue formats in that the focal point in deontology is on the goodness act, and not the goodness of the actor, as in the virtue ethical theories.

As God is the author of what are considered morally good actions from the Christian perspective, deontological models are sometimes referred to as 'divine command ethics'. By focusing on the command of God, the duty aspect of deontology is highlighted. An example that illuminates this is God's demand for Abraham to sacrifice Isaac (Gn 22:1–3), as this would be a good action according to the theory of strict obedience (Jones, Cardinal & Hayward 2006). In the following text, the term 'deontology' is used for the description of the different versions of Christian-based ethical models, as this terminology better illustrates the authority of God as an ethical guide, rather than the command aspect, which may give connotations of blind uncritical obedience and perceptions that God could command anything, and that would be acceptable. After all, from the biblical context, it will appear that Abraham was not commanded to sacrifice Isaac in the end, and it could be that God was merely testing Abraham's loyalty.

Different Christian models in the deontological tradition of Christianity are described further, and those found to be practically viable approaches for banking actors' decisions are presented, within a constructive version of Christian ethical theory. The purpose of this elaboration is to explain how seemingly similar deontological schools of thought may differ in practice.

Situation ethics

Joseph Fletcher (1905–1991) is the most recognised proponent of the ethical philosophy called situation ethics. This is a theory that can be situated between the legalist views of deontology and the normless relativisms of antinomianism. However, in accordance with the philosophy and its followers, it could as well be located within the deontological paradigm, as it does recognise one law, given from God – the law of love. Fletcher (1966), in his *Situation Ethics: The New Morality*, describes this law, stemming from God, as ultimate and normative, and he emphasises that the biblical Greek term 'agape' best describes the love derived from God, as opposed to the secularly watered-out term 'love'.

According to Fletcher's brand of situation ethics, the only measure of morality is to follow the norm of love, and the concept of inherently good actions is lost, leaving the resultant consequence to determine the action's goodness. In contrast to the pure relativism of the consequentialists, according to situation ethics, the moral yardstick would be what best serves the aim of love, and as such, acts otherwise seen as immoral, such as lying to protect someone or perhaps extramarital sexual activity, could be morally good acts, best serving the love principle if the situation dictates it.

Fletcher asserts his ethics in four main presuppositions explaining his moral philosophy: *pragmatism, relativism, positivism* and *personalism*, which can briefly be explained as:

- Through applying a *pragmatic* approach, Fletcher claims that his philosophy is inspired by ethical pragmatism, and that serving the love principle is best performed if pragmatically aiming for the maximum love, no matter what other consequences the action may lead to; like relativism, a teleology of love is what is sought.
- The *relativist* element of the philosophy lies in its assertion that in order to gain the maximum amount of love from an action, and to elect what is the right and good moral avenue to follow, the action may need to be compared to alternative actions. To distinguish this brand of ethics from the secular consequentialist, Fletcher (1966:45) explains that the ultimate criterion is 'agapeic love' as derived from God.
- The concept of *positivism* includes the notion that people emotively derive their values not from nature but from their feelings. Through the norm of Christian, God-given love, any moral materialisation can be justified and defended. Fletcher (1966:49) emphasises that Christian faith is the real foundation for love, and that in Paul's phrase 'faith working through love' (Gl 5:6) is found 'the essence and pith of Christian ethics'.
- The concept of *personalism* involves the idea that humans are beings of superior moral value, and that humans are the only inherently valuable beings. Other than humans, there are no other morally valuable entities,

according to Fletcher, and he refers to Immanuel Kant's (1724-1804) maxim – that people should never be treated as means, but only as ends – as an illustration of this presupposition.

As can be seen from the above, situation ethics holds on to the deontological camp only by a thread, and its inclusion in this part of this treatise may as much be due to the theory's self-professed Christian deduction of divine authority as the basis for its ethics, as what academic analysis might conclude. Due to the situational relativity of any action condoned by situation ethics, albeit judged against the yardstick of biblical agapeic love, situation ethics conflates into a form of consequentialism, which is not acceptable as viable ethics under the Reformed paradigm.

Unqualified absolutism

Central to deontological ethical models is the idea of inherent values of good or evil actions. The idea that to lie is sinful, and inherently wrong, could here serve as an example, based in Scripture, and thus, binding as a norm for human conduct. A notable historical proponent of unqualified absolutism is Augustine of Hippo (354–430), who argued that telling a lie, for example, is always a sin, and thus, his absolutism is without any qualifications or exceptions of any kind. Augustine argued that lying for the purpose of avoiding a consequence, for example to save someone from murder, is still a lie in his systematic, if the lie has the goal of deceiving the recipient. On the other hand, if something untrue is said, for example as a joke, and without the intent of deception, it will not be a lie, and thus, not an inherently immoral act (Augustine 1887a). Deceitfully telling what is untrue is seen as sinful and inherently bad, with no apparent exceptions, and it is this position that characterises this brand of absolutism as 'unqualified'.

A further consequence of Augustine's unqualified version of absolute morality can be found in his interpretation of David's oath to God (1 Sm 25:21-22) where Augustine notes that Scripture records the making of an immoral oath but does not condone making it. Further, to Augustine, Lot's handing his daughters over to the Sodomites (Gn 19:1-11) did not represent a sin on Lot's part, but merely that Lot's actions invoked sin on the part of the Sodomites. He maintained that to commit a crime of one's own to avoid another could never be considered good moral conduct (Augustine 1887b).

In modernity, Kant was a central supporter of an unqualified absolutist position pertaining to morality. To Kant, morality was unconditional, and an immoral act could never be allowed for creating a better outcome, or to avoid greater sin. He explained his 'categorical imperative' in several versions, including the fact that humans are always to be treated as ends and not as means. He saw morality as intrinsic, and that any action is either good or sinful, so that to tell a lie could never be acceptable, even to save lives. This implies the existence of *a priori* knowledge, which would ordinarily be connected with religious belief, for Kant however, it was the other way around, as he saw religion leading to morality. Reason, then, was given a privileged and superior position compared to theological affirmations. His position was that telling the truth is an unqualified obligation, and that the right to decide whether to tell the truth, or to whom, does not rest with humans (Kant 1947, 2007; Morgan 2011).

Geisler (2010), who explains the unqualified absolutist position to be typically connected to Anabaptist confession, posits that in this version of absolutism a central aspect is the belief in the providence of God, and his ability to free humans from the moral dilemmas this unqualified position will necessarily pose, through offering a 'third moral alternative' – third in the sense that none of the (two) alternatives posing the perceived dilemma need be chosen. For example, he explains, this could be illustrated from Scripture when Daniel is asked by the pagan king to violate God's law by partaking of wine and meat, and Daniel chose vegetables and water, and was blessed by God for this (Dn 1). Geisler further explains the main tenets of this brand of absolutism to involve:

- God's unchanging character as the foundation of moral absolute rules.
- The unchangeable morality of God is demonstrated in his law.
- It is not possible that God contradicts himself.
- By this position, absolute moral laws can never be in conflict.
- And from this again, all moral dilemmas only represent apparent and not real conflict.

Geisler concludes that unqualified absolutism is not viable under the Reformed paradigm because of its legalistic and sometimes unmerciful absoluteness, and that the proponents of the philosophy constantly attempt to create exceptions and qualifications for the purpose of modifying its results. To Geisler, the main argument is that it is necessary to accept the fact that moral dilemmas exist in real life, and that to withdraw into the unqualified will not aid the honest attempts of solving moral conflicts in practice.

Conflicting absolutism

In contrast to the position of unqualified absolutism, the typical Lutheran position is that moral conflicts are not just apparent, but real, and that they therefore need be resolved by humans in practice. This position may be labelled 'conflicting absolutism', as it resolves the conflict by allowing the sinner to choose one of the (two) alternatives and accepting that this choice involves still considering the chooser to be a sinner. The position entails the fact that both alternatives are open and inherently immoral, and that the person acting is obligated to elect the alternative that includes the lesser sin. The colloquial expression is 'to choose the lesser of two evils'. In his *Letter to Melanchthon,* Luther (1521) famously states:

> Be a sinner, and let your sins be strong, but let your trust in Christ be stronger, and rejoice in Christ who is the victor over sin, death, and the world. (n.p.)

The quote describes the position that in a fallen state, humans are unavoidably sinners, and that to sin can in itself be seen as a part of God's design, permitting humans to make the best possible moral choices in any given real-world dilemma and remain in sin even when the best possible choice is elected. It is important to note that there is no redemption or excuse for choosing the lesser evil, and the only way out for the sinner is to seek the forgiveness of God for the transgression. Geisler (2010) sums up the most important aspects of this direction in Christian ethical philosophy:

- The law of God is absolute and unbreakable through its perfection (Ps 19:7). Just as it is impossible for God to lie (Heb 6:18), it is always inexcusable for humans to lie, no matter the motivation or alternative.
- Because of human depravity, it is unavoidable to be confronted with moral conflict and dilemmas. On account of our fallen state, we are entangled in a never-ending web of sinfulness and therefore inevitably meet situations in which committing sins is the only alternative, as we are obligated to adhere to both conflicting moral demands.
- We have the duty to perform the lesser evil, or sin. This can be scripturally founded in what Jesus explained to Pilate, 'the one who handed me over to you is guilty of a greater sin' (Jn 19:11).
- As sinning is sometimes unavoidable, humans can always reach for the forgiveness of God through Christ. A consequence of our sinful world is that our sins lead us to Christ for forgiveness, and this is the path leading out of our moral conflicts and dilemmas.

It is of importance to note, from the above stance, that being in moral conflict is unavoidable, and to solve these conflicts by choosing the lesser evil is an obligation. To determine what is the lesser evil could then imply returning to the application of principles from consequentialism and situation ethics, as the conflict necessitates a relative perception of what is the smaller and greater sin or evil (Jn 19:11).

Geisler (2010) explains the conflicting absolutist position, typically connected to Lutheranism, as a nonviable ethical alternative under the Reformed paradigm, for several reasons. One important aspect is that if moral conflict is unavoidable, then Christ also will have sinned, and this is something that cannot be accepted under Reformed theology, as it contradicts scriptural sources (Cor 5:21; Heb 4:15). He posits that to propose that sinning is unavoidable is absurd as part of moral theory, and that it defies logic, because if moral dilemmas are unavoidable, then Christ must have faced them as well, and they necessarily would have to make him a sinner, and if he was not so confronted, he would not be our perfect example. On these grounds in particular, the model of conflicting absolutism cannot be accepted under the Reformed paradigm and must be rejected as a guide to ethical behaviour.

Graded absolutism

Modifying some of the troublesome and illogical elements of the previously discussed options, graded absolutism remains a viable option for the Reformed exegete to consider. Graded absolutism shares some historical foundations with conflicting absolutism, and it would be prudent to present a few words on the historical background.

Augustine, albeit instrumental and foundational in theories pertaining to unqualified absolutism, not least when telling the truth and lying is considered, held the position that a hierarchical order of sins exists, and that some are worse than others. Thus, he may be considered a forerunner of graded absolutism. In Augustine's love-centred theology, it is clear that God deserves more love than humans do, and the logical moral pyramid of love places God on top, then humans in the middle and finally, things at the bottom. It would be pertinent to note here, that based on this line of thinking, animals would be considered as things (Augustine 1887c). Augustine further recognises that moral obligations may conflict, and that there can be different levels, or classes, of moral duties, making up the foundation of his version of graded absolutism. He does, for example, accept Samson's suicide, although principally wrong, by explaining that divine authority may sometimes grant exceptions to the moral rules, and that such exceptions may follow from general law if specific allowance is given as an exemption to the individual (Augustine 2003).

Another notable theologian proposing ethics resonating with graded absolutism is Charles Hodge (1797–1878), who from an absolutist starting point allows for the wilful falsification of the truth under certain circumstances. To Hodge, in principle, truth is sacred and all things counteracting it are in opposition to God, but he maintains that, as with the Hebrew midwives (Ex 1) and (1 Sam 16), there are scriptural foundations for the justification of wilful deception and deviation from the path of truth. Other examples that can explain deception as moral for Hodge, would be when misleading an enemy army for the purpose of saving people from harm because a higher moral obligation would absolve a lower, which is then subordinated (Hodge 1873).

Geisler (2010) explains the central tenets of graded absolutism as follows:

- There are moral laws of higher and lower order, as Jesus described some matters of the law as 'more important' (Mt 23:23); he used the term the 'least' (Mt 5:19) of certain commands, and Pilate was told that Judas' sin

was greater than his own was (Jn 19:11). The idea of all sins having equal weight cannot be accepted, as the scriptural references provided clearly allocate different weight to different manners and categories of sin.
- Unavoidable moral conflicts exist, and the individual will not be able to obey both moral obligations. It follows from Scripture that such conflicts are recognised, and examples may be found in the story of Abraham and Isaac (Gn 22), Samson's suicide (Jud 16:28-30), conflicts pertaining to the Cross and the punishment of the innocent (Ezk 18:20) and Christ's punishment for the sins of humanity (Is 53; 2 Cor 5:21; 1 Pt 2:24, 3:18).
- There is no guilt imputed for unavoidable actions, as God does not pass responsibility onto individuals in unavoidable conflict, if they choose to follow the higher law among the alternatives. Further, individuals are not culpable if they do not keep an obligation that was not possible to hold without violating a higher obligation.
- In concluding that the above establishes the graded absolutist position as the scripturally correct one, Geisler raises the question as to how we can then navigate this hierarchy, and sets out the following basic rules:
    - Love for God is to be placed above love for humankind, as this follows, for example, from the teaching that one's love for God should be so much more than one's love for parents (Mt 22:36-38) as this love in comparison would appear as 'hate' (Lk 14:26).
    - God should be obeyed over governmental authority, as this can be permitted by a higher principle than that of obeying the government, which normally should be followed, even if the rulers are evil (Rm 13:1-2; Tt 3:1). For example, no governmental law against prayer (Dn 3) or preaching (Ac 4-5) can be respected, as the authority of God supersedes that of worldly authority.
    - Mercy overrules veracity, in that despite all scriptural commands of telling the truth and avoiding falsehood (Ex 20:16; Pr 12:22, 19:5), to deceive and speak falsely can be the right moral choice, serving the higher moral principle. The narrative of the Hebrew midwives can serve to be a good example of this principle, as God commended them and awarded them families of their own (Ex 1:20-21).

Summing up, graded absolutism entails the fact that moral principles are derived from the absolute moral character of God, and they can be divided among the higher and lower categories. When such principles are in conflict, we are bound to follow the higher moral law according to the guidelines set out above, and we are not culpable for any moral transgression or otherwise held responsible for breaking the lower moral law or principle. However, what we are awarded by God are not exceptions to the rules, as these remain valid and binding, but we receive an individual exemption from suffering the consequences of sinning that would otherwise follow breaking the rule. As explained in relation to conflicting absolutism above, moral conflicts are unavoidable under graded absolutism also. When in conflict, the guide is to follow the higher moral law, but this will not leave us completely free from considering aspects of consequentialism and situation ethics, as the determination of what the higher law is may imply the consideration of the practical facts at hand, and their subsequent impact on possible human suffering. Graded absolutism would represent the correct and widely acceptable overall moral model under the Reformed paradigm and is the one espoused in the remainder of this treatise.

Reformed position
Revelation

After establishing how to assess and apply different models of ethical principles, new questions arise: how should we determine the relevant concrete rules of conduct in a Christian perspective, and how can we extrapolate such rules and norms from Scripture? A further matter to evaluate is how the different ethical rules should be practised: by way of first seeking Scripture for guidance, or to define a problem and then consult Scripture, or both? As is described in this and the next section, within the Reformed paradigm, there is space for both the strict scriptural and inerrant view, where ethics may be expressed through negation, as well as for the constructive perspective, where the focus is on how the Christian can contribute constructively to society as guided by Scripture.

In consulting Scripture for ethical guidance, it is considered prudent under the Reformed tradition to seek out general and specific revelation regarding ethics (Geisler 2010). A well-known starting point for general revelation in this deontological tradition is found in Paul's statement (Rm 2):

> Indeed, when Gentiles, who do not have the law, do by nature things required by the law, they are a law for themselves, even though they do not have the law. They show that the requirements of the law are written on their hearts, their consciences also bearing witness, and their thoughts sometimes accusing them and at other times even defending them. (vv. 14–15)

This is a clear example of the existence of a universal natural law, common for all people populating our world, and is readily visible and comprehensible for all to follow. Aquinas (2010) was aware of this, and to him, the natural law pertained to the first, or higher principles, which he considered to have universal authority and visibility, without consideration of nationality or religious affiliation. The existence of a universal natural law pertaining to morality can also be seen as expressed in Kant's (1947) categorical imperative, and in the notion that humans are to be treated like ends and not means. Calvin also recognised the natural law, as knowable for all humans, and that it was created before the Fall, indicating the divine superiority and universal status of natural law as a bond between God and humans through innate conscience, and standing above the laws created by humans (Billings 2005; Calvin 2012:*Inst.* 4.10.3). To Calvin (2012:*Inst.* 2.8.12), the revelation of God is presented in natural law, clarified in Scripture, and summarised in the Decalogue. The concept of natural law in Reformed thinking has not been without contention and has gained wider acceptance in modern Neo-Calvinist theories, and in particular as a means of developing modern social theory under a contemporary two-kingdom doctrinal view (VanDrunen 2012). Leading up to this doctrinal point was the heated debate between Karl Barth and Emil Brunner (1889–1966) in the inter-war period, where Barth posited a Christocentric view based on the scripturally confirmed self-revelation of God in Christ, denouncing natural theology and thus, the concept of natural law. Brunner's position was that of accepting the notion of natural theology, allowing the knowledge of God to be present in all humans without reference to scriptural special revelation, and that between God and humans there is a point of contact in nature, knowable for all. This position was strongly rejected by Barth, on the grounds that natural theology then would imply human participation in his own salvation, something Barth's staunchly Christocentric stance rendered unacceptable (Brunner & Barth 2002; Holder 2001). As per Geisler's (2010) thinking, a particular consequential point here is that we are judged not only for our actions, which are fallible anyway, but also for what we do not do unto others. From Paul (Rm 1), we learn that it is through the universality of God's law that he can judge all, including the non-believers, as he says:

> For since the creation of the world God's invisible qualities – his eternal power and divine nature – have been clearly seen, being understood from what has been made, so that people are without excuse. (v. 20)

From the starting point of accepting the existence of natural law pertaining to morality, the Christian exegete needs to seek out specific guidance towards making concrete ethical decisions from scriptural special revelation. For the Reformed, the Bible represents the inscripturated divine truth of God, demonstrating the moral character of God as equally revealed in all people's hearts and in nature. An expression of this if found in 2 Timothy 3:16–17, where it is stated that 'All Scripture is God-breathed and is useful for teaching, rebuking, correcting and training in righteousness, so that the servant of God may be thoroughly equipped for every good work'. Regarding the relationship between general and special revelation, it must be determined whether they are harmonious or can be in conflict. It would follow for the believer that as God is the source of both revelations, his perfection determines that there cannot be conflict between general and special revelation. This also follows from several scriptural passages, for example, when Jesus gives the Golden Rule as a summarisation of Old Testament laws, stating: 'So in everything, do to others what you would have them do to you, for this sums up the Law and the Prophets' (Mt 7:12).

Although not in conflict but in concert, general and special revelations are not identical. General revelation is known by and apparent to all people irrespective of religious, national or ethnic background (Rm 2:15), and all are subjected to God's judgement under this realm of revelation, as we are all 'without excuse' (Rm 1:20). Special revelation, on the other hand, is not known or apparent to all people, as it appears in the Bible, is written, and 'God-breathed' (2 Tm 3:16), as opposed to natural law, which does not appear in such a form. The special revelations are infallible as the 'word of God' (Mt 15:6), and 'cannot be set aside' (Jn 10:35), and this is not the case for general revelation or natural law. Special revelation is more specific in its instructions, as for example the Golden Rule is a general statement covering the specifics of the more detailed commands of the Ten Commandments. Finally, from a soteriological perspective, following and adhering to the instructions of special revelation is what provides salvation (Jn 15:6–8), something not offered by merely following rules found in general revelation or natural law.

Summing up this section, the moral laws of God as expressed in the Old and New Testaments are harmonious and in concert, as are the general and special revelations. The written law of God is superior and above the natural law, as the written law is infallible and explicit, as opposed to the universal natural law.

Constructive ethical attitude

As the elaboration above will have shown, ethical guidance acceptable under the Reformed paradigm may be retrieved from Scripture as illuminated by general and special revelation. However, this is only a starting point for assessing what the practical application of such revelation would be, and what kind of dutiful activity this induces in the believer. It is a tendency among certain Reformed ethicists to let revelation be the moral guide, but yet to maintain focus on what is forbidden, rather than what is permitted. Geisler (2010) can be seen as a proponent of this line of thinking, as much of his writings focus on what would be non-acceptable, as revealed from Scripture either as directly prescribed or by antithetical negation. By following this line of thinking, the reader is left with an impression that it somehow can be the best moral option of conduct to do nothing.

Other contemporary ethicists demonstrate a more constructive ethical methodology, as they search out what guidance can be found in Scripture for proactive moral societal participation, in answer to the needs of individuals and groups in the collective that is our global community. An example that may illustrate the different approaches to moral questions may be drawn from the difference between how Jesus and Confucius explain the Golden Rule of reciprocity. Jesus says: 'So in everything, do to others what you would have them do to you, for this sums up the Law and the Prophets' (Mt 7:12), and Confucius (1979:135) says '[d]o not impose on others what you yourself do not desire'. As is clearly demonstrated from this juxtaposition of the two versions, Jesus urges towards action and proactivity, whereas Confucius promotes a passive approach towards others. In a sense, the way of Jesus can be seen as promoting reciprocity in a soteriological perspective, whereas the Confucian version can be seen as an expression of the same from an eschatological vantage point.

A promotion of a proactive approach in ethical matters for Christians is found in the writings of Vorster (2007, 2017a), who, from his vantage point of post-apartheid South Africa, envisions a participatory and inclusive role in the development and re-creation of his nation as one of benevolence and liberal democracy. According to Vorster (2007), the aim of the Christian is to attain a constructive attitude towards society and the individual, and this is the correct path to take from a Christian ethical perspective.

According to Vorster (2007), the central tenets of Reformed Christian ethics are found in the scriptural teachings of gratitude. Believers should attain a grateful attitude as their response to receiving the gift of redemption from God, following the fall of humanity. Vorster maintains that redemption through Christ promotes a change in the sinner, who is then moved to act according to the benevolent commands of God. This change will stimulate the believer to live in gratitude to God, as opposed to a life dedicated to self-service, and this new life will be lived not to earn the love of God, but to perform good acts in response to receiving God's gift of grace in Christ. In gratitude for this gift, we no longer need to live in sin, 'but the fruit of the Spirit is love, joy, peace, forbearance, kindness, goodness, faithfulness, gentleness and self-control' (Gl 5:22–23). From this starting point of gratitude, Vorster explains what attitude of ethics should be sought to guide ethical choices and actions under the Reformed tradition. His account could superficially be termed a 'theory of virtue ethics', albeit firmly located within the deontological paradigm. However, such a description would not be accurate, as Vorster's scripturally based theories are not marred by the difficulties of virtue ethics proper, where the foundations for chosen actions are obscure, relativist and situational.

The initial point of cognition for Vorster's (2007) constructive soteriological-based perspective is Scripture's revelation calling Christians to imitate the attitude of Christ in an expression of their gratitude. For example, followers are urged to take up Christ's yoke (Mt 11:29), and disciples are called to wash each other's feet (Jn 13:12–17) and to love each other as he loved them (Jn 13:34). Vorster (2007) further develops the productive ethical position from Philippians 2 which, for clarity, I include in full:

> In your relationships with one another, have the same mindset as Christ Jesus: Who, being in very nature God, did not consider equality with God something to be used to his own advantage; rather, he made himself nothing by taking the very nature of a servant, being made in human likeness. And being found in appearance as a man, he humbled himself by becoming obedient to death—even death on a cross! Therefore God exalted him to the highest place and gave him the name that is above every name, that at the name of Jesus every knee should bow, in heaven and on earth and under the earth, and every tongue acknowledge that Jesus Christ is Lord, to the glory of God the Father. (vv. 5-11)

This powerful expression of Christian attitude, where verses 6-11 represents a hymn, forms the basis for the four main principles Vorster (2007:18-19) develops for his constructive Christian ethical approach. The position can be explained thus (Vorster 2007):

- **Love.** The first principle to be derived from the hymn is that of agape, or all-inclusive love, involving being humane and compassionate, and making oneself available for others in rendering comfort, dignity and respect.
- **Stewardship.** The second principle is that of assuming the role of a servant, and through imitating Christ as revealed in Scripture, for example in John 13:12-17, to attain an attitude of service for the community and thus strive for a just and moral order of peace and social justice.
- **Self-denial.** The third principle is that of humility and self-denial, in that Christians should imitate Christ in his self-denying attitude in social relations, by exuding a willingness of personal sacrifice for the enhancement of the principles of the kingdom of God.
- **Obedience to God.** The fourth principle explains the fact that living in obedience to the will of God as expressed in Scripture entails, for Christians, seeking a chaste life and a moral social order.

Summing up his position, Vorster (2007) explains how he perceives the above four principles as guidelines that are complementary to other hermeneutical principles of scriptural interpretation pertaining to ethics, and which he advocates to be relevant in any context and at all times.

For the purpose of this treatise, the constructive ethical position explained by Vorster is of substantial use, as it mainly informs the interpretations that are made. The productive approach given under this paradigm will fit well the need of any banking actors, as they typically will have a professional and mandated obligation to act, and the opposite option of inactivity as shown by Geisler cannot be seen as a viable option for banking practice.

The plenitude of deontology

The above elaboration has outlined some of the main ethical philosophical options that could possibly inform human activity, from virtue, consequentialist and deontological perspectives. It has been shown that the relativity of the virtue formats renders these empty and futile, and it has also been demonstrated that although utilitarianism may imply a greater degree of flexibility compared to deontology or 'divine command', and although deontology may imply staleness and impracticality on account of superficial connotations of 'decided once and for all', this apparent dichotomy is not real; in fact, deontological and utilitarian solutions will often coincide. It is clear, both from the above, and from the following exploration in subsequent chapters, that there are no grounds to defend the notion that deontological ethics are not useful, practical, dynamic and up to date. On the contrary, the deontological model demonstrated and espoused here reveals the fact that the attitudes of global constructive participation in any human context, adhering to scriptural principles of love, stewardship, self-denial and obedience to God, will contribute substantial insights that will foster the expression of Christian life.

■ Pastoral trajectories

There are different vantage points on what constitutes pastoral theology, and consequently, some variations in what is focused on among different thinkers, both over time, and in current academic discourse. What is of interest here is not to develop a systematic elaboration of such differences, nor to adjudicate what would be the most advantageous locus of interest. In this treatise, it is the pastoral norms, and how they would be applicable in real life practical situations, such as in banking, which are at the forefront. The pastoral norms pertain to how Christians are to exert and express love towards others, and through this, apply Christian learning into different practices. Pastoral norms have been sought and developed by theologians and practising Christians; such norms have been based not only on the New Testament, but also from Old Testament sources. Both Testaments point to how Christians are to lead their lives in a practice of leadership, and to how exerting moral leadership and teaching by doing is a continuous theme found throughout the complete biblical corpus (Tidball 1997).

▨ Old Testament
☐ God's ministry

In pastoral theology, the metaphor of the shepherd is a central theme, which would lead us to understand how Christians are to act in order to guide others, and to distribute the love message, which is essential for the Christian believer. In the Old Testament, we meet the shepherd motif already in Genesis 48:15, where Jacob, in his ponderings on God and his relationship to humans, talks of 'the God before whom my fathers Abraham and Isaac walked faithfully, the God who has been my shepherd all my life to this day'. This quote points us to the continuum of the pastoral ethos, as Jacob clearly expresses how God has led 'his fathers' in the past, and that Jacob is awarded the same continued guiding by God, as his 'shepherd'. Other Old Testament passages where God is referred to as shepherd of his people by direct use of the shepherd motif is found in Genesis 49:24, 'the Mighty One of Jacob, because of the Shepherd, the Rock of Israel'; in Psalm 23:1, 'The Lord is my shepherd, I lack nothing'; and in Psalm 80:1 where we learn of the 'Shepherd of Israel, you who lead Joseph like a flock'. What strikes one as particularly notable in these quotes is how here it is God who is the shepherd, and not the believer, and this could be seen as the ministry of God, which would be the normative yardstick for human believers to adhere to when exerting pastoral ministry (Tidball 1997).

Further fortifications of the shepherd metaphor are inversely expressed in several passages, where humans are described as sheep to be herded, for example in Psalm 100:3, where we learn of 'his people, the sheep of his pasture', and in Psalm 119:176, where it is expressed that 'I have strayed like a lost sheep'. Further, from Psalm 44:22, we understand that when we have lost our way, we become exposed and weak and 'we are considered as sheep to be slaughtered'. These early quotes on the shepherd and his flock, the sheep, could perhaps be seen as a kind of proto-ministry, which in the initial stages is performed by God himself, for humans to learn from by example.

In describing God's ministry, the shepherding and herding motifs do not comprehensively elucidate God's care and guidance of his people. An important adjacent metaphor for explaining God's ministry is the use of the father imagery, where God cares for his people as if they were his children, and he has to raise them like children by sometimes exerting encouragement and praise, yet at other times by chastisement and discipline. A striking and moving example of the father metaphor is found in Hosea 11:1–11, where we learn of 'God's love for Israel'; that 'when Israel was a child, I loved him, and out of Egypt I called my son'; that when the people of Israel were in need, God 'bent down to feed them'; and when 'they refuse to repent a sword will flash in their cities'. The love God expressed for his people is not characterised by sentimentality and leniency, and as already evident from the above quotes, the father–child relationship of the Old Testament requires obedience on the side of the people, and also discipline and patience on the side of God. This is evident, for example, in Deuteronomy 28:1–68, where it is initially stated that 'If you fully obey the Lord your God and carefully follow all his commands I give you today, the LORD your God will set you high above all the nations on earth', and where the rest of the passage elaborates different aspects of obedience/reward, and disobedience/punishment.

The use of the father/child imagery could perhaps be interpreted as an extension of the shepherd metaphor, as by inserting the familiar facets of family life and raising of children, the important element of responsibility on the side of humans is emphasised. By solely utilising the shepherd and sheep metaphors, the responsibility on the side of the 'herded', the humans, could be lost, as an expected perception among readers would be that livestock are not capable of taking responsibility in a human manner. This would be very different when family life is used as the basis for literary imagery, where not least in early agrarian societies, all members of a family would be expected to have and take responsibility for different aspects of the family's total daily chores.

Another aspect of God's proto-ministry described in the Old Testament is that of God as saviour. As a result of disobeying God and ignoring copious warnings, Israel was punished through God's judgement, by way of being exiled (Ez 7:1–9). From Isaiah 50:1, we understand that the estrangement from God was not meant to be final, as the question there is posed: 'Where is your mother's certificate of divorce with which I sent her away?' Further, we learn, in Isaiah 52:2, how the Assyrian captivity was ended by a second exodus, when God instructed, 'Free yourself from the chains on your neck', and in Isaiah 52:12, God as saviour is demonstrated by the promise that when leaving exile, 'the Lord will go before you, the God of Israel will be your rear guard'. The magnitude of this deliverance was substantial, and in Isaiah 60–65, its glory is elaborated and celebrated in soteriological terms. What may be drawn from this great salvation could be how already from the inception it had been up to God alone, in his special relationship with Israel (Dt 7:7–8), whether his grace would be bestowed upon them.

From these initial interpretations, it could be inferred that the ministry of God involved guidance and care through his shepherding, discipline and instruction through his fatherhood, and salvation to be granted by his grace alone. It could be considered a prudent interpretation, then, to conclude that all following ministerial learning and activities were to be informed and led by the example of God's proto-ministry as described above (Tidball 1997). Indeed, in the Old Testament we are shown numerous examples of how humans took God's lead and exerted leadership and pastoral care over their people, inspired by God's own ministerial works.

☐ Moses

A natural starting point in describing early examples of ministry in the Bible would be to consider how Moses led the Israelites. His leadership was crucial; he acted as a prophet (Dt 18:15), leading them out of Egyptian exile during the first exodus; he conveyed the Ten Commandments as handed from God (Ex 20; Dt 5) with whom he spoke directly (Ex 33:11), and he was a pivotal figure in the formation of the nation of Israel (Wright 2009b). Of the many leadership tasks Moses carried out, his pastoral vision is not least evident in the narrative of the golden calf, where he chastises and sets straight the wayward Israelites, who had been without their leader for 40 days

(Ex 24:18, 32:19-26). Scripture renders other examples on how Moses used his leadership to guide his people by teaching and not dictating, which is exemplified in Deuteronomy 30:19, where Moses explains how his people have to make their own choices: 'I have set before you life and death, blessings and curses. Now choose life, so that you and your children may live'. This quote not only inspires people to make choices, but also points to the rewards of making the right ones.

The model of Moses' pastoral ministry is clearly mirrored in his successor Joshua, who, in Joshua 24:14-24, skilfully outlines to the Israelites their options and freedom to choose. His teaching leads the people freely to choose to 'serve the Lord our God and obey Him'. The pastoral principle of leading humans through offering insights on their free will could be said to be at the core of Old Testament pastoral ethos and should serve as a template for any pastoral and ministerial activity for all subsequent Christians who take on a leadership role, through promoting learning, realising and celebrating (Hiltner 2000).

Other leadership figures

Following the demise of Joshua, disorder broke out in Israel, and for the following era there, an established formal leadership in Israel would not exist, but the nation was influenced by judges through their varied degrees of emergent leadership. These judges did not have a permanent or formalised position in leading the nation, but nonetheless contributed guidance and teaching to the Israelites. After the period of the judges, Israel returned to the monarchy as the ruling system, and again a sense of restored order emerged (Collins 2014).

With the monarchy, we learn from Jeremiah 18:18 that there were three other categories of leaders that had appeared as the spiritual leaders of the nation, namely, the priests, the wise men and the prophets. The priests were mainly concerned with passing on the law of the covenant, as for example in Ezekiel 44:23, and their guidance may have been seen as narrower and more formal in comparison to that of the other pastors of Israel (Tidball 1997). Among the prophets, who were not formally instituted or appointed on the basis of heredity to exert their guidance but were called by God as individuals (Weber 1978), the guidance sought would have been broader. This individual aspect of the prophets' activities was sometimes expressed through the prophets receiving oracles from God, something that may be seen as an individually experienced divine communication (Collins 2014). Notable writing prophets were Ezekiel and Jeremiah, each awarded their own books in the Old Testament canon. The wise men of Israel were a category of pastors that deviated from the aforementioned, in that they did not reside in a formal place in society, but rather rendered useful practical advice and guidance for everyday situations with which their followers were troubled. The unrivalled example of an Old Testament wise man would be Solomon, who 'was wiser than anyone else' and whose 'fame spread to all the surrounding nations' (1 Ki 4:31).

The family

The final but not least important description of pastoral care in the Old Testament is connected to the family. As the family is the fundamental institution in society, focused in both Testaments, we learn already in Deuteronomy 4:9 of 'the things your eyes have seen', that they be taught 'to your children and to their children after them'. Further, we learn in Deuteronomy 6:6–7 that God's 'commandments' are given with the instruction to 'impress them on your children' and to 'talk about them when you sit at home'. Without delving any deeper here, it would be clear from the quotes that pastoral care and guidance are to be distributed at the most personal and private level, in the family, and that dispensing such pastoral care is not to be limited to formal and/or religious institutionalised settings.

The Old Testament abounds with norms and instructions on how to dispense pastoral care and guidance, and these instructions provide valuable inspiration for all subsequent pastoral ministry, including that which is detailed in the New Testament books. As always, the Bible is a collection of texts to be interpreted as a combined whole and in context (Vorster 2017b).

New Testament
Different literary strands

Without doubt, the New Testament is a premier source for pastoral learning, as Christ himself would be considered the premier minister, and following his lead and example is crucial to understanding the dynamics of pastoral leadership. The pastoral theology found in the New Testament is represented in two different versions: one as a theology directly pertaining to the expression and establishment of the church, and the other dealing with the church's ministry. The instructions and descriptions of the church as a practical forum for worship constitute the explicit pastoral strand of these two and has traditionally been receiving maximum attention from theologians and scholars. The implicit pastoral strand is nonetheless informing and important, and it is this strand that could lend most insights when seeking to mine out pastoral norms and principles from the New Testament (Tidball 1997). In the following text, it is mainly the implicit pastoral stand that is highlighted.

☐ Synoptic gospels

Among the synoptic gospels, Matthew is clearly focused on pastoral aspects in his writings, and he mentions the church explicitly in Matthew 16:18 and Matthew 18:17. However, Matthew does not maintain that the congregations of the church should be left without pastoral instruction, and he expands both directly and indirectly on how the leaders of the church are to lead, teach, learn and encourage faith. There are numerous examples in Matthew to illustrate this. For example, in Matthew 10:5–42, Jesus gives detailed instructions to his flock, and the aspect of teacher and pupils stands out as a leading pastoral relationship. In these passages, it is clear that by taking in the instructive teachings, the faithful pupil who is willing to learn will be rewarded, as Jesus says that 'Whoever welcomes a prophet as a prophet will receive a prophet's reward' (Mt 10:41). Clearly, then, the teacher and pupil both need to be diligent, and both sides of the relationship need to be responsible and trusting. A further and even more prominent example would be the Sermon on the Mount that is found in Matthew 5–7, which directly places Jesus as the teacher/leader, using monologue for guiding his listeners. The use of the leader/led speaker/listener imagery fits well within the wider social structure of the patron/client relationship, which was a cornerstone of the Roman society. This patron/client relationship permeated all aspects of Roman society, both within and outside of the legal realm, and most, if not all, Roman citizens, high or low, would typically reside within such social structures. Every person would be both a patron and client, as the father was the patron of his children, and the father was the client of someone higher, for example, a landowner, who in turn was a client for another patron, maybe an official or military person of authority. The key aspects of this patron/client relationship were that it was a binding commitment for both parties, and involved rights and responsibilities for both (Roniger 1983). When Matthew elaborates the core of discipleship in Matthew 8:23–27, this patron/client relationship is evident, as when their boat was sinking, 'the disciples went and woke' (Mt 8:25) Jesus, and Jesus then 'rebuked the winds and the waves, and it was completely calm' (Mt 8:26). From this passage, we understand that the leader is expected to lead the followers, and that the followers must trust their leader.

It must be noted that in the pastoral theology of Matthew, the role of the pastor is not one of authority and instruction solely, but more a position of participating as a humble servant to their flock, or as a guide, according to the example of Christ. Examples here could be Matthew 10:24, where we learn that 'the student is not above the teacher, nor a servant above his master', or Matthew 20:26–27, where we are informed that 'whoever wants to become great among you must be your servant, and whoever wants to be first must be your slave'.

The implicit pastoral strand is less visible in Mark than in Matthew, but nonetheless, there is significant pastoral learning to be taken from Mark also. When Mark addresses the aspects of suffering as a core element of discipleship, it is not his teaching that suffering is a punishment to be avoided, but rather, something to endure and withstand, for receiving compensation and exoneration in the after-world. We learn about this in Mark 13:16–27, which predicts that, when 'the sun will be darkened, and the moon will not give its light' (Mk 13:24), then the 'people will see the Son of Man coming in clouds with great power and glory' (Mk 13:26). The message would be that the faithful were to identify their own sufferings with those of Christ, and to relate to this the value of their own endurance, as their sufferings would be less than those of Christ. Examples here could be found in Mark 8:31, where it is stated that 'the Son of Man must suffer many things' and that 'he must be killed and after three days rise again', and in Matthew 10:40, where Jesus explains that 'to sit at my right or left is not for me to grant. These places belong to those for whom they have been prepared'. Mark's use of the term 'Son of Man' may have been a method for relating that Christ was indeed human, and thus, that his sufferings were not any less than those of other humans. Making this point would have been of importance in order to stave off heresies of Ebionist and Arian character, where Christ's humanity was not accepted or assured (O'Collins 2009).

In Luke and Acts, the place of the church is juxtaposed against contemporary society, and notably, the church is not presented as an authoritative or hierarchical institution run by the few. However, Luke and Acts are not renowned for matters of historical accuracy, and as a whole, these two volumes may be viewed as a ministerial project, where the focus is on the example of Jesus and his ministry. Luke and Acts provide several examples of individuals and their deeds, as model examples, such as the generous Barnabas, the suffering Paul and the evangelical Phillip (Tidball 1997). In Acts, there is an emphasis on matters that arose in the early church, where practicalities and instructions of different kinds are described. As part of this emphasis, the focus is on how to perform the duties as pastor, and in Acts 20:17–36 we learn of Paul and his exemplary pastoral vocation. For example, in Acts 20:19 we learn how Paul 'served the Lord with great humility and with tears', and in Acts 20:27, how he has 'not hesitated to proclaim to you the whole will of God'. Paul instructs his listeners to 'be shepherds of the church of God' (Ac 20:28), and against their opponents, his message is to 'be on your guard!' (Ac 20:31). At the end of the narrative, Luke refers to Paul's forward-gazing hope for the pastoral congregation, the church, when he commits them 'to God and to the word of his grace, which can build you up and give you an inheritance among all those who are sanctified' (Ac 20:32).

John

When reading the Gospel of John, it becomes evident that John's main aim is to direct attention to the greatness of God, and to instil in the reader the sense that only through believing comes individual salvation. The focus in John, then, is on the individual rather than the communal, and John does not address church matters or formal ministry. Consequently, when searching for pastoral guidelines, we need to look at John's technique of conveying these through the numerous examples of Jesus' acts and teachings. Of crucial pastoral importance are the narratives that tell of the good shepherd (Jn 10:1-21) and the washing of the disciples' feet (Jn 13:1-17).

In the parable of the good shepherd (Jn 10:1-21), Jesus uses the shepherd/flock metaphor and describes how only the true shepherd will be lawfully let into the pen, and then, 'the sheep listen to his voice' (Jn 10:3). Further, in keeping with the pastoral ethos of John, Jesus explains that 'I am the gate; whoever enters through me will be saved' (Jn 19:9), and when relaying the responsibilities of the leader, Jesus explains that 'the good shepherd lays down his life for the sheep' (Jn 10:11). The good shepherd parable clearly outlines foundational pastoral principles of belief, faith, leadership and reciprocal obligations of the leader and the led, which, as described below, are of central value when directing pastoral practice and care.

When Jesus washes the disciples' feet (Jn 13:1-17), the aspect of pastoral leadership as service is made further evident to the readers. The passage renders direct pastoral instruction, as when Jesus as the disciples' 'Lord and Teacher' (Jn 13:14) had washed their feet, the instruction was 'I have set you an example that you should do as I have done for you' (Jn 13:15). The perceived lowliness of washing someone else's feet elegantly elucidates the serving aspect of the pastoral role, and firmly to establish the egalitarian qualities of true leadership. Jesus says that 'no servant is greater than his master, nor is a messenger greater than the one who sent him' (Jn 13:16).

Paul

Among those who took their learning directly from Christ's earthly ministry, we know more about Paul than anyone else. The wealth of teachings and instructions left us by Paul then lend his authorship particular interest, not least when exploring Scripture seeking for pastoral inspiration (Chadwick 1907; Ridderbos 1997). Although Paul was concerned with theological aspects of faith, there are numerous pastoral directives and inspirations to be drawn from his written legacy. In Paul's view, establishing the church and formulating faith would be two sides of the same coin, something that is evident in 1 Corinthians 3:1-9, where he explains that 'we are co-workers in God's service;

you are God's field, God's building' (1 Cor 3:9). Clearly, then, the tasks of living in, dispensing and accepting faith are joint pastoral tasks for all believers to partake in.

In Paul, the mutually and universally binding patron/client motif as described above is particularly in use, and is evident in several places, albeit in different literary contexts. For example, in 1 Corinthians 4:15, we find in use the metaphor of father/child; in 1 Thessalonians 4:7, the adjacent nursing mother/child; in Colossians 1:28, teacher/student. The serving aspect of Paul's pastoral theology builds up under the reciprocal and communal responsibility of pastoral duties, and he frequently places the pastor in a serving role towards fellow believers. This is represented, for example, in Ephesians 3:7, where he describes himself as 'a servant of this gospel', and in Colossians 1:23, where Paul has become a 'servant' of the gospel. To further expand on the service aspect of pastoral obligations, Paul uses the steward metaphor, as in 1 Corinthians 4:1, where he says that he is among the 'servants of Christ'.

A final observation on Paul's pastoral theology is that his method of guiding and distributing his pastoral vocation was one that used examples as much as direct instruction (Wolter & Brawley 2015). This distinguishing factor of Paul's didactic ministry is represented in passages like 1 Timothy 4:11, where we are advised to 'set an example for the believers in speech, in conduct, in love, in faith and in purity', and in Titus 2:7, where the instruction is to 'in everything set them an example by doing what is good'.

☐ Pastoral epistles

The general epistles, in their varied scope and subject matter, offer pastoral insights and inspiration, and we find use of the collaborative ethos of the shepherd/flock metaphor, as well as the adjacent pastoral method of utilising examples and not relying exclusively on teleological instruction.

The use of leading by example is clearly elucidated in Hebrews 11, where biblical narratives are restated to exemplify faith, such as in Hebrews 11:8, where Abraham, when called by God, 'obeyed and went', and in Hebrews 11:31, Rahab, who 'welcomed the spies, was not killed with those who were disobedient'. The crux of the complete exhortations in Hebrews 11:1–39, is found in verse 39, where we learn that 'these were all commended for their faith, yet none of them received what had been promised'. How better to explain how to lead by selfless example, and to exert a pastoral attitude though living in faith, and expressing it in practice?

The shepherd/sheep motif is in use in Hebrews 20:20, 'Lord Jesus, that great Shepherd of the sheep', but more prominently in use in Peter. In Peter, we find the pinnacle of biblical shepherd symbolism, where the term 'Chief Shepherd' is introduced for Christ in 1 Peter 5:4 (Tidball 1997). That pastoral responsibilities are on the community, and not solely on certain individuals, may be extrapolated from 2 Peter 3:17-18, where the instruction is to 'be on your guard', and 'grow in the grace and knowledge of our Lord and Saviour Jesus Christ'. Clearly, this is an instruction to every believer, not left as the prerogative or responsibility of only a few.

Historical development
A post-Christ focus

After outlining some essential aspects of pastoral instruction from scriptural sources, the next point of interest is to explore how these biblical teachings have inspired and informed the practical-pastoral understanding over the subsequent millennia. In doing so, it will not be concentrated on the development in Old Testament times, as the locus of interest in this section is the development of the Christian practical-pastoral tradition after Christ.

The early centuries

In the first centuries of Christianity, the practice of love and care was central to all Christian activity, and a central aspect was that of leadership. The leadership image of the shepherd caring for his flock could be a suitable metaphor for how the early Christians perceived their lives as mission, and their mission to be their lives. In a sense, then, to paraphrase Gandhi (1959), their lives were their message, and this caring and shepherding praxis was a joint activity among all Christians (Tidball 1997). Thus, in the first era after Christ, the pastoral ministry of the early Christians and their first church structures were perceived and developed as a communal task among the constituents. This communal and incisive aspect of the early church, and its constituents, included both genders, which is evidenced in 1 Corinthians 11:5, where we learn of 'a woman who prays or prophesies' and in 1 Timothy 3:11, where in the context of deacons, it is stated that 'the women are to be worthy of respect'. The latter quote may be an indication that the early church had female deacons. The principle of gender equality is equally emphasised in Galatians 3:28 and in 1 Corinthians 11:11-12. That pastoral ministry was a dual gender activity in the early centuries after Christ was also evidenced by the important place women had in missionary activities and their place in pastoral care. The communal aspects of pastoral and missionary agency did not mean that there was no emergent leadership among the early Christian congregations, as in the early churches there seem to have existed numerous local leaders, such as evangelists and teachers. There are also indications of leadership above the local levels, and Paul may have been a representative of this. In the early stages, these leaders were not appointed in a formal process in the churches, but pastoral ministry was regarded as a charism, where the community may have had a role in recognising such gifts of leadership (Bernier 2015). This collaborative and inclusive version of the church was to end with Emperor Constantine's (272–337) conversion to Christianity when the church became a state organisation, after which time women outside religious orders fell to the margins of organised church ministry (Heitink 1999).

With the church becoming a state matter, Christian history was appropriated by the imperial state, and Constantine used this annexation project to affirm his authority in the leading position of the church, with Byzantium and Rome as official stages for the associated divine appointment. Further institutionalising aspects of the drive towards organisation and formality were found in the active recreation of a Christian Holy Land with Jerusalem in the centre, a Jerusalem which, until then, had been a provincial backwater in the empire (MacCulloch 2010).

Leading up to Christianity becoming the state religion in the Roman Empire, there had been a development towards institutionalised order and organisation of the church, but the picture was rudimentary. For example, the role of leadership among the few, as opposed to pastoral ministerial duties of the many, was not moulded into the traditional church hierarchy we would know in later history. The pre-Constantine church did, however, use titles such as bishop and presbyter, but here it is of importance to note that in these early stages, ministries were held in private homes, and did not move into separate buildings for worship until after 300 AD (Selby 2012). In this stage, ministerial ordinations occurred, but they did not entail the formality and uniformity which we would understand in a later context (Bernier 2015).

In the Constantinian period and beyond, as the organisation of the formal church gained traction, thoughts on pastoral activity increasingly became connected to the formal offices of the church, and there was less emphasis on the communal task it had been perceived as previously. An important contributor of this era was John Chrysostom (349–407), who was Archbishop of Constantinople, and is considered one of the early church fathers (Hitchcock 2012). Between 380 and 386, Chrysostom wrote the *Six Books on the Priesthood*, wherein he outlined his views on pastoral theology and his perceptions on the pastoral office of the church. What is notable in Chrysostom's authorship is how he understood pastoral theology solely in the spiritual and theological realm, at a distance from the pragmatic and practical concerns of church operations (Purves 2001). This brand of pastoral ethos placed Chrysostom firmly in a New Testament pastoral tradition, where the priest is not a leader above the people he guides, but integral with them, like the dynamics of a shepherd and his flock (Chrysostom 2017).

Augustine, as the seminal Western Christian he was, imprinted his mark on the development of pastoral theology and practice in the Western churches. He acted as a role model in keeping close to the ordinary people, in that he personally lived a monastic life lacking the luxuries of the elite, and in his prolific and substantial authorship we find traces of his pastoral theology, where the focus was on teaching and guiding. His quest to integrate Scripture into the developing of an organised church is particularly evident in his *City of God*, where he outlines this connection, and among his expressed goals is the task of encouraging faltering believers and leading heretics back onto the true path (Augustine 2003). As Augustine was also concerned with the ordination of clergy, his influence on the development of the church led to a firming-up of the formality of the role of the pastoral leader, the pastoral office as posterity knows it. Thus, with Augustine, the acceptance of the communal pastoral ministry came to an end, and thereafter ministry became a task for the few who had been formally ordained by the church authority. In a sense, at this stage, the Western church had attained a position on the pastoral task more like that of the Old Testament priests than that of the corporate ministry of the New Testament (Tidball 1997).

With the emergence of the formalised and increasingly authoritarian church, and with pre-Constantine roots, there was a parallel development of monastic orders among Christians, which on some levels, may be viewed as a counter-formal movement. In the monastic movement, there was a perception that in the close-knit and exclusive world of these monastic orders the constituents were living more like the early apostolic Christians, in small groups on the margins of organised society, where only the true believers could belong. With the growth and organising of the Christian church, the group of Christians was increasingly widened, and consisted of members from different backgrounds and with various degrees of resolve in their Christian beliefs. To some of the monastic societies, the growth of the church represented a weakening of the church's pastoral impact, and the wider church collective could not measure up to the religious 'top athletes' of the monastic communities (MacCulloch 2010).

☐ Medieval era

With the fall of the Western Empire, the church entered the medieval era with answering calls to replace the secular rule of the West Romans, as there was no secular organisation in place to uphold the Roman institutions that previously had represented the organisation of Western Europe. Following this need, the church became increasingly entwined in worldly matters. In a Reformed context, it would be typical to write off the whole era as one of ecclesiastical decay and degeneration (Tidball 1997). Such a stark view of nearly 1000 years of European church evolution would be a grave misrepresentation of history, and not least, of the pastoral contributions the church made to society in that age.

If we are to accept that the church did fall into what we later see (with modern post-Reformation eyes) as disrepair in a pastoral context, there is still room for acknowledging the pastoral care and guidance that was extended to the populations of Western Europe by the church during the medieval era. Among these pastoral tasks that the church undertook were the missions to the northern regions, where the classical teaching ethos of Scripture was expressed; and how better to care for people than leading them onto the path of Christianity (Hitchcock 2012)? Other examples of societal shepherding are to be found within the monastic orders of the era, and within the Knight Templars mentioned above, in their protection of pilgrims, and not least, in developing useful banking structures with lasting beneficial importance to society. To delve deeper into the technological advances that were created within the medieval church and monasteries, including those of agriculture, horticulture and engineering, would fall outside the scope of this treatise (Baumol 1990). In addition to the technological advances that were created under church rule, the medieval church also upheld a functioning legal system, a certain level of education and literacy, as well as creating demand for a wide array of services connected to its buildings and religious services, which was foundational for the development of the arts and crafts (Hitchcock 2012; MacCulloch 2010). They are mentioned here to only emphasise the pastoral shepherding qualities of the church and her constituents during an age where later history so often takes the view of darkness and decay.

The above notwithstanding, one early medieval thinker who is widely recognised as authoring one of the most influential works on pastoral theology is Gregory the Great (540–604) who became Pope in 590, with his publication of the *Pastoral Care*. The *Pastoral Care* became the dominant publication on pastoral theology for 1000 years, from its publication around 590 until the Reformation, and is considered the most read work on pastoral theology within Christianity, next only to the Bible (Purves 2001). In *Pastoral Care,* Gregory distinguished between the bishops' role as church nobles, and their role as pastors of their congregations, and he further instructed the readers that a pastor must live as he preaches (Gregory 1890). This leading-by-example ethos could be seen as a harkening back to the early Christian pastoral values, where the pastor and his flock are equals in their belief and life experiences. However, even if Gregory's pastoral ethos was normative for the churches' ministerial offices in the medieval era, there can be no doubt that the church during this time grossly corrupted the pastoral assignment of the church. Examples of this are well-known, such as the practice of lay investitures, selling indulgences and the gross amassment of worldly goods in the hands of the church and its monasteries (Tidball 1997).

Chapter 5

☐ The reformation

By the time of the early Renaissance and the discoveries of the 'new world', for a multitude of complex reasons, the stage was set for the social, political and religious revolution we have come to know as the Reformation, which is typically attributed to the revolutionary acts and works of Martin Luther (MacCulloch 2004). Often, Luther's (maybe legendary) posting of the 95 theses on the Wittenberg church door in 1517 is attributed seminal importance in setting off the Reformation and was an act of superlative symbolic importance in a time when oppositional views on religious matters were not welcomed (McNally 1967).

Within the scope of this treatise, it is not the Reformation history that is in focus, but rather, how this movement influenced religious thinking on pastoral theology. Martin Luther (1483–1546), in his active life in service, was highly focused on his pastoral responsibilities, and his theology democratised the church to become a ministry of the word, and not of formal institutions. For Luther, the church was where the word of God was, and a seminal contribution to this manner of ministry was aided by his translation of the Bible into the German language. This act may be seen as an act of Reformed pastoral care, as by letting anyone gain access to Scripture first-hand, the church of the word could become a reality (Tappert 2007). In addition, allowing the Bible to be widely read also furthered the use of biblical imagery, proverbs and narratives to a new group of artists and authors, by allowing biblical passages to be used in references in the vernacular language (Nord 2001).

Central to Luther's own pastoral ministry was the ministry of consolation and aiding the sick, and there are numerous examples of his personal active ministry in this area. It is worth noting that although Luther proclaimed the church of the word, he was as capable of supporting his theology in practice, and again, the church would be in touch with its constituents, and its priests working among them (Tidball 1997). This aspect of the priests now again working and living in direct contact with and among the believers was further supported by the clergy's newfound right to marriage (MacCulloch 2004). By letting the priests marry, they would truly become engrained in society, and their pastoral guidance could be expressed in action yet again. This could be seen as a return, in part at least, to the communal pastoral responsibilities of the early Christians described above.

A contemporary of Luther was the Strasbourg-based protestant reformer Martin Bucer, who made considerable imprints on the development of Reformed thinking, influencing Lutheran and Calvinist Protestant theology, not least through his works on pastoral theology. He converted to Lutheranism in 1518, was among the first Reformers to get married and was of considerable influence on Calvin when he lived in Strasbourg (Tidball 1997). His most important contribution to pastoral theology is his *Concerning the True Care of Souls*, which sets out a theology based on biblical and Reformation foundations (Purves 2001). Bucer's vision of the church was one of democracy, and this was expressed, for example, by how laypersons could be appointed as elders and deacons, and how the different ministerial offices were given assignments of pastoral character (Heitink 1999).

In *Concerning the True Care of Souls,* Bucer outlines the themes of his pastoral vison. The word of God is at the centre of his theology, and a pluralist approach towards leadership is attained. Essential to the pastors would be exegesis and the practical application of the scriptural insights that this would yield. The leaders should be selected from all societal strata, and the reason therefore was that no one person would have all gifts bestowed upon them. On pastoral discipline, Bucer states that to care for sinners is the duty of all Christians, but the pastor has the highest responsibility for this task. To aid his flock in spiritual growth, Bucer maintains that the pastor should promote this goal through teaching and guidance, thus giving his pastoral vision a scriptural didactic approach (Bucer 2009).

John Calvin is of substantial importance to the development of Reformed pastoral practice and theology. He diligently worked in Geneva from 1536 to 1564, except for his five years in Strasbourg, as teacher, preacher, pastor and author, and during this period, he contributed widely to the development of a broad field of what is later considered Calvinist Reformed theology (Partee 1995). Among his most influential work is the *Institutes of the Christian Religion*, and together with the *Ecclesiastical Ordinances*, this is where we find Calvin's pastoral theology presented. The pastoral ideal of Calvin was guidance through teaching and instruction (Tidball 1997). This didactic ideal is eloquently represented in his *Institutes*, where he (Calvin 2012) states:

> We see that God, who might perfect his people in a moment, chooses not to bring them to manhood in any other way than by the education of the Church. (*Inst.* 4.1.5)

Calvin is aligned with the early Christian ideal of community and dispersal of Christian teaching among the believers, wherever they are. On this, he says in his *Institutes,* that pastors should '… exhort and admonish from house to house, whenever their hearers have not profited sufficiently by general teaching …' (Calvin 2012:*Inst.* 4.12.2).

Calvin's pastoral ministry had its place in Geneva, where he worked tirelessly on his pastoral duties, and, as part of his teaching activities, he placed great emphasis on caring for the sick, proclaiming that people should feel free to call their pastors when in need, and not have to wait until they were on their deathbeds (Tidball 1997). Like Bucer, Calvin divided the clergy according to their assigned roles, and allowed lay members to be appointed deacons and elders, where elders performed home visits and church discipline, and the deacons were in charge of handling social needs. The diaconate branch of the church was responsible for caring for the poor, the sick and those in need. Calvin's systematisation of church affairs included a division into minister, deacon, elder and teachers, which was followed by the Dutch churches for their organisations (Heitink 1999).

The Reformation thus profoundly influenced the ideals of pastoral theology, and it could fairly be stated that the vision for pastoral care returned to its early Christian roots, where the democratic and corporate responsibility for pastoral guidance was at the forefront.

Modern era

The Reformation made a powerful imprint on the re-creation of pastoral theology and practice into the modern era, and substantially parted from the development of the Catholic Church in this regard. The Reformed churches now allowed a new impulse to be introduced from the emerging natural and social sciences, and the Catholic Church remained true to the more institutionalised authority of the formalised church offices, the sacrament and liturgy as foundational in their pastoral ministry, at least up to the Second Vatican Council of 1962–1965 (Bernier 2015; Tidball 1997).

Among the evangelical revivalist authors/practitioners, John Wesley (1703-1791) contributed invaluable insights to the developing field of pastoral practice and theology. In his sermon, *The Ministerial Office*, Wesley outlined his principles for prudent ministry. One of the main points is that the roles of preacher and pastor should be delineated. In his view, the elevated role of the priests was not compatible with the pastoral role of the minister, as this would be perceived from scriptural exegesis. The basis of the sermon refers to Hebrews 5:4, where the ministerial instruction is that 'no one takes this honour on himself, but he receives it when called by God', and the intention was that the pastors should not seek ministerial positions for the worldly glory attached, but should see themselves as embedded among the community of believers (Wesley 2018). It was a substantial ethos in the pastoral principles of the Wesleyan Methodism that widespread participation in pastoral activity among the lay members was sought out. There was an evangelical renaissance of social engagement and spiritual care, where the format of small groups, so-called 'class meetings', were the most important forum for teaching and pastoral guidance. The core tenet in this movement was love for God and neighbours, and this neighbourly love would find many forms connected to social needs and spiritual guidance. The movement instigated homes for orphans and widows, free health stations, food supply to the poor, interest-free loans and cottage-industry employment, as well as home visits to administer prayer. In this movement, both men and women were recruited with great skill to participate in the collective shepherding of the flock, and their core qualification was the ability to exert their love and belief in God while partaking in the pastoral activities (Albin 1995). This distinction between the ordained priests and the lay pastoral practitioners was, however, challenging to uphold, even among the Wesleyan Methodist pastors, and increasingly they sought and were extended ordinations by the Church of England (Tidball 1997).

In the evangelical revivalist period, the focus on systematising the role of ministers was increasing and works of this period led to the formation of the academic field of practical theology. Friedrich Schleiermacher was a substantial contributor to this development, and in his *Brief Outline on the Study of Theology*, Schleiermacher explains his pastoral theology. His ethos was that the theological should not be separated from the pastoral, lest the ministers become mechanical purveyors of superficial Christian truths only. With this foundation, the goals of pastoral activity were to better and balance the community, and to influence its constituents through promoting theological truths in practice (Schleiermacher 1966). Systematic teaching was to be central in the ministry, so that the homiletics would promote Christian self-awareness though the dispersion of dogmatic learning (Schleiermacher 2011).

Schleiermacher's influence on subsequent theologians was substantial, and examples of proponents of this development can be found in the authorship of Jan Jacob van Oosterzee (1817–1882), who in 1877–1878 published *Practical Theology: A Manual for Theological Students*, where he outlined all the different tasks of the ministerial office in a comprehensive and detailed manner. Although he claimed to take a scientific vantage point on practical theology, he emphasised homiletics, in other words, the teaching/guiding aspect of the ministry office (Heitink 1999; Van Oosterzee 1878). Another prominent example of the development of pastoral theology in this age of systematisation is Washington Gladden (1836–1918), who, through his various sermons and published works, oriented pastoral theology towards the social economic trends of the day. To Gladden (1916), shepherding and pastoral guidance were viewed as the key tasks of the pastor and preaching and devotion as a peripheral aspect of pastoral practice. Although he did not espouse socialism, his idealism made him seek a societal balance of harmony and equity, and political issues such as labour rights and social equality were focus areas in his brand of pastoral theology (Dorn 1993).

It would be clear from the above text that the development of pastoral theology in the post-Reformation modern era was one of increased systematisation, and that the Reformation's recreation of the lay participation and scriptural foundations for the ministerial office was maintained and further enforced. The pastor in this era remained one with his flock, and one who increasingly partook in the societal challenges of the flock.

☐ Twentieth century and onwards

Karl Barth contributed substantially to developing Reformed theology during his prolific authorship, and although his most prominent works were on dogmatics, he also contributed to advancing pastoral theology as relevant in the 20th century. Barth has been widely praised as perhaps one of the most influential Protestant authors since the Reformation, and many labels have been stuck to his authorship, such as, for example, 'dialectical theology' or 'neo-orthodoxy'. It should be noted that his thinking went through different phases, and that he perceived theology as a freestanding realm, where responding to God's revelation was at the core (McGrath 2012). Barth's theology focuses on the redeeming and reconciling works of Christ, and the core aspect is grace, where human acts of righteousness are only a reflection of the righteousness of God, and human righteousness cannot replicate or fulfil that of God. As opposed to the Lutheran dogmas, Barth saw the gospel as above the law, as the law cannot prepare for gospel, but he maintained that gospel would allow for a new perception of the law (Bloesch 1995).

In his somewhat church-critical *The Epistle to the Romans*, Barth (1968) outlines some pastoral principles, and the fellowship and community among the followers of Christ is seen among the central tenets in the pastoral vocation, as well as the didactic method of pastoral care. Here, he points out how the letter to the Romans was given to all parts of society, as it was 'addressed to men and women, to Greeks, Romans, and Jews, to masters and slaves' (Barth 1968:536), and through this communal distribution, the teaching became available to all, as a living theology. To Barth, then, a scripturally based pastoral theology founded on the communal collaborative principles of the early Christians was clearly the ideal mode of pastoral practice.

A major influence in 20th-century pastoral theology was the inclusion of other social sciences, such as sociology and psychology, into pastoral practice (Purves 2001). A substantial thinker of this school of thought was Seward Hiltner (1909–1984), who included concepts of psychotherapy in his brand of counselling theology and used real-life case studies in his teaching of theological students. His pastoral approach was client-centred, and his emphasis was on the whole person (Hiltner 1969). At the core of his pastoral theology was the shepherding of the community, including healing and guiding, and thus, the counselling aspects were to be downplayed in the pastoral tasks (Hiltner 1949). His pastoral theology has received criticism for overemphasising the shepherd metaphor, and for diffusing the delineation between theology and psychology (Hurding 1995b).

One such critic is Thomas Oden (1931–2016), who reacted against Hiltner's theology by proposing a return to a scriptural basis for pastoral theology, although he did not completely refute any claims of psychology. He accepted that psychology could be a gateway for exposing Christian truths, but that this would be the only role of psychology, and not the opposite, as could be derived from Hiltner's theology (Oden 1978). For Oden, the core of the pastoral office is connected to shepherding the congregation, in an inclusive and embedded fashion, which could be seen as a loyal harkening back to the scripturally based collaborative mode of ministry of the early Christians (Oden 1983).

Eduard Thurneysen (1888–1974), a Swiss theologian who was a personal friend of Barth, was the proponent of a pastoral theology where Scripture was at the core. Thurneysen's proposition was that the word of God was the only element to be considered in pastoral practice, and that the fundamental aspect of pastoral activity is the conversation. The conversation, he maintained, in itself represented preaching in a wider sense, and would lead the believer from the vantage point of the word of God, and on to the discipline and sanctification of the individual. It would be fair to state that Thurneysen further bolstered the biblical basis of pastoral theology, but his critics maintain that his demotion of adjacent sciences was too strict, and that not allowing a broader view of the individual than the strictly theological was too limiting (Atkinson 1995a; Thurneysen 2010).

Jay Adams (1929–2020) was a theologian who moved even further away from accepting extra-scriptural inclusions in pastoral practice; his brand of pastoral counselling rejects all forms of psychotherapy, and his introduction of the nouthetic counselling paradigm comprises a total repudiation of Freudian theory. All that Adams deems necessary for forming behavioural attitudes, values and belief systems, appears in the special revelation found in Scripture. The foundational aspects of Adams' theology are found in the Old Testament, from where he draws on the didactic methodology of admonition, warnings and advice (Adams 1986). The anti-Freudian stance of Adams is criticised not only for its dismissal of adjacent counselling fields, but also for its apparent neglect of the aspects of comfort and encouragement, which typically is connected to New Testament theology (Hurding 1995a).

It is evident, then, that during the 20th century, the field of pastoral theology was under pressure from secular influences, in particular within the realm of pastoral counselling. With the plethora of tools on offer in contemporary pastoral practice, it is of interest to elaborate how this would extrapolate to a prudent pastoral-theological practice under the Reformed paradigm for the 21st century, both for the setting of the individual counselling practice, as well as in the wider role of shepherding the community of believers.

Contemporary praxis model

With the historical background as described above, the question arises: what is the reigning Reformed pastoral-theological model of today? That is, of course, if such a question can even be answered convincingly and uniformly, where there will be one single line of practice that is the general Reformed pastoral model. It is clear that the post-Reformation development, has moved in a direction away from the elevated and distant clergy of the medieval era, where the ordination was at the core, where the pastor was among the few and the flock left to be informed at the will of the elevated minister. With the politicised and secularised societal discourse of the 20th century, the traditional pastoral theology was challenged by secular impulses, and the answer was typically one of seeking the other extreme, as the anti-psychiatry stance of Adams shows. It is of interest to examine a few contemporary authors to elucidate how they interpret and synthesise this 20th-century discourse.

Before venturing onto the contemporary authors, it is of interest to investigate further the thinking of Oden, who was a moderating 20th-century voice, as his theology seems aligned with Barth and Calvin, in that his focus was on the communal shepherding of the believers, and also, that he was not confined to an extreme biblicist exegetical praxis (Tidball 1997).

To Oden, the core of pastoral theology was found in Scripture, and the leadership and guidance task was, in his view, best represented in the shepherding metaphor. He elaborates on this metaphor, finding a basis in John 10:1–18, and questions whether the shepherd is a figure that may be understood by modern humans. His conclusion here is clear, as he describes how it would be an underestimation of people to distrust their understanding of this pivotal analogy. On the contrary, he explains how the intimacy in the relationship of the shepherd and his flock clearly mimics that of the prudent pastoral office, and how the pastor is to guide the constituents onto a safe life path, just like the shepherd when he leads his flock onto fresh pastures. He further explains how the shepherd/pastor has authority, but that this is an authority that is drawn from the service of leadership. In other words, the pastor's leadership is seen as a service to the constituents, in Christ (Oden 1983).

The image of leadership as service is a core element of Reformed pastoral theology, and Osmer (2008), for example, supports this perception, describing the pastoral office as servant leadership. Another central aspect of the modern Reformed pastoral ethos is community and collaboration. Based on scriptural sources such as 1 Corinthians 11:5 and 1 Timothy 3:11, it is evident that among the early Christians, ministry was a communal task, unlike the elevated Old Testament priesthood, and as demonstrated above, this mode of communality was continued with strength by the Reformation (Bucer 2009; Heitink 1999). The place of laity and both genders has been a core concern of Reformed pastoral expression, although not all Reformed churches have allowed women the gift of ordination. However, the development has increasingly moved toward ordination of women in Reformed churches, and already Oden (1983) supported the place of all in ministry, irrespective of gender, so that women should be ordained. However, the ordination of women is still controversial in certain conservative Protestant circles, and the Dutch Reformed Church in 2017 was suspended from its membership in the International Conference of Reformed Churches because it opened up all church offices for women (International Conference of Reformed Churches 2017). It is difficult to accept this conservative stance as representing responsible scriptural exegesis, as it appears in several scriptural locations (e.g. 1 Cor 11:5 and 1 Tm 3:11) that both genders took part in the early Christian ministries, and leading contemporary Reformed writers like Vorster (2017b) see such gender-excluding interpretations as nonviable.

Among modern Reformed pastoral thinkers, Heitink (1999) attains a functional perspective on the pastoral vocation under the practical theology umbrella and outlines how ministry could be viewed according to its practical societal location, rather than against secular impulses. In fact, according to him, it is the context of ministry, rather than dogmatic anchoring, which forms the basis for analysing pastoral theology and its practical uses. Heitink consequently sees Christian life and Christian logic as the two cornerstones of theology. In this framework, Heitink includes elements such as the traditional pastoral shepherding, learning, celebration, Scripture, ethics, psychological theology, aesthetical theology and comparative theology, to mention but a few (Heitink 1999). Such a holistic perspective of the pastoral task is also expressed by Whipp (2013), who underscores the contextual and provisional nature of the pastoral vocation, to be aligned with the needs of believers in their life stages and situations. Within this broad attitude, topics such as use of language and power perceptions are included in the consideration made in ministry, and terms such as theological anthropology are used as auxiliary to those of the traditional shepherding nomenclature (Whipp 2013).

As will have appeared in this section, there is no single and coherent mode of pastoral practice that can convincingly define a uniform one-size-fits all mode of pastoral practice within the Reformed paradigm. Thus, for the purposes here, it will be necessary to outline a pastoral model that is aligned with sound Reformed theology, undergirded by Scripture, and which resonates firmly with practical life and modern-day considerations.

Espoused pastoral-ethical model

Introduction

After perusing the above-presented philosophies and moral models that may elucidate banking practice from a pastoral and theological-ethical perspective, it is of paramount importance how these different impulses may be expressed in acceptable pastoral-ethical terms that are defendable under the Reformed paradigm. In this section, I elaborate on the pastoral-ethical model that is used here when engaging in the pastoral argument, and which is the basis for the interpretations and elaborations throughout this treatise, both connected to Scripture and practical life.

Inclusive and constructive model

From the above elaboration in this chapter, it has appeared that a valid pastoral theology and practice within the Reformed tradition will need to be rooted firmly in Scripture, to be collaborative and inclusive, to include both formal clergy and lay members of both genders and will need to be didactic and helpful in guiding believers in all areas of their lives. Such a practice is securely guided by the scriptural shepherding metaphor and is well aligned with the constructive ethical theology of Vorster (2007, 2017a), where the concept of stewardship (Jn 13:12–17) is pivotal, and which clearly mirrors the leadership call that is placed on the pastoral vocation. Such constructive leadership needs to pay heed to the central Christian motif of love, which is expressed in numerous scriptural passages, and that would place the pastoral activity in direct connection to key biblical events and theological principles, as we learn from 1 John 4:19 that 'we love because He first loved us'. From such an image, it may be concluded that individual and social inclusion in a constructive societal frame is at the centre of any viable Reformed Christian praxis model. As the ethical stewardship principles outlined above are unbreakably connected to the pastoral love principle of Scripture, and as both sets of norms are immersed in scriptural soteriology, the proposal here is that ethical (moral) action is essentially pastoral action, because it has to do with promoting the good for the benefit of all people.

Praxis and context oriented

Although the scriptural foundations from both Testaments will always be at the centre, it is not acceptable to close off other adjacent bodies of knowledge, secular or ecclesiastical, as this could be contrary to fulfilling the pastoral leadership task that must be respected at all times. An example here could be found in contemporary management theory, which typically is inclusive and collaborative, just like the pastoral vocation in the early Christian biblical tradition (Raelin 2003, 2010). It would be reasonable to expect that, for Christians, partaking in banking activities could sometimes be experienced with some unease, because the outside world may perceive their professional activities with some suspicion, as they may be seen to 'serve both God and money' (Mt 6:24). Despite some scripturally based eschatological impulses (e.g. Rv 21), a constructive pastoral approach is of practical importance, as the focus remains on the soteriological, such as the redemptive qualities found in the serving ethos (e.g. Lk 22:27), and the constructive message of the creation narrative and the human task-oriented place in the world (e.g. Gn 1:28, 2:15). For bankers, as for any other business people, such a Christian ethical and pastoral model may be suitable and give meaning to their profession of choice and everyday work life (Higginson 1994).

When applying scripturally grounded ethical and pastoral principles, it is of importance to utilise a context focus, as although the scriptural norms are universal, their application may not be clear from a literal reading of biblical passages, not least as here, when viewing them in light of modern-day banking practices. Clearly, as Scripture was authored nearly two millennia or more ago, many of the moral dilemmas that appear in our modern everyday work life may be connected to a set of real-life circumstances not known to the scriptural authors. The interpretive task then is to extrapolate these universal norms onto the professional practice of contemporary society. Only then, will our practice be aligned with Heitink (1999:6), who explains practical theology as 'the empirically oriented theological theory of the mediation of the Christian faith in the praxis of modern society'.

In this treatise, such a scripturally rooted holistic, inclusive, didactic, constructive and functional version of practical theology is used, where the performance of good deeds in appropriate contexts and the development of a praxis of promoting the good to the benefit of all people is at the core. I expect this to be well-suited to elucidate and inform the development of Christian banking as rooted in the Reformed tradition. The leadership attitude of constructive participation that banking professionals can adopt towards banking adhering to principles of love, stewardship, self-denial and obedience to God, will through their scriptural foundations shed light on how to move the banking activities forward in a soteriological perspective.

Chapter 6

Scriptural foundations

Keywords: scriptural grounding; borrowing; lending; interest; *imago Dei*; human rights; equal opportunities; animal welfare.

■ Introduction

In this chapter, I explore the scriptural basis for ethical and pastoral norms, as these may relate to banking, with all its practices and connected products. The chapter is divided according to conventional topics of interest typically discussed within Christian and secular spheres, and this elaboration is expected to yield useful insights on pastoral-theological and ethical positions leading to useful scripturally based policies pertaining to banking. Thus, the topics that have been elected to be highlighted are believed to be of interest for the practical banking professional and especially for the Christian reader (Birch & Rasmussen 1989). The subjects highlighted will pertain both directly to what is known as traditional banking practices, and also to what is assumed to guide banking practice on a general level, as to inform what pastoral and ethical stances need be respected when engaging with customers or products, whether this be in general or by sectors. Without a clear understanding of scriptural ethical and pastoral positions, the assessment of what is accepted and unaccepted banking practices as expounded in Chapter 7 will not be possible. It is, however, realised that selecting topics and motifs from the vast source that is the Bible is subject to choices, and to balance breadth against

How to cite: Bøsterud, M., 2021, 'Scriptural foundations', in *A treatise on Christian banking*, pp. 119–194, AOSIS, Cape Town. https://doi.org/10.4102/aosis.2021.BK263.06

width within the confines of this treatise would be a trying task. However, the chosen topics are thought to be of general utility for a wide tract of banking operations in the Western realm.

At this stage, it is useful to note that global capitalism, with its industrial, technological and mercantile development, happens at a high pace, and that the general ethical and pastoral positions that are extrapolated from Scripture in this chapter should be subject to ongoing interpretation and updating for practical application. It should suffice to point to the technology-driven opportunities of information distribution offered by the Internet, to serve as an example for how scriptural principles need be applied to hitherto unknown arenas of human interaction and commercial activity.

■ Moneylending

Context

When addressing matters pertaining to moneylending from a Christian vantage point, it may be too comfortable just to take the concept of lending and borrowing as a given and to assume that it is a wholly acceptable social construction. In the Western economic systems, the widespread use of capital belonging to others could easily lead to the conclusion that moneylending, with or without charging interest, is an acceptable mainstay in the socio-economic makeup of the Western societies. In light of this, it is prudent to start out by elaborating whether the concepts of lending and borrowing are morally acceptable activities at all, as seen from the aspects related to both the borrower and lender, and this is the starting point when searching out scriptural positions pertaining to moneylending.

Lending or giving – To the needy only?

The matter of lending is touched upon in the Old Testament, and as we find stipulations pertaining to lending already in the Pentateuchal books, it may be inferred that the matter is of substantial importance in Scripture, as these early biblical books pertain to binding laws directly handed over by God to his people. For example, from Exodus 22:25, we understand that the Israelites could 'lend money to one of my people among you who is needy', and in Deuteronomy 15:8–7, we learn that God's people should 'not be hard-hearted or tight-fisted' toward the poor and needy. Rather, they should be 'open-handed and freely lend them whatever they need'. These quotes are clearly seen from the aspect of the lender, and there is also a hint of charity involved, as the focus is on the need of the borrower. It should further be inferred from the quotes that the lending described points to the fellow Israelites, and this could be a reflection of the tribal society that the Israelites lived in, rather than being a statement of a moral imperative leading to the prohibition of helping other needy groups by way of lending (Buckley 1998). However, in the New Testament, where the teaching becomes more universal, the message is repeated, for example in Matthew 5:42, where we are instructed to 'give to the one who asks you, and do not turn away from the one who wants to borrow from you'.

From the above quotes, it would appear that the act of lending could in itself be seen as an acceptable action, from a biblical point of view. This conclusion may not be as obvious as it may superficially seem, as it would be prudent to ask whether the lender should not merely give away from his surplus what is needed by the borrower. This, however, does not seem to be founded in the scriptural sources mentioned, and on the contrary, the act of lending is in itself seen as an act of charity when extended to the poor and needy. This would not least appear from Proverbs 19:17, 'Whoever is kind to the poor lends to the Lord, and he will reward them for what they have done'. To lend, then, is morally acceptable, and if to the poor and needy, it would be an act of shepherding societal constituents, leading them onto a path of needs satisfaction. However, a question about lending remains: is it only acceptable to lend to the needy, or may it also be acceptable to lend to those not needing to borrow, but who want to borrow?

On lending to those not in need, we learn from Exodus 22:25 that to 'lend money' may be considered 'a business deal' and then the concept of interest is introduced as acceptable. From the New Testament, we learn in Luke 6:35 how Jesus advised that even when dealing with our 'enemies' we should 'lend to them without expecting to get anything back'. It would appear from these quotes that the lender is not obligated to lend only to those in need, but can also lend to those not in need, and even to his enemies. Whether or not the enemies may be in need does not appear from the context of the scriptural passage, but a reasonable interpretation would be that at least we cannot know whether our enemies are in any need, as we cannot be expected to know them as well as we know our own people. On this basis it could be concluded that the act of lending also to those not in need could be considered an acceptable act from an ethical and pastoral perspective.

Borrowing – A moral act?

Although it has now been demonstrated that lending money is an acceptable activity, this does not answer the question whether it is considered equally acceptable to receive a loan, and thus, to be the borrower in the transaction. Connected to this question, it may be asked whether it matters if the borrower is in need, how this need is brought about or if it is acceptable to borrow even when not in need.

Scriptural foundations

The scriptural passages quoted above concerning lending instil a sense in the reader that being in need is often the situation of the borrower, although the business loan is also described. To this, it should be mentioned that, among the Old Testament Hebrews living in a basically agrarian society, the typical social situation for borrowing would be when in need, and the loan would frequently be given by relatives and other near-standing lenders (Buckley 1998). As has already been demonstrated, Scripture recognises the concept of lending when not in need (e.g. Ex 22:24; Lk 6:35), and, as there are clear warnings in Scripture about accepting loans, it would be reasonable to infer that receiving a loan is not completely unambiguous from a moral perspective. Examples of this may be found in Proverbs 22:7, where we learn that 'the borrower is slave to the lender', and in Habakkuk 2:7, where it is asked, 'Will not your creditors suddenly arise?' and if so, 'then you will become their prey'. These warnings are also represented in the New Testament, where in Romans 13:8, it is stated in a universal manner, 'Let no debt remain outstanding, except the continuing debt to love one another'. To guarantee the borrowing obligations of others is in Scripture likened with borrowing for oneself, and in Proverbs 22:26, we are warned not to 'be one who shakes hands in pledge or puts up security for debts', for if we do, the consequences may be dire (Pr 22:27), and conversely, 'whoever refuses to shake hands in pledge is safe' (Pr 11:15). From the foregoing, it could be understood that to take on debt is not something to be taken lightly, and, that borrowing carries a heavy burden on the borrower for repayment.

The repayment aspect is pivotal when borrowing is described in Scripture; for example, in Psalm 37:21 we learn that 'the wicked borrow and do not repay', and in Psalm 15:4 we are instructed to be the one 'who keeps an oath even when it hurts'. Similarly, if a guarantee has been given to a neighbour and he has not made good on his debt obligation, we learn in Proverbs 6:3 that the guarantor should 'go – to the point of exhaustion and give your neighbour no rest!' The morally ambiguous quality of making others guarantee on their own behalf is described in Proverbs 6:2, where the guarantor is depicted as having 'been trapped' and 'ensnared' by the words of the guarantor to give his pledge. Clearly then, according to Scripture, to enter into debt and not intend to repay is considered immoral, and to make sure that this obligation is understood would be a task of shepherding the morally weak. From this it may be inferred that, according to scriptural sources, to enter into debt with the intention to repay can be seen as acceptable from a moral standpoint as an overriding norm, but to induce others to guarantee to repay or be liable for the debt of others may be considered immoral. This is regardless of the fact whether the borrower is in need or not, and if in need, no matter how such need is brought about. However, this does not mean that any form of borrowing is acceptable, and a prudent question may be asked whether borrowing for highly speculative ventures may represent a form of greed or covetousness (Lk 12:15; Pr 11:6) as discussed further, which in itself could render such borrowing, and indeed, such lending, an unsound practice from a scriptural perspective (Chewning 1995).

Duration and security

Although the scriptural sources referred to above support the legitimacy of moneylending and borrowing as principally acceptable societal institutions, it is not given that any format of lending and attendant conditions may be deemed acceptable as seen from an ethical and pastoral perspective. For example: when does lending become so long-term that in reality it represents rent, or economic serfdom, and when does the transaction become so risk-laden that it could represent economic ruin for the borrower if something fails? These questions are relevant to Western countries, when it is regularly necessary to borrow as part of housing needs, by way of mortgages, when financing education through student loans, when entering into more frivolous consumer lending, but even more so when considering how Western lenders could send developing countries into lasting economic bondage through lending, especially if the borrowing country has poor national governance (Collier 2008; Easterly 2002).

The matter of duration on loans is mentioned in several biblical passages, and a natural starting point is Deuteronomy 15:1, where it is stated that 'at the end of every seven years you must cancel debts', and this is followed up later in Deuteronomy 31:10, where Moses specifies that this is to be done 'during the Festival of Tabernacles'. That the time of debt-cancelling was set to a festive occasion was not coincidental, as becoming free of debt was seen as an occasion for celebrating the return to freedom for the individual and families. The ethos of limiting debt duration was introduced to protect the assumed weaker position of the borrower against the lender and represents the cognition that the perceived stronger lender was to care for the best interest of the borrower too. This practice entails a strong pastoral dimension, as it infers the task to take care of the needy and the vulnerable. The set maximum duration of loans would put the onus on the lender to consider how heavy a debt burden the borrower could carry, and if tempted to overload the borrower, this would be at the cost of the lender (Chewning 1995). The ethos of the strong looking after the weak permeates the biblical pastoral ethos. For example, in Proverbs 29:7, we are told that 'the righteous care about justice for the poor, but the wicked have no such concern', and in Matthew 5:42, we are instructed to 'give to the one who asks you, and do not turn away from the one who wants to borrow from you'.

Another expression of the protection of the assumed weaker position of the borrower against the lender is found in the biblical systematic of the jubilee year, again allowing the borrower and lender to set their economic relationships back to a new starting point. The jubilee year and its different provisions are stipulated in Leviticus 25:8–55, where it is stated that the year of the jubilee is set at the end of seven seven-year cycles, the 50th year, on the Day of Atonement (Lv 25:9). The purpose of this debt-cancelling social institution was not only to clear individual debts, but more so to reinforce the family units and safeguard their integrity. If the individuals were to be left under debt bondage, the families would be broken up, with dire societal consequences. It is not known whether the jubilee year was effected in practice, and if so, with what force, as there is no other narrative evidence of its practical application (Wright 1995). However the jubilee year was practically used in Old Testament Israel, it is clearly presented as a biblical ideal whether considered utopian or not, and similar institutions of debt cancellation and slavery release are known in Mesopotamian Akkadian (2400 BC to 2200 BC) and Old Babylonian (1900 BC to 1600 BC) sources; these were, in fact, really practised (Gnuse 1985).

The cognition that the lender is considered the more powerful one in the lender/borrower relationship, and that the pastoral responsibility of consideration is on the lender, is also represented in other biblical passages. For example, when considering what may be taken as security or collateral for loans, we find in Deuteronomy 24:6, 'Do not take a pair of millstones – not even the upper one – as security for a debt, because that would be taking a person's livelihood as security'. From this quote, we again understand how the borrower is perceived to be in a weak position, and that the lender is to exert pastoral shepherding of the weaker, by not introducing added risk to the economic stability of the borrower. Similar instructions are found in Exodus 22:26–27: 'If you take your neighbour's cloak as a pledge, return it by sunset, because that cloak is the only covering your neighbour has'. These instructions do not entail that pledges may not be taken by lenders, as they are expressly allowed in Proverbs 20:16 and Proverbs 27:13, albeit seen as morally ambiguous and perhaps not exactable in Ezekiel 18:16. The passages pertaining to collateral may seem antiquated to a modern reader; however, as there is no doubt that Scripture allows the taking of collateral for debts, the obligation on the lender is to shepherd and care for the borrower, and exert societal stewardship in this regard. This also applies in a modern-day interpretation of Scripture on this point (VanDrunen 2015). When a borrower wants to borrow more than his financial status can bear, it is sometimes the case that loans are given against pledges from third parties, by way of co-signing the loan, posting security or collateral or similar (Chewning 1995). However, when the pledge is given by someone other than the borrower, the scriptural instruction is stricter, as we see from Proverbs 22:26–27, which reads: 'Do not be one who shakes hands in pledge or puts up security for debts; if you lack the means to pay, your very bed will be snatched from under you'. Clearly, from this quote, which is mirrored in Proverbs 6: 1–5 and Proverbs 11:15, here the stance is plain to see, and the inclusion in loan agreements of any form of third-party security taking, co-signing, guarantee or similar is not acceptable, and this position must be the one to accept in modern-day interpretation of Scripture relating to this matter.

When viewing the above scriptural passages on loan duration and collateral, it becomes evident that Scripture remains ambiguous on the construction of loans, and that the onus is on the lender to care for the interest of the borrower, and not to set the latter in a bondage-like economic situation, as such may be considered detrimental for family and societal values. The fact that a loan must have a duration where it is likely that it can be paid back is of central importance, and this has been given such a weight in Scripture, that in the Old Testament era, if not paid back in seven years, the loan would be cancelled with no recourse against the borrower (Dt 15:1). Further, we have seen, from the above quotes related to collateral and security, that there should be stipulated times for loan repayments, but even within this limited duration, the loan should not threaten the economic well-being of the lender (Dt 24:6).

Summing up this section, it has appeared that when giving loans the lender should ensure that loans are not given with overly strenuous conditions while they run, and that the durations must be such that the borrower will be able to pay back the loan in full within a reasonable time. Furthermore, collateral may be accepted or demanded from the borrower, but any use of third-party pledge is always immoral.

Charging interest

It has been demonstrated above that the scriptural position on moneylending is one of general acceptance, if due considerations are given to the ethical and pastoral caveats described, but there is still a question whether charging of interest is acceptable to appear among terms to a loan, and if so, what level may be charged.

Before venturing into this further elaboration, it is prudent to define a little more accurately the terms 'interest' and 'usury'. In today's economic society, interest could typically be defined as in *Definitions* above, 'the act of charging for the privilege of borrowing money or receiving credit, typically expressed as annual or monthly percentage rate' (Merriam-Webster's online dictionary n.d.:n.p.). The term 'usury' would today typically be seen as a situation in which an interest rate is so high as to be considered exploitative. As per the Merriam-Webster's online dictionary (n.d.), we find usury defined as 'the lending of money with an interest charge for its use; especially the lending of money at exorbitant interest rates'. As explained in Chapter 2, in the Christian pre-Reformation era, 'usury' was used synonymously with 'interest', as the theological position then was that all charging of interest was considered exploitative and immoral. In this treatise, usury is defined as 'the lending of money at exorbitant interest rates'. Whether usury is to be considered immoral is a separate question, and here, 'usury' is merely defined in contrast to the adjacent term 'interest'.

The Old Testament starting point on charging interest is that interest is considered immoral when charged on loans to fellow countrymen in need (Ex 22:25; Lv 25:35-35; Dt 23:19). The background hereto could be found in the perception that those not in need, who were able to lend to their neighbours in need, had themselves been graced by God in their needs satisfaction, and were obligated to pass this benefit onto their neighbours. Not doing so, by charging interest, would be considered usury, no matter what level of interest was charged. The viewpoint, then, was that charging interest would exacerbate the plight of the needy borrower (Chewning 1995). This initial position was already modified in Old Testament passages when the loan was connected to business, as appears in Exodus 22:25, where it is antithetically stated that when a loan is not 'a business deal' one should 'charge no interest'. In other words, when entering into business-oriented loans, the charging of interest in itself is not to be considered immoral. This point is further underscored in Deuteronomy 23:20, where it is clearly stated that 'you may charge a foreigner interest', which would indicate a typical business situation, when personal and family aspects are removed from the transaction, and the loan becomes part of making added profit, and not for alleviating the plight of the borrower.

In addition to the aspect of interest on business loans as a way of sharing financial 'upsides' among the parties, foundational roots of the permission to charge interest in this type of transaction may be found in the general principle of *Lex talionis*, which was found in the Sumerian laws, the code of Hammurabi and was a standard template for settling compensation claims in the Old Testament era in the Near Eastern region (Kim 2009). According to this principle, when a loss was incurred, the guilty party was to compensate the damaged party in kind, and at least with the same value; in other words, it was a form of equity principle. In the Old Testament, we find traces of *Lex talionis* in Leviticus 24:19-20, where we learn that 'anyone who injures their neighbour is to be injured in the same manner: fracture for fracture, eye for eye, tooth for tooth'. As one could imagine, the Israelites could not ban foreigners from lending to the Israelites with interest charged, and the *Lex talionis* principle would then lead them to charge similar fees from foreigners (or in business), when the situation was reversed (Buckley 1998). Allowing interest, then, could be seen as a reciprocal fairness when in business, as would the non-charging be when among family and outside the realm of business. The *Lex talionis* would work in both situations, and equity would thus prevail.

Although the Old Testament passages reveal insights directly pertaining to the morality and pastoral aspects of interest on loans, the New Testament is less informative on the matter. However, we do learn from several passages that money and lending was not pastorally or ethically neutral, but, as the New Testament was written in the Roman era, society had become increasingly complex, and the Roman affinity for business and commerce was apparent. A striking difference from the Old Testament teaching, which typically relates to those who *need* to borrow, is that in the New Testament, we find references to those who merely *want* to borrow. This is described in Matthew 5:42, where Jesus instructs people not to 'turn away from the one who wants to borrow'. In contrast to Exodus 22:25, for example, where the potential borrower is described as 'needy', the Matthew text refers to the ones who 'want' to borrow. Further, when reading Luke 6:34–35, it becomes evident that New Testament teachings on lending attain a universal perspective, where we are instructed to lend even to our enemies, something that could be seen to mean, in plain terms, 'to anyone'. For if we can lend to our enemies, surely, we can lend to anyone. With this universal perspective in an economically complex Roman society, and with a myriad of different nationalities involved and several currencies in use, the New Testament reveals further insights on how moneylending and banking is perceived. It could superficially be tempting to read into the parallel narratives found in Matthew 21:12 and Mark 11:15, where we learn of how Jesus cleared the temple of the moneychangers, and to conclude that dealing with money in a banking manner should be seen as either outright immoral or at least highly morally dubious. Such an interpretation would, however, be taken out of context, as it is clear from the connected passages, both in Matthew and Mark, that Jesus' aim was to chastise those who had corrupted the temple by turning it away from its religious foundation; he explains in Matthew 21:13 and Mark 11:17, 'My house will be called a house of prayer' (Dale 2007).

New Testament passages specifically pertaining to banking are to be found in the two parallel parables of Matthew 25:14–30 and Luke 19:11–27. In these parables we learn of a wealthy man, who, when setting out on a journey, entrusted his three servants with amounts of money (in Matthew, different amounts) which they were to take care of while the master was away. Upon the return of the master, the servants had managed their entrusted funds differently, and in both stories, two of the servants had invested it and made a profit, while the third had not invested the money, but had kept it as it was given, and subsequently returned to the traveling master the exact amount he had been given. In both parables, the two investing servants are praised by their master, and the third non-investing servant is chastised for being passive with the funds. In both versions of the parable, the master states similarly to the derided servant that 'you should have put my money on deposit with the bankers, so that when I returned I would have received it back with interest' (Mt 25:27).

Scriptural foundations

The parables are laden with soteriological semiotics pertaining to Christ's earthly departure, the journey as the era of the church, the return as the return of the Son of Man, the reward to the good servants as reward for faithfulness in belief, and the chastisement of the passive servant as an eschatological vision of the consequences of sins of omission (Dale 2007). The references to Christ's ascension and *parousia* may not be as clear in Luke's version as in Matthew's, for in Luke, there is a subplot that pertains to claiming a kingdom, which may be inspired by 4th-century BC Roman real-life events (Franklin 2007). However the parable may be understood in an allegorical fashion: there is no doubt that the mentioning of earning interest as not only acceptable, but even outright commendable, may not be disregarded. It would be a hard-won interpretation that such central New Testament topics as the ascension and return of Christ could in any way be connected to allegorical semiotics of a negatively-laden character, even with the least chance of connecting the narrative to Christ. In the universalistic New Testament theology set in an economically complex Roman society, to interpret that charging interest is deemed acceptable would be a natural exegetical result. To conclude the opposite, as was done during the medieval era up until the Reformation, would seem forced and unnatural.

Coming out of the medieval era, the church was stuck in its somewhat stale economic worldview, where Catholic teaching was shaped to interact with a stagnant society, based on ethics of material distribution rather than engaging with problematics concerning the production of goods and services. The church's cognition on money matters was stuck in premodern patterns and was bound in a fascination with the community and hierarchy of the then feudal Europe, to such a degree that the starker sides of feudalism were largely overlooked (Novak 1990). The medieval church doctrine that prevailed was that any charging of interest on loans was immoral exploitation, and as such was considered usury, as the term is used in this treatise. In other words, any interest charged was too much.

Among the topics discussed among the early thinkers of the Reformation, was the charging of interest, and whether this should be allowed despite the medieval church's theological position. In the early stages of the Reformation, Martin Luther supported the medieval church's stance on interest, considering any charging of it immoral, and he maintained this stance no matter what the economic circumstance without exceptions (Luther 1824). Calvin, on the other hand, contributed to the relaxation of the Reformed view on interest, as he encouraged it when used in business loans, something that would take hold in Reformed doctrine, and gradually, the distinction between commercial and private loans disappeared, so that now interest has become the expected and perceived moral practice, and free market ideology has become the mainstay economic ideology among Reformed Christians (Chewning 1995; Cramp 1995). Since Calvin has been considered to be foundational for developing Protestant views on work, thrift and capitalism (for example, by Max Weber), it would be of interest to look a little more closely here at how Calvin expressed his views on the charging of interest (Weber 2012).

In his *Harmony of the Law*, when discussing the morality of interest, Calvin (1852b) refers to the scriptural equity principle as expressed in Matthew 7:12: 'So in everything, do to others what you would have them do to you'. He (Calvin 1852b) then goes on to outline:

> Whosoever has any ready money, and is about to lend it, he will allege that it would be profitable to himself if he were to purchase something with it, and that at every moment opportunities of gain are presenting themselves. Thus there will be always ground for his seeking compensation, since no creditor could ever lend money without loss to himself. (p. 159)

This quotation clearly refers to the practice among business people, and even so, Calvin (1852b) urges the terms to be equitable:

> Hence it follows that usury is not now unlawful, except in so far as it contravenes equity and brotherly union. Let each one, then, place himself before God's judgment-seat, and not do to his neighbour what he would not have done to himself, from whence a sure and infallible decision may be come to. (p. 161)

In a letter to one of his friends, *De Usuris Responsum*, Calvin (1545) sums up his position on usury, and defends his position in the following terms:

> It could be wished that all usury and the name itself were first banished from the earth. But as this cannot be accomplished it should be seen what can be done for the public good ... Therefore, usury is not wholly forbidden among us unless it be repugnant both to Justice and to Charity. (n.p.)

It would be fair to infer from the above extracts that, even though Calvin saw charging of interest as a practical necessity in his contemporary societal setting, he did not embrace the concept of interest with great enthusiasm. To him, the idea of equity was at the core when entering loan agreements, and not least, each lender would have to realise how he would be answerable to God if he transgressed (Wykes 2003).

Calvin's scriptural interpretations on usury and interest have stood the test of time in Reformed theological circles, and the position under this paradigm is that, in principle, charging interest is considered wholly acceptable and moral in any loan agreement (Cramp 1995). However, the principle of equity, as promoted by Calvin and the ancients, would firmly establish that usury as defined in this treatise would be deemed immoral.

■ Risk and stability
Context

When exploring the moral qualities of banking, the adjacent fields of risk and societal and individual economic stability are central in arriving at conclusions relevant to this treatise. From history, we know of numerous examples of banking failures that led to widespread societal, social and individual disruptions of economic stability and safety. In some cases, for example, after the great stock market crash of 1929, with its subsequent long-lasting economic depression in the West, such economic instability may also have contributed to large-scale unrest and warfare (Galbraith 2009). Since the latest financial market collapse in 2007–2008, there has been increasing political and social instability in the Western countries, and uprisings and warfare in non-Western countries may well have been direct results of the societal unease that has followed in the path of the market disruption (Krugman 2008; Varoufakis 2016). Against this background, there can be no doubt that banking plays a pivotal role in maintaining societal economic stability, and when disruptions occur, they may lead to societal tensions, representing grave threats to all areas of human lives. To investigate scriptural positions on the morality and pastoral quality of safeguarding stability and acceptable levels of financial risk-taking, would then be of interest to the topics covered by this treatise.

Scriptural stance

That material wealth is a good to be enjoyed by humans is represented in Scripture in several passages, for example, in Deuteronomy 8:18, where we learn that material goods are a gift from God, 'for it is he who gives you the ability to produce wealth, and so confirms his covenant'. The principle that sufficiency of material goods is a good, and that it is morally acceptable to enjoy it, is further developed in Ecclesiastes 5:19, where it is expressed that 'when God gives someone wealth and possessions, and the ability to enjoy them, to accept their lot and be happy in their toil – this is a gift of God'. In Psalm 23:1–6, we understand how 'the Lord is my shepherd, I lack nothing', and how God will 'prepare a table' before us, so that we 'will dwell in the house of the Lord forever'. Clearly then, to receive and enjoy the gift of wealth from God is part of our covenantal duties, and as humans, we are instructed to maintain this gift with gratitude. The Old Testament also warns of the consequences of falling into poverty, as Proverbs 22:7 reveals how 'the rich rule over the poor, and the borrower is slave to the lender'. This latter descriptive quote is probably as true now as when it was written, and it suffices to say, the obligation to maintain God's gifts of wealth, and not willingly fall into poverty, is still an instruction to be heeded. In banking practice, this instruction will inform how not to practise in a manner where the gift of God may be jeopardised without reason.

The matter of material stability is also represented in New Testament passages. From the Good Shepherd metaphor in John 10:10, we learn how stability and safety is emphasised by Jesus: 'The thief comes only to steal and kill and destroy; I have come that they may have life, and have it to the full'.

That societal and material stability is a quality we receive from God, is further represented in James 4:2, where we learn that 'you do not have because you do not ask God'.

Even though wealth is a gift from God, we cannot sit back idly and wait for his gifts to be handed to us without effort. In 2 Thessalonians 3:10, it appears that 'the one who is unwilling to work shall not eat', and in Proverbs 14:23, 'All hard work brings a profit, but mere talk leads only to poverty'. No doubt this indicates our own obligation to participate in maintaining ourselves materially, and that our effort will mirror our outcomes. This leads on to the question of what risks we are supposed to be willing to take, and whether increased risk leads to increased material outcomes. These questions are answered directly in 2 Corinthians 9:6, where we learn that 'whoever sows sparingly will also reap sparingly, and whoever sows generously will also reap generously'. Clearly then, we are encouraged to take risks in our pursuit of material needs satisfaction, and the more risk we take on, the more likely will the outcome proportionately increase.

The above quotes should suffice to develop the scriptural positions on work ethic, material stability and risk-taking, but the parallel parables referred to above, found in Matthew 25:14–30 and Luke 19:11–27, illustrate the biblical pastoral ethics on this point by using allegorical imagery directly connected to banking which would be fully understandable for today's readers. In these parables, we learn that not only is the idle servant chastised for his idleness and risk-aversity, but the risk-taking servants are rewarded for their initiative, personal effort and level of risk-taking. This becomes particularly clear in Luke (19:16–19), where the servants' rewards are in direct proportion to what their investments yielded. The overall position of the two parables on personal effort and initiative is summed up in Matthew 25:29: 'For whoever has will be given more, and they will have an abundance. Whoever does not have, even what they have will be taken from them'.

Luther was sceptical of the early forces of capitalism in his time, and he was largely informed by the medieval thinking on economic society and by the poverty ideal of the medieval church. Not only did he believe that charging of interest was immoral, but he was equally sceptical of all manner of market manipulation and price coercion, as to honour such behaviour would destabilise society at the cost of its weaker constituents. Luther's views on what was considered fraudulent and market-manipulating coercion were far stricter than what later thinkers considered fraudulent and immoral market activity, which could be attributed to the scholastic influences on his economic worldview (Langholm 2009). According to Luther, the best and most secure method of safeguarding price and market stability would be to let the civil authorities elect a few honest and insightful men, let them decide what were to be fair prices on all manner of goods and services and what the allowed maximum prices would be (Luther 1824). To Luther, then, the allowance and acceptance of free market forces to influence prices, supply and demand, by taking and distributing risk, was a highly unwanted societal practice, and to allow it would, in his understanding, increase market fluctuations and destabilise the economy to a degree where the strong preyed on the weak. This was in part due to a typical Lutheran strand of thought connected to the principle of loving one's neighbour, which was based on Matthew 5:40, for example: 'And if anyone wants to sue you and take your shirt, hand over your coat as well'. To Luther, the businessperson informed by the new mode of capitalism would exploit these principles and, on the behalf of good men, be violating the scriptural principle of loving one's neighbour (Langholm 2009).

For Calvin, the restrictive economic thinking of Luther was not wholly satisfactory, and to him, already by allowing charging of interest, the free and unregulated market forces were not seen as inherently immoral in their working. Calvin's Geneva was a multicultural crossroads where business was conducted among a multitude of nationalities, and the city was renowned for hosting a shrewd business community. It was in this cosmopolitan city that Calvin's views on trade and business came to deviate somewhat from those of Luther, and although they shared a common position in that trade not should be allowed to roam free without limits, Calvin's theology would provide the impetus for a more dynamic development of business and trade, hereunder banking and financing. Calvin's influence on Geneva was based on his *Institutes*, and not least, his defence of the Ten Commandments therein. From this would follow that a true Puritan Christian should be astute in business and also a generous benefactor of the weak (Foster 1908).

Like Luther, Calvin was also concerned with the welfare of the less fortunate, but the principle in Matthew 5:40, so hailed by Luther, was seen in conjunction with the merits of hard work and shunning human idleness. Calvin was himself a hard worker, and we know from his substantial authorship and pastoral activity that he truly lived what he preached in this regard (Gordon 2011). The notion of the Protestant work ethic has been addressed by Weber (2012). Whether it has been emphasised as too central for Calvin's theology will not be discussed here, but there can be no doubt that, unlike Luther, Calvin placed a substantial value on work, and to him, people would receive deservedly and according to their effort. If deserving of wealth, one should be allowed to enjoy it, even if not all could reach the same standard of enjoyment (Stone 2009).

To shed some light on Calvin's ideas on work, idleness and enjoying the fruits of labour, Calvin (2012) has this to say in his *Institutes*:

> No work will be so mean and sordid as not to have a splendour and value in the eye of God. (*Inst.* 3.10.6)
>
> ... nor idle men receive what ought to be distributed to the poor. (*Inst.* 4.5.4)
>
> Let everyone then live in his own station, poorly or moderately, or in splendour; but let all remember that the nourishment which God gives is for life, not luxury. (*Inst.* 3.19.9)

The above quotes, without being comprehensive, outline well Calvin's theology on work and its well-deserved fruits, and also indicate that added effort, even added risk, was not only acceptable, but was the right way to enjoy the gift of God that was wealth. This has had major influences on the development of Calvinist Reformed doctrine on trade, commerce, banking and finance, and has been adopted in Reformed circles to this day. To accept risk and thrive in the free market has become fully acceptable and should be considered the main position under the Reformed paradigm (VanDrunen 2015). This said, to allow risk and uncertainty at all levels may not be according to accepted Reformed pastoral ethos, as there will have to be limitations to the level of risk in use, for both the individual and the larger society.

To illustrate the other side of risk-taking is to consider whether risk-taking may be so substantial and uncontrolled that, in reality, it is tantamount to gambling. When a risk becomes a gamble, it may greatly influence the well-being of individuals, families and other societal stakeholders. Outside the realm of banking and financing, the negative effects of gambling are well evidenced; gambling is controversial in Western society and is widely considered to be immoral (Hoffmann 2000).

As explained in more detail in 6.11.4, gambling may not be specifically forbidden in Scripture, but the essence of it is considered in several locations, which all will explain all forms of gambling as immoral. That earning money through excessive risk-taking and pure chance by gambling is sinful is widely accepted in Reformed theological circles, and Geisler (2010), who discusses gambling extensively, finds substantial support for concluding that gambling is sinful, and against core societal values. That this pertains directly to banking and financing is further accepted as a valid Reformed position, which will thus act as a guide for avoiding inappropriate risk within the banking realm (VanDrunen 2015).

On the basis of the scriptural quotes and theological positions of the authors referenced above, it can be concluded that utilising moderate risk in business life and banking is acceptable. However, excessive risk-taking is never deemed acceptable, and there are obligations to care for society, and to safeguard others from destabilising the economy as a result of entertaining any level of financial risk.

■ Truthfulness

Context

When practising commercial activities such as banking, the matter of safeguarding prudent levels of information among all involved parties is of importance. Only when all parties are aware of the same risks and terms connected to a transaction will they be able to ascertain whether the risk is worth taking on. This may not be specific to banking, as such considerations are assumed to be important in all commercial activities. However, for banking, the parties acting truthfully is of particular importance, as the lender may be in a better position than the borrower to fully understand all aspects of a loan, such as duration, compounded interest, risk of market fluctuations on connected collateral and risk of fluctuating interest rates. On the other side, the borrower may be more knowledgeable regarding his own intentions or abilities to pay back the loan, at all or in a timely fashion, and information connected to this would be of importance to a lender when considering a given loan.

Scriptural stance

It is of interest to investigate what Scripture reveals on truthfulness, and how influential theological thinkers within the Reformed paradigm have interpreted this. An obvious place to start is the Decalogue, and in particular, the ninth commandment (Ex 20:16), where teaching on truthfulness is set out. The commandment in itself, as it is written superficially, pertains directly to the obligation that we 'shall not give false testimony' in a court of law situation. Although the commandment seems to be directed to a specific life situation, there has been no doubt when interpreting the passage, that the obligation goes beyond the courtroom, and obliges us to be truthful in all parts of our lives. Further, the mentioning of the 'neighbour' in the passage indicates that we are obligated to be truthful not only to our closest family and friends. The circle of persons to benefit from our truthfulness is not to be restricted to our own closest kind, as we learn in Proverbs 25:21 that we should also care for our enemies: 'If your enemy is hungry, give him food to eat; if he is thirsty, give him water to drink'. Our pastoral obligation to truthfulness is further explained in Ephesians 4:25, where we are instructed to 'speak truthfully to your neighbour, for we are all members of one body'. To stay truthful when dealing with opposing parties in business transactions would naturally be included, for as we do this with our enemies, surely, also our business partners need be considered 'members' of our own 'body' as well (Eph 4:25). The ninth commandment will typically be considered the main scriptural instruction related to truthfulness; we are not to lie, but to stay truthful in all situations, to everyone, and in every situation, and to remain in this state regardless of whomever we interact with (Douma 1996).

Our ethical and pastoral obligation to stay truthful in our interaction with others is emphasised and illustrated further throughout the Bible. In Proverbs 6:16-17 we learn that 'the Lord hates ... a lying tongue', and in Proverbs 19:9, that 'a false witness will not go unpunished, and whoever pours out lies will perish'. In Proverbs 24:28 it appears that we should not use our 'lips to mislead', and the topic of deceit is further specifically mentioned in Leviticus 19:11, where it is expressly stated, 'Do not deceive one another'. The specific instructions pertaining to deceit are of direct import to the topics in this treatise, as they point to interaction with others in a manner where one party understands that the other does not have a complete understanding of the implications of entering into a transaction, and/or when one party is leading another into a state of not realising the full truth. Clearly, then, to stay truthful means more than not telling direct lies, for it also implies representing the truth in a responsible manner. That truthfulness is rewarded in Scripture follows directly from Proverbs 12:19, for example, where it is stated clearly that 'truthful lips endure forever'.

Calvin's works will shed further light on the Reformed position on truthfulness and deceit. In his *Institutes,* Calvin (2012) writes:

> By malignant or vicious detraction, we sin against our neighbour's good name by lying; sometimes even by casting a slur upon him, we injure him in his estate. It makes no difference whether you suppose that formal and judicial testimony is here intended, or the ordinary testimony which is given in private conversation. For we must always recur to the consideration that for each kind of transgression one species is set forth by way of example, that to it the others may be referred, and that the species chiefly selected is that in which the turpitude of the transgression is most apparent. (*Inst.* 2.8.47)

The above extract refers to general aspects of lying and staying truthful, and for the context of this treatise, where banking and commerce is at the core, it is of interest to see what Calvin wrote more directly pertaining to this subject matter. Calvin (2012) addresses matters of truthfulness and deceit on commercial life from the angle of theft, and the rich oppressing the poor. With regard to the eighth commandment (Ex 20:15), he writes:

> But not to dwell too long in enumerating the different classes, we know that all the arts by which we obtain possession of the goods and money of our neighbours, for sincere affection substituting an eagerness to deceive and injure them in any way, are to be regarded as thefts. Though they may be obtained by an action at law, a different decision is given by God. He sees the long train of deception by which the man of craft begins to lay nets for his more simple neighbour, until he entangles himself in its meshes. (*Inst.* 2.8.45)

The above extract well illustrates Calvin's position on market speculation and the rich oppressing the poor and was directly influenced by what he observed in the Geneva of his time, where wealthy traders exploited poor people, including migrant workers escaping to Geneva from poverty (Valeri 1997). It is here noteworthy that Calvin's scepticism towards unchecked capitalism may have been more substantial than later interpreters of his works have accepted, and even with his fundamental acceptance of the constructive free market forces, he did not condone exploitation of the weak or gains gotten by deceit. That Weber (2012) and others have awarded Calvin the honour of inventing modern capitalism may not have been as much founded on his own writings as on the works of later authors in his tradition, not least, within the English Puritan movement (Graafland 2009).

It is evident, then, that the Reformed position on truthfulness and lying comprises a clear obligation to stay truthful and to avoid deceitful attitudes in all realms of life, including the realm of banking. There can be no doubt that under the Reformed paradigm, we are instructed to live out and love the truth as the main rule (Gushee & Stassen 2016). There may be some small exceptions to this main rule, as when we are under professional obligations to keep secrets, for example, in a counselling or advisory situation, where we would be breaking our promise to keep the secrets entrusted to us, which in itself would represent lying in the first place. However, such acceptance of concealment does not allow us to deceive others by way of utilising our especially entrusted knowledge gained under these unusual circumstances, and for Christian participants in a banking context, this norm will be the overriding one (Douma 1996).

■ Greed
Context

When exploring the moral and pastoral obligations connected to banking, aspects of greed among the partakers, and consideration of its morality and effects, are of interest to interrogate to this treatise. As banking pertains to money in all its form, it will be the assumption here that the phenomenon of greed will lurk in the back of the minds of many a participant, and that if this impulse is left unchecked, it may permeate the banking sector and its connected actors. Thus, when involving in banking practice, all actors need be aware of the flaws of the human psyche that is greed.

Scriptural stance

Greed and problems connected with it are mentioned in numerous passages in Scripture. For example, in Psalm 10:3, we learn how 'the wicked man … blesses the greedy and reviles the Lord', and in Proverbs 21:25-26, how 'the craving of a sluggard will be the death of him … but the righteous give without sparing'. From Proverbs 23:4, we are informed, 'Do not wear yourself out to get rich', and in Proverbs 28:20, we learn of the consequences of greed: 'One eager to get rich will not go unpunished'. The latter instruction is enhanced in Proverbs 15:27, with 'The greedy bring ruin to their households'. These timeless truths appear as general in the Old Testament, which largely reflects the economic society of the Hebrews, who lived in a basically agricultural and tribal society (Barton 1996; Rogerson & Davies 2005).

In New Testament times, when Scripture was written in the context of the more affluent, money-oriented Roman society, scriptural passages on greed are more concretely connected to money matters and are increasingly associated with the search for ways to amass wealth. For example, in Hebrews 13:5 the instruction is, 'Keep your lives free from the love of money and be content with what you have', which is followed up by 1 Timothy 6:10, 'For the love of money is a root of all kinds of evil'. From Luke 12:15, we are urged to 'be on your guard against all kinds of greed; life does not consist in an abundance of possessions'. These quotes clearly warn against greed and the search for overconsumption. With direct reference to overconsumption, Proverbs 25:16 explains that 'if you find honey, eat just enough – too much of it, and you will vomit', and in 1 Corinthians 10:31: 'So whether you eat or drink or whatever you do, do it all for the glory of God'.

With regard to thirsting for money, Ecclesiastes 5:10 informs us that 'whoever loves money never has enough', and the consequences thereof are revealed in Matthew 6:24, 'No one can serve two masters. Either you will hate the one and love the other … you cannot serve both God and money'. Clearly, then, in both Testaments, we find an abundance of sources explaining how the greed for wealth in general, and for money in particular, will make us turn away from God, and shun our societal task of caring for everyone and everything found in God's creation (Gn 2:15).

In his *Harmony of the Law*, when commenting on how the Israelites built the tabernacle as described in Exodus 36, Calvin (1852b) points out that the Israelites were a role model, and he highlights their thrifty use of materials:

> Their prudence is shewn in the distribution of the materials among them; their diligence in the quickness with which they commenced the work, without waiting until they had enough for its completion; whilst this testifies to their extraordinary integrity when they voluntarily declared that enough had been given, and put a stop to the offerings, lest they should be more than they required. (p. 338)

Connected with this, but on a general note, Calvin (1852b) writes:

> We know how few restrain themselves when an opportunity is given of thieving without detection; and, even if there be no disposition to deceive, yet most people are tempted by ambition, greedily to long for more to pass through their hands than they need. (p. 338)

From the above discussion, it appears that Calvin perceived thrift as a virtuous human quality, and as thrift may be seen as the opposite of greed, it may be inferred that even though Calvin may have accepted wealth as a gift from God, and something to enjoy, when enjoyment becomes gluttonous, it is not acceptable. On this matter of gluttonous luxury, he (Calvin 2012) was clear:

> Luxury causes great care, and produces great carelessness as to virtue; and it is an old proverb: Those who are much occupied with the care of the body, usually give little care to the soul. Therefore, while the liberty of the Christian in external matters is not to be tied down to a strict rule, it is, however, subject to this law – he must indulge as little as possible; on the other hand, it must be his constant aim not only to curb luxury, but to cut off all show of superfluous abundance, and carefully beware of converting a help into an hindrance. (*Inst.* 3.10.4)

The above extract is written directly in the context of gluttony, and this may cast valuable light on Reformed cognition related to greed, consumption and the responsible search for needs satisfaction. That gluttony is a form of greed cannot be doubted, and its sinfulness is stated in the Westminster Larger Catechism, where it is described as a sin in the seventh commandment (Westminster 2015). Calvin's thoughts on greed and gluttony were well founded in Scripture, and here, Luke 12:15 is relevant: 'Watch out! Be on your guard against all kinds of greed'. We cannot know whether the modern-day minimalist ethos of 'less is more' would have been welcomed by Calvin, but surely, we would expect that to him enough will always have been enough.

Calvin's views on greed and gluttony as sinful have remained the focus of the Reformed tradition to this day, and it has stood the test of time, through vastly changing Western societies, and his promotion of thrift and moderation is of substantial guidance when establishing a prudent Christian framework for banking (Gushee & Stassen 2016).

■ Covetousness
Context

Greed and covetousness are frequently seen as near synonyms, and there clearly are overlapping aspects of these two attitudes. However, as greed typically pertains to an individual wanting more, or too much for that matter, covetousness, or desire, could be seen as wanting what we do not already have, and this want may well be instilled in others, actively and openly, or covertly and indirectly. In a modern-day commercial setting, covetousness may be promoted through marketing advertising and influences in social and other media (Douma 1996). In the context of banking, to instil in others a desire to acquire material goods may be a powerful motivator to lead them into financial agreements which they may not benefit from or may outright be harmed by. For this treatise, then, to excavate norms from Scripture pertaining to desire and covetousness, will shed valuable light on central aspects connected to banking practices.

Scriptural stance

The natural scriptural starting point on covetousness may be Exodus 20:17, which forms part of the Decalogue as the tenth commandment, and pertains directly to matters of desiring what we do not already have. This commandment has a wide scope, as it refers to 'anything that belongs to your neighbour', and it relates to coveting both material goods ('your neighbour's house, ox or donkey') and carnal desires ('your neighbour's wife'). As with greed, it appears that in the Old Testament era, the Israelites lived in an agrarian non-monetised society, and the focus of the commandment reflects this by use of examples and imagery. This notwithstanding, the passage is connected with all forms of desire, and with its location in the Decalogue, it may be inferred that this instruction is at the highest level of importance (Thompson 1996). The central ethos of the commandment, in contrast to pure greed and gluttony, relates to the desire to possess what we do not have, rather than more of what we already possess. We may want to take something from others, or just get it for ourselves regardless of its source (Houston 2007). In the Old Testament era, the economic perception may have been one of scarcity, so that what one person obtained was thought to be lost by another, but in our time, when we realise that there may be sufficient resources for everyone if politically and commercially organised, the focus may be on the desire for acquiring more in general, whether we want more of what already belongs to others, or want it to be produced just for our benefit (Bøsterud & Vorster 2017). The focus in this treatise is the desire for responsibly added material wealth, no matter whence it derives.

In the New Testament, passages warning against desire and greed are in abundance. For example, in Colossians 3:5 it is stated that 'evil desires and greed' should be 'put to death'. In 1 John 2:17, the obligated priorities of the believer are explained with the statement, 'The world and its desires pass away, but whoever does the will of God lives forever', and in 1 Timothy 6:9, 'Those who want to get rich fall into temptation and a trap and into many foolish and harmful desires that plunge people into ruin and destruction'. Finally, the instruction in Luke 12:15 cannot be misunderstood: 'Be on your guard against all kinds of greed; life does not consist in an abundance of possessions'. Clearly, then, without further exemplification needed, the scriptural position is that we should not succumb to desiring what we do not need, and do not have.

In *Commentary on Matthew, Mark, Luke*, Calvin (1845) comments on the wider scriptural position on greed and desire:

> But all this does not hinder us from being fed by the undeserved kindness of God, without which men might waste their strength to no purpose. We are thus taught, that what we seem to have acquired by our own industry is his gift. (p. 284)

And (Calvin 1845):

> Men are grown mad with an insatiable desire of gain. Christ charges them with folly, in collecting wealth with great care, and then giving up their happiness to moths and to rust, or exposing it as a prey to thieves. What is more unreasonable than to place their property, where it may perish of itself, or be carried off by men? ... particularly, when God allows us a place in heaven for laying up a treasure, and kindly invites us to enjoy riches which never perish. (p. 291)

Again, the priority of the believer is clear, and Calvin reminds us of the close connection between greed and desire, where one may lead to the other, and create a destructive evil circle for the individual and society (Pigott 1995). This theological position remains the Reformed one, and holds true today as always, but the pressures of destructive consumerism may instil a new form of covetousness in the general public for an ever-increasing spending and acquiring of material goods, something which may be spurred on by different modes of marketing and moneylending, which is all too available to the modern-day Western citizen (Douma 1996; Gushee & Stassen 2016). For the banking context here then, contributing to the acquiring of material goods that are not needed is thus considered a form of covetous immoral self-indulgent hoarding.

■ Sanctity of life

Context

Many areas of commercial activity available for banking and financing may pertain to and influence humans negatively in the most direct and fundamental manner, as such opportunities can be found within military and arms suppliers, medical companies manipulating the human genome and health care providers offering services of abortion and/or assisted euthanasia. Such products, services and practices may be found in a wide area of business life but may frequently challenge core Christian values in ways that may be difficult to clearly identify because of intentional or coincidental opaqueness of the underlying activities. For example, pertaining to capital punishment, connected opportunities could be found in prison providers, medical manufacturers, real estate and other asset categories, in connections that to the untrained observer could appear unexpected and surprising. The will to connect banking activities to basic ethical topics such as the sanctity of life may be scant, and temptations of superficial and simplified interpretation could prevail. Such problem spheres may be derivative and indirect, as for example when involving in real estate and the tenants could be partaking in controversial and unethical practices, or when originating or trading in bonds, where the ultimate beneficiaries could fall within the same categories. Conversely, there will be an equally substantial realm of banking opportunities where humanity is affected in a positive manner, such as when aiming at caring for the sick, generating and promoting education, medical innovations that cure diseases, to mention but some examples, and within this area of commercial life, there may be equally complex structures for bankers to choose from.

Imago Dei

A natural entry point for the elaborations on biblically-based ethics is to establish the main scriptural principle regarding the value of humanity and God's intention for the human family. Prior to addressing topics such as abortion, war, euthanasia, among others, this topic needs to be resolved on an overarching level.

In Genesis 1:27, it appears that 'God created mankind in his own image, in the image of God he created them'. This is the *imago Dei* expression, wherein it is explained that God created humanity in his own image, and this position is evident in several other scriptural locations, such as Genesis 5:1, 9:6; 1 Corinthians 11:7; Colossians 3:10 and James 3:9. The expression *imago Dei* is not self-explanatory, something which may lead to various interpretations, and has therefore been subject to widespread interpretation throughout the ages. It would appear that God gives mankind a privileged position among all the creatures he created. From a literal interpretation, this can be seen in several ways:

- **Representative Perspective.** According to this perspective, which was indicated by Augustine, humans have formal properties and a nature that represents God. Thus, humans enjoy qualities and characteristics, spiritual and rational alike, which liken humans to God (Augustine 2015; Clark 2001).
- **Relational Perspective.** Under this perspective, supported by Barth, humans reflect God more than other creatures when it comes to relational capabilities (Feinberg 1972).
- **Functional Perspective.** From this vantage point, which was typical for the pre-Christian philosophers and Hebrew thinkers, the *imago Dei* reflects what humans do, rather than what they are. From this perspective, it would be expected that humans attain dominion of nature and represent God on earth. Thus, humans most clearly express the divine image of God through practical action, and this is the main reason for the creation of humanity (Middleton 2006).

All the above perspectives render explanations and evoke images of humanity's place with God, but they all have strengths and weaknesses, as explained by Grudem (1994): for humans to fully appreciate the concept of *imago Dei* is not possible, as it would imply a comprehensive understanding of God's nature and true being as well as a full understanding of human nature. As he indicates, we cannot achieve this, as God alone can reach such insights. He further contends that even in the fallen state, we are still in the image of God, and that this pertains to all humans, be they old, young, physically or mentally disabled, sick or unborn, and he concludes that all human states are encompassed by *imago Dei* and protected by God. This stance is firmly based on the teachings of Calvin (2012:*Inst.* 1.15.4), who asserted that even with all the human depravity that followed the fall, we remain in the image of God, and are bearers of his dignity, as this has not been distorted by the expulsion from Eden. For Calvin, this was confirmed in Ephesians 4:24, where Christian believers are instructed to 'put on the new self, created to be like God in true righteousness and holiness'. It would be reasonable to infer from the above remarks that humanity has a privileged and responsible position in creation as given by God, and that from this would follow both rights and responsibilities (Gn 1:29–29, 2:15).

The *imago Dei* was of importance for Calvin's theology, and in his discussion of the possible physical and spiritual similarities between humans and God, he (Calvin 2012) stated:

> Accordingly, by this term ('image of God') is denoted the integrity with which Adam was endued when his intellect was clear, his affections subordinated to reason, all his senses duly regulated, and when he truly ascribed all his excellence to the admirable gifts of his Maker. And though the primary seat of the divine image was in the mind and the heart, or in the soul and its powers, there was no part even of the body in which some rays of glory did not shine. (*Inst.* 1.15.3)

It is thus clear that in Calvin's opinion the 'primary seat' of the *imago Dei* is in the spiritual properties of humans, and that this then would be at the centre of attention when assessing the impact of humankind being created in the image of God. Humans, then, however faintly, reflect the greatness and glory of God, and responsibilities are inherent in this image.

Berkhof (1958), in his exploration of *imago Dei*, employs a method of scriptural interpretation including sources from both the Old and New Testaments. He explains that the words 'image' and 'likeness' are used synonymously in the Bible, and he illuminates this by pointing to Genesis 1:26, where both words are used, and to Genesis 1:27, where only 'image' is in use, as with Genesis 5:1 and Genesis 5:3, where a similar interchange of the terms coexists. From the New Testament, he directs the reader to Colossians 3:10 for the sole use of 'image' and to James 3:9 for using 'likeness' only. Berkhof's understanding of *imago Dei* is centred on the spiritual aspects of the divine character of humanity in creation, and points to scriptural sources of soteriological weight, such as Genesis 1:31, explaining that God's creation was 'very good', and Ephesians 4:24, explaining that humanity is made to be like God in a state of 'righteousness and holiness'. The special relationship of humans and God is duly demonstrated through these sources as per Berkhof's view.

Jenson (1997) presents an anthropological perspective in his explanation of *imago Dei* and connects it to what it means to be human in dialogue with God. He posits that through *imago Dei*, we are awarded a unique place in creation, and that the only justification of this uniqueness is the likeness with God, as explained in Scripture (Gn 1:27). He further contends that as we are given this special place with God, we should not consider ourselves as separate beings in this uniqueness but need to constantly relate our being to God in continuous conversation. Thus, if we do not possess ourselves, we are self-transcendent in the dialogue with God, which necessitates humans to be mutually available for each other. The likeness to God is then a gift to us, and needs to be viewed in a soteriological light, explaining human uniqueness as a mystery, leading to a continuous seeking of inner perfection for pleasing God through actions.

It would follow from the above elaboration that the human relationship with God is unique and special as revealed through the *imago Dei* doctrine, regardless of physical or mental states or gender (Lazenby 1987). That humanity has a special place in dialogue with God, is clear; however, full knowledge of our own 'holiness' cannot be reached, as this privilege resides with God alone. The *imago Dei* doctrine does not fully explain and demonstrate the Reformed stance on the sanctity of life, or how life should be protected and what consequences transgressions against God's creation of humanity should have, but this doctrine serves as a foundational starting point for extended scriptural interpretations.

Sixth commandment

A logical expression of humanity's privileged position in creation is the sixth commandment, 'You shall not murder' (Ex 20:13). In the literal superficial meaning, it would be evident that 'murder' points to the wilful taking of human life, as opposed to accidental and unintentional. On this level, the commandment is a simple one, which commands only to refrain from a certain action, namely murder, and in itself does not lend further explanation as to how to honour human life. Whether the literal interpretation is correct as the true meaning, and whether exceptions or exemptions could be embedded in the commandment, needs further analysis and exploration for the purpose of guiding the ethical principles sought in this treatise.

Calvin (1852b), in his *The Harmony of the Law*, connects the sixth commandment with Leviticus 19:14, and uses these verses as a vantage point for his stance on the sanctity of life:

> Since the Law comprehends, under the word murder, all the wrongs whereby men are unjustly injured, that cruelty was especially to be condemned by which those wretched persons are afflicted, whose calamity ought rather to conciliate our compassion. For, if any particle of humanity exists in us, when we meet a blind man we shall be solicitous lest he should stumble or fall, and, if he goes astray, we shall stretch out our hands to him and try to bring him back into the way; we shall also spare the deaf, for to insult them is no less absurd or barbarous than to assail stones with reproaches. It is, therefore, gross brutality to increase the ills of those whom our natural sense impels us to relieve, and who are already troubled more than enough. Let us, then, learn from these words, that the weaker people are, the more secure ought they to be from all oppression or injury, and that, when we attack the defenceless, the crime of cruelty is greatly aggravated, whilst any insult against the calamitous is altogether intolerable to God. (p. 30)

It is of special interest to note that Calvin here uses an interpretive technique of describing what is expressly forbidden in the sixth commandment, that is murder, in conjunction with what is positively encouraged in Leviticus 20:14, positively to defend those weaker than ourselves. This would be an important stance to notice in the following, when addressing ethical matters comprising power imbalances among the involved actors.

Calvin's position on human life is taken further in the Westminster Larger Catechism, where the sixth commandment is explained by both the connected duties and sins. On the duties of humanity, it is stated that our obligation is (Westminster 2015):

> [T]o preserve the life of ourselves and others by resisting all thoughts and purposes, subduing all passions, and avoiding all occasions, temptations, and practices, which tend to the unjust taking away the life of any; by just defence thereof against violence, patient bearing of the hand of God … . (p. 24)

And, on the forbidden sins that they include (Westminster 2015):

> [A]ll taking away the life of ourselves, or of others, except in case of public justice, lawful war, or necessary defence; the neglecting or withdrawing the lawful and necessary means of preservation of life … Whatsoever else tends to the destruction of the life of any. (p. 24)

For Geisler (2010), it is evident from scriptural interpretation that suicide is equal to murdering another person, and can be seen as a particularly grave crime, because it violates God's sovereignty and the sanctity of life, but also indicates that the perpetrator does not accept responsibility for the life entrusted to him by God. He further maintains that suicide contradicts Paul's teachings that all humans must show basic self-respect, as demonstrated in Ephesians 5:29, which reads: '… no one ever hated their own body, but they feed and care for their body'. Although it is difficult to find direct literal scriptural sources forbidding suicide in particular, Geisler's interpretation would represent a responsible interpretation of the sixth commandment and the *imago Dei* doctrine, as seen in context. Grudem (1994), who directly infers from Exodus 20:13 that suicide and murder are equally severe transgressions against God, supports this view.

Another more recent ethicist addressing contemporary issues through a scriptural lens is Douma (1996), who gives a comprehensive account of the Ten Commandments applied to modern-day ethical challenges. While sharing Geisler's basic view on the gravity of unethical aspects of suicide, he reminds us of cases of depression and mental illness, indicating that society sometimes can carry a part of the responsibility for not rendering the sick person sufficient support. He further maintains that there could be cases where suicide can be seen as an act of self-sacrifice, as explained in John 15:13, 'Greater love has no one than this: to lay down one's life for one's friends'.

The above have further elucidated scriptural positions in the value of human life, and in conjunction, the *imago Dei* and the sixth commandment indicate a high value on life, and command us not merely to refrain from taking life, but also to protect human life in all its forms. From this, we need to determine what the consequences of transgressing the scriptural elevation of human life would be.

Consequences of transgression

The sanctity of human life is further explained in scriptural sources describing reactions against transgression of the value of human life in all its forms. To delve further into this, a natural starting point would be to seek out what the Bible explains as the obvious reaction to taking another life by murder. To murder another human being is the wilful act of taking human life, and it is not possible to conceive a more direct attack on the value of life as God has explained through creation and the sixth commandment. In Exodus 21:12, it is simply stated that: 'Anyone who strikes a person with a fatal blow is to be put to death'. This is as clear an expression as can be given for what God sees as the natural and obvious reaction against attacking and destroying human life, and thus, the 'image' of God (Gn 1:27). The verse is absolute in its form and would, by a strict literal interpretation, lead to capital punishment even in instances of manslaughter and self-defence. This would be a difficult position to defend; for example, in Genesis 21:13, this main principle is modified by explaining that: 'However, if it is not done intentionally, but God lets it happen, they are to flee to a place I will designate'. Further, in Numbers 35:11, free havens are designated for those who are guilty of manslaughter, and thus innocent of murder in the sense of the sixth commandment. From these scriptural passages, it is already clear from the outset that God values human life at the highest level, but also that he is just in the distinction of the perpetrator's intention as the determining factor for suitable punishment.

Even if the taking of life is wilful and intentional, as in the case of war, Scripture accepts such acts not to be considered murder, and as such, the acts will not be seen as transgressing the sixth commandant. The Pentateuch, in several passages, describes God in war as a 'warrior' (Ex 15:3) and in Numbers 21:14, the term 'Book of the Wars' is used in early Hebrew history. These wars can be seen as commissioned by God, in acts of cleansing the world of sinners, and for introducing divine justice to humans. For example, in Exodus 32:25-29, Moses is commanded to send some Hebrews into their own camp to kill the unrighteous, and it could be interpreted that when God exacts war in this manner, it is to effect capital punishment for committed sins (O'Mathuna 2003). The topic of war in the context of this treatise is expounded upon in 'War' section and is not discussed here further in the context of establishing the Reformed view on the sanctity of life.

It is evident from the discussion in this section that Scripture holds human life at the highest value, as the main punitive reaction for murder is capital punishment, and that murder can be accepted with lesser punishment only if the act is unintentionally performed or performed in the conduct of war.

Value of life

From the above elaborations covering the topics of the *imago Dei* doctrine, the sixth commandment and reactions for transgressions, it appears from Scripture and literature cited that the Scriptural position on the value of human life is that of sanctity. It is clear that life is held at the utmost and highest value, regardless of race, gender, nationality, health condition or mental faculties. All humans are created in the image of God (Gn 1:27), and there are no stipulated exceptions from this. From this principle, it can be inferred that all human life is to be treated with the utmost care and respect, and that our responsibility is not merely to refrain from murder or harm others or ourselves, but to actively protect and preserve life and health. In particular, the powerful should be seen as having a special responsibility to protect the weaker (Calvin 1852b). It has also been demonstrated that transgressing God's image in creation will invoke consequences, but that these will be meted out according to the intention of the perpetrator or the circumstances of the acts. Through these distinctions, the God of the Covenant is represented as just.

On the basis of the above explanation of the scriptural position on the sanctity of life, it will be explored how this principle should be applied to specific situations of ethical difficulty or moral ambiguity, as far as we are expected to be prudent in the context of banking practice.

Capital punishment
Context

The topic of capital punishment is relevant to banking practice in two ways: connected to participation in involved industries (pharmaceutical, prison providers etc.), and concerning what kind of regimes and political environments the morally concerned banker can acceptably be involved in. The topic is elaborated here in relation to the sanctity of life, but it is also relevant in the exploration of governments and civil disobedience below, as this may pertain to political issues connected with banking practice. It is worth mentioning, that most all of the traditional central Christian thinkers up until modernity have accepted capital punishment, and this includes theologians such as Augustine, Thomas Aquinas, Martin Luther, John Calvin and more (Elshtain 2004). In the modern-day academic and political discourse relating to the question of capital punishment, argumentation pertaining to its efficacy is often presented, but for my purposes here, this is not expected to shed any further light on the main questions of this treatise, so I will not address any such arguments in the following explanation.

Prescribed, allowed or prohibited?

The general discourse in theological circles will gravitate around the question whether Scripture prescribes, allows or prohibits capital punishment, and regularly, this debate has its starting point in *imago Dei* doctrine (Van Ness 1995). Geisler (2010) presents an outline of Christian positions relating to capital punishment, and describes the main theories as follows:

- **Rehabilitationism.** Under this philosophy, the criminal needs to be rehabilitated and not punished, and the main focus of the government should be on remedial efforts and not on retribution and punishment. This stance applies to all crimes, not only the capital ones, and the proponents do not distinguish governmental remedies according to the gravity of the crime. Typical biblical support for this position is sought in Ezekiel 18:23, posing the question, 'Do I take any pleasure in the death of the wicked? declares the Sovereign Lord. Rather, am I not pleased when they turn from their ways and live?' From this, it is interpreted that God seeks to rehabilitate rather than destroy the sinner. Further support can be solicited in Matthew 5:38–39 where Jesus declares, 'But I tell you, do not resist an evil person. If anyone slaps you on the right cheek, turn to them the other cheek also'. Again, retribution is not presented as the main remedy for transgression.
- **Reconstructionism.** Under this paradigm, capital punishment is mandatory for all major crimes, and in particular, those mentioned in the Bible. The aim is punishment and retribution, and not rehabilitation. The classical followers

of this theory, who are sometimes referred to as theonomists, claim that the Old Testament Mosaic law should form the basis for a reconstruction of our societies. The Old Testament names more than 20 crimes calling for capital punishment, ranging from what would be understood as grave crimes in modern secular societies, such as murder (Ex 20:13) and rape (Dt 22:25) to breaching ancient ceremonial law (Nm 4:15) that has no application in any modern society. The strict proponents of the reconstructionist theory, the theonomists, maintain that modern governments are under obligation by scriptural instruction to exert capital punishment on all the offences mentioned in the Bible, no matter whether the described transgressions can be considered of material, social or ceremonial character.

- **Retributionism.** Under this philosophy, capital punishment is allowed and necessary for certain crimes, the capital ones, and not for the lesser ones. As opposed to the theonomists, the followers of retributionism do not claim that Mosaic Law related to the use of capital punishment binds modern civil governments. The position of retributionism can be seen as a compromise between that of rehabilitationism and reconstructionism, and the proponents seek support in the same scriptural passages as both the former theories, through adopting a more moderate stance regarding their implementation, by evaluating the appropriateness of mercy and possible rehabilitation. However, the concept of retribution is still at the forefront of the theory, and New Testament thinking as in Matthew 5:38–39 is allowed for lesser crimes only; thus, this philosophical position is better aligned with variations of modern Western secular thinking (Tonry 2001).

For the Reformed Christian, Calvin's position on capital punishment would be of interest. Calvin, in his *Institutes*, accepts that governments have the right and obligation to punish as they 'do not bear the sword for no reason' (Rm 13:4), and uses Old Testament references in explaining the Christian use of capital punishment. Calvin (2012) can, however, not be taken as a supporter of the theonomist reconstructionist stance, for he says:

> The magistrate must guard against both extremes; he must neither, by excessive severity, rather wound than cure, nor by a superstitious affection of clemency fall into the most cruel inhumanity, by giving way to soft and dissolute indulgence to the destruction of many. (*Inst.* 4.20.10)

Among modern Reformed ethicists, Vorster (2017a) presents a moderate view, in which it is accepted that biblical sources and the teachings of Calvin acknowledge capital punishment, but that society should be urged to consider alternative means of punishment, such as life imprisonment, when the situation allows for it. To Vorster, it is problematic for society to defend and protect human life on the one hand and to take it away on the other. Douma (1996), who points out that capital punishment should be permitted in modern society, but that not every capital offence automatically should lead to this highest level of punishment, also shares this moderate view.

The position of moderate retributionism best reflects responsible scriptural interpretation, Calvin's teachings and the moderation urged by Vorster (2017a). Thus, on the basis of the above scriptural sources and literature, it will appear that within the Reformed tradition capital punishment is acceptable under certain circumstances.

■ War

Context

The possibility to contribute financially in industries and technologies related to military activities in war and violent conflict is prevalent, and it would be a fair assessment that bankers throughout history have played a vital role in initiating and upholding war and armed conflict. As war represents the ultimate level of violent conflict, and often threatens the very core existence of the affected societies, it is not surprising that financing the involved parties in their acquiring of arms, technologies and allied support can involve vast amounts of capital. It would be reasonable to expect that the warring parties would attempt to gather as much capital as is necessary and possible to amass, as the perception rightfully may be that they will not be given another chance to win. From modern Western history, USA can serve as a good example. Graeber (2012) explains that since 1790, the US Federal debt, in 2008 at more than $12 000 billion, in reality has been a war debt, and that the US spends more than all other nations of the world put together on its military forces – in 2008 alone, more than $800 billion. He further contends that the US military spending is so vast and involves such wide tracts of the total federal budget, that without this item, the US budget may not experience the recurring deficits currently incurred. It suffices to say from this example, when extrapolated to a global level, that when involved in banking, it is of utmost importance to clarify what the Christian stance on war is.

Scriptural sources pertaining to war and violent conflict are plentiful, and in the context of this treatise, the aim is to explore whether involvement in war can ever be an acceptable banking practice. To elucidate this point, in the following sections, I explain three possible positions towards the morality of participating in warfare: pacifism, activism and selectivism.

■ Pacifism

In some Christian traditions, the statement of the sixth commandment would imply that all taking of life is forbidden, and that there can be no exceptions or exemptions from this rule, because of its clear and direct wording in Exodus 20:13. Further scriptural arguments for pacifism are drawn from Matthew 5:39 where it is stated: 'But I tell you, do not resist an evil person. If anyone slaps you on the right cheek, turn to them the other cheek also'. On the other hand, there are numerous scriptural sources pointing to God's initiating and utilising war as a remedy, such as Joshua 6, Joshua 10 and Psalm 44, and staunch pacifists need to explain how these correlates with the anti-war scriptural passages that serve as basis for their theology. There is some evidence that the early Christians were pacifists, at least prior to Constantine's decision to make Christianity the state religion of the Roman Empire. From Constantine's conversion, the Christian doctrine has been directed towards the acceptance of war in certain and rare circumstances, where the main peacekeeping pacifistic assumption permeates all interpretation of theology and the actual situation. To state that there is a great gulf between pacifism and the just war doctrine would be incorrect both from a historical as well as theological perspective (Hoekema 1986). It is of importance to note, though, that the historical evidence open for interpretation is scarce, and for the period up until AD 170 there is no real evidence to speak of, and from then on to Constantine's conversion, evidence of active Christian soldiers appears. Christian objections against military service were most prevalent in the Hellenistic Eastern part of the Empire, and Northern African Christians were divided on the matter. Prior to Constantine's conversion, the most extensive of Christian participation in war was to be found in the eastern frontier areas (Bainton 1946). As will appear from the following sections, the acceptability of Christians participating in war was to increase despite sound biblical arguments against this, both from direct passages and from the total love ethos of Scripture. The total pacifist stance is today found only outside the mainstream Christian denominations, among groups such as the Anabaptists, Mennonites and Quakers (Rempel 2005). The position of pacifism is not in accordance with the Reformed ethical stance on war.

Activism

In contradiction to the theological stance of complete pacifism is that of activism, which, in Geisler's (2010) explanation, entails the fact that individuals must always obey their government, even when ordered to participate in war. Under this paradigm, he posits, individuals will not commit sin when killing in war if their own government duly orders them. This is a position based on the view that Scripture commands obedience to government; Genesis 9:6 and 1 Corinthians 14:33 and 40 will serve as the biblical foundation for the theology. The main thought is that God is the God of order and not of chaos, and Genesis 1:28 bestows societal dominion on humanity by giving the instruction to 'rule over every living creature that moves on the ground'. That God accepts war as a suitable means of protecting the innocents is further explained from Genesis 14, where Abraham engages in war to rectify the unjust aggression perpetrated against his nephew, Lot.

From the scripturally based argumentation outlined above, Geisler (2010) continues to highlight the activist position by means of philosophical and political argumentation, drawing from sources of ancient philosophy. He does not, however, describe any contemporary proponents of the activist position, and I have not been able to find any church society or academic literature openly adhering to or even defending in part the activist position on war from a Christian vantage point. On the contrary, the notion that individuals can act with impunity if they are instructed by superiors is not even accepted in secular legal thinking, according to what is found, for example, in the context of International Humanitarian Law (IHL) pertaining to war. The Red Cross (International Committee of the Red Cross n.d) is an important proponent of the promotion of IHL, and on its home page, the principle of legal responsibility of the individual is described in the following:

> Criminal prosecution places responsibility and punishment at the level of the individual. It shows that the abominable crimes of the twentieth century were not committed by nations but by individuals. (n.p.)

The position of activism is not a defensible Christian norm, and it opposes fundamental international conventions pertaining to war, war crimes and the responsibility of the individual.

Selectivism – Just war

As the theological positions of pacifism and activism do not align with Reformed norms pertaining to war and morality, the concept of selectivism, or the doctrine of 'just war', needs to be explained. This theological philosophy can be seen as a practical-theological application to the harsh realities of the existence and persistence of war in our societies in historical times and in our contemporary global political reality.

The narrative outlined in Exodus 32:25–29, where Moses is instructed to send some Hebrews into their own camp and murder the unrighteous, is in traditional theology seen as justification for the doctrine of 'just war'. This theology maintains that war can be acceptable under certain circumstances, for both society and the individual, and it resonates well with secular philosophy and practice to this day (Lee 2012).

Augustine, in his *City of God*, was among the first theologians to refer to the just war theory, and he acknowledged the fact that it was acceptable for a Christian to serve honourably in the military to protect his country. He further posited that to resort to violence should not be the first choice for Christians, but that God has given government the sword (Rm 13:4) for just reasons. Augustine did not elaborate all the necessary conditions for what constitutes just war, but he did coin the term, and contended that a wise man would fight just wars, but at the same time lament fighting them (Augustine 2003).

The just war theory was further developed by Aquinas in his *Summa Theologica*, where he built on the argumentation of Augustine, and explained some basic conditions for when warfare can be considered just. Aquinas (2010) defined three basic requisites for just war:

- **Proper authority.** A state or other formally created authority must institute the war. In this thinking, proper authority is assumed to represent the common good of its people, which can only be to achieve peace, which will lead to the highest aim of humans, God.
- **Just cause.** The second condition is that the waged war must be for a just and good reason, which cannot be purely for self-gain. Just causes could be to restore lost territory or property, or to discipline wrongdoers for their evil deeds.
- **Right intention.** The third condition is that the waged war should have as its main justification and aim to achieve peace. This intention must be shared by both the government and involved soldiers, for the intention to qualify as just.

Among Reformed theologians, Calvin's stance on war is of particular interest for the purposes of this treatise. In his *Institutes of the Christian Religion*, Calvin builds on the theories of Augustine and Aquinas, and to him, for a government to wage war to protect the central values of its citizens is not only permitted, but at times, a duty as well. On the matter of when war can be justly waged, he (Calvin 2012) has the following statement:

> As it is sometimes necessary for kings and states to take up arms in order to execute public vengeance, the reason assigned furnishes us with the means of estimating how far the wars which are thus undertaken are lawful. For if power has been given them to maintain the tranquillity of their subjects, repress the seditious movements of the turbulent, assist those who are violently oppressed, and animadvert on crimes, can they use it more opportunely than in repressing the fury of him who disturbs both the ease of individuals and the common tranquillity of all? ... Natural equity and duty, therefore, demand that princes be armed not only to repress private crimes by judicial inflictions, but to defend the subjects committed to their guardianship whenever they are hostilely assailed. Such even the Holy Spirit, in many passages of Scripture, declares to be lawful. (*Inst.* 4.20.11)

As an answer to the pacifist stance, Calvin (2012) has the following to say:

> For (to use the words of Augustine) 'if Christian discipline condemned all wars, when the soldiers asked counsel as to the way of salvation, they would have been told to cast away their arms, and withdraw altogether from military service. Whereas it was said (Lk 3:14), Concuss no one, do injury to no one, be contented with your pay. Those whom he orders to be contented with their pay he certainly does not forbid to serve'. (*Inst.* 4.20.12)

Calvin assumes that war can be fought justly, and aligned with scriptural sources, but he does not outline detailed conditions for when warfare can be seen as just and be fought with moral impunity.

The above Christian thinkers all build on the assumption that wars can be justly fought and that governments under certain circumstances can and even should initiate them. It is, however, an underlying assumption that to resort to violence represents a means of exception, and therefore, to establish from Scripture what would be the acceptable situations, and thus, the needed conditions for just warfare, is necessary.

Geisler (2010) refers to the just war theory as selectivism and defines several categories and conditions for when wars can be fought within what is acceptable for Christians and in accord with scriptural sources. For just war, he defines the following rule set:

- **Defending the innocent.** To wage war to defend the innocent is just, and to fight an aggressive invader is normally justifiable. Genesis 14 can be seen as supporting this stance, but war can only be fought as long as it is necessary to retrieve the lands and possessions of the innocent.
- **Exerting justice.** When war is fought to execute justice, it is just. This means that it can be initiated for punitive reasons, and even invasions can be defended under this paradigm. Geisler does not present any scriptural support for this stance, but points to the Allied invasion of Nazi Germany in World War II as an example of justifiable punitive warfare.
- **Government is needed.** To be accepted as just, a war must be fought by government, as God awarded authority to governments, and not to individual citizens (Rm 13:4). Any military engagement among individuals must therefore be initiated and executed by governments and can only be declared by governments to be considered just. This does not, however, deprive individuals of their right to defend themselves violently, as is explained, for example, in Exodus 22:2.
- **Must be justly fought.** Even though a war can be defined as just, it does not follow that any act committed on the just side is defensible. The war must thus be fought justly, and as mentioned above, there are secular international humanitarian rules for warfare, guiding the conduct of acceptable violence, going back to the ideas of Emer de Vattel (1714–1767) in his *The Law of Nations*, later developed and culminating in the Hague and Geneva Conventions (Reichberg, Syse & Begby 2006). Scriptural expression of this principle can be found, for example, in Deuteronomy 20:19, where when engaged in long time siege of a city, the sieging party shall not 'destroy its trees by putting an axe to them, because you can eat their fruit. Do not cut them down'. This can be taken as an instruction to fight humanely, as the victor should not deprive the defeated of their possibility to sustain themselves from their land.
- **Reasonable prospect of victory.** A war cannot be just if there is no reasonable prospect of winning the war. This rule pertains no matter what just cause the initiated war may serve, as fighting a futile and useless war may be equivalent to mass suicide. This stance may be indicated in Luke

14:31–32 where Jesus says that if victory is not expected, the warring party will 'send a delegation while the other is still a long way off and will ask for terms of peace'. If no victory can be expected, surrender is then the moral choice to be made.
- **Peaceful remedies exhausted.** A war cannot be initiated unless all other peaceful efforts have been tried and have failed. In Scripture, this can be found as expressed in Deuteronomy 20:10, where Israel had to offer peace prior to attacking, and in Romans 12:18 where it is stated: 'If it is possible, as far as it depends on you, live at peace with everyone'.

Acceptable moral position on war

The above-described theological theories, from the early medieval era up to the current day, have explained how war must be seen as the last resort for Christians and that to live in peace and forgiveness is the highest principle (Aquinas 2010). It is of utmost importance here to underscore that Christians are always called to achieve peace, as we are under obligation to also love our enemies (Holmes 1995). The position presented by Geisler (2010) with all his elaborate conditions, I would believe to be an acceptable stance towards warfare, as it balances the blind uncritical obedience of activism and the sadly unpractical pacifism, in a manner by which conflict can be an acceptable choice of Christians. Thus, the position of selectivism is in accordance with the Reformed ethical stance on war.

For the purposes of this treatise it is not necessary to clarify all the different aspects of selectivism and just war theory, as the above elaboration in itself will have demonstrated that war and violence are unwanted among Christians, and accepted only as a last resort when all other peaceful avenues of negotiation have been exhausted. It is, however, of importance to be aware of the main tendencies pertaining to this important area of life, as banking practitioners will need to consider the participation in war on a regular basis, and to perceive this as indirect and remote may be tempting for reasons of complacency. It will be clear, however, that any participation in war by governments, individuals or indeed bankers, is unwanted, and cannot be seen as unproblematic by anyone.

Health and disease

Context

As the medical industry globally is a major capital-intensive sector, matters pertaining to practices of hospitals, producers of medicine and health service providers are of interest, as this sector would be relevant to consider in banking practice. It is difficult to estimate the total size of this sector on a global scale, as the medical sector is divided among private and public providers, and this can vary from country to country. However, as this sector is substantial, participation may be a typical opportunity frequently contemplated by Western bankers.

Caring for the sick

Ethical considerations on the practice of medicine is not a realm exclusive to Christendom, as such ethical reflections may for example be connected to Hippocrates (c. 460 BC to c. 377 BC), and not least, to Judaism which mostly has harboured a positive outlook on the medical crafts. Despite King Asa's reluctance to seek God's help when ill (2 Chr 16:12), Judaism has mainly viewed the medical arts as an illustration of the creative union between God and the human family, and indeed, some leading rabbis were physicians in the pre-Christian era (Higginson 1995).

When searching for scriptural illumination on matters of health, disease and healing, it should be noted that illness was not a part in the original state of humanity in the Garden of Eden, and that the intention of God for his creation was that all his creatures would live in perfect physical and spiritual well-being (Gn 1–2). From a biblical perspective, illness and disease came into the world as the result of original sin, and with the Fall came human mortality, as well as broken relationships between God and humanity, within humanity, within one's individual selves and with the very world we live in (Gn 3). As we live in a fallen state, humanity cannot take good health for granted, because this can only be received as a gift from God, flowing from his grace. It must further be emphasised that Scripture does not depict God as the author of disease and illness, but God uses disease as a method for testing the faith of humanity and also as an opportunity for human growth (e.g. Rm 5:3-5; 2 Cor 7:11; 1 Pt 1:6-7). Illness and disease are something that mainstream Christian theology has urged believers to fight and not succumb to, as death is the ultimate result of illness, and thus, not fighting it may be seen as a rejection of God's gift of life (Cook 1995; Moseley 2016).

The necessary cooperation between God and humanity concerning health and healing, is clearly evident in Exodus 15, which reads:

> If you listen carefully to the Lord your God and do what is right in his eyes, if you pay attention to his commands and keep all his decrees, I will not bring on you any of the diseases I brought on the Egyptians, for I am the LORD, who heals you. (v. 26)

That Israel trusted God's healing powers appears in for example Numbers 12:13, concerning Miriam's skin affliction, when Moses cried out to the Lord, '[p]lease, God, heal her!'. The focus on caring for and healing the sick is present in several other Old Testament passages, as for example in Jeremiah 30:17, concerning the restoration of Israel, where we learn that the Lord 'will restore you to health and heal your wounds' and in Psalm 103:3, the Lord is presented as the one who 'heals all your diseases'.

The New Testament shows in numerous passages how Christ was a great healer and physician, who through his healing ministry brought wholeness and health to the human family in a manner that aligns with the good health and well-being God originally created humans to enjoy (Cook 1995). Of passages evidencing the healing powers of Christ may be mentioned Mark 5:21–43, where Jesus raises a dead girl and heals a haemorrhaging woman, the exorcism of the Gerasene demoniac described in Mark 5:1–17 and Luke 8:26–37 (also in Matt 8:28–34), and not least in Matthew 8:1–3 where Jesus heals the leper, to mention but a few examples covering physical and mental disease. The example of Christ's healing ministry had substantial influence on the apostles and the early church, something that is expressed in James 5:14, with the instruction 'Is anyone among you sick? Let them call the elders of the church to pray over them and anoint them with oil in the name of the Lord'. In James 5:15, we understand how the church had a special place in caring for the sick with the expectation that 'the prayer offered in faith will make the sick person well; the Lord will raise them up'. As like Christ, the early churches perceived the concept of health as both a matter of physical as well as mental well-being, as appears in 3 John 1:2 'I pray that you may enjoy good health and that all may go well with you, even as your soul is getting along well' and in 2 Corinthians 7:1 with 'let us purify ourselves from everything that contaminates body and spirit'.

The motif of suffering and pain as a post-fall state of humanity, and with it the possibility of God's healing powers, is further expressed in the Eschaton narrative in Revelation, where it is described how with the second coming of Christ there will be no more illness, disease or death (Rv 21:3–4, 22:1–3, 7:13–17).

To Calvin, the concept of caring for the sick needed to be clearly separated from the act of healing the sick, as this in his view was not open for the Christian believers to perform. This position of delineation was by Calvin seen in a dialogue with the Catholic Church, which at Calvin's time, and later, ascribed healing effects to mundane acts of human works, such as the Extreme Unction, which was among those church institutions he perceived as false sacraments. On the matter of healing the sick, Calvin (2012) explained how:

> Mark relates that the apostles, on their first mission, agreeably to the command which they had received of the Lord, raised the dead, cast out devils, cleansed lepers, healed the sick, and, in healing, used oil. He says, they 'anointed with oil many that were sick, and healed them' (Mark 6:13). (*Inst.* 4.19.18)

Furthermore (Calvin 2012):

> Therefore, even were we to grant that anointing was a sacrament of those powers which were then administered by the hands of the apostles, it pertains not to us, to whom no such powers have been committed. (*Inst.* 4.19.18)

Of the position of the Catholic Church related to healing, Calvin (2012) made his position particularly clear when stating:

> They make themselves ridiculous, therefore, by pretending that they are endued with the gift of healing. (*Inst.* 4.19.19)

Notwithstanding Calvin's position on healing, he did not oppose the pastoral activity of caring for the sick. On the contrary, active and participatory pastoral ministry was at the core of Calvin's theology, and to him, a pastor needed to be present with his flock as much as possible and at all times in a constituent's life. According to Calvin's teachings, the sick should always be visited in their homes by their pastors, no later than three days after they fell ill. Not only were the sick to be visited by their pastors, but they should if necessary, also be lodged in hospitals and cared for, as this was prevalent in the ancient Christian traditions Calvin promoted (Calvin 2006). In Geneva, the city hospital was established well before the time of Calvin and the reformation, but Calvin's visionary ideas for the hospital would point well outside the contemporaneous practice of merely caring for the sick. To Calvin, it was also important to care to the generally infirm, the aged, the dependant and widows without support. Thus, the practical aspects of ministry as Calvin envisaged it would express his wider perception of what a caring ministry meant. Calvin's pastoral theology did not then only exist in theory, but through his involvement in the city hospital of Geneva, become one of practice as well (Greene 1923).

As will have appeared from the theological positions of Calvin relating to illness and health, the focus in Reformed theology is that of *caring* for the sick, and it is therefore important to keep distance from the theology of healing ministries found in certain other denominations, such as for example among the Pentecostal churches, which will fall outside what is the viable and generally accepted Reformed position. In the Reformed tradition, there has been an understanding that sin and disease are evil, and that sickness and death have entered the world as a result of original sin, and thus, that the healing ministry of Christ as described in the New Testament is an expression of God's victory over sin. The Reformed reaction to death and disease has therefore not been one of indifferent acceptance, and to focus on the caring aspects when dealing with the sick has been a mainstay and core value and should be seen as an important task for the Christian expression (Groenhout 2006; Moseley 2016).

Abortion

The matter of abortion is a subject of substantial contention, and in some regions of the world such as in the West it is typically debated from a secular perspective, and in relation to the possibility for a pregnant woman freely to choose whether to carry the foetus to full term. In other regions, it may not be as simple as a matter of choice, as the woman may be under pressure to abort,

Scriptural foundations

due to gender preferences connected to expected offsprings in different cultures. Such questions will not be further debated here, as the matter at hand is viewed through a Christian lens, irrespective of cultural idiosyncratic variations.

On abortion, there are three typical stances: that a foetus is subhuman, and thus, that abortion is always permitted; that the foetus is potentially human, and thus, that abortion is sometimes permitted; and that a foetus is fully human, and thus, that abortion is always immoral (Geisler 2010). All of these positions are debated from both secular and theological vantage points, and in the following text, I elaborate on some scriptural sources shedding light on the matter.

The proponents of the stance that abortion is always permitted seek scriptural support in Genesis 2:7, where it is started that 'the Lord God formed a man from the dust of the ground and breathed into his nostrils the breath of life, and the man became a living being'. From this passage, it is posited that life is present in a human only when breathing. Further support for the stance is sought in Job 34:14–15, where it appears that 'if he withdrew his spirit and breath, all humanity would perish together and mankind would return to the dust'. Both of these passages superficially indicate that without breathing, humans cannot be seen as living. In other words, humans become humans, and thus represent the image of God, only when we are born.

The proponents of the position that abortion seek scriptural support in (among others) Exodus 21, which reads:

> If people are fighting and hit a pregnant woman and she gives birth prematurely but there is no serious injury, the offender must be fined whatever the woman's husband demands and the court allows. But if there is serious injury, you are to take life for life. (vv. 22–23)

This passage is then interpreted to indicate that if only a foetus is injured, financial reparation is the remedy, but if the life of the mother is taken, the reparation is by capital punishment. Thus, the proponents argue that a foetus is of lesser value than that of a living person, the mother, and this indicates that a foetus is only potentially human and can sometimes be aborted. A similar argumentation is drawn from Hebrews 7:9–10, where 'Levi … paid the tenth through Abraham, because when Melchizedek met Abraham, Levi was still in the body of his ancestor'. The main argument for this position then is that a foetus is not a real human being, and not protected by God and his laws.

The final position always considers abortion to always be immoral, and against God's will and his laws. The position here is that all humans are an image of God, and thus equally protected, even when unborn. The Bible has several passages clearly evidencing this position, in addition to the higher principles of God's creation and the special place in it of humans in the image of God. For example, foetuses are called 'baby' in Luke 1:41-44 and described as created by God in the 'mother's womb' in Psalms 139:13. From Psalm 139:15-16 it appears that God knows his subjects already in their mothers' womb. Seen in context and in conjunction with the creation narrative and the *imago Dei* doctrine, there cannot be any doubt that, in Scripture, the unborn are considered humans as much as any other living persons.

Calvin (1852b), in his *The Harmony of the Law*, addresses the matter of abortion in relation to the passage in Exodus 21:22-23, and has the following to say:

> This passage at first sight is ambiguous, for if the word death only applies to the pregnant woman, it would not have been a capital crime to put an end to the *foetus*, which would be a great absurdity; for the *foetus*, though enclosed in the womb of its mother, is already a human being (*homo*) and it is almost a monstrous crime to rob it of the life which it has not yet begun to enjoy. If it seems more horrible to kill a man in his own house than in a field, because a man's house is his place of most secure refuge, it ought surely to be deemed more atrocious to destroy a *foetus* in the womb before it has come to light. On these grounds I am led to conclude, without hesitation, that the words, 'if death should follow', must be applied to the *foetus* as well as to the mother. (pp. 51-52)

That abortion is a practice that cannot be defended, and represents a clear violation of the sixth commandment, is supported by Douma (1996), who in his elaborations also points to the difficult situation some women may be in and warns not to use strong judgemental language when approaching those in difficulty.

The above sources are just a highlighted and brief extract of the existing theological debate regarding the morality of abortion. The referenced scriptural sources, when interpreted responsibly, all describe the unborn as humans in God's image. The sources used by the abortion proponents do not lend any counter argumentation that can be seen as valid and cannot support a stance that abortion can be acceptable for Christians. The position of Calvin, referred to above, is as eloquent an explanation of this as conceivable. The conclusion on this topic is that abortion is always immoral and cannot, under any circumstances, be allowed or promoted (Vorster 2017a).

Euthanasia

Euthanasia can be divided into passive and active euthanasia, where the passive version entails leaving someone to die by denying them available medical assistance, and the active, to positively assist in taking someone's life (Rachels 1975). For adults, it is conceivable that both active and passive euthanasia can be both consensual and non-consensual, but when it comes to minors, all euthanasia needs to be viewed as non-consensual.

Scriptural foundations

Euthanasia is performed on infants in hospitals when the medical staff perceive that the new-born is irrevocably ill, or highly disabled (Verhagen & Sauer 2005). In this section, it is delineated against abortion, in that euthanasia by definition will happen outside the womb. From a scriptural perspective, to take a life actively is murder, and as discussed in previous sections, is in direct conflict with the sixth commandment (Ex 20:13). Thus, in its active form, to euthanise a new-born is clearly unacceptable from a Christian perspective. When it comes to passive euthanasia of newborns, this can be by way of denying the child natural means of survival such as food and water, or unnatural means, such as medicine and technical support. It cannot be open for debate that to deprive someone of food and water and other natural sources of subsistence is equal to murder, and in the case of children, this must be seen as unacceptable and immoral under all circumstances (Geisler 2010). When the consideration pertains to denying a new-born unnatural means of survival, such as medicine and medical treatments, the matter will still be similar, as the infant cannot have its own opinion about its suffering, quality of life and its further possibilities (Robertson 1975). Therefore, in the case of newborns and children, unnatural passive euthanasia will also be considered immoral (Douma 1996; Geisler 2010). In this connection, it is worth mentioning the UN Declaration of Human Rights, Article 3, which states, 'Everyone has the right to life …' (United Nations n.d.). This can be viewed as a secular expression of the Christian position on the sanctity of life and should be seen as particularly important when addressing euthanasia of newborns and children, who themselves cannot have any influence on such matters.

When evaluating euthanasia among adults, the matter can be perceived from a different perspective, as adults to a larger degree will be able to form opinions on their own life, and the possible duration of their suffering. To some, life loses value when suffering becomes substantial and lasting, and suicide may seem the best solution. When it comes to assisted suicide, there are clinics and organisations in Switzerland (for example) that will assist certain types of sick individuals in taking their lives (Dignitas n.d.). Among some secular people then, assisted suicide can be acceptable under given circumstances. From a biblical vantage point, however, this cannot be acceptable, as it follows from Genesis 1:26 that humans are mandated as rulers and caretakers of creation, and thus, are obligated to protect God's creation. All human experiences, including suffering, come from God. God uses suffering in educating people to attain greater trust, as it is demonstrated in Deuteronomy 32:10–12 and James 2:1–8. Another perspective is that of hope: by choosing euthanasia, people are devoid of hope because they do not trust in God, and have more regard for death than for life, and this may as well be seen in conflict with what may be explained as a biblical Christian anthropology (Banner 1998). From a scriptural perspective then, it is clear that active euthanasia is immoral, and in conflict with basic Christian values (Vorster 2017a).

The matter of passive euthanasia for adults may evoke some different perspectives than that of active assisted suicide. As is the case for children, to deprive someone of natural means of sustenance, such as food and water cannot be seen as moral, but to let someone die a natural death, and not give them the required medical treatment, which may only be life-prolonging, should possibly not be seen to be in conflict with acceptable Christian teachings (Geisler 2010).

Summing up the above, euthanasia is immoral as human life is protected and created in the image of God, but under some circumstances, to allow passive euthanasia for adults may be permitted. Even under such circumstances, the decision should not be taken lightly, and the dying should consider their circumstances thoroughly (Geisler 2010; Vorster 2017a). However, from a Christian anthropological perceptive as described above, such circumstances will evoke particular interest, as to become unwilling to live goes against this fundamental understanding of the value of life in all its forms (Banner 1998).

■ Biomedical challenges
Context

Advances in modern medicine and technology have introduced new kinds of ethical questions to consider, both as individuals in our daily lives. For banking practitioners, matters of bioethics can come into play when involvement is contemplated in medical and educational assets.

With modern research and scientific development, possibilities for manipulating natural processes have evolved to a hitherto unknown level, and where humans in previous historical times had scarce opportunity to manipulate life and nature, this has now increasingly become acceptable to secular interests, industry and governments. The possibilities today related to manipulating life, human and otherwise, abound, and include *in vitro* fertilisation (IVF), surrogate mothers, organ harvesting and donations, gene splicing, cloning, human genome manipulation (eugenics), pre-natal diagnostics, hybrids and chimeras (Geisler 2010; Sutton 2008).

Manipulating life

Under the consequentialist secular humanist view, no divine creator is recognised, and quality of life rather than sanctity of life is the key. A typical tendency under this philosophical and political paradigm is that the ends justify the means, and that humans are the sovereign rulers of life and nature (Geisler 2010). However, due to the atrocities carried out by Nazi Germany, and their research on and with humans, an increasing interest in the ethical aspects of science and its tampering with life evolved during the second half of the 20th century and beyond (Sutton 2008). So-called secular humanists have been allowed a substantial place in this ethical discourse, which has led to a myriad of new life-tampering technologies being accepted as beneficial for humans and society. In this thinking, there is no divine creator, and the human being is seen as the height of rationality, and capable of making the best choices pertaining to all ethical questions that are or will be presented for answering (Kurtz & Wilson 1973). This grandiose perception of human cognition, and the ability to make wise choices and overview all possible consequences of scientific progress and development, is prevalent. A typical proponent of this stance would be Singer (2011) who is a self-professed preference utilitarian, and for him, it is difficult to determine that anything can be intrinsically moral or immoral; consequently, his writing is permeated with tendencies to accept that the ends justify the means.

For Christians, the area of new medical and scientific possibilities poses many new realms of ethical considerations, but answers still need to be sought in Scripture, and to be based on the core Christian values revealed there. To search for support among theologians from the past, such as Calvin, could be seen as futile, as the possibilities offered in contemporary science can be assumed to go beyond the imagination of all thinkers from the past. This factual state will also pose problems in financial activity, as what is not conceivable or possible today may soon be, and in the future, consequences of seemingly unproblematic contemporary technologies may lead to immoral practices.

Any viable position that aims to assess bioethical problematics pertaining to human life will need to be founded in scriptural revelation connected to the creation, *imago Dei* and the sanctity of life as discussed above. To point out any specific scriptural passage for any conceivable biomedical or technical possibility will not be possible; however, the general scriptural instructions will more than suffice for humanity to stay informed, so the main view needs to be founded on the affirmation that God is the creator of all things (Gn 1:31), and be based on our stewardship obligation in creation as stipulated in Genesis 1:28. That our stewardship obligation connects to all of creation without any exemptions is further evidenced from Psalm 24:1, 'the earth is the LORD'S, and everything in it, the world, and all who live in it'. As always, for Christians then, the ends cannot justify the means if they contradict scriptural revelations of the sanctity of life and stewardship in creation. Mere utilitarian considerations pertaining to what is beneficial to an individual or group in the short term should not outweigh the Christian stance and acknowledgement that God is sovereign over life and creation. This stance must be the guide when considering biomedical matters, in our lives and in banking practice (Geisler 2010). We should serve God, not play God.

Human rights
Context

To evaluate the Christian positions pertaining to human rights could be of importance in banking when considering participation in certain countries and regions where it is uncertain whether basic human rights are observed. To observe such matters could seriously affect where and with what regimes and political systems bankers should allow their practice to be included. It is the assumption here that how banking practitioners act in this regard is important, as more powerful actors can be seen as a role model for other others and even other regimes and political movements. Further, in some cases, considerations of human rights can be important to assess the quality of the specific target area, as observing issues such as authorisation of trade unions, payment of fair wages, maintenance of political neutrality and use of child labour can all be topics to be addressed in a company prior to getting involved, no matter what formal financial instrument is being considered.

The human rights construct

Human rights with a secular foundation can be found comprehensively expressed in the UN's Universal Declaration of Human Rights as dated 10 December 1948, the 'Declaration' where central civil liberties are proclaimed as universal, and as such, should be available for all persons globally (United Nations n.d.). In the time of adoption by the general assembly by its resolution of 1948, the Declaration was seen as a substantial forward step for the collaboration of politically and religiously diverse and oftentimes conflicting regimes, who were based on divergent traditions and systems, but regrettably the resolution of the General Assembly did not have a legal force. As not legally binding on the signatories, the Declaration was of programmatic value only, and it was open for wide and varied interpretations and operationalisations. Because of the non-binding character of the Declaration, the UN Commission of Human Rights already initiated and proposed additions to the Declaration by way of multilateral human rights treaties in 1947. This led to two International Human Rights Covenants, one concerning economic, social and cultural rights, and one on civil and political rights. The covenants were adopted in 1966 and came into force in 1976 (Office of the High Commissioner for Human Rights n.d.; see also Vorster 2017a). This near three decades long delay may have been caused by the fact that several Western states maintained their colonial practices, and were reluctant to allow the rights universality, because such rights would then have to be extended to their subjects in the colonies (Robertson 2012). Although they are not formally founded in Christian ethics, it is of interest to use these rules as a background for what kinds of rights should be assessed in a Christian banking setting. It is well-known that these rights are by no means universally available today, but for banking practitioners, it is of particular interest to understand what these rights are, and the extent to which they are based on Christian values and norms. In the following text, some key issues of human rights are discussed, as they are deemed important in the context of this treatise.

Education

In today's Western societies, to receive education is mostly taken for granted as a given, at least on the primary and secondary levels, and in most places tertiary education is widely available for most. That this has not always been the case in the West, and sadly, to this day still not in many places in the world, is also well known. Education as a good deserving human right status was understood by the signatories of the Declaration, and in Article 26 (1) (United Nations n.d.) it is stated that:

> Everyone has the right to education. Education shall be free, at least in the elementary and fundamental stages. Elementary education shall be compulsory. Technical and professional education shall be made generally available and higher education shall be equally accessible to all on the basis of merit. (art. 26[1])

For ethically concerned banking practitioners, these rights would be seen as central values to uphold, and it is of interest to explore scriptural sources pertaining to such rights.

Connected to the special covenantal position humans have under creation is the dignity that rests in the ability humanity has been bestowed by God to reason and learn, and education has remained a mainstay part of the Christian and Judaic tradition. This tradition is abundantly represented in both the Old and the New Testaments as well as in Christian practice, which would be known by Christian readers from their experience in church, Sunday school, conformation preparations, Bible study groups, the Christian school and university movement et cetera. Learning is of the utmost value for Christians in their journey to know God, and this gift of learning may be understood best through the example of Christ in his master–apprentice approach to his pupils, whoever they were. The concept of education in a purely Christian context is not what will be of interest to elaborate here, as the realm of education is broad and will cover a wide area of financial opportunities, so it will be the Christian tradition of participating in and generating education that will be of intertest in the following. The Judaic and Christian focus on education runs deep, and its core area of focus would be to offer moral education to the human family, and to enable humanity to serve and love God and their neighbours. Jewish tradition holds that schools were already organised in a systematic manner in the 1st century BC in Palestine by Simeon ben Shetah (Atkinson 1995b).

In the Old Testament, the family is a venue where the law of God is explained, as for example expressed in Deuteronomy 6:1–7, where we learn of 'the commands, decrees and laws the Lord your God directed me to teach you to observe', and how the listeners are instructed: 'Impress them on your children'. In the Wisdom literature, moral education is highlighted, like in Proverbs 3:1, where it is stated 'my son, do not forget my teaching, but keep my commands in your heart'. The importance of knowledge is further highlighted in Daniel 1:17, where we learn how 'God gave knowledge and understanding of all kinds of literature and learning', and in Ecclesiastes 7:12, where it is simply put that 'Wisdom preserves those who have it'.

Education and teaching are given substantial emphases in the New Testament, where Jesus teaches his disciples in numerous passages, such as in the introduction to the Sermon on the Mount, where we are informed how 'His disciples came to him, and he began to teach them' (Mt 5:1–2). This is a model passage, from where we can infer not only that Jesus taught the disciples, but also that they 'came to him' to receive the teaching, which illustrates the obligation of Christians to seek knowledge and accept it as a gift. The understanding that teaching is a gift to receive was well accepted in the early church, and in Ephesians 4:11 we learn that to build the church for the service of humanity 'Christ himself gave the apostles, the prophets, the evangelists, the pastors and teachers'. The knowledge-as-gift motif is also developed in 1 Timothy 4, where the instruction goes:

> Until I come, devote yourself to the public reading of Scripture, to preaching and to teaching. Do not neglect your gift, which was given you through prophecy when the body of elders laid their hands on you. (vv. 13–14)

The importance of knowledge and teaching has followed the development of the church and its institutions from the earliest of days, and in the medieval era, the Western church was the core societal institution to uphold literacy and learning, and from this practice were developed schools and universities where Western traditions of philosophy, law, art, architecture, music and more were maintained (Hitchcock 2012). The Western church hegemony in teaching and knowledge distribution was not truly broken until the late medieval era, when secular teaching institutions were developed to challenge the church within certain areas, not least in the teaching of law, where the first European university was formed in Bologna in 1088 (Long 1994; Università di Bologna n.d.). With the Reformation, the Catholic Church was challenged further in its teaching activity, and through the translation of the Bible into vernacular languages, the Christian ethos of democratic distribution of teaching and knowledge as a gift to receive was further significantly developed, respected and promoted (Bunkowske 1985).

For Calvin, the importance of knowledge was connected to knowing God and how all knowledge flowed from God, and thus, Calvin's authorship is permeated with emphasis on teaching and learning. For example, in Calvin (2012), he explains how:

> Our wisdom, in so far as it ought to be deemed true and solid Wisdom, consists almost entirely of two parts: the knowledge of God and of ourselves. (*Inst.* 1.1.1)

Furthermore (Calvin 2012):

> [/]t is evident that man never attains to a true self-knowledge until he has previously contemplated the face of God, and come down after such contemplation to look into himself. (*Inst.* 1.1.2)

That the teaching ministry of Christ was to be seen as a perfect template for human ministry becomes clear when he (Calvin 2012) expounds:

> [B]ecause Christ performs the office of teacher under a head, he applies the name God to the Father, not for the purpose of destroying his own Divinity, but for the purpose of raising us up to it as it were step by step. (*Inst.* 1.13.24)

To Calvin, theology was never merely a theoretical and distant entity, but something to apply in practice. Thus, Calvin was active within the field of education, and during his period of pastoring in Geneva he founded a college in 1559, which was divided into a public school and a seminary. The public school was known as Calvin College, and the seminary became known as the University of Geneva, and because they were tuition free, this initiative may be seen as a harbinger of the public education later to become common in Europe. Not only concerned with the practical aspect of the college, Calvin recognised the connection between the Christian faith and education, and to satisfy this line of thought he authored a catechism to be used by parents to teach their children alongside any secular education they were given (Hall 2008; Parker 2006). That the University of Geneva exists to this day with around 17 000 students from 150 different nationalities as Switzerland's second largest university offering more than 500 programs, is testament to the lasting legacy Calvin has had in the field of education (Université de Genève n.d.).

On the basis of the scriptural quotes and the longstanding firm church tradition of teaching, not least as evidenced in Calvin's authorship and personal example, it can be concluded that education represents a core Christian value that needs to be promoted, respected and protected.

Freedom of speech

In Western society, liberal societal freedoms aligned with the UN's Declaration of Human Rights are generally recognised, and this includes freedom of speech, which is seen as a vital part of the political discourse and is increasingly taken for granted. That this is not the case in large parts of the world is well known. The Declaration, Article 19 states (United Nations n.d.):

> Everyone has the right to freedom of opinion and expression; this right includes freedom to hold opinions without interference and to seek, receive and impart information and ideas through any media and regardless of frontiers. (art. 19)

Article 20(1) secures that (United Nations n.d.) '[e]veryone has the right to freedom of peaceful assembly and association'.

For ethically concerned banking practitioners, these rights would be seen as central values to uphold, and it is of interest to explore scriptural sources pertaining to such rights.

A natural starting point related to expressing opinions could be 1 Peter 2:16, which urges, 'Live as free people, but do not use your freedom as a cover-up for evil; live as God's slaves'. Another important passage of relevance for free speech is John 8:32, which in the context of following the teachings of Jesus states, 'Then you will know the truth, and the truth will set you free'. Vorster (2017a) points out that this verse could be seen in a soteriological perspective, but maintains that for developing true and just societal development, the expression of truth is a central ingredient. Vorster's interpretation is of special interest here, as it pertains to the reconciliation process performed when his native South Africa was transformed from an apartheid state to one of liberal democracy. The relevance of his interpretation could not be stronger, as to utter opinions freely without the risk of persecution would be necessary to carry out such a vast societal project of democratisation.

Calvin (1969:92) touches on the matter of free speech in the context of his time, and in his *Commentary on Seneca's de Clementia*, he states that '[i]f there is anything free in man, it is his tongue. A man is thrust into utter slavery when his freedom of speech is taken away'.

It suffices to say that in Calvin's time of reformation and major political and religious upheaval in Europe, he would have first-hand knowledge of the value of free speech and the right of uttering alternative political and religious opinions, leaving his writings as a lasting legacy in Western democratic thought (Witte 2007). It would, however, be prudent to point out that in this time in European history, general suffrage did not exist, and the statement need be seen more as a promotion of a free discourse than of general democracy in the modern liberal Western manner.

On the basis of the above scriptural quotes, and Calvin's direct instruction, the conclusion is that general freedom of speech for all is a protected value as aligned with core Christian values.

Freedom of belief

Another aspect connected to liberal freedom, and directly related to freedom of speech, is that of freedom of religious affiliation and expression. The UN Declaration of Human Rights, Article 18, states that (United Nations n.d.):

> Everyone has the right to freedom of thought, conscience and religion; this right includes freedom to change his religion or belief, and freedom, either alone or in community with others and in public or private, to manifest his religion or belief in teaching, practice, worship and observance. (art. 18)

The position here is clear, and again, what scriptural sources say is of interest.

Both the Old and New Testaments abound with passages insisting that there is only one true God (Ex 20:3), and to worship others is seen as transgression of the laws (Ex 20:4). Jesus speaks of 'the kingdom of heaven' (Mt 4:17), and of the duty of proclaiming it (Mt 28:19–20), and thus it would be difficult to responsibly extract a principle of general religious freedom from Christian scriptural sources. For the Reformed Christian, then, the matter is whether we should accept that there is no religious freedom in a society, and indeed actively promote such a state, or whether we should perceive the freedom of religion as a necessary extension of the freedom of speech, or perhaps simply promote such a value for pragmatic reasons.

In Calvin's time, the matter of religious freedom would have been deferent as compared to today, as in the Reformation era, the inter-Christian schisms were at the fore, and what would be pertinent then was whether the Western individual could freely choose her Christian confession. This as opposed to today, where not only will there be questions connected to inter-Christian disputes, but also connected whether to accept other religions and belief systems, which during the height of the Reformation would only pertain to peoples living in other parts of the world, or that would not yet even have been heard of or invented. When we then look at Calvin's authorship on the subject of religious belief, 16th century European Zeitgeist need be noted, and also, how liberal freedoms that we recognise today were only in their seminal beginnings. On the matter of individual beliefs, Calvin (2012) explained:

> Therefore, lest this prove a stumbling-block to any, let us observe that in man government is twofold: the one spiritual, by which the conscience is trained to piety and divine worship; the other civil, by which the individual is instructed in those duties which, as men and citizens, we are bold to performs. (*Inst.* 3.19.15)

Despite the understanding of the twofold government of humanity, Calvin (2012) would not promote what we perceive as true religious freedom today, which would follow from the following quote:

> I no more than formerly allow men at pleasure to enact laws concerning religion and the worship of God, when I approve of civil order which is directed to this end – viz. to prevent the true religion, which is contained in the law of God, from being with impunity openly violated and polluted by public blasphemy. (*Inst.* 3.20.3)

Although it is fair to criticise Calvin for not realising the logic of the twofold government image in relation to religious freedom, it can be argued, that his authorship on this point equipped later proponents of allowing true religious freedom with a useful theological framework (Wilken 2019).

Vorster (2007, 2017a) discusses freedom of belief thoroughly in the context of creating a South Africa with a space for all groups and describes different models of state and privately run and governed religious activity. His conclusion is that to utilise a system where the government and religion are separated, but where religion should function in the public realm, will best allow for a peaceful and amicable development of society, with the best result for all involved groups. He terms this position the 'active plural option'. Vorster (2017a) seeks some scriptural support for this stance in 1 Timothy 2:2, 'that we may live peaceful and quiet lives in all godliness and holiness'. This position will allow for all groups, including the Christians, to carry on their worship freely, educate their children in the faith and partake in missionary activities in accordance with scriptural obligations (Mt 28:19–20). The stance may seem pragmatically motivated, but the context of writing is that of evaluating human rights, so I assume it is not purely motivated by utilitarian considerations, but that it remains within viable Reformed Christian paradigmatic philosophy. The conclusion is, then, that to allow freedom of religious expression and affiliation for all citizens is the only acceptable moral norm pertaining to religious freedom.

Equal opportunities

Outside the realm of freedom of religious expression, but still connected, is the matter of what liberal rights are awarded to societal minorities. Although women cannot be considered a minority, it would be natural to include gender issues related to their rights in this section. The UN Declaration of Human Rights (United Nations n.d.) is permeated by the equality principle; as for example, already in the preamble it becomes clear that both genders are seen as equal, in stating that the:

> United Nations have in the Charter reaffirmed their faith in fundamental human rights, in the dignity and worth of the human person and in the equal rights of men and women … . (n.p.)

Further, Article 23 (2) states that (United Nations n.d.) '[e]veryone, without any discrimination, has the right to equal pay for equal work'.

In any society, social stratification can appear to be based on a multitude of different outer characteristics connected to gender, ethnicity, religion, financial strength, profession, race, age, disability and religious and political affiliation, to mention but a few (Bottero 2005). Relating to gender, it must be emphasised that from Scripture, we know about God's creation of humanity that 'male and female he created them' (Gn 1:27). Therefore, in a time of popular and media focus on so-called transgender problematics, alleged gender fluidity and adjacent purported rights, nowhere in the Bible can we find recognition of any other gender variation than that of woman and man. A responsible scriptural interpretation, *tota Scriptura*, will then be that humans can only be seen in the created genders, and no support for rights based on transgender or fluid gender identity can be drawn from Scripture. Any further discussion on gender transgender issues or gender fluidity will fall outside the scope of this treatise.

The protection of the weak and marginalised is considered in several scriptural passages. Relating to the poor, we are informed in Exodus 23:6, 'Do not deny justice to your poor people in their lawsuits' and in Exodus 3:11, we learn that it was an obligation to let the poor 'get food' from the owner's agricultural land in years of sabbath. In James 2:5, it says, 'Has not God chosen those who are poor in the eyes of the world to be rich in faith and to inherit the kingdom he promised those who love him?', something which clarifies the scriptural stance on the weak in society. A perceived weak social group that is mentioned in several scriptural locations are foreigners (Dt 15:3; Ex 18:3), and in Deuteronomy 24:14 it is instructed, 'Do not take advantage of a hired worker who is poor and needy, whether that worker is a fellow Israelite or a foreigner residing in one of your towns'.

Within Christian Reformed circles, the view on women and their place in society has brought controversy, as some attain a strict biblicist vantage point (Vorster 2017a). The Old Testament contains copious entries that on the surface may describe women as inferior in society when compared to their male counterparts. Examples of such readings are Exodus 20:17, where women are perceived as the husband's property likened with other physical assets, and in Numbers 30:4–5, the woman's legal capacities are explained as limited and secondary. It should however be noted that these references are all from the post-fall human state, as in Genesis 1:27, it is shown how God created both woman and man with equal value, equal creational significance, and 'in his own image'.

The New Testament, significantly changes and augments women's position in society. This as for example exhibited, in Galatians 3:26–27: 'So in Christ Jesus you are all children of God through faith, for all of you who were baptised into Christ have clothed yourselves with Christ'. Vorster (2017a) explains how this passage represents a clear expression of the New Testament ethos of gender equality.

Vorster (2017a) outlines how within certain biblicist groups, the increasing trend is to accept gender-based inequalities, and he points to how churches of our time continue the unjust practices of the past. Further, the New Testament abounds with examples of women being given the most important societal and religious tasks imaginable. For example, it was women who were the first to meet the risen Christ (Mk 16:9; Jn 20:14), who were appointed to notify the disciples of the resurrection (Jn 20:17) and not least, it was a woman who gave birth to and raised Christ in this world (Bøsterud 2019a). Further from the New Testament, it can be argued that Galatians 3:28 was a revolutionary expression depicting the complete dismantling of all forms of social hierarchical superiority and the inauguration of a new foundation for human relationships. The argument then is that Galatians 3:28, as contextually seen *tota Scriptura*, renders a valuable vantage point on the equality of all humans and this perspective offers a scaffolding for the global value of equality. This relationship will be valid between all, irrespective of gender and therefore, to limit the rights of women in any way cannot find justification in a *tota Scriptura* reading of Scripture (Vorster 2019).

Because of the above, and in particular the New Testament sources and Vorster's position, it is the contention here that to promote societal inequality on the basis of gender, race, religion, age, disability or any other marginalising characteristics, cannot be defended in a Reformed theology. To discriminate against any societal group, no matter for what reason, will then be considered immoral. The conclusion is, then, that to promote societal equality among all groups and individuals is the only acceptable moral norm pertaining to equal rights.

Working conditions

Another area of particular interest to banking is that of fair wages and working conditions. In the UN's Declaration of Human Rights (United Nations n.d.), it is stated in Article 23 (3) that '[e]veryone who works has the right to just and favourable remuneration ensuring for himself and his family an existence worthy of human dignity', and in Article 24 (United Nations n.d.) that '[e]veryone has the right to rest and leisure, including reasonable limitation of working hours and periodic holidays with pay'.

The quotes are a suitable vantage point from which to explore scriptural sources pertaining to fair wages. Romans 4:4 states: 'Now to the one who works, wages are not credited as a gift but as an obligation', and from this it can be inferred that to receive a wage is a right for the worker, and this is also expressed clearly in Leviticus 19:13, 'Do not defraud or rob your neighbour. Do not hold back the wages of a hired worker overnight'. From this quote, it can be inferred that holding back wages is akin to robbery, indicating the legitimacy of the worker's claim for his wage. In Luke 3:4, the instruction to the soldiers is to 'be content with your pay'. This instruction indicates that not only wages are due, but also that by mentioning 'contentment', it can be inferred that the level of the wage would be sufficient for on which the worker (soldier) and his dependants can subsist. How else could they be instructed to be content?

Connected to rest and leisure time, we know from Genesis 2:3 that 'God blessed the seventh day and made it holy, because on it he rested from all the work of creating that he had done'. That rest from work is obligatory in Scripture is further demonstrated in Exodus 20:9–10, 'Six days you shall labour and do all your work, but the seventh day is a sabbath to the Lord your God. On it you shall not do any work'. There can be no doubt, the provision in UN's declaration Article 24, is well aligned with scriptural norms, and thus, respecting rest and leisure time is in concert with Christian- ethical principles.

Calvin, commenting on the eighth commandment (Ex 20:15), addresses the topic of wages from the angle of the rich oppressing the poor. He (Calvin 2012) explains:

> But not to dwell too long in enumerating the different classes, we know that all the arts by which we obtain possession of the goods and money of our neighbours, for sincere affection substituting an eagerness to deceive and injure them in any way, are to be regarded as thefts. Though they may be obtained by an action at law, a different decision is given by God. He sees the long train of deception by which the man of craft begins to lay nets for his more simple neighbour, until he entangles himself in its meshes. (*Inst.* 2.8.45)

The above quote illustrates Calvin's stance on oppression of the poor, and he found several expressions of this in his contemporary Geneva, where wealthy traders took advantage of the poor, not least migrant workers escaping poverty in other places (Valeri 1997). As will appear then, although Calvin viewed capitalism positively in a moderate and constructive form, his stance was one that did not promote exploitation of the weak.

From the above sources, and with particular weight given to Calvin's teachings, the position here is that under the Reformed paradigm, to deprive workers of a fair level of wages or reasonable rest and leisure must be seen as immoral, and as violating responsible biblical interpretation. The ethical norm is that workers' rights to rest and leisure time and to receive fair wages for their work, to a degree where they can support themselves and their dependants with dignity needs to be promoted, respected and protected.

Child labour

Another issue of particular practical interest to consider is the use of child labour. That children participate in the working force is unfortunately very common on a global scale, and according to UN statistics, in 2008 there were approximately 208 million children aged 5–17 involved in industrial production, depriving them of the childhood that is taken for granted by most in the West. Of these children, approximately 115 million were involved in hazardous work, implying that they participate in what the UN terms 'the worst forms of child labour' (United Nations n.d.). The statistics further tell us that by sector, child labourers work in agriculture (60%), in services (25.6%), in industry (7%) and in undefined sectors (7.5%).

Child labour is touched on in Article 4 of the UN Declaration of Human Rights (United Nations n.d.), where it is declared that '[n]o one shall be held in slavery or servitude; slavery and the slave trade shall be prohibited in all their forms'. In Article 26 (1), it is stated that (United Nations n.d.) '[e]ducation shall be free, at least in the elementary and fundamental stages. Elementary education shall be compulsory'.

It follows from the above quotes that the espoused values will not allow for children to partake in a professional, market-based or industrial workforce, and it represents responsible interpretation to conclude that children have a right to enjoy childhood. Of particular scriptural significance here, I find the passage in Matthew 19:14: 'Jesus said, "Let the little children come to me, and do not hinder them, for the kingdom of heaven belongs to such as these"'. In addition, Romans 9:12, '[t]he older will serve the younger'. These quotes explain how no person should be 'hindered' in experiencing faith, and furthermore, it is the duty of the parents and society to care for the children, and not the opposite. These quotes illustrate how Scripture guarantees children preservation from harm, and a protected position in society.

Calvin's authorship does not contain much directly pertaining to the lives of children, and often, 'children' is in his writings used as a metaphor for humanity. There are however some passages where children are considered not only metaphorical, such as in his *Letter to Viret 1842* (Calvin 1542):

> The Lord has certainly inflicted a severe and bitter wound in the death of our infant son. But he is himself a Father, and knows best what is good for his children. (n.p.)

Another passage where children are considered is found in *Commentary on Psalms V*, where Calvin (1849b) explains that:

> [U]nless men regard their children as the gift of God, they are careless and reluctant in providing for their support, just as on the other hand this knowledge contributes in a very eminent degree to encourage them in bringing up their offspring. Farther, he who thus reflects upon the goodness of God in giving him children, will readily and with a settled mind look for the continuance of God's grace. (p. 96)

Furthermore, the quote taken from Calvin above in 6.9.7 with regard to taking advantage of the less fortunate, may also illuminate a vantage point on child labour (Calvin 2012:*Inst.* 2.8.45). While Calvin berated how adults in poor situations were being taken advantage of by the better positioned, it is challenging to imagine how he would condone exploitive practices of any kind connected to children.

As education is a value mentioned in the UN's Declaration as touched upon in the section on 'The human rights construct', it is of interest to peruse some scriptural sources pertaining to children's education. Daniel 1:17 relates to the young and learning, and reads, 'To these four young men God gave knowledge and understanding of all kinds of literature and learning', and Ecclesiastes 7:12 states that 'Wisdom is a shelter as money is a shelter, but the advantage of knowledge is this: Wisdom preserves those who have it'. From these quotes, it is clear that educating children is a central Christian value, not least as

Scriptural foundations

knowledge is attributed higher value than material possessions. To deprive anyone, and children in particular, of education would thus not be aligned with Scripture.

It is frequently discussed whether moderate use of child labour can be beneficial to individuals and societies, and in particular to societies undergoing economic development. The argument is that child labour can lead to the development of human resources previously not existing with the individual or the society, so that, to a certain degree, child labour can contribute to the alleviation of poverty in developing economies. However, research is scarce and ambiguous; so, to hastily conclude that child labour carries some benefits cannot be substantiated in any viable form (Akabayashi & Psacharopoulos 1999). The position here is clear: children have a right to childhood and this right must be respected at all times and under all circumstances.

The scriptural quotes and cited sources above have shown that child labour cannot be seen as beneficial for the involved children. The biblical position, in conjunction with Calvin's warning against exploiting the unfortunate, leads to the conclusion that to benefit from or promote child labour would be immoral, and that it should always be avoided.

Senior constituency

When humans reach old age they can also be in a weak position and in need of special protection and attention. This is of importance in the setting here, as senior citizens to a large extent participate in the work force, but also, that they can be discriminated against in acts of 'ageism', and pushed out of professional life and consequently lose their ability to fend for themselves. To this should be noted the fact that in developing and emerging nations, for the elderly to continue working after retirement age is a way to fend off poverty rather than a choice. In low-income countries, this is the case, as less than 20% of the senior population receive pensions (International Labour Office 2017).

In the UN Declaration (United Nations n.d.) it is stated that:

> Everyone has the right to a standard of living adequate for the health and well-being of himself ... in the event of ... old age or other lack of livelihood in circumstances beyond his control. (art. 25[1])

It will be clear from this provision that the elderly have the right to fully contribute to society, and that this will include partaking in the work force and being able to include a life on dignity.

That we are to respect seniority and our seniors is already evident from the fifth commandment: 'Honour your father and your mother, so that you may live long in the land the Lord your God is giving you' (Ex 20:12). Not only for this command, but also elsewhere in Scripture there is ample support for respecting, including and honouring the seniors of society, as this is among core traditional Christian values. For example, in Proverbs 16:31 we learn that 'Gray hair is a crown of splendour; it is attained in the way of righteousness', and in Job 12:12, the following leading questions are asked: 'Is not wisdom found among the aged? Does not long life bring understanding?' Our obligation to include and care for the seniors will be evident from Psalms 71:9, 'Do not cast me away when I am old; do not forsake me when my strength is gone' From the New Testament we are for example informed in 1 Timothy 5:1 that 'Do not rebuke an older man harshly, but exhort him as if he were your father', and 2 Corinthians 4:16, explains 'Though outwardly we are wasting away, yet inwardly we are being renewed day by day'. The quoted biblical passages are but a very small sample of what are numerous scriptures that will underscore the point here, we are to respect, include, honour and care for the senior members of society, at all levels and in all realms of life, and not honouring this obligation will be immoral.

It is clear that the ethos of the human rights declaration is aligned with scriptural norms, and that such provisions are necessary is well picked up in the academic field of gerontology, where the concept of ageism has been coined and is compared to that of racism. This in the sense that ageist attitudes stereotype the elderly, and imply they have nothing to contribute in society and that those who have lived far for some years somehow are different from the rest of the population. Sadly, such attitudes are prevalent in larger groups of Western society, and this is something that needs to be addressed and rectified (Butler 1969; Moss 1995). Clearly, to practice ageism in the workplace or in any other social arena is immoral.

Following the above, it can be concluded that the inclusion of the elderly on all societal arenas is aligned with core Christian norms and needs to be promoted, respected and protected.

Private property ownership

For civil society, the respect of private ownership to property, of any kind, is of core importance for allowing the society to function in an orderly manner where individuals will be able to benefit from the fruits of their labour and capital. The concept of private property as held by individuals has been touched upon in Chapters 2 and 3, and as this was a creation of the Roman antiquity, it will be important to note that the concept is not connected to humanity as a law of nature, but rather, that it is a social construct for developing wealth in society, and, a concept where ownership to assets may be reached by each societal constituent as a result of their efforts. This of course if other societal institutions will not create barriers for such ownership, or, as in some well-known cases like that of the communist countries in the post-World War II era in Europe and elsewhere, governments worked against the concept of private ownership, or outright forbade it (Howard-Hassmann & Donnelly 1986; Markussen 2008).

When formulating the UN Declaration of Human Rights, the principle of respecting private ownership was recognised as worthy of being protected as a universal human right, and is formulated in Article 17 as:

1. Everyone has the right to own property alone as well as in association with others.

2. No one shall be arbitrarily deprived of his property.

This part of the declaration was not in complete concert with the societal order and moral political values among all signatories, and, Article 17 is one of the human rights that has been used to undergird the line of criticism of the UN declaration as being Western-centric, and thus, lacking in universal value (Griffin 2008). This criticism is unfounded, because as the concept of private ownership may not be guaranteed in any societal order or political dispensation, this will not make the concept a typical Western one, as also in the Western world throughout history the citizens have been arbitrarily deprived of their properties by way of expropriations and other forms of third-party arrogations from governments or other institutions, at times labelled as taxation. That this was viewed as problematic and in conflict with democratic thought in modernity is evidenced for example in the Norwegian Constitution of 1814, which in its section 105 on eminent domain guarantees property rights and freedom from arbitrary appropriations, and where any expropriations are taking place they need to be fully compensated by the state (Constitution 1814).

Although society as depicted in the Old Testament can largely be described as a traditionalist society where the individual filled roles based on tradition rather than on individual traits, and as such did not enjoy individual rights to the same degree as we in the later Western tradition have come to know, the concept of private property was well-known (Howard-Hassmann & Donnelly 1986). However, private property in this historical state would not necessarily be considered as solely belonging to the individual, but rather (also) to the tribe or group. Thus, the position of private property in the Old Testament may have been connected to the tribe through tradition, and not only to the individual, and in the ultimate sense the land of Israel belonged to God, as explained in Leviticus 25:23: 'the land is mine and you are but aliens and my tenants'. Despite this derived position of ownership, there is no doubt that property could be held privately, as it appears in Leviticus 25:25 that property generally may be sold, and in 25:29, where it is explained that 'a house in a walled city' may be sold. That not only real property is protected as private property appears for example in Proverbs 19:14, 'Houses and wealth are inherited from parents', as well as in Proverbs 14:23, where it appears about industriousness that 'All hard work brings a profit, but mere talk leads only to poverty'. Clearly then, in the Old Testament ethos, property could be held by private actors both as individuals and as groups. Further, it will be clear from the language and contexts used in the Old Testament that private property was enjoyed and accepted, and the concept of ownership permeates the Old Testament, as for example the word *Nachalah* – 'possession, property, inheritance' occurs no less than 224 times (Battle 2008). It would be a responsible interpretation to view all human ownership to any type of property, real or movable, as resulting from being rewarded by God the ultimate owner, and, that private ownership thus must be respected and revered, both by the owners who are given dominion over the owned goods, as well as by other societal actors (Kaiser 2012).

The concept of private property in the Old Testament is also described as an exclusive position, and there is no doubt that a property would be protected against the uses of the non-owners, as follows not least from the eight commandment, 'You shall not steal' (Ex 20:15; Dt 5:19). Further, this exclusiveness appears in several other Old Testament passages, like for example in Deuteronomy 27:17 'Cursed is anyone who moves their neighbour's boundary stone', and in Exodus 22:3 'Anyone who steals must certainly make restitution'.

In the New Testament era, the concept of private property ownership had been further cemented through the Roman developments of individual private property rights in the legal system and through mercantile practice. Therefore, when looking for passages of property in the New Testament, it will be of importance to note that not only are the main subject matters therein of a different character than in the Old Testament, but also, the market oriented Roman economy that relied on the respect of ownership rights may be seen as presupposed. For example, when Jesus in Mark 10:23 states 'How hard it is for the rich to enter the kingdom of God!', it is the love of money that is at the centre of attention and not money itself, as will appear when seen in conjunction with 1 Timothy 6:10 'For the love of money is a root of all kinds of evil'. The two parallel parables of Matthew 25:14–30 and Luke 19:11–27, where the servants of the absent master are entrusted with managing the master's wealth, and the more successful the management the more praise is bestowed on the servant at the master's return, clearly describes that private property is accepted by Christ, and that prudent stewardship of God's material gifts will be rewarded.

Calvin worked in Geneva at a time when it had already become a centre for commerce and banking and was concerned with socio-economic matters, not least on how the rich treated the poor. As part of this focus, Calvin elaborates on private property ownership in his authorship, and he viewed this under the doctrine of the common grace of God. As mentioned above, all wealth and goods we as humans possess are enjoyed as gifts from God. Calvin elaborates on this in light of Exodus 16:9–18, where the Israelites were fed manna and quail, as this reveals how possessing something, like foodstuffs, heightens our relationship and knowledge of God. Calvin (1852a) expounds on this that:

> [F]or it is necessary for the preservation of human society that each should possess what is his own; that some should acquire property by purchase, that to others it should come by hereditary right, to others by the title of presentation, that each should increase his means in proportion to his diligence, or bodily strength, or other qualifications. (p. 255)

That privately owned possessions flow from the bounty of God and were to be protected by civil society was clear for Calvin (1849a), and he explained on this that:

> He who acquires rejoices, and he who is compelled to sell suffers some degree of sorrow; and sometimes the man who is deprived of his lands and possessions tears out as it were his own entrails. It is natural therefore for the buyer to rejoice, and for the seller to lament. (p. 260)

Calvin's clear stance on the individual's right to own property privately and exclusively may be seen against the position of the Anabaptists, who in Calvin's time promoted the principle of communally-owned property, and also against the contemporaneous feudal societies that did not protect and respect the right of individuals to own property. Thus, Calvin brought forward theologically founded principles of private rights of property ownership to be protected by civil authorities that would prove to be of substantial importance for the further development of the civil and political order in Geneva and France (Forster 1995; Vorster 2017a). The idea that communally-owned property aligns with Christian moral norms in a superior manner as opposed to the individual and privately held ownership is by some Christian thinkers drawn from Acts 2:44–45 'All the believers were together and had everything in common. They sold property and possessions to give to anyone who had need', and Acts 4:32, where it appears that in the Jerusalem church 'No one claimed that any of their possessions was their own, but they shared everything they had'. A Christian preference for communally held property cannot responsibly be inferred from the passages; however, a prudent interpretation would be that what is described is a way of jointly managing their properties, and that the members showed selflessness in making their goods available for the church. There are however no indications that legal or otherwise binding structures were put in place which would deny the church members to hold property as privately and exclusively owned. In other words, to propose that private property ownership is not fully aligned with the Christian message, and that forms of communal ownership would be somehow preferential, like in communist ideology for example, cannot be defended from scriptural interpretation (Douma 1996; Negus 1995).

On the basis of the scriptural quotes and theological positions of the authors referenced above, it can be concluded that private property ownership is aligned with core Christian norms and needs to be promoted, respected and protected.

Government – Civil disobedience

Banking practitioners need to consider whether to be involved with states that do not have or do not promote sufficient democratic rights for their citizens. For convenience here, the term 'democracy' is used several times in this treatise, but it should be noted that the term may include several degrees of freedom, and that the traditional Western liberal democracy in this treatise may serve as a loose template for what could be an ideal. Often, political conflicts lead to different levels of blockade and embargo, which was the case with apartheid South Africa, and the US embargo of Cuba may serve as an example as well (Cain 1994; Coulibaly 2009). For banking actors, it may not be sufficient to rely on formal political embargoes to guide their decisions, but assessments of the states and countries that are involved should be performed on an individual basis. Therefore, in the following text scriptural sources on government and civil disobedience are explored, as it is expected that both of these perspectives are able to shed valuable light on where and with whom bankers should engage.

That humanity should live in a state free from oppression was of the utmost value when the UN Declaration (United Nations n.d.) was authored, and already in the preamble, the following is stated:

> Whereas it is essential, if man is not to be compelled to have recourse, as a last resort, to rebellion against tyranny and oppression, that human rights should be protected by the rule of law. (n.p.)

There can be no doubt then, that in the ethos of the Declaration, the loyalty and obedience populations and individuals are to show to their governments is limited. This not least when relating to unjust regimes, something that would have been all too familiar in the aftermath of World War II when the Declaration was pronounced.

To be loyal to government is promoted in several instances in Scripture, and a typical quote to examine is Romans 13:1, which states, 'Let everyone be subject to the governing authorities, for there is no authority except that which God has established. The authorities that exist have been established by God'. This direct and powerful statement is mirrored in Titus 3:1: 'Remind the people to be subject to rulers and authorities, to be obedient, to be ready to do whatever is good'. From these quotes it could superficially be extrapolated that citizens always need to obey their governments, and that any disobedience or revolt is wrong. This starting point is modified, however, in Psalm 22:28, which instructs us that 'dominion belongs to the Lord and he rules over the nations', and in Acts 5:29, 'We must obey God rather than human beings!'

From these quotes, it would appear that citizens are not obligated to follow their government in all its commands, and that it may, in fact, be immoral to do so if governmental instructions go against the will of God.

Luke's nativity narrative reports Augustus' assertion of power as the first Roman emperor, through an empire-wide census of all its citizens. This event expresses an extreme exertion of governmental influence, as all citizens would then become taxable and controllable (Lo Cascio 1994). When Herod wanted to kill the new Messiah, the Magi 'outwitted' him (Mt 2:16) by returning 'to their country by another route' (Mt 2:12). This shows that to disobey government can be moral, and indeed, an obligation. Further support for this scriptural position may be taken form Exodus 1:17, where the 'the midwives … feared God and did not do what the king of Egypt had told them to do'. For this passive resistance, God rewarded the midwives and 'gave them families of their own' (Ex 1:20).

As a summing up of the scriptural stance on government, and their due loyalty, a clarification is given in Romans 13:7, 'Give to everyone what you owe them: if you owe taxes, pay taxes; if revenue, then revenue; if respect, then respect; if honour, then honour'. From this passage, we are again reminded that our main obligation is to God and his laws, and that our obligated loyalty to governments stretches only as far as what is instructed within the limitations of God's realm and authority.

Calvin's position on government and civil disobedience was based on a literal reading of Romans 13, and in principle, he advocated almost blind loyalty toward government, no matter what its merit or democratic quality. A suitable extract from his writing (Calvin 2012) on this topic could be the following:

> Let no man here deceive himself, since we cannot resist the magistrate without resisting God. For, although an unarmed magistrate may seem to be despised with immunity, yet God is armed, and will signally avenge this attempt. (pp. 4, 20, 23)

From these direct words, Calvin does modify, however, and sees rulers as God's agents, and his expectation is that they be just. If not so, in his thinking, unjust rulers may be overthrown, in a suitable punishment from God, and on the abuse of power, he (Calvin 2012) states:

> So far am I from forbidding these officially to check the undue licenses of kings, that if they connive at kings when they tyrannize and insult over the humbler of the people, I affirm that their dissimulation is not free from nefarious perfidy, because they fraudulently betray the liberty of the people, while knowing that, by the ordinance of God, they are its appointed guardians. (pp. 4, 20, 31)

Geisler (2010) elaborates different positions of practical and political character pertaining to the contemporary real-life application of the above teachings and scriptural quotes. He explains three principally different views:

- **Radical patriotism.** Among the most extreme biblicists, the view is that of radical patriotism, where the obligation of the citizens is to obey their government under all circumstances and adhere to all its edicts. The rationale is that it is commanded by God in Scripture. Pragmatically, this position shuns any revolt or revolutions, and will most likely be for the benefit of stability in society, and not least, of its weakest constituents. For the radical patriot, central scriptural support emerges from Romans 13:2: 'Consequently, whoever rebels against the authority is rebelling against what God has instituted, and those who do so will bring judgement on themselves', which then is understood as conclusive for all circumstances.
- **Antipromulgation position.** The proponents of this line claim that it is the right of citizens to disobey the government whenever the given laws or instructions are seen as contrary to God's word. This line would reflect that of the more radical liberation theology, which advocates that Christians and the church should take an active part in the shaping of a more just society. This ideology was prevalent among Catholics in Latin America in the 1960s and 1970s and beyond. This radical movement took its cue from the situation in Latin America at the time and declared that, in the past, the church had sided with the powerful and thus contributed to the ongoing oppression of the poor. This line of theology perceives Scripture as a liberation narrative, with particular focus on the liberation of Israel from Egypt's bondage, the prophets' rebuking of oppression and Jesus' proclamation of good news to the marginalised (Gutiérrez & Muller 2015; McGrath 2011).
- **Anticompulsionist position.** Under this stance, the citizens are given the opportunity to resist their government only when their rulers compel the citizens to perform evil. If an instruction is merely against God's laws, resistance cannot be justified under this paradigm.

Geisler's further explanation on the suitable Christian position seems to indicate a stance somewhere in between the position of antipromulgation and anticompulsion. Geisler seems, however, to be drawn to the side of the biblicist stance of radical patriotism, as he perceives the American Revolution, for example, as unjust.

On the basis of the above sources, it would be responsible to conclude that the Reformed position on government and civil obedience is that civil disobedience is sometimes permitted, and that sometimes it is also an obligation to disobey government. From Matthew 2:12, we learn that passive resistance as performed by the Magi can be preferred, and this resonates well with the position of Geisler (2010), that violence and anarchy should be avoided, as these will seldom benefit the weak in society. It must be concluded then, that the ethical norm is that to promote evil and unjust governments must be seen as immoral and should always be avoided.

Scriptural foundations

■ Nature and ecology
Context

As human activity necessarily impacts nature, to assess banking practice from the perspective of ecology is important. Several of the possible options for financial participation pertain to manufacturing, chemical production, infrastructure development, real estate development and industrial farming, to mention but a few that may influence the natural environment.

Animal welfare

Human interaction with animals has traditionally been in the context of hunting, farming or leisure, and the modern aspects of industrial farming and research laboratories have not been areas of much ethical concern. In recent decades, the question of how we treat animals, and indeed, whether animals themselves have rights is controversial, and will benefit from being viewed from a Christian vantage point. In this treatise, the term 'animal' will include all living organisms, such as land and sea mammals, birds, fish, crustaceans, insects, et cetera.

From Genesis 1:26-27, we understand how humans alone were created in 'the image of God' and it is typically perceived in an exclusionary fashion, only relating to the human family. Even though animals may not be seen as created in God's image, this does not dismiss the human duties towards them. In Genesis 1:28 it is explained how we should 'fill the earth and subdue it. Rule over the fish in the sea and the birds in the sky and over every living creature that moves on the ground'. The words 'subdue' and 'rule' may describe our commission to rule the natural environment and everything in it (Geisler 2010). Although humanity is authorised to rule over other living creatures, from Psalm 24:1 we learn that 'the earth is the LORD'S, and everything in it, the world, and all who live in it'. Here, the human stewardship duties towards nature are clarified, and instead of attaining a mentality of use and exploitation towards nature, we understand how we are obligated by God to care for all aspects of creation (Kearns 1996).

When searching for Calvin's stance on animal welfare, we find animals mentioned frequently in his authorship, and not least in his creation theology. Some critics of Calvin find his use of animal and natural metaphors as purely decorative, that his theology of creation is either anthropocentric of theanthropocentric and that his theology made way for the massive desacralisation of nature that has happened in modernity. This could not be further from the truth, and with careful reading of Calvin's authorship, we will find that Calvin's theology engages with the natural world in a much closer manner than present in many modern theologies on creation. Although Calvin may not be seen as in complete concert with 21st century Eco theologies, his theology does not include the anthropocentrism represented in vast tracts of mainstream Christian creation theologies on animals and nature. Calvin did not contemplate a role for animals in God's redemptive plans, but he placed animals at the fore in his theology and authorship, something that reveals how non-human creatures played a pivotal role in his theological inspiration (Deane-Drummond 2008; Huff 1999). This vivid animal imagery is for example present in Calvin's (1849c) *Commentary on Romans*, where he informs:

> Thus the condemnation of mankind is imprinted on the heavens, and on the earth, and on all creatures. It hence also appears to what excelling glory the sons of God shall be exalted; for all creatures shall be renewed in order to amplify it, and to render it illustrious. But he means not that all creatures shall be partakers of the same glory with the sons of God; but that they, according to their nature, shall be participators of a better condition; for God will restore to a perfect state the world, now fallen, together with mankind. (pp. 264–265)

The utilitarian Bentham, as explained above, had as his ethos that the good human acts were those that increased happiness. As we have seen, happiness in this thinking was not merely confined to humans, and animals were equally recognised as being able to experience happiness and pain. Already in Bentham's time, the topic of animals and their cognitive faculties was being discussed, and to some, it was of importance whether animals could think or not, to decide whether we at all needed to consider how to treat them. For Bentham, however, the question was 'not, Can they *reason?* nor, Can they *talk?* but, Can they *suffer?*' (Bentham 1907). An important clarification that sheds further light on the matter is made by Regan (1985), who explains that animals may be subjected to suffering both by being actively inflicted with harm, and by being deprived of necessary means to fulfil physical needs and satisfaction.

In contemporary philosophical discourse, Singer (1995) has become the main proponent of promoting animal welfare, and, to him, it would be pertinent to award rights to animals akin with human rights. He builds his arguments mainly on the animals' capacity for feeling pain and suffering and uses examples from research and factory farming to elicit sympathy for his philosophical stance. His argumentation fails on some points, as he seems to ignore the principle that if someone has rights, others have corresponding obligations to honour them. Such obligations would then rest with humans, and the point to argue should rather be what obligations humans have towards animals and their suffering, and from where such obligations may be drawn. For a utilitarian like Singer, the problem then becomes that there is no higher authority from which to instil obligations in humans, so his focus needs to stay solely on the rights side of the discourse. Waldau (2006), on the other hand, examines the connection between religion and concern for animals, and his outlook is more positive, as he recognises that several world religions acknowledge the plight of some animals, and that it is human responsibility to care for nature, including our fellow beings, animals.

Scriptural foundations

The theological stance that humans are obligated to exert responsible dominion over animals is a widely accepted position among Christians, still, there are those who claim that Christian life and religious adherence prescribe veganism. This position is scripturally founded, and is explained through that in Eden, the only available foods for humans were plant-based, and that this was under instruction from God as expressed in Genesis 1:29: 'Then God said, "I give you every seed-bearing plant on the face of the whole earth and every tree that has fruit with seed in it. They will be yours for food"'. The perception under this paradigm will be that consuming animal-based food is a post-fall phenomenon in the history of humanity (Gn 9:3), and in conflict with the Edenic diet that was originally prescribed for humans (Calvert 2008; Wirzba 2019). This hard-line vegan position is not aligned to by all proponents of Christian vegetarianism, and some posit that we cannot know from scriptural sources if Jesus consumed meat. However, there are solid indications in Scripture pointing to Jesus eating fish (Horrell 2008).

Suggestions of fish consumption are found in the narratives where Jesus feeds the many (e.g. Mt 14:13–21; Mk 6:31–44), and in the miraculous catch (Jn 21:6; Lk 5:4–7). These narratives may not positively describe Jesus consuming fish, but it is a viable interpretation to infer that he did not reject the eating of fish. Furthermore, in Mark 7:19, it is described how Jesus discarded the food laws of the Hebrew scriptures. From Romans 14:3 we understand how the early Christian were concerned with dietary matters: 'The one who eats everything must not treat with contempt the one who does not, and the one who does not eat everything must not judge the one who does, for God has accepted them'. Furthermore, Romans 14:6 explains 'whoever eats meat does so to the Lord, for they give thanks to God; and whoever abstains does so to the Lord and gives thanks to God'.

When read in conjunction, the above scriptural locations explain the stance that for Christians, it is fully acceptable to consume foods based both on animals and plants. However, it must be emphasised, that choosing a vegan lifestyle is wholly acceptable for any Christian. In my view, this is a viable position, and to focus on the human obligation rather than the rights of other creatures places responsibility where it is due. In fact, it may be argued, as in Bøsterud (2019b), that not only do we as humans have an obligation to care for our fellow beings from creation, the animals, in accordance with our stewardship obligations as stipulated in Scripture, but also that we as individuals are so bound to such religious obligations that being denied the opportunities to honour them may be a breach of our human rights as Christians. The cognition then is that as individual consumers, if we are not able to consume animal-based foodstuffs or other products in a manner which aligns with the stewardship obligations as set out in Genesis 1:28 and Psalm 24:1, we are in reality being denied our rights to live and practise as Christians, which is a right guaranteed in the UN Declaration of

Human Rights, Article 18 (United Nations n.d.). We have seen that Singer's theories are tainted with the lack of higher authority to care for nature, thus his focus on awarding rights, but this problem is solved within the realm of Scripture through the human obligation toward nature as God's caretakers. Animals have no other way to protect themselves than through the obligation of humans, and through these obligations, animals do not need to be subjected to imposed artificial rights. Bentham's focus on the capacity to suffer, and the corresponding human obligation not to inflict suffering, would be a pertinent norm for the Reformed dispensation. This will also entail that we refrain from certain practices when in contact with animals, whether connected to commercial production, science, education or recreational activities such as hunting, fishing and keeping pets. It must particularly be noted that killing or hurting animals for human entertainment is always immoral, something that includes practices connected to recreational catch-and-release fishing, recreational hunting, bullfighting, cock fighting, feeding with live animals and sadly, much more. In relation to hunting and fishing, it is the entertainment aspect that must be seen as affronting God in creation, through the forfeiting of the human stewardship obligation as explained above, as when such activities are performed by groups who live a basic lifestyles where hunting and fishing is necessary for their sustenance, it will not be against God's plans for creation. However, under such circumstances the hunters and fishers are always obligated not to inflict any unnecessary pain on their prey. Furthermore, when keeping animals for pets, we are still under the absolute stewardship obligation where the infliction of pain and possible deprivation of their natural needs are seen as an unacceptable and immoral practice, and this will pertain to all forms of keeping, breeding, feeding and trading in pets.

The conclusion for the purposes of this treatise would be that the human obligation is to care for animals and not to inflict suffering on them, and not to deprive them of their basic, natural needs.

The natural environment

From the above section, it appears that humanity has a stewardship duty for nature, because it belongs to God and not us (Ps 24:1). In 1 Timothy 4:4, nature is expounded as good: 'For everything God created is good, and nothing is to be rejected if it is received with thanksgiving'. Seen in concert with the human caretaking commission over nature (Gn 1:28) it becomes clear how we are nature's stewards. Genesis 2:15, explains the keeper duties: 'The Lord God took the man and put him in the Garden of Eden to work it and take care of it'. To be assigned stewardship over nature makes us the keepers of God's gifts, and not the exploiters of them. These duties are also explicated in 1 Corinthians 4:2, 'Now it is required that those who have been given a trust must prove faithful' and Job 41:11, where God informs Job, 'Everything under heaven belongs to me'.

Calvin (2012) was a seminal thinker who appreciated the natural environment, and how this perfection was to be seen as an extension of God's glory and infallibility. Consider for example his (Calvin 2012) statement:

> The Lord is manifested by his perfections ... Hence it is obvious, that in seeking God, the most direct path and the fittest method is, not to attempt with presumptuous curiosity to pry into his essence, which is rather to be adored than minutely discussed, but to contemplate him in his works, by which he draws near, becomes familiar, and in a manner communicates himself to us. (pp. 64-65)

And in how to handle the perfection that is creation, Calvin (1847) had the following instructions:

> Let him who possesses a field, ... endeavor to hand it down to posterity as he received it, or even better cultivated. ... let every one regard himself as the steward of God in all things which he possesses. (p. 77)

Vorster (2017a) discusses the aspect of human stewardship in nature and argues that important societal institutions need to be involved in caring for the natural environment. Of particular interest for this treatise is his position that as corporations and their stakeholders benefit from the natural environment, they should be responsible for establishing a balance between production and environmental impact and pollution. He continues that a portion of corporate profits should be set aside for the alleviation of its harmful effects on the environment, and that this is a special concern in developing countries. This means that industrial activity needs to be environmentally sustainable over the longer term, and in particular, corporate stakeholders should be expected to consider the poor and unfortunate in this world. Geisler (2010) supports the above position on humans' obligation to care for nature and contends that if we sin against God's creation, we also sin against ourselves and our fellow humans, as this is God's earth, and it is needed to sustain ourselves and our brothers and sisters, including those of the future.

From the above sources, the conclusion must be that we as humans have the obligation to care for nature and exert prudent stewardship of our natural environment, and that to contribute to its destruction in any form is immoral.

Bioethical challenges

Connected to nature and ecology, it will have become clear both from the elaborations on animal welfare and pollution, that humans as part of creation do not only have a part in nature, but as well have been given the task of stewardship (Gn 1:28). Biomedical challenges have been raised in the section on 'Biomedical challenges', but there mainly relating to human beings and our integrity in creation. In connection with animal welfare and the natural environment, it will be of utmost importance to reiterate the scepticism raised against modern-day scientific abuse of nature, by way of gene splicing, gene modifying organisms, as well as species creation, introductions of alien species and more, will raise as many objections as those of biomedical character concerned to humans. Some of such disruptions of the natural environment, be they resultant of commercial or scientific activity, may be intentional, whereas others may be side effects of human interventions where the natural world has not been perceived sufficiently important to consider (Sutton 2008).

Although bioethical challenges we experience today did not appear in Calvin's time, it will be clear from his quotes connected to animal welfare (Calvin 1849c:264–265) and the natural environment (Calvin 1847:77, 2012:64–65), that nature and its conservation was emphasized in his theology as a matter of morality. For the contemporary Christian then, it should be noted that it was not necessary for Calvin to experience the horrific destruction of the natural environment we are witnessing now, nor to be frightened by claims of climate change, looming ecological disasters and more, for him to care for the natural environment as handed to us through creation.

There can be no doubt then, that any form of bio-scientific disruption of nature, no matter in what form it comes is immoral.

■ Societal morality

Context

Many opportunities open to the banking sector will influence societal morality, by way of promoting or counteracting values pertaining to family life and moral values connected to family, the individual and society.

Family

That family values are central to Christians may not need much documentation, but modern mass consumption, marketing and mass media are areas where the bankers can be expected to participate, and to elaborate some sources of the Christian perception of family is necessary.

God created humans to belong together in pairs, and the family is the obvious theme in Genesis 1:27; 'male and female he created them', and it was from this beginning that humankind should 'be fruitful and increase in number' (Gn 1:28). The natural manner in which this propagation was to happen was through marriage, between woman and man as evidenced in Genesis 2:24, 'That is why a man leaves his father and mother and is united to his wife, and they become one flesh'. There can be no doubt, there can be found no foundation in Scripture for same-sex marriages, and the augmented media attention given to the gay and so-called Lesbian, Gay, Bisexual and Transgender (LGBT) movement is completely without any biblical support. Furthermore, it will be clear that same-sex marriage is against the concept of family as described in the Bible, not only through reading the above quote in isolation, but also through a contextual and *tota Scriptura* interpretation of the biblical version of family. Thus, allowing or promoting same-sax marriages and families must be considered immoral, and as counteracting core aspects of the Christian message.

From the New Testament, the most noteworthy expression of family is found in the narrative of Jesus – how he was born into a family situation (Mt 1) and brought up in this social framework. The concept of the traditional family permeates the biblical narratives of both the Old and New Testaments, and is especially noted in Ephesians 3:14–15, 'For this reason I kneel before the Father, from whom every family in heaven and on earth derives its name'. Further, we can learn how Jesus perceived marriage as an unbreakable union between man and woman and of the highest importance, as for example stated in Matthew 19:6 (with reference to Gn 2:24), 'So they are no longer two, but one flesh. Therefore what God has joined together, let no one separate'. From this we learn that marriage is not a civil contract between two individuals, but is a divine bonding.

Calvin (1849d) understood marriage as instituted by God, and its sublime covenantal location in the relationship between God and humanity is described:

> God is the founder of marriage … when a marriage takes place between a man and woman, God presides and requires a mutual pledge from both. Hence Solomon, in Proverbs 2:17, calls marriage the covenant of God, for it is superior to all human contracts. So also Malachi declares, that God is as it were the stipulator, who by his authority joins the man to the woman, and sanctions the alliance. (pp. 556–557)

Kostenberger (2010), a central Christian author on family matters, explains the institution of marriage as derived from Genesis 1–3, as a representative expression of the *imago Dei*, where the unity of man and woman is central in carrying out human responsibilities before God. From this starting point, Kostenberger defends the marriage-centred family as a core Christian value and expresses his worry that the church in contemporary society has relaxed the doctrinal view on the unit that is the family. To him, the weakening of the family and its attendant values that have developed in the secular world is not sufficiently counteracted by the church. He calls for a new, scripturally based strengthening of the marriage-centred family and uses the *imago Dei* doctrine to make his agenda clear.

A contemporary attack on traditional Christian family values comes from the secular acceptance of different modes of homosexual practices, such as promoted in the wider LGBT movement. To discuss homosexuality in detail will fall outside the scope here, but it needs to be pointed out that such practice is condemned persistently throughout both Testaments (e.g. Gn 18–19; Lv 18,20; Rm 1:24–25; 1 Tm 1:10), and thus, that it is considered immoral and as affronting God (Douma 1996; Kostenberger 2010). For the purposes here, it will suffice to say that the desertion of natural sexuality through homosexual practice is morally unacceptable and, that this would be the firm stance under the Reformed paradigm. However, although homosexual practice is sinful, this would not mean that individuals who define themselves as homosexuals should be condemned, but be accepted as full members of the Christian collective if they so wish, and in any case, be viewed as bearers of God's image (Vorster 2007). Homosexual practice is a forgivable offence (1 Cor 6:11), and abstention from such practices will represent homage to the instruction given in 1 Corinthians 6:20, 'Therefore honour God with your bodies'. Without further references or elaboration, it should be safe to establish that, under the Reformed paradigm, the traditional family based on same-sex marriage is a core societal institution that should be promoted, respected and protected, and that to counteract family values must be seen as immoral.

Pornography

With the advent of the Internet, financial involvement in media can be assumed to have reached hitherto unknown levels, and the distribution of information has never before been more efficient than today. Such ease of distribution allows the wide dissemination of pornography, as substantial profits may be generated from this media sector (Rea 2001; Schlosser 2003). Defining what constitutes pornography may not be simple, as individual societal sensibilities differ and change over time, and that there will be an interface against what is considered freedom of artistic expression. This not least as many artistic representations we do not consider pornographic will present nudity and powerful erotic depictions. However, what will typically be considered pornographic will include dehumanizing, aggressive and taboo-braking content and sexual exploitation, often paired with powerful emotive and suggestive media technologies (Court 1995). For the purposes of this treatise, it will not be necessary to define pornography any further, as it is matters of morality that will be at the fore here. I further highlight some sources on the morality of pornography, which would be of interest for banking practice.

To distribute pornography in any modern format was of course not known in biblical times, but sexual immorality is not new, and sources pertaining to this are readily available in Scripture. Hebrews 13:4 urges that 'marriage should be honoured by all, and the marriage bed kept pure, for God will judge the adulterer and all the sexually immoral'. This is a clear statement that extramarital sexual activity is immoral, and thus, that pornography at its core is against God's laws. It can further be argued that viewing and distributing pornography will cultivate lust and adultery as indicated in James 1:4, 'but each person is tempted when they are dragged away by their own evil desire and enticed'. Paul also writes: 'Do not think about how to gratify the desires of the flesh' (Rom 13:14). Furthermore, in 1 John 2:16 we are infirmed that 'the lust of the flesh, the lust of the eyes, and the pride of life – comes not from the Father but from the world', and in Ephesians 4:16, we are instructed not to give ourselves 'over to sensuality so as to indulge in every kind of impurity', and finally, Galatians 5:16 instructs: 'walk by the Spirit, and you will not gratify the desires of the flesh'. Following a responsible interpretation, the scriptural instructions could not be clearer: to indulge ourselves in pornography, or enticing others to do so, is immoral.

Calvin (2012) may not have written about pornography directly, but his views on formication and chastity will illuminate the matter as discussed here. On personal chastity he (Calvin 2012:*Inst.* 2.8.43) states 'the Lord prohibits fornication, therefore he requires purity and chastity'. And on tempting others, 'therefore, while he forbids fornication, he at the same time forbids us to lay snares for our neighbour's chastity by lascivious attire, obscene gestures, and impure conversation' (Calvin 2012:*Inst.* 2.8.44)

Clearly, the above quotes will be directly relevant to pornography, and again, Calvin's thoughts are of value in our contemporary media and societal setting.

The above sources should suffice to demonstrate the biblical stance on pornography, and the position would then be that to consume, produce, distribute or market pornography is immoral.

Gambling

Another business sector that has greatly benefitted from the advent of the Internet and its ease of distributing information is the gambling industry, which holds out great financial rewards for its promotors (Marshall 2003). Gambling can be defined as an activity that involves betting something of material value, where the outcome is not certain and based on chance, and where the transaction leads to gain for one party and a loss for another party. Gambling today is ever present in the West, and there are several avenues for this including: casinos, sports betting, online poker, gambling vending machines, lotteries of different forms and much more. Some of these gambling formats are organised by professional for-profit organisations, while others are organised by governments or NGOs. As with pornography, gambling may greatly affect the well-being of families, the individual and society, and to consider the morality of the sector should be of interest, since its negative effects are well documented, and gambling remains controversial among large tracts of society (Hoffmann 2000). For example, the disastrous effects gambling can have on individuals is evidenced through the necessity of organisations like Gamblers Anonymous, which is an international organisation that has as its purpose alleviating the personal difficulties and outright tragedies gambling can cause (Gamblers Anonymous n.d.).

In Scripture, gambling may not be directly forbidden, but aspects of its essence are covered in several passages. The ethics of work as an obligation for making our living harkens back to Genesis 3:19: 'By the sweat of your brow you will eat your food', and this principle is mirrored in 2 Thessalonians 3:10, 'The one who is unwilling to work shall not eat'. Seeking quick earnings is warned against in Proverbs 13:11, 'Dishonest money dwindles away, but whoever gathers money little by little makes it grow'. Then, 1 Timothy 6:10 explains: 'For the love of money is a root of all kinds of evil. Some people, eager for money, have wandered from the faith and pierced themselves with many griefs'. In 1 Corinthians 4:7 Paul asks: 'What do you have that you did not receive?' These quotes quite clearly indicate that to attempt to earn money by gambling, and not by trusting the providence of God, is contrary to the way recommended in the Bible.

Luther discusses gambling in connection with usury, and his judgement is clear, Money won by gambling … is not won without self-seeking, self-love, and sin (Luther 1824:137). Luther (2018: Loc:10066) further connected gambling to a number of other sins of similar magnitude, such as '… loafing, gluttony, and drunkenness, gambling and other evil deeds'.

Calvin outlawed gambling in Geneva, and made it punishable by fines, and this strict view on gambling as sinful has with some few exceptions been the mainstay position of protestant churches to this day (Douma 1996; Rogers 2005). Geisler (2010) discusses gambling extensively and finds ample support for recognising gambling as leading to serious societal problems; his conclusion is that gambling is sinful, and against central family and societal values.

The strict views held by Calvin and Luther on gambling are in concert with several biblical passages, and also with central aspects of the Christian message. For example, we learn from 1 Corinthians 14:33, 'For God is not a God of disorder but of peace – as in all the congregations of the Lord's people', and through this, we know that we should have trust in God for him to provide for all our needs. To leave our financial well-being to chance, like when gambling, will exhibit distrust in God's order and his satisfying our material needs. Further, to promote gambling, as done by private for-profit organisations, governments or NGOs, will also represent a promotion of greed and covetousness in others, which will go against the tenth Commandment, Exodus 20:17, which is mirrored for example in Luke 12:15, 'Then he said to them, "Watch out! Be on your guard against all kinds of greed; life does not consist in an abundance of possessions"'. Despite these clear scriptural instructions, some Christians propose that gambling is not always such a bad thing, and argue that state lotteries and other kinds of fundraising initiatives involving gambling can, and have, been used to realise important projects beneficial for the whole of society. Examples mentioned can be the Sydney Opera House, the Montreal Olympics and the London Metropolitan water supply were all realised through lottery funding (Field 1995). This could not be further from the truth, and even the most casual readers of this treatise will recognise how flawed this proposal is, and see it for what it represents; a consequentialist ends-justifies-the-means argumentation, where core aspects of the Christian message are suppressed for the here-and-now immediate and gluttonous gratification.

On the basis of the above biblical quotes, the positions of leading theologians, the longstanding tradition in Reformed churches, as well as the societal damage caused by gambling, it is the conclusion here that participation in gambling and its promotion should be perceived as immoral at all levels regardless of who organises it.

Drugs, alcohol and tobacco

To evaluate whether the use, production and marketing of drugs, alcohol and tobacco is moral should be of interest to the banking sector. In this connection, drugs will refer to the recreational use of drugs for intoxication purposes, and not their medical application. All drugs, alcohol and tobacco are subject to different levels of cultural meanings and importance in different regions of the world. It is well-documented and evidenced that abuse of drugs, alcohol and tobacco globally leads to adverse health effects, and substantial added societal cost (Degenhardt et al. 2008).

To treat our bodies with respect would follow from the *imago Dei* doctrine alone, but Scripture also relates to the matter of abusing the body and using intoxicants in several passages. For example, in 1 Corinthians 19:20 Paul states, 'Do you not know that your bodies are temples of the Holy Spirit, who is in you, whom you have received from God? You are not your own; you were bought at a price. Therefore honour God with your bodies'. Further, on intoxication, 1 Peter 4:7 commands, 'Therefore be alert and of sober mind so that you may pray'. This is mirrored in Ephesians 5:18: 'Do not get drunk on wine, which leads to debauchery. Instead, be filled with the Spirit'. The cited quotes are clear in that we need to treat our bodies with caution, and that to seek intoxication will interfere with our relationship with God, and thus, to seek intoxication is immoral on both accounts.

For Calvin, the consumption of alcohol was not banned, and in his cognition, enjoying alcoholic drinks was part of life's pleasures. Alcohol consumption is to Calvin (2012) connected to the enjoyment of life, as for example expressed:

> [N]or was it ever forbidden to laugh, or to be full, or to add new to old and hereditary possessions, or to be delighted with music, or to drink wine. (*Inst.* 3.19.9)

However, even though alcohol consumption was allowed in Calvin's (1850) practice, overindulgence and drunkenness was strictly forbidden:

> For the drunkard delights in drinking, but afterwards by vomiting he suffers the punishment of his intemperance, when his head, his stomach, his legs and other members shake and tremble. (p. 34)

Luther (2018: Loc:39276) was neither a teetotaller, but to him also drunkenness was an unjustifiable aberration to be likened with other sins, saying 'here you see that he who lies day and night in drunkenness has no more inheritance in the kingdom of God than the whoremonger, adulterer, and such like'.

The use of intoxicants is a controversial topic among Christians, and it would be safe to state that recreational use of drugs would be seen as immoral by most evangelical Christians. For instance, in the thinking of Geisler (2010), because an increasing number of Christians are consuming alcohol, the best position is to refrain from drinking it altogether. It cannot be concluded that to refrain from all intoxicants is against common Reformed moral theory, but surely, to seek intoxication would be. Therefore, any recreational use of drugs is immoral, and to incite others towards intoxication should also be seen as unethical. Tobacco may not traditionally have been seen as an abusing intoxicant, but modern research shows that many of the adverse effects connected to drugs and alcohol are connected with tobacco abuse also (Marrero et al. 2005). Douma (1996) explains that tobacco has a detrimental effect on people's health, and that to use it could be seen as an expression of irreverence for human life, in an extension of his sixth commandment interpretation, and to him, the use of tobacco should be refrained from altogether.

The position is then that to use, produce or market tobacco and drugs for recreational use is always perceived as immoral. To use alcohol is immoral only when it is abused, and when the goal is intoxication. Thus, to promote abuse of alcohol is always immoral.

Consumerism

As an extension to the above topics on societal morality, and also connected to stewardship of nature and all its gifts, an aspect to consider is that of human consumption; how much can and should we responsibly consume? Among Christians, consumerism has been met with scepticism, even though some links may be observed between Christian currents and increased consumerism (Trentmann 2004). To observe scriptural sources on consumerism should therefore be of interest for the topic of this treatise.

From Scripture, we are urged in Hebrews 13:5 to 'Keep your lives free from the love of money and be content with what you have', and in Luke 12:15, 'Be on your guard against all kinds of greed; life does not consist in an abundance of possessions'. Both quotes clearly warn against overconsumption and can be seen in conjunction with our obligation to exert proper stewardship over natural resources. With direct regard to overconsumption, it is stated in Proverbs 25:16 that 'if you find honey, eat just enough – too much of it, and you will vomit', and in 1 Corinthians 10:31, 'So whether you eat or drink or whatever you do, do it all for the glory of God'. The latter quote demonstrates that gluttonous consumption can be seen as breaking with our keeper role in nature (Gn 2:15), and thus should be perceived as immoral.

Calvin (2012), as explained above, may not have been opposed to capitalism, but gluttonous behaviour was not acceptable to him. On the matter of luxury, he wrote:

> Luxury causes great care, and produces great carelessness as to virtue; and it is an old proverb: Those who are much occupied with the care of the body, usually give little care to the soul. Therefore while the liberty of the Christian in external matters is not to be tied down to a strict rule, it is, however, subject to this law – he must indulge as little as possible; on the other hand, it must be his constant aim not only to curb luxury, but to cut off all show of superfluous abundance, and carefully beware of converting a help into an hindrance. (*Inst.* 3.10.4)

Although the above is written in the context of gluttony and not in the context of modern mass consumption, the extract sheds valuable light on Christian thinking related to consumption and the responsible use of resources. That gluttony is considered sinful is also expressed in the Westminster Larger Catechism, where it is described as a sin in connection to the seventh commandment (Westminster 2015).

The above sources are presented in light of consumerism and mass consumption, and are relevant for bankers who are concerned about how banking practices can promote mass consumption, and about the degree to which unnecessary and gluttonous consumption can be defended, even if in the short term it can contribute to increased production and wealth. It will appear from the above elaboration that to participate in or promote overconsumption and gluttony is immoral.

Chapter 7

Banking praxis

Keywords: banking practices; borrowing; lending; interest; *imago Dei*; human rights; equal opportunities; animal welfare.

■ Introduction

In this chapter, I address the application of Christian ethical and pastoral principles to different typical banking practices and demonstrate how they fit with the two strands of immoral and beneficial practices. Namely, those that will be considered immoral and thus should be shunned, and those that will be considered beneficial and may be considered to align with Christian norms, as these may bolster benign societal values, and thus, are deserving of continued promotion. The immoral will be termed 'unacceptable practices' and the beneficial will be termed 'acceptable practices'. Following this, the acceptable banking practices may be seen in contrast to the unacceptable practices, without the acceptable practices appearing dependent or parasitic on the unacceptable ones. Any sound Christian banking practice must be based on its own solid scriptural foundations.

There will certainly be categories of banking practices that are not covered, as the scope of this treatise does not encompass the adjudication of the moral quality of all conceivable manners of banking. The aim of this treatise is to develop a Christian norm-based structure for the kinds of banking practice that should be sought out by the banking professionals

How to cite: Bøsterud, M., 2021, 'Banking praxis', in *A treatise on Christian banking*, pp. 195–247, AOSIS, Cape Town. https://doi.org/10.4102/aosis.2021.BK263.07

and the general public in real-life situations. Further, it must be pointed out that all the banking categories mentioned need to be assessed, in principle, on their own direct merit, no matter what type of underlying asset is involved, as this should in principle not change the stance on the potential prudence of the utilised banking practice. For instance, if it is found that to finance a certain type of activity is considered morally acceptable, as for example financing students by way of giving student loans, the moral position will not change according to the financing rationale, as any banking activity will need to be subjected to the same scrutiny and moral standards. It is of the highest importance to make this distinction, because if not, certain banking categories, which on account of their perceived morality (e.g. loans to developing countries, microfinancing or housing for the poor) would otherwise escape the scrutiny they deserve from a Christian moral perspective, as financing such needs could be perceived to be morally acceptable to an untrained eye. Further, the focus here is on the typical situation where at least one of the parties is a professional actor, but all the highlighted Christian principles are equally relevant in a purely non-professional setting, although these may not be the typically recurring situations.

The following outline is meant to inform the use of Christian banking principles in real-life practice, in a manner that illuminates the different categories addressed in the following, for the reader to follow my thread of logic, and through this, be able to appreciate the constructive and shepherding character of the principles that underscore the Christian banking paradigm.

■ Moneylending

Unacceptable practices

☐ Lending

As Scripture allows lending to those in need as well as commercial transactions, we may be led to think that any lending is acceptable, no matter what the position of the borrower is. However, even though Scripture allows both to lend to those in need and those in 'want', the main position as uncovered in Chapter 6 (e.g. Ex 22:25) points to the element of helping the needy to get out of the unfortunate situation they are in, and not to exploit them. Lending to those not in need is not problematic and is only viewed according to other standards, such as greed or covetousness. The consideration here is whether we may always lend to those in need, or whether such a practice may sometimes be immoral. In a sense, then, the question is: Could there be a distinction as to whether the borrower is motivated by desperation or aspiration?

Within the Western societies, we do not expect that lending to people motivated by a real desperation for needs satisfaction is at the core of the problem, as these societies are expected to contain numerous protective structures backed by their governments, and in many cases, their welfare states render true desperation impractical to consider for lenders (Galbraith 1989). However, in the West, there is a practice of lending to other countries, and some of these may be in a state of real desperation because of unstable political situations, war or natural disasters. The question then becomes whether it is moral to lend to such desperate borrowers, often developing countries, or if the proper remedy in such cases would be to give from the surplus of the West to those urgently seeking needs satisfaction. In the West, there are also examples from modern history, where the now powerful European countries were in desperate need, like the substantial Marshall plan initiated by the US government, where certain European countries were aided in recreating their infrastructure and liberal democracies after the devastations of World War II. This was an aid package of large proportions, where the central element was financial aid rather than purely lending (Neal 2015). To answer the question on the basis of Scripture, a prudent passage to use as guidance could be the first section of Matthew 5:42, where we are instructed to 'give to the one who asks you', for we are encouraged to show ourselves as charitable when we can. For the purpose of this treatise, it is not necessary to conclude exactly when lending to those in urgent need is acceptable or not, but interpretation of Scripture leads to the conclusion that lending to truly desperate borrowers is not acceptable, as we are in these cases morally obligated to give rather than to lend. I note here that Christians are not obligated to lend or give, if they are not in a position of surplus themselves, so that if we can lend, we can also give.

An extension of the above topic is also relevant for the movement of so-called microfinancing, which in the West is often viewed as a way to lead individuals in developing countries towards a state of self-sufficiency not previously enjoyed (Khandker 2005; Morduch 1999). Without probing more deeply into this topic, the conclusion would be (as with lending to developing countries) that if the borrower is taking loans on an aspirational basis, it is acceptable, but if the borrower in reality is in desperate need, the lender should be obligated to give rather than to lend.

On the basis of the findings from Scripture in Chapter 6, it would be a responsible interpretation that banking practices that include lending to those in a state of urgent and desperate need must be considered immoral.

Borrowing and deposits

The above is seen from the angle where the lender is perceived as the more powerful party of a transaction, but, as examined in Chapter 6, the borrower's participation also needs to be considered from a moral and pastoral point of view. To do this, a useful example could be the situation in which a bank takes a deposit, and the depositor is the lender, against interest, to the bank, who then is the borrower of the transaction. As established in Chapter 7, to borrow is in itself acceptable, but the borrower is under a moral and pastoral obligation to ensure that the loan can be paid back as agreed. For the banks in the West, there are quite detailed legislative rules regarding the level of security the banks must have on their books to operate, and which will give them the right to earn banking licences. Such rules vary slightly, and there are stricter rules in Europe than in the United States of America for what the banks need to comply with in terms of liquidity and capital assets. In Europe, these rules of capital requirement are referred as the Basel rules, which state that banks need to be able to accommodate liquidity for 30 days, and to have a so-called 'core capital' or 'countercyclical capital buffer' that serves as a safeguard against a fall in the values of the bank's own assets (Angelini et al. 2015; Repullo & Saurina 2011). The point here is that, like any other borrower, the bank needs to have sufficient assets and expected earnings in their plan to pay back their lenders, and also to ensure that their own debtors may accommodate their obligations towards the bank by making good on their debt to them.

On the liability side of the balance sheet of a bank, there will typically be retail deposits, corporate deposits, interbank deposits, equity issues, share issues and past profits saved, and on the asset side, cash, liquid securities, money market instruments, loans, fixed assets and other holdings (Casu, Girardone & Molyneux 2015). Such balance sheets would be similar to those of many other businesses, and typically, the valuations on both sides of the balance sheet might be prone to value fluctuations in tune with the general market, and to the specific development of each separate business. However, what makes the banks stand out is that their main liabilities refer to money lent to them by others, and thus, the prudence of the banks' business practice will determine whether the loans may be paid back or not. Further, as in most cases, when credit is extended to a business, the creditor may realise there is a risk connected, and will perhaps not pay in full until full delivery is performed, but with banks, the credit is extended through borrowing, and the scriptural considerations described in Chapter 6 need to be attended to. That risks connected to deposits are covered by governmental deposit protection schemes (as, e.g., in the EU, where €100 000 of a deposit is insured/covered) does not liberate the banks from acting as any other prudent borrower need do, as this is society's way of protecting the depositor, who has the same status as any other creditor when loans are to be paid back (Gros & Schoenmaker 2014). If anything, such protective schemes could serve as a warning that the banks may not be as prudent borrowers as could be expected, with all the regulatory frameworks they are surrounded with, such as the Basel rules and other regulations (Allen et al. 2012). Further, with the numerous bailouts of the banks that have been evidenced in several financial crises, not least after the crisis of 2007–2008, it would appear that banks are acting as borrowers without due consideration to their obligation to pay back their loans to the depositors or other lenders (Neal 2015). As explained in Chapter 6, it is up to the lender and borrower to ensure that their transaction is responsible, and may be settled in an orderly fashion, and thus, for others to end up bearing the burden for failures, like society via the central banks, is not viable from a Christian perceptive. The bank bailouts we have seen in Western markets several times during market crashes will therefore have to be considered resultant of immoral borrowing on the part of the banks, and to be violating central norms as found in Scripture. All risk of failed debt, then, has solely been carried by the creditor who has extended such credit, who, in some cases, has been the depositor who has trusted his bank with his money. The societal ramifications that have appeared in the aftermath of such banking crises have been serious and substantial, and serve to inform any borrower, banks included, to be prudent when borrowing, and not to borrow recklessly, possibly at the cost of the lender and the greater society (Barofsky 2011; Bhattacharya & Nyborg 2013).

On the basis of the findings from Scripture in Chapter 6, it would be a responsible interpretation that banking practices that include borrowing without safeguarding sufficient means to pay back to the lender must be considered immoral.

Duration and security

Although lending and borrowing may be performed in a prudent manner, taking care not to exploit the desperately needy, and with due regard to repayment capabilities, this does not automatically entail that any such construction is aligned with Scripture in a pastoral or moral fashion. Two pertinent questions arise: what security is acceptable to charge for a loan, and what is an acceptable duration of a loan?

In the Western world, the typical long-term loan taken on by individuals will be connected to their purchase of a home, as mortgage. The duration of mortgages varies from country to country, but as the main rule, they tend to run for 10 or more years. In the United Kingdom, for example, 25 years is common, and 30 years or more duration on a mortgage is not uncommon there (Stiastny 2014). In dealing with real estate transactions, there will be an element of the property lasting longer than the loan duration, as typically perceived, so that the risk of being unable to repay any residual amount may not be considered as large. However, if the mortgage's loan-to-value (LTV) ratio is high, market fluctuations may put the borrower at risk for not being able to repay the mortgage, and thus the borrower may become a 'slave to the lender' (Pr 22:7). This risk of being caught in a situation where the LTV ratio becomes negative may be more prominent when lending is connected to immovable objects, such as cars or durable household goods, where the asset will be expected to depreciate all the way to zero, as opposed to the expectation of appreciation connected to real estate. It could be argued that the longer the duration of a loan, the larger the risk of diminishing LTV ratio caused by market fluctuations or other external economic shocks. This would indicate, as aligned with the scriptural passages mentioned in Chapter 6, that there should be responsible durations on loan agreements, so that they in reality can and will be paid back, and not unduly put the borrower at risk of entering into a bonded serfdom-like relation to the lender.

As evidenced in Chapter 6, Scripture not only perceives the borrower as vulnerable with regard to duration but also with regard to having his economic situation destabilised by way of the creditor making use or taking of given collateral. Although the biblical quotes refer to another historical era, focusing on millstones (Dt 24:6) and pieces of clothing (Ex 22:26–27), the message is clear; the creditor must exert due pastoral stewardship over the borrower, and not take as security anything that may be of vital importance to the economy or physical well-being of the borrower. Clearly, in the Western world of today, with all the above-mentioned safety nets put in place by different governments and welfare states, it would be difficult to imagine a situation in which the lender could not repossess a car or a durable good if the borrower reneges on his obligations. Further, with the current regime of collateralisation as a means of securing reasonable mortgages, not to accept the property of a borrower to be posted as security would be counterproductive to our financial system, and be detrimental to the interests of the borrower, and the possibility of his acquiring housing for his family (Casu et al. 2015). However, even if such security taking is considered acceptable, there is a question as to whether a lender should be able to evict a borrower from his home if in default on a secured loan. This type of situation may not only relate to a mortgage default, but also to other debts that may be duly secured against property. As the scriptural findings above would indicate, the interest of the borrower is at the core when considering security, and if there are no other dwellings available for the borrower than the collateralised property that is his home, a lender should not be able to evict without breaking scriptural norms. The matter of pledges becomes even more severe a loan depends on the pledges of people other than the principal borrower, such as family or friends, as such third-party guarantors may not understand that their pledge only imposes obligations on themselves, but does not provide them with any benefits (Pr 22:26–27, 6:1–5, 11:15). It could be argued that when third-party pledges are given, the principal borrower may be put in a position where s(he) is able to purchase something useful that could not otherwise be possible. However, there are only two ways to see this from the side of the lender; either the principal is not deemed able to pay the loan as it matures, or, the third-party pledge is taken on a 'just-in-case' basis, and thus, is superfluous. If the former is the case, then, the loan should not be given, as it will already from the outset be clear that it is too much to bear for the borrower. If the latter is the case, then, the bank need not take the pledge, as it could rather adjust the interest rate to a higher level to compensate for the uncertainties they deem connected to the security of the loan. There can be no doubt that to accept or demand third-party pledges, co-signing or collateral of any kind as part of loan extensions must be seen as unacceptable banking practice.

On the basis of the findings from Scripture in Chapter 6, it would be a responsible interpretation that banking practices that include lending duration beyond a reasonable time for paying back, and, when connected to a purchased asset, not within the expected time of value depreciation of a connected asset, or where the security puts the borrower at economic risk or risk of losing his home, or when relying on third-party pledges, must be considered immoral.

Acceptable practices
Lending

When operating in the core area of banking, which is the activity of lending money to those who need or want it (Mt 5:42), the onus is on the practitioner to perform such activities in a constructive and non-exploitative manner. This entails that the scriptural norms discussed earlier need to be observed, and that loans should be given to those who are in need, but only to the degree that they are not in a state of desperation, where other more charitable alternatives for aiding the potential lender would be prudent. When the lender extends a loan, it would be necessary to match this with the capabilities of the borrower to repay the loan, and to ensure that this is possible by mutual agreement, so that the borrower can maintain his dignity throughout the duration of the loan. When the need of the borrower attains the character of 'want', such as in a business transaction (Ex 22:25), the balance between the parties may be more even, and thus, the lender may rely more on the discretion of the borrower as to whether he will be able to repay, and not least, how this will affect his economic well-being. Taking risks is acceptable and encouraged in business (Mt 25:14–30; Lk 19:11–27), but the lender also needs to exert a certain stewardship in the situation, by displaying an attitude of pastoral leadership towards the borrower if the lender has more experience than the borrower (Tidball 1997; Vorster 2007). This shepherding role of the lender will also extend to acting responsibly when extending loans, be they in business or to private individuals, because if the lending bank does not observe caution when giving loans, their potential repayment failures may destabilise the bank's balance sheet, and thus harm their other customers, borrowers and depositors alike if the bank fails (Neal 2015).

From the above, it follows that to extend loans to those who are able to bear the cost and will be capable of repayment, is well within a sound Christian banking strategy.

☐ Borrowing and deposits

The obligation of the banking practitioner to act responsibly and to exert shepherding leadership and societal stewardship is even more salient when borrowing to finance a bank's operations, not least by taking deposits from the general public. Borrowing must be performed in a responsible manner, and the banking professionals must ensure that the bank has sufficient funds, both as long-term capital reserves as well as short-term liquidity to make good on its obligations to its lenders. Such responsibility is not observed only by aligning with official capital requirements as mandated by governmental regulatory bodies or private agencies, but rests with the individual banking practitioner in each case, as only 'the wicked borrow and do not repay' (Ps 37:21).

That the official capital requirements have been insufficient to safeguard the depositors' money in bank lending will have been clear for all to see during the banking crises of the 20th and 21st centuries, and still after years of fine-tuning the Basel rules, even in the latest crash of 2007–2008, we saw runs on the banks, and only through government bailouts were the depositors' money paid back. In the Western cognition on banking, it may seem that a situation where banks cannot pay back the depositors' or other creditors' money is accepted as if a rule of nature. It is interesting then, to note, that already in the 1930s, in the aftermath of the great crash of 1929, a school of thought arose where the ideal was that banks should be obligated to hold capital reserves covering 100% of the depositors' money. This is referred to as *The Chicago Plan*, and was first described by economists of the University of Chicago (a forerunner to the later Chicago School of economists), most prominently by Irving Fisher (1867–1947). According to this plan, by keeping 100% capital reserves, this would eliminate many troublesome aspects of our current state of banking and monetary system, such as by avoiding runs on banks and largely eliminate inflation. As we know from later history, this systematic has never been adopted in Western banking, and the theories have been largely forgotten, until the IMF revisited the theories after the crash of 2007–2008. Interestingly, IMF's findings as presented in their research paper confirms the validity of the Chicago Plan. Whether such high-level acceptance of the framework will lead to real changes in capital requirements remains to be seen, but as of yet, little indicates such a development (Benes & Kumhof 2012; Fisher 1935).

The ability to repay is a central tenet when borrowing, and any banker needs to observe this individual obligation when taking deposits and other means of borrowing. Clearly, the Chicago Plan if implemented in practice would involve an ideal level of security, but even without such a responsible level of capital reserves, the theories presented in the Chicago Plan certainly should guide as aspirational inspiration for any morally concerned banker. When taking deposits, it also becomes clear that the banking practitioner needs to observe obligations of guidance to the less professional, to explain that money may be lost even in deposits, and to shepherd those who need to understand the ramifications of this. Some may be well served by being guided to invest rather than risk their money on low interest-bearing deposits, particularly if the deposits are large, and may thus fall outside the minimum deposit insurance schemes that may be relevant in the different cases (Gros & Schoenmaker 2014). To guide someone towards understandable risk could be considered good shepherding, not least if the outcome is that the money will be constructively used by others (Bøsterud & Vorster 2017). Prudent bankers, then, only take deposits and borrow when they are certain that their repayment obligations will be observed in full.

From the above, it follows that to borrow and take deposits with certainty of repayment is well within a sound Christian banking strategy.

☐ Duration and security

When entering into a loan agreement, it is important that this includes a duration that is appropriate in terms of both the possible depreciation of associated financed assets and the financial horizon of the parties. If the duration becomes longer than the existence of a financed asset, or the remaining loan amount is higher than the value of a depreciating asset, the loan agreement will attain characteristics of rent or investment, and then other types of terms should apply. There is no need for loan agreements to be set in stone or as a one-size-fits-all regulation as expressed in Deuteronomy 15:1, but it is the onus of the banking professional to shepherd the less professional actors so that a loan agreement becomes functional and possible to repay (Pr 29:7). Regarding taking security, which can only be taken or demanded from the borrower, it is important that such security does not deprive the borrower of essential needs satisfaction such as housing and food, and even if a lender has a legal right to take security to use, this may only be performed without inflicting reduced needs satisfaction on the lender (Dt 24:6; Ex 22:26–27).

From the above, it follows that to lend money with a duration that is responsible in terms of depreciation of the financed asset, the financial horizon of the involved, and based on reasonable pledges from the borrower only, is well within a sound Christian banking strategy.

■ Charging interest
Unacceptable practices

As has been demonstrated in Chapter 6, charging of interest is accepted as morally and pastorally permissible within the Reformed paradigm. The question here, then, will be: what constitutes immoral usury, or in other words, when does the interest payment connected to lending become exorbitant, and thus unacceptable from a Christian perspective (Cramp 1995)? In most Western countries, there have been different modes of regulation on the financial industry, such as levels of interest or consumer protection schemes. Since the widespread deregulation of the Western financial markets during the 1980s and 1990s, a wave of new financial products has been launched, and, with this, calls for new regulations have followed, which in some cases have been followed up by legislation (Neal 2015).

Despite the quite extensive regulation, the financial industry is subjected to in the Western markets, there are still large areas where charging of interest may be problematic because of the level of interest in use. This will not typically be found within the stable market for the comfortable middle classes, but rather, within the realms of the lower classes, and amongst those who may have fallen on hard times for different reasons. This market is typically referred to as the sub-prime market, which indicates its place in relation to the prime market, where the borrowers are considered good risks for the lender. In this sub-prime market, there will also be different levels of risk taken on by the lenders, and different expectations of payment for such risk by way of interest charging. The sub-prime market is not uniform or tied to certain types of credit, as lenders within most sectors will be willing to lend if the risk is duly compensated through interest. Sub-prime financing is found within mortgages, car loans, personal credits and more (Investopedia n.d.). An example from the lower range of the sub-prime lending market is that served by the so-called payday lenders. A payday loan is a small uncollateralised loan, typically between $100 and $500, and is meant to carry the borrower financially until his next payday. A typical mode of practice in markets where cheque books are still in use is that the borrower issues a post-dated cheque to the lender, who then cashes it directly when the payday arrives (Stango 2012). A typical borrower in a payday lending scheme will be a person who is in need, perhaps desperation, and may not have access to other sources of short-term credit such as credit cards (Investopedia n.d.). What stands out in a payday lending scheme is the unusually high level of interest paid by the borrower. In such loans, interest rate of more than 1000% p.a. is not unusual, and may in some cases run into several thousands of percent when annualised. It is possible for the borrower to roll his credit forward to subsequent paycheques for extra fees, and through this, the borrower may be caught in a situation where he might not be able to get out of debt, and the loan will continue running at such high interest rates for long-term. It is a fair assumption that borrowers will only accept such high levels of interest out of desperation, as there are no other alternatives available for them. Additionally, they may not be able to calculate the interest levels for themselves when this is not properly explained by the lender (Martin 2010). I use this example here to illustrate that what exactly an acceptable level of interest is and what an exorbitant one is will vary with the practical circumstances and general level of interest in the market, but when it gets into the thousands, there is no doubt that it is exorbitant and exploitative.

Situations not as extreme as the payday loans, but where the lender is preying on the weakness of the borrower may also be found within typical consumer financing, when credit cards and/or deferred payment or third-party uncollateralised finance is provided (Karlan & Zinman 2009). With deferred payment for consumer goods, the borrower may not be in a desperate state, but may not be able to calculate the real interest charged. With credit cards the situation is more regulated, but also here, the interest rates may run high, often 25% p.a. or more.

As the above examples show, the charging of high interest from individuals is a possibility in the financial markets, and, through the extending of initial small-amount short-term loans, individuals may be trapped in a long-term loan where the level of interest becomes extremely high. Even though the Reformed paradigm accepts interest as moral, to exploit the needy may not be acceptable. Here, Exodus 22:25 weighs in; we are obligated to lend to the one 'among you who is needy' and in Deuteronomy 15:7, we learn that towards the poor we should 'not be hard-hearted or tight-fisted'. The imperative instruction here would be that charging interest that is as high as possible from one in 'need' would have to be considered 'hard-hearted' and 'tight-fisted', and thus, to exploit someone in such a manner, could not be considered viable from a Christian vantage point. For loans to individuals outside the realm of commercial financing, then, charging exorbitantly high interest may be seen as immoral usury, and thus, not permitted without breaking scriptural norms. As it is difficult to assess exactly the limits of an acceptable interest rate, it should be clear that when the interest rate runs into the hundreds of percent per year, this would be an impermissible 'hard-hearted' banking practice of immoral usury. However, here it is solely the establishment of the principle of immorality that is in focus, so, detailed elaborations of acceptable and unacceptable levels of interest fall outside the scope of this treatise.

For loans in commercial situations, it is difficult to imagine how someone may be in 'need' in the above sense of the word. Being 'hard-hearted' or 'tight-fisted' in a business transaction is just part of the game, and typical to the risk scenario for which anyone who enters this realm of life should be prepared. Risk is a central aspect of business, and risk means what it sounds like: the possibility of losing some or all of what is put at stake. To entertain such risk is well within what is acceptable for the Christian believer (VanDrunen 2015).

On the basis of the findings from Scripture in Chapter 6, it would be a responsible interpretation that banking practices outside the realm of commercial financing that include charging interest rates that exploit the need of the borrower in an exorbitant manner must be considered immoral.

Acceptable practices

When extending credit in any form in a professional setting, the mainstay in the Western world is to charge interest as the means to pay for the credit and alleviate some of the perceived repayment risk on the part of the lender (Casu et al. 2015). As interest charging is considered acceptable under the Reformed paradigm in principle, the question here is not where a line may be drawn for when charged interest becomes too high, or exorbitant, so that it falls outside what would be morally acceptable, as merely refraining from charging immoral levels of interest does not mean the practice can be seen as beneficial. Rather, the question here is when is interest charged at a responsible and morally acceptable level, so as to qualify as contributing beneficially to stewarding the interest of the borrower, as well as wider society. As with the topic of duration, it will not be possible to determine where such a line should be drawn once and for all, but the issue for the concerned banking professional would be how to exert sound stewardship and give guidance when entering into dialogue and/or agreements with borrowers. A good guide here may be the talionic principle (Lv 24:19–20) where both parties should be giving and taking in equal measure. In other words, a concept of 'value-for-money' or equity needs to be applied when shepherding borrowers who will enter into credit. A prudent banking professional, then, will apply such a principle of evenness when guiding a potential borrower, and make certain that the borrower understands what the cost will be, and how this compares to the benefit reaped from entering into a loan. If this principle is adhered to, and the borrower is not in a state of desperation, no situations should arise where the interest charged could reach a level where it would be considered immoral usury or exorbitant.

From the above, it follows that to lend money against interest, in a situation where the interest level is set at a responsible rate which can be considered as equalling out the benefits of the loan for the borrower, is well within a sound Christian banking strategy.

■ Risk and stability
Unacceptable practises

Although risk-taking and utilisation of financial structures may be not only acceptable, but also called for in Scripture (Mt 21:12; Mk 11:15), it is not within our right to insert risk into the lives of others, nor onto greater society, as our enjoyment of material goods 'is a gift of God' (Ec 5–19). The questions, then, are: What is an acceptable level of risk to take on, and what kind of financial risk-taking and structuring would be seen as breaking with scriptural norms?

In the professional banking market, there are numerous structures that serve to increase liquidity, ease trading in shares and commodities, offer credit, alleviate risk, protect against unwanted risk, amongst others. In reality, the number of different financial instruments existing and being made is limitless, as the financial actors create new products and tools in line with the development of the underlying markets they aim to serve and/or exploit (Stiastny 2014).

To elucidate financial instruments, their use and potential pitfalls, a suitable example would be how financing of share trading could be structured, and how attendant risk might increase with elaborate financing structures. In trading of shares, the trader may bet on the likelihood that a share will rise in value, and thus buy it at a price, and hope to sell it later when it has appreciated. This activity is in the trading nomenclature called taking a 'long' position (Stiastny 2014). Conversely, if a trader believes a share will fall in price, he will of course sell such a share, but he cannot do this if he does not already own it. This problem is solved in the market through share loans, where a trader borrows shares from another, and promises to deliver them back at a later fixed date. The motives for the lender could be to make some extra money, as the loan will carry interest, and the typical lender is one who has as a strategy to own the share long-term, whether it depreciates or appreciates in value. Such strategies are common for entrepreneurial owners, who plan on owning their shares indefinitely, and for investment funds which have a strategy to own certain types of shares no matter the wider market situation. When the borrower has received the shares to his account from the lender, he is free to sell them in the market, and wait for the share to fall in value, and then buy back the correct number of shares in the market and deliver them back to the lender. If the share has fallen in value in the meantime, the borrower, the 'short seller', has made a profit from his 'short' position (Downes & Goodman 2014). At times there have been criticisms voiced against short selling, but when it is deconstructed as above, selling shares whether owned or borrowed will amount to the same, as the market bet is that the seller sells shares he expects to drop in value. The market actors should be free to sell their shares, to lend them out, borrow or buy, and the risk for such transactions will only, in principle, reside with the market actors. In addition, when the wider market falls, short positions will dampen the fall, as all the short sellers then will be buying back the shorted shares in order to take profit and hand back the shares to their owners. In falling markets, short sellers may be amongst the very few who buy shares, and this is rarely acknowledged amongst critics of short selling (Mallaby 2010).

The structure of share lending is a financial instrument that is similar to the financing that is given to the long trader as well. A long trade may be leveraged with debt according to the market capitalisation of the share, its expected liquidity and the perceived strength of the share in the market. To utilise financing, whether going long or short in the market, is in itself acceptable, as lending and borrowing is aligned with Scripture in principle, but when the borrowing becomes reckless, it may become immoral and go against sound pastoral principles pertaining to societal stewardship. Examples here may be taken from the hedge fund industry, where the fund managers typically utilise both short and long positions in their strategies. It is customary to use high degrees of financial leverage in these funds, and banks and brokers willingly extend generous loans to buy shares to take long positions, where the collateral will be the shares themselves. The risk involved is typically perceived as low, as the lender can sell the shares in the market if the value falls close to the level of financing (LTV), and thus avoid losing if the borrower's strategy fails. With shares enjoying high liquidity, this perception could be acceptable, but, as the hedge funds will also borrow shares for selling short, the short selling will mean that the short seller receives money for the short sale. This money will go into the account of the short seller, who then will be able to use this 'new' money as collateral for buying even more shares, adding to his long positions. Through such financial structuring, the degree of leverage may reach as high as a hundred times the size of the capital invested by the owners. The point then is that the real money in use may be that of the short sale, and in theory, there need not be any risk capital required from the owners at all (Krugman 2008). For example, with a leverage of 99% LTV ratio, then, only a 1% rise in the positions will double the money invested, and conversely, 1% fall will wipe out all the invested capital. With such high financial leverage, the real underlying risk of the owners will in reality be transferred on to other market actors and lenders, and in addition, such structures become so vulnerable to value fluctuations that they may lead to hurried and desperate activities that may unduly destabilise the market, and consequently hurt the wider societal economy (Danielsson, Taylor & Zigrand 2005). In addition to the level of financial leverage taken on, the typical hedge fund will be based on an enumeration of management where the management receives a 'carried interest' of 20% of the fund's profits as remuneration, but the management will not share in any losses the fund might incur. Such renumeration mechanisms, where the managers only have interest in the potential profits and no downside risk, may in themselves spur on excessive risk-taking, as the decision-making managers will have only negligible risks for losses compared to near endless possibilities on the upside.

A well-known example of such potential pitfalls is the collapse of the fund Long Term Capital Management, in 1998, which had an LTV ratio of more than 25:1, had borrowed $125 billion on its own capital (c. $5 billion), and taken positions worth $1 trillion when it imploded. When the structure started to collapse, the expected market disruptions were on such a scale, both for the United States of America and the world economies, that the US government found it necessary to intervene and arrange a bailout of the structure (Edwards 1999). In other words, the cost of the reckless borrowing and high financial leverage was passed on to others, who in turn had had no part in any earning potential profits from that fund. For the purposes of this treatise, it is not necessary to adjudicate what would be the exact level of acceptable financing leverage, but only to point out that when risks become severe, both for those involved and most of all for the general society, such financial structuring will be unacceptable, and be disrespectful to the 'gift of God' (Ec 5–19) that is our material well-being.

The above example is based on the use of share trading, but the financial markets have many other more exotic financial instruments on offer. For example, shares or other forms of equity positions may be taken by way of derivatives, which are structures where a contract is connected to the performance of an underlying asset. For example, an option to purchase a share, currency or a commodity will be a derivative of such an asset, and the contract/derivative will fluctuate in value in line with value fluctuations of the underlying asset (Downes & Goodman 2014). For example, if a contract gives an option to purchase a share at the price of 100 within the next year, to have this right may come at a cost of 5, for example, and then, as soon as the share is valued at more than 105, the option is worth money, and the owner of the option is 'in the money'. As will appear then, such derivative structures may offer possibilities for financial leverage, as instead of purchasing the real underlying asset, to acquire the derivative will cost less, and give the same risk exposure, only at the cost of the option premium.

Derivatives have been developed over a wide financial spectrum, covering most of the conceivable financial risk-taking. Well-known examples are derivatives connected to mortgages and consumer loans, where such derivatives may have been structured with collateral. The collateralised debt obligations (CDOs) and their place in the run-up to the US housing boom in the early 2000s, and their subsequent effect on the 2007–2008 wider market crash are worth considering here in brief. A CDO is a financial instrument represented by a bond or note, which is backed by a pool of different fixed-income assets, where the rights to the cash flows from these assets go to different investors who are organised in accordance with different levels of risk derived from the pool, so-called 'tranches' (Stiastny 2014). What makes such structures of interest for investors is that they provide a way to invest in a security representing what is inherently an illiquid asset, for example a housing loan or mortgage, and such a process of creation and origination is frequently referred to as 'securitisation' (Gotham 2009). Such CDOs are in use in order to raise money for lending purposes, for example, and can be structured to accommodate widely different risk appetites. When deconstructed, it will appear that such instruments may consist of principal loan risk from one source, and interest risk from another (Demyanyk & Van Hemert 2009; Neal 2015). In other words, through such financial engineering, an investor may have the rights to receive cash flows from the principal lending payments of a group of nurses in Texas, for example, and interest payments from the loans given to a group of firefighters in California.

The above method has made it possible to create and originate investment grade papers based on the over-collateralisation effect that could come with pooling of risk, and has in turn made it possible to raise vast amounts of capital which has then been lent out to homebuyers, for example. Such an augmentation of available loans to homeowners was a main driver in providing loan capital which was utilised in what became the US sub-prime mortgage bubble of the late 1990s and early 2000s. The originators of the CDOs were motivated to lend out more and more, as they in turn could sell the papers on to investors at good prices (Purnanandam 2010). This created an unhealthy cycle, whereby, in 2006, house prices in the United States of America had risen substantially and to unsustainable levels, as resulting from a debt-driven purchase spree amongst homebuyers. The US housing bubble in itself wiped out values of around $8 trillion, which was divided between $7 trillion for the home buyers and $1 trillion for the financial CDO investors (Krugman 2008).

The fallout from the US sub-prime crisis was felt worldwide in most financial markets, and societies and individuals around the world are still struggling with the longer-term effects, where whole countries like Greece and Spain are still working to iron out their relationships with creditors and stabilising their national economies (Varoufakis 2016). The crisis that led up to the wider market fall was to a large degree driven by advanced financial engineering, where the real risks were divorced from the directly affected parties (lenders and borrowers), and thus, where economic stability was sacrificed in order to maximise short-term financial profits. The cost of this instability has to a large degree been passed on to Western taxpayers, who have had to finance the different bailout schemes devised by Western governments in the aftermath of the crisis (Neal 2015). From the perspective of this treatise, there can be no doubt that the kind of financial structuring that was involved in the sub-prime crisis gravely put at risk our ability to enjoy material well-being 'in the house of the Lord' (Ps 23:6), and was instrumental in dividing risk and profits unevenly, such that the risk was left with those who had not taken it on (borrowers, investors and taxpayers). This would be an unacceptable practice in light of scriptural norms.

On the basis of the findings from Scripture in Chapter 6, it would be a responsible interpretation that banking practices that include exaggerated risk-taking and attendant financial structuring that transfers risk onto others and/or society must be considered immoral.

Acceptable practices

As the application of credit has become a pivotal social technology for the advancement of the Western economies, to ensure that it is practised in a responsible manner without posing undue risk on the direct participants, third parties or wider society have become a matter of substantial importance. This importance is evidenced through the many different financial bubbles and subsequent crashes that have appeared in the Western economies over the centuries, where wider society has had to bear the burden of losses incurred by reckless market actors (Galbraith 2009; Neal 2015). When utilising banking technologies as a means of societal or individual economic advancement, a full appreciation of how this is connected to risk and societal stability will lead to the structuring of financial instruments and their application in a manner where the risk of destabilising the economic systems in which they are applied is minimal. This would entail the use of utmost care when originating derivatives and obscure financial structures and necessitates that all involved parties fully understand the societal reach and financial magnitude of each instrument in use, as well as only issuing such instruments in a volume the market can assimilate without irresponsible risk build-up. This will mean that CDOs connected to mortgages, for example, should only be issued for the purpose of ensuring a stable supply of mortgage lending to potential house buyers (Gotham 2009).

In addition to the careful application of financial instruments, it is also important to be responsible when applying financial leverage in trading and investment operations in order to safeguard human enjoyment of material goods (Ec 5:19). This is especially important when performing speculative market operations connected to trading in securities and other assets, as the prudent use of leverage may lead to optimisation of capital in the best interests of society and the individual (Mt 25:14–30; Lk 19:11–27), but the opposite may have financially devastating consequences for the societal economy and a wide group of stakeholders (Edwards 1999). The aim, then, should be to apply financial leverage with care, and utilise stewardship principles with extra-party stakeholder interests at heart when applying financial leverage in trading and investment operations. In any banking operation where financing is involved and when structuring financial products of any kind, the actors need to focus not only on those directly involved, but also to employ a shepherding attitude where wider societal interests are considered. Through this, issuance, origination, trade and investment in structured financial products would be useful for the individual and society in obtaining and enjoying material goods, which God has supplied us with the ability to receive (Dt 8:18).

From the above, it follows that to structure, originate, issue, trade in or invest in societally useful financial products for responsible use in market operations and raising of debt, is well within a sound Christian banking strategy.

■ Truthfulness
Unacceptable practices

When utilising any form of financial instruments or performing any act of finance, honesty and transparency are important factors for such practices to be acceptable from a Christian perspective. Banking practices involve many stakeholders, some of whom are willing participants in the involved risk, and others of whom become subjected to risk they do not welcome, and sometimes are not even aware of. An example here could be mortgage securitisation mentioned above, where the sub-prime financed house buyers were not aware of the price bubble build-up that was created by the incessant CDO originations carried out by the banks.

To handle matters of transparency in banking has been a concern of governments for decades, and, for example, in the United States of America, there have been regulations on truthfulness in banking through the Truth in Lending Act of 1968, the Truth in Savings Act of 1991, and most recently in the so-called Dodd-Frank Act of 2010. The Dodd-Frank Act was designed to rectify some of the excesses that led to the 2007–2008 financial crash, and is a comprehensive framework regulating a substantial tract of financial activity, including consumer protection, insurance and credit rating, and has introduced new governmental agencies, with monitoring and regulatory tasks, into the financial markets (Dimitrov, Palia & Tang 2015; Downes & Goodman 2014). Such legal regulations are found in most of the Western nations, and typically focus on regulations for such things as consumer protection, correct marketing of interest, loan duration and avoidance of hidden costs. Only to a small degree are topics discussed in this treatise focused, such as depositors' risk of losing money because of banks' reckless borrowing, the real level of bank capitalisation and what it means for stakeholders, whether the parties in a loan have realistic expectations to each other, and more. Such topics have mainly been left to the parties to regulate, and consumer protection has been seen as the main remedy (Wilmarth 2004).

In a Christian perspective, being truthful is a sought-after quality in any line of business, but when it involves banking and financing, the societal ramifications of being untruthful may be severe, and the wider group of involved stakeholders may be larger than in most, if not all, other lines of commercial activity. When the directly involved parties are not truthful, as when a borrower is reckless or the lender avoids letting the borrower know his intentions of creating a long-term situation out of a short-term one (e.g. payday loans), they will violate scriptural norms (Ex 20:16), put others at risk financially, or ensnare them in a web of dishonesty for financial gain (Calvin 2012:*Inst.* 2.8.45).

On the basis of the findings from Scripture in Chapter 6, it would be a responsible interpretation that banking practices that include hiding the truth of a transaction, and/or contribute to misleading others who may be affected, must be considered immoral.

Acceptable practices

To stay truthful in all realms of business life may be challenging at times; for example, negotiating commercial deals with others may entail a certain economising with the truth. However, when it comes to banking and financing, to stay truthful and transparent is of utmost importance from a Christian perspective. As evidenced in Chapter 6 this is informed by scriptural norms. Topics concerning truthfulness in relation to banking may involve all aspects of credit giving and receiving, and examples here may be to ensure that a borrower is aware of all terms of a loan agreement, such as duration, fees, security and the real interest rate per year. Some of these aspects may be connected to wider marketing activities such as advertising credit cards or consumer loans, but also to how the actual interparty dialogue is handled in a professional business setting (Douma 1996). It should be noted here that for the individual banking practitioner involved in such marketing and utilisation of banking products, solely to adhere to formal governmental regulations, such as the US Truth in Lending Act, in itself will not suffice to align with scriptural norms (Downes & Goodman 2014). Here, scriptural obligations to attain a shepherding attitude towards the individual and society are informed solely by the norms set out in Scripture. Thus, all banking activity needs to be truthful and transparent, and banking practitioners need to apply the truth in all aspects of their practice, and at all times (Ex 20:16).

From the above, it follows that to remain truthful and act truthfully in all circumstances when originating, marketing and utilising transparent banking products is well within a sound Christian banking strategy.

▎Greed

▎Unacceptable practices

When assessing the place of greed in banking, the task is to view the general activity through the lens of greed in a scriptural sense. Central topics here pertain to the involved actors trying to make more of what is already there, in other words, to maximise profits to a degree and/or in a manner not aligned with scriptural norms (e.g. Lk 12:15; Pr 28:20).

In many of the above examples, greed was a factor, as for example when banks stay undercapitalised to make more on their capital, and this could lead to their creditors, depositors included, being at risk of incurring losses, something which constitutes reckless borrowing on the side of the bank. Other examples could be exaggeration of the securitisation of banking assets to such a degree that it creates a bubble in underlying markets, as in the early 2000s US housing market, charging of exorbitant interest and fees as with the payday lenders, and utilising risk at a level that is not responsible compared to the capital invested by the initial risk-taker, as with the actions of Long Term Capital Management (Danielsson et al. 2005; Krugman 2008).

On the basis of the findings from Scripture in Chapter 6, it would be a responsible interpretation that banking practices that include the promotion or utilisation of greed must be considered immoral.

▎Acceptable practices

When banking practices are to be assessed in connection with greed, the matter relates to the issue of leadership on the part of the banking professionals, both when communicating with less professional actors, and also amongst themselves. The sphere for applying Christian leadership is substantially connected to greed and desire within the financial industry, and a shepherding activity would be to guide potential borrowers as to whether they need to obtain more material goods (Ex 20:17) by way of financing, and for the bankers, whether earning more money through extending more credit really is necessary (Lk 12:15).

For the banking professionals, one important aspect would be to ensure that their banks stay sufficiently capitalised, in order to ensure that their creditors, depositors included, are not put at risk of incurring losses. This despite the fact that, if more thinly capitalised, the bank and its owners may have a higher rate of return on their own capital in use, something that would be tempting and could be induced by succumbing to greed, something which constitutes reckless borrowing on the side of the bank. The ideas promoted in the Chicago plan could be inspirational in this regard. Other examples could be to be prudent when securitising of banking assets to such a degree that it will not create a bubble in underlying markets (as occurred in the early 2000s US housing market); be diligent in setting and charging interest and fees, despite possibilities to increase these (as opposed to the payday lenders); and to accept risk at a level that is responsible compared to the capital inserted by the initial risk-taker (Danielsson et al. 2005; Krugman 2008).

When dealing with professional borrowers, such as corporations, it is of particular value to ensure that their capitalisation is sufficient, so that if possible, the lender through such requirements will dampen greed on the borrower's side, as the temptation there might to maintain a minimal level of capitalisation, in order to receive higher returns on capital in use. Through such financing demands, banking will promote a frugal and diligent practice of capitalisation and borrowing in the corporate realm, which will be based on constructive and pastoral guidance from the lender (Osmer 2008; Vorster 2007).

Further extension of such didactic guidance would entail the promotion of financial diligence and responsible borrowing to potential customers and practitioners, and to ensure that all marketing and structuring of banking products follows such an understanding. It is realised that, to some, such evangelising may seem somewhat misplaced in a professional and/or consumer setting, but, as financial diligence and responsible borrowing and capitalisation represent the opposite of greed, and, as financing such benign choices may also be profitable, promoting such stewardship in a banking setting will create an authentic, practically oriented ministry, where norms founded in Scripture are at the core.

From the above, it follows that to promote financial diligence and responsible borrowing and capitalisation in all aspects of a professional or consumer banking setting is well within a sound Christian banking strategy.

▪ Covetousness
▪ Unacceptable practices

While greed and covetousness may be seen as adjacent, if not overlapping, moral topics, it has been shown in this treatise how greed may pertain to all actors in the market wanting more of what they have, but covetousness is here seen as the impulse to try to acquire what is not already there. The focus here is more on how finance may be used to induce individuals to want to possess material goods not already enjoyed (Ex 20:17).

A typical area where banking practice may promote and/or prey on covetousness is within the sale of consumer goods and services, where the consumer does not have the money at hand to make the desired purchase. As evidenced in Chapter 3, certain parts of consumer banking have derived from the production and sale of durable consumer goods, and financing of consumption has increased during the post-war era and onwards to the present day (Boczar 1978; Ryan, Trumbull & Tufano 2011). The practice of financing consumption, be it in the form of durable goods, travel or short-term general credit, is not in itself in violation of any scriptural norms, but when such financing becomes predatory and aggressive, the matter changes rapidly. There are numerous examples of consumer credit being offered, where the marketing may not be fully transparent, and where the incentives to make financed purchases clearly relate to luring individuals to make purchases by making them want to own something out of peer pressure promoted through speculative marketing (Douma 1996).

Amongst speculative tactics to initiate covetousness and subsequent financed purchases is the practice of offering finance through so-called 'cash-back' discounts or credit schemes. In the cash-back schemes, the purchaser is tempted by receiving money from the seller as a kind of bonus. In other words, not only can the purchase be made on credit, but the purchaser will also receive ready money from the transaction (James, Lahti & Zettelmeyer 2006; Zinman 2009). It is difficult to interpret anything else into such schemes other than attempts at making people want to buy something they do not already have through financing, and giving money out to consumers would only be devised to make them 'fall into temptation' (1 Tm 6:9).

On the basis of the findings from Scripture in Chapter 6, it would be a responsible interpretation that banking practices that include the promotion of covetousness must be considered immoral.

Acceptable practices

A typical area where banking practice needs to be aware of impulses of covetousness is within the sale of consumer goods and services, where the consumer does not have the money at hand to make the desired purchase. The practice of financing consumption, be it in the form of durable goods, travel or short-term general credit, needs to be done in a manner where thrift and frugality is at the forefront, and where the borrower is guided to purchase via financing only goods and services that may be deemed useful and/or necessary for him, and at the very least, not allow any financing for frivolous purchases. A banking practice where the potential borrower is guided towards using his own money for purchasing solely necessary goods and services, will promote thrift and responsible consumption and lending both.

The beneficial consumer credit to be offered then will be one where the marketing is fully transparent, and where the incentives to make financed purchases clearly relate to the sensible practical need of the borrower, such as with durable consumer goods, which is the motivating factor for the borrowing.

Any marketing of the potential lending needs to be in a fashion where the focus is on sensible utility, so there will be no chance for promoting that potential borrowers will 'fall into temptation' (1 Tm 6:9). Through such a shepherding attitude to the potential customers, the banking professionals will promote what may be seen as sound banking practice, for the benefit of a wider group of societal actors. Focusing on thrift and responsible borrowing will also be a central point in a beneficial banking practice when dealing with the professional market. Some of the examples mentioned above under the treatment of greed are of value also when assessing possible covetousness, and here, the two terms typically may substantially overlap. As in the consumer market, the role of the banking professional is to promote a sound banking practice based on thrift and responsible acquisition, for the benefit of a wider group of societal actors (Osmer 2008; Vorster 2007, 2017a).

As related to greed, further extension of such didactic guidance would entail the promotion of thrift and responsible acquisition to potential customers and practitioners, and to ensure that all marketing and structuring of banking products follows such an understanding. It is realised that, to some, such moral proclamations seem out of place in a banking setting, but, as thrift and responsible acquisition represents the opposite of covetousness, and, as financing such choices may also be profitable, promoting such stewardship in a banking setting will create a real-life praxis-oriented ministry, where scripturally based norms are foundational.

From the above, it follows that to promote thrift and responsible acquisition in all aspects of a professional or consumer banking setting is well within a sound Christian banking strategy.

■ Sanctity of life
Unacceptable practices
☐ Prisons

The global economy will present numerous opportunities for the banking industry to partake directly or indirectly in prisons and correctional facilities, by way of public and private initiatives, or in outright private prison operators (Engel, Fischer & Galetovic 2013). Other corporate actors may offer services pertaining to operating sub-supplies to prisons such as catering and janitorial services, and yet others to participate in the construction and practical operations, without being specifically aimed at prison services. The pertinent moral questions such involvement raise is whether it is morally acceptable to participate, and in particular, such questions are related to whether the facility is involved in capital punishment and/or cruel or unusual punishments (Bonta & Gendreau 1990).

From the norms explained in Chapter 6, it is clear that under the Reformed paradigm capital punishment is permissible, albeit not a preferred punishment option, and only if related to serious, capital crimes, and to use cruel and unusual punishment methods would also contradict this norm. Thus, to use capital punishment other than for capital offences, or applying cruel and unusual punishment methods, would be immoral under the Reformed paradigm and should not be permitted under any circumstance (Geisler 2010; Vorster 2017a).

The conclusion connected to prisons and correctional facilities would be that the 'best practice' banking strategy of any would be to avoid the prison industries that are involved in capital punishment other than for capital offences or that allow cruel and unusual punishment methods.

☐ Weapons production and sales

As I noted in Chapter 6, the *imago Dei* doctrine dictates the sanctity of human life, and to be involved in assets pertaining to arms production should therefore, in principle, be avoided and be seen as immoral from the outset. However, as the just war doctrine in certain circumstances allows for the taking of life (Ex 20:13), to elaborate the topic of weapons production as a possibly acceptable type is necessary (Geisler 2010). In the following, references to arms production are related to weaponry designed to be used against humans and societal interests, and also for recreational hunting.

From the just war doctrine, it appears that killing is acceptable in certain situations, and that it has to be performed justly, with acceptable means and levels of violence. These provisions are of central importance for participation, as they would limit to whom weapons could be sold, and what types of weapons should be allowed to be produced, and consequently be financed. The limitations on what kind of weapons are considered just and fair is neither a recent consideration, nor of Christian origin, as ancient Hindu codes already prohibited the use of poison arrows in warfare, and later, the 1925 Geneva Convention prohibited the use of poison gas and bacteriological weapons (Lee 2012).

To finance arms production connected to fair warfare and self-defence of a people would not be in conflict with the just war doctrine, and thus in principle should not be considered immoral from a Reformed perspective. However, when bankers are contemplating participation, it could be difficult to ascertain that the involved arms are only to be used fairly, in self-defence and only in warfare initiated through governmental involvement. As we know from recent history, the global political situation is not stable, and weapons that today rest safely in the hands of a just government for the purpose of self-defence may soon change hands if the government is overturned (Shane & Hubbard 2014).

When financing assets connected to arms production, it would also be necessary to assess the likelihood that the producer manufactures only weaponry that can be considered part of just warfare, and that different types of mass destruction weaponry are not produced against the just war principles. For example, cluster bombs and certain types of high-capacity arms can frequently be used illegally against civilians, on account of their deterrent effects (Macintyre et al. 2000). Typically, such weapons will represent at the very least an ambiguous proposition, as their quality in terms of 'just' use is borderline and allows for situational discretion on the part of the user. As weapons of mass destruction and/or weapons aimed against civilians could not be deemed acceptable under the just war doctrine, to be involved in any assets pertaining to such weapons would be immoral under the Reformed tradition.

Regarding weapons sold to private individuals or groups for self-defence, the matter may not be much different from when intended for warfare. There are places in the world where it is customary to keep arms privately, for example in the United States of America, and where it is also historically and socially acceptable and expected (National Rifle Association n.d.). When comparing to the just war doctrine, it could be argued that if a state can defend itself justly, then, also a private citizen should be awarded the same privilege. It is difficult to argue against this logic, and manufacturing and selling arms to individuals for protecting themselves or their families cannot be seen as immoral.

When it comes to weapons used for recreational hunting, the matter becomes simpler. The killing of animals for entertainment is always immoral, and to contribute to such activities in any form is immoral. However, there will be groups who hunt for a living, and in a sustainable way, and manufacturing and distributing weaponry to them will be deemed morally acceptable. The same will be the case for those using arms to kill humanely wounded wild animals as will be the case for certain specialised government agencies and park rangers.

It would be a reasonable and responsible interpretation of scripturally based ethical principles such as the *imago Dei* doctrine and the just war doctrine, to maintain that participation in arms production should generally be deemed immoral and contrary to central Christian values. However, as this category can be morally defensible in certain narrow situations, it can in these situations be tolerable; however, the acceptability of such activities as moral would be the rare exception.

The conclusion connected to weapons production and sales would be that the 'best practice' banking strategy of any would be to avoid arms production.

☐ Medical service providers

Within the realm of medical service providers, including hospitals and clinics, the topics of abortion and euthanasia are of particular interest in the context of this treatise. Globally, the number of artificially induced abortions is around 42 million, according to Antommattei, Khanfar and Mujtaba (2011), and in the Netherlands alone, the annual number of euthanasia procedures was around the 10 000 mark already 20 years ago (Onwuteaka-Philipsen et al. 2003). These disturbingly high numbers demonstrate the prevalence of such medical practices and explain the global market as vast and presumably profitable, leaving bankers numerous opportunities to participate. Abortion is always deemed immoral under the Reformed paradigm, and euthanasia can only be permitted in rare and mutually informed circumstances. Even in the rare acceptable situations permitting euthanasia, the lack of hope and trust in God evokes moral considerations that explain the ambiguous character of the practice and shows how practitioners should approach such a practice with the utmost caution (Banner 1998). Further, Vorster's (2007) perspective on what would represent love and societal stewardship would indicate that to partake in practices involving euthanasia could still conflict with Christian principles. To finance any medical service providers performing or promoting abortion would be immoral and should not be permitted under any circumstance. To cooperate with medical service providers who perform or promote euthanasia is generally immoral, even if it may be allowed under certain rare circumstances.

The conclusion connected to medical service providers would be that the 'best practice' banking strategy of any would be to avoid medical service providers performing or promoting abortion, as well as medical service providers who perform or promote euthanasia, as such practice may only be allowed under rare circumstances.

☐ Medical products

Although the concept of caring for the sick would be well within core Christian values, the manufacturing of medicine and its marketing may prove morally problematic and ambiguous. A typical example could be when a product that has been developed for one purpose is being used (abused) for others, and when this is a situation known to and exploited by the producer. For instance, this was the situation with Misoprostol (Cytitec), which is a medicine designed for use against stomach ulcers, but that has side effects, making it an effective pill for inducing abortions. To market this pill knowing that it can be used for immoral purposes would then be problematic; this example demonstrates a particular challenge of the medical products industry (Antommattei et al. 2011).

The matter of the abortion pill is relevant when considering banking participation, as to some societal actors, its marketing and promotion will aid the health of women worldwide, but to others, its marketing and use remain immoral. The RU-486, which was the product name of the abortion pill prior to its final marketing in the global market, reveals another complication. Even though the company Roussel Uclaf, which back in the 1980s held the patent, hesitated to market the pill for moral and market reasons, it was forced by the French government to release the pill into the market, as the obviously secular French government took the position that its marketing was the best moral choice (Badaracco 1998).

The difficulties described above pertaining to the use and abuse of medical products for abortions can be expected to be found in other cases as well, and to fully assess the level of abuse of prescription drugs, and the knowledge of the producer, will be difficult for any practitioner (Compton & Volkow 2006; McCabe, Teter & Boyd 2006). Similar problems could be connected to the use of medical products in warfare, immoral experimentation, immoral research and punishments, and to the banker, the task would be to monitor and assess the real-life practical use of the involved products, and the level of knowledge that exists related to possible abusive use. For informal abuse by private citizens, the banking practitioner cannot be responsible, unless it is clear that the producer is exploiting this.

The conclusion connected to medical products would be that the 'best practice' banking strategy would be to avoid medical products designed to counteract Christian norms or when the producer knowingly exploits the market for abuse that transgresses such norms.

Biomedical science and products

As with the medical sector, participating in industries using modern-day biomedical practices can be problematic, as this may well be in breach of Christian norms. Such opportunities may be found in private corporations, and within educational institutions, pertaining to a wide range of situations, such as IVF, surrogate mothers, organ harvesting and donations, gene splicing, cloning, human genome manipulation (eugenics), pre-natal diagnostics, hybrids and chimeras (Geisler 2010; Sutton 2008).

For practitioners, it can be problematic how and where to draw the moral line, as questionable biomedical products and practices may be hidden in many different industries, and under several layers of research, material inputs and suppliers. For example, the derivation and use of human stem cells in medical treatments and in medical products may well be in conflict with the *imago Dei* doctrine, and the use and/or production of such medical products may be difficult for the banker to observe (Parson 2006).

It can be difficult to conclude comprehensively what types of activities should be considered immoral within the category covered by biomedical and scientific concerns, and a particular concern is that education and scientific endeavours have been central church activities for centuries (MacCulloch 2010). To limit educational involvement in an overly strict manner could therefore possibly counteract other central Christian values. Based on the brief elaboration here, and in conjunction with the scripturally based norms, the conclusion is that it is immoral to partake in activities or products using or promoting scientific or biomedical practices or products in violation of such norms. The concerned banking practitioner needs to observe these norms, and refrain from involving when it is evident that central Christian norms are violated.

The conclusion connected to biomedical science and products would be that the 'best practice' banking strategy would be to avoid activities or products utilising or promoting scientific or biomedical practices or products in violation of Christian norms.

Acceptable practices
Women and family

When addressing opportunities that would support Christian norms of the sanctity of life, women and family considerations would be a natural starting point. The family is a core societal unit, and women are at the centre of caregiving and activities connected to subsistence of life and family-oriented activities, and the support of these values should be given the highest priority (Kostenberger 2010). Aspects bankers should look for would be whether involvement could be seen as supporting values pertaining to the maintenance of human life, and to the fulfilment of our human obligation under the creation covenant (Gn 1:26).

It is unfortunate that women could be surrounded by social conditions driving them to seek abortion when pregnancy is an aspect that should be considered when determining how to participate in a manner that promotes human life and its scripturally explained sanctity (Gn 1:27; Ex 20:13). Glander et al. (1998) found through their substantial study amongst women in the United States of America that as many as 39.5% of the women seeking abortion amongst their study subjects reported that they were victims of domestic violence, and they conclude that this could be amongst the factors that motivate the abortion choice. In other cultures, cultural pressures on women, brought on by poverty or offspring gender preferences, for example, could also lead to women terminating their pregnancies (Agadjanian 1998). On the basis of these overall arguments, it would be prudent to argue that to aid women in their social and material circumstances, allowing them the freedom to choose life in a benign social environment, could lead to fewer abortions, and thus, advance human life in its state of God-given sanctity.

How to support life through aiding women and families is touched upon below in connection with several of the suggested asset categories, and at this stage, the direct measures could be related to the immediate social environment of families. Support for women and their right to freely continue their pregnancies could be aided through allowing them to have personal economic prospects through equal opportunities for education and work. One direct measure that can be influenced by banking participation would be the alleviation of one of the difficult aspects of poverty, namely sufficient housing. Buvinić and Gupta (1997) posit that in developing countries there is a prevalence of poverty in female-headed households, and that targeting women to enhance their economic conditions would be a prudent method of supporting these families. They further explain that to intervene constructively in families in developing countries led by women is a more efficient method of poverty reduction compared to targeting the male-headed families, as this would add further economic trickle-down effects in society. Urbanisation is a growing trend, and today approximately 55% of the world's population live in cities, and the projection for 2030 is 60%. In the wake of such a strong trend is a high and unmet demand for housing in the urban areas. The global urbanisation has developed rapidly: in 1955, there were 90 cities in the world with a population exceeding 1 million; in 1995, the number was 336; in 2016, the number was 512, and by 2030, the projected number is 662 (Moore, Gould & Keary 2003; United Nations n.d.). Amongst the new urban dwellers migrating to a new life, the need for housing is substantial on a global scale, and lack of housing leads to a series of poverty related problems, such as lack of water, poor sanitation and subsequent health risk and scarce education opportunities.

To outline comprehensive categories to support women and families would be difficult, but to focus assets related to family and women's needs would be a prudent manner of supporting the maintenance of our population, motivating childbirth without terminating pregnancies, and allowing for the safe upbringing of children. Obvious assets to involve in towards this end would be in the construction industry, housing and infrastructure directed at developing new global urban growth, as this would support the family, and thus life, long term and constructively. This market is large and diversified, and the projected value of engineering, procurement and construction (EPC) market worldwide in 2019, is $7.6 trillion (Statista n.d.).

Involvement connected to construction, the development of housing and infrastructure directed at developing the new global urban growth, is well within Christian historical tradition, and would fit in under a Christian banking strategy.

☐ Promoting peace – Trade and technology

For the support of human life, counteracting war would be a central aspect to consider in financing activity. As has been established, merely refraining from financing conflict and partaking in arms production would not suffice; the question is how to promote peace through financial involvement.

For promoting peace, it is relevant to suppress the impulse of initiating war because for humans to go to war against someone we are friendly with is not as tempting as with those we loathe (Var, Brayley & Korsay 1989). Consequently, it would be expected that to promote cultural exchange between people of different nationalities, races, religions and cultures would aid sustained peace, and thus minimise the risk of war. I do however realise how my assumption may not always hold true, as the horrors of the civil wars in Rwanda and Ex-Yugoslavia of the late 20th century would well exemplify. Typical modes of distributing intercultural knowledge would be through travel and tourism, and pertaining to this could be travel agencies, airlines, ships and ferries, hotels, accommodation and hospitality providers. In addition to such traditional assets, cultural exchange can be expected to have been accelerated by information technology, and further distributed by the added efficacy of the Internet (Takahashi et al. 2008). It could be expected that there are multitudes of technologies that would support cultural exchange, such as educational providers and travel and tourism-oriented technology, and that for practitioners, there should be good opportunities to contribute constructively.

In addition to the foregoing, trade is a traditional mode of cultural exchange, and we know from examples such as the Silk Road of antiquity that trade can make people rely on one another, and get to know one another, and that such trade presupposes trust amongst the involved actors (Christian 2000; Lee & Turban 2001). It is reasonable to expect that there would be available assets in this category, such as trading platforms pertaining to shares and commodities, by way of both traditional formats and those based on technology.

Involvement with actors promoting cultural exchange, such as by way of travel, tourism and trade, is well within Christian historical tradition, and would fit in under a Christian strategy.

☐ Medical service providers

The development of hospitals stems from medieval monasteries in Europe, and knowledge of medicine was passed on and furthered in church-run universities, and Calvin's interest in this sector is demonstrated in Chapter 6 (Antić 2010). Within this proud Christian tradition, there should be many opportunities to contribute in this sector. Such involvement could conceivably be directed towards shares in health service providers, such as operators and owners of hospitals and clinics, insurance companies offering health coverage, as well as in the form of real estate and infrastructure connected to such activities. In countries where the health services are nationalised, different public–private partnership (PPP) schemes, for financing and owning hospitals and health service infrastructure would typically represent opportunities in this sector (Klijn & Teisman 2003).

The global healthcare sector is of substantial size, and in 2016 was estimated to involve a total spending of approximately $1000 for every person in the world, with an average spending of approximately 10% of the total global Gross Domestic Product (GDP). This number includes private and governmental actors and should give a brief indication as to the scale of the sector and its connected industries (World Bank Group n.d.). There are opportunities in this sector in abundance, and such may be sought in most markets globally.

Involvement in the healthcare services industry is well within Christian historical tradition and would fit in under a Christian banking strategy.

Pharmaceuticals and medical equipment

An obvious starting point here would be the pharmaceutical industry, which supplies the consumption of vast proportions, with a global spending in 2018 alone of $1.2 trillion (Statista n.d.). This industry would render many opportunities falling within a Christian banking strategy. A natural extension of the pharmaceutical industry is the sector of medical equipment, where all manner of specialised equipment and tools for service providers is produced. Typical equipment here will include items such as CT scanners, X-ray machines, special lighting and fittings, diagnostics equipment and operating tools. In its own right, this is a massive industry, and as it is not as clearly delineated and regulated as the pharmaceutical industry, it is difficult to assess its global annual turnover, but the global size of the medical technology sector alone for 2018 is estimated at $430 billion (Statista n.d.). This is also a sector where ample acceptable opportunities should be found. A further extension within this industrial realm would be products aimed at alleviating the suffering of the disabled and handicapped, such as prostheses, wheelchairs and hearing aids. As this industry encompasses outputs ranging from directly connected products to more distantly connected ones such as building access ramps, specialised locks, alarm systems and doorbells, it would be even less clearly delineated than the medical equipment industry, and I expect it would be challenging to fully estimate its total global size, although it can be assumed to be substantial.

Involvement in the pharmaceutical and health products industry is well within Christian historical tradition and would fit in under a Christian banking strategy.

☐ Health-promoting assets

In addition to the conventionally defined medical sector, there is a growing industry pertaining to promoting good health, which is expressed by way of health centres and gyms, manufacturing and distributing specialty products, fitness technology, sporting equipment and nutritional supplements.

This sector can collectively be seen as a natural extension of the medical services and products industries mentioned above, and is aligned with prudent Christian values, connected to the exertion of prudent societal stewardship and caring for creation, and the acceptance of good health as a gift flowing from the grace of God. To assess the total annual turnover of this sector on a global basis would be difficult, as it represents a collection of different yet associated opportunities. The nutritional supplements industry alone has an estimated global turnover of $132.8 billion in 2016 and is predicted to reach $220.3 billion in 2022 (GlobeNewswire n.d.), and the fitness club industry had a global annual turnover in 2018 of $80 billion (Statista n.d.). If these substantial numbers are extrapolated and expanded onto a wider sector perception, it would appear that this is an industry of vast proportions, offering immense possibilities.

Involvement in the health-promoting products and services industry is well within Christian historical tradition and would fit in under a Christian banking strategy.

■ Human rights
Unacceptable practices
☐ Unjust regimes

In the academic discourse pertaining to international business and ethics, there has been slight interest in developing cross-cultural standards to follow, and the level of general agreement is low (Robertson & Athanassiou 2009). A prevailing tendency amongst business theorists has been for different cultures and countries to develop their ethical norms incrementally and on a contextual basis. This should explain why there is a lack of adherence to equal moral norms in all markets (Gick 2003). In addition, it should be pointed out that the main tendency is to adhere to consequentialist moral philosophies, and to some, this entails the option to negotiate the lowest common moral denominator amongst the involved stakeholders, manoeuvring the different extant moral norms, and leaving the outcome at a minimum acceptable level for all involved (Korthals 2008). Such ethical theorising could not be seen as acceptable from a deontological perspective.

As demonstrated in Chapter 6, central human rights such as access to basic education, private property ownership, freedom of speech and freedom of belief should be seen as central Christian values worthy of respect. Yet, as explained above, the current international business climate is one where it is not necessary to adopt the highest moral standards once business is taken across national and cultural boundaries, and bankers are free to participate regardless of whether such values are represented in the country of the target activity. It could be argued that as long as this state of moral relativism in international business is allowed to persist, it would not contribute to any real development of freedom of speech and belief, but rather, it may contribute to the perpetuation of the undesired state instead. If left as it is, the recipient regime will benefit from the business activity through taxation and general increased economic output, and thus strengthen its government and authoritative power. On this basis and taking into account the Reformed position pertaining to education, freedom of speech and religion, it should be seen as immoral to involve commercially in unjust countries and regimes where these basic human rights are not respected.

The conclusion connected to unjust countries and regimes would be that the 'best practice' banking strategy would be to avoid unjust countries and regimes where basic human rights are not respected.

Child labour

Another matter pertaining to human rights and treatment of individuals involves the use of child labour in industrial production and economic activity in general. This practice prevails in many countries around the world, and may exist within any country or regime, regardless of their formal position or express intentions. For practitioners, this situation evokes particular consideration, and involves scrutiny and evaluation of the target assets and their supply chains. The matter of child labour is an important consideration, as children are the weakest of societal actors, and because they represent the future, their treatment determines what development can be expected in the relevant country. Thus, any form of exploitation of children will be viewed as immoral and in breach of core Christian norms, as well as breaking with central secular perceptions of universal human rights. The Reformed ethical position on child labour is that it should be avoided, and thus it should be seen as immoral to contribute to any activity or asset if this can be seen as promoting or utilising any form of child labour.

The conclusion connected to child labour would be that the 'best practice' banking strategy of any would be to avoid activities that can be seen as promoting or using any form of child labour at any level.

Labour rights, gender and racism

When participating on a global scale, to observe that the involved labourers receive fair wages, have the rights of unionising and that all societal actors have equal rights of participation regardless of race, gender, ethnicity, age, disability, political or religious affiliation, is another matter that can represent difficulties of assessment for the concerned banking practitioner. Social division and inequality can permeate a society, and these can be based on all the aforementioned social characteristics and markers and more (Bottero 2005). To fully assess such social mechanisms in a society may be difficult, and it should be expected that social division and inequalities exist in all societies, but the aim should be to avoid promoting increased social injustice or perpetuating such undesired societal states (Banerjee & Duflo 2012; Kymlicka 1995). A particular problem is that inequalities can be highly politicised within each country, and bankers should not be obligated to take part in any internal societal discourse on social justice on a superficial and merely political or theoretical level (Rawls 1971). To promote inequality on the basis of race, ethnicity or gender, or any other marginalising characteristics, cannot be defended in a Reformed ethical theology, and banking should not contribute to perpetuating structural injustices or to contribute to such conditions. Further, workers should receive fair wages for their work, allowing them to support themselves and their dependents with dignity, as denying them such level of wages will be deemed immoral.

The conclusion connected to labour rights, gender and racism would be that the 'best practice' banking strategy would be to avoid structures that support or perpetuate grave social injustice based on race, gender, ethnicity, age, disability, political or religious affiliation, and to avoid structures where the involved labourers do not have sufficient rest and leisure time, do not receive fair wages or do not work under fair working conditions.

Acceptable practices
Educational service providers

Promoting education and rendering educational services is a strong and longstanding scripturally founded Christian tradition, which is at the core of the values of the Christian church and the Reformed tradition. In its current state, actors ranging from governmental agencies, religious institutions, eleemosynary organisations and private for-profit corporations offer education in a competitive environment (Marginson 2006). For the banking practitioner, it is the latter category that is open for participation and in the following, some angles and examples are presented for consideration.

Within the education sector, there will be private actors rendering education services directed at the consumer, the student and those who produce support services to the primary provider by way of sub-supplies and technological solutions or physical real property and adjacent infrastructure. All of these categories are open for consideration. With the advent of the Internet, information technologies have been used to an increasing degree to support education rendered on different learning platforms. This opens up new and promising opportunities in addition to the direct involvement in established, privately owned education facilities of the traditional type. Examples here could be privately owned education providers operating within the higher education market and educational technology provider to this market, supplying technological infrastructure aimed at campus and online learning facilitation. Other examples could be companies that render educational services online or by way of apps, of which there is an abundance to choose from, ranging from specialised providers focused for example on language education, to those covering a wide range of educational topics.

Involvement in educational providers and attendant technology and infrastructure is well within Christian historical tradition and would fit in under a Christian banking strategy.

Emerging nations

We live in a world with substantial socio-political instability in some regions, and at the time of writing, there is great unrest in the Middle East, North Africa, with the NATO members at odds with Russia over the Ukraine and other matters. No matter what the background of such crises, and what the outcome might be, in these regions people live with needs common to everyone. It would be important, then, to assess how financial activity could contribute positively to the development of such countries, be it under current or new rule. The focus here is on how to secure societal development without meddling in the domestic political discourse, and to promote the sound development of a society where human rights as described above are secured.

Emergent nations often need to go through a stressful political process. For example, the emergence of the post-apartheid South Africa necessitated substantial social reforms and judicial procedures, including that of the Truth and Reconciliation Commission, as part of the nation-building process (Vorster 2017a). The relative success of this peaceful transition in a country with many different ethnic and religious groups should serve as an example of nation-building through peaceful discourse. Outside actors, however, should leave the emerging nation to attend to the internal and contentious matters of politics and historical interpretation. On the other hand, as described above in Chapter 6, it is not consistent with the Christian stance to sit still and accept the societal misfortunes of others, but to accept that sometimes civil disobedience and regime change should be supported.

Support for emergent nations in their democratic development through financial engagement should be focused on necessary elements of infrastructure that could be missing. Typical projects that have been performed with success in PPP pertain to the development of roads, hospitals, schools, bridges, ports, airports and more (Osborne 2000; Savas 2000). It could be argued that contributing to the establishment of such necessary societal foundations would be an important step in securing the establishment and maintenance of basic human rights in the emergent state, as new societal upheaval could jeopardise the newfound societal goods and efficacy made possible through the PPPs. Further, this effect of the PPP could be seen as a benign and non-intrusive method of exerting a minimum of international governance on the emerging nation (Börzel & Risse 2005). In the very nature of PPP-based infrastructure development lies the almost limitless extent of its scalability, as such projects may include construction and development on the grandest scale, and thus, there should be plentiful opportunities within this category.

Involvement in PPP-based infrastructure projects in emerging nations is well within Christian historical tradition and would fit in under a Christian banking strategy.

☐ Information technology and media

As has been demonstrated in Chapter 6, certain human rights such as basic education, private property ownership, freedom of speech and freedom of belief are core values protected under the Reformed paradigm. The promotion of such values should then be included in banking practices, and the concerned practitioner should seek out opportunities directed at this goal.

A traditional manner of subduing citizens' rights of free speech and belief has been through the control of media, information technology and information distribution, which has given rulers the opportunity to muffle, quieten or silence unwanted societal voices that often belong to minorities and perceived societal out-groups (Augoustinos, Walker & Donaghue 2006). In the context here, 'media' will include all manner of media that distribute any kind of information, whether they be connected to news, education, science, entertainment, religion, politics, map services and many more. The traditional manner of distributing information has been connected to physical objects and artefacts, such as newspapers, books and art, and this mode of storing and dispersing information has made governmental suppression relatively simple. Since the advent of the Internet, however, information is flowing more freely than ever before, and authoritarian governmental control measures have proven difficult to exert. It could be argued that this lack of control is a central cause of the negativity and fearmongering often promulgated by authorities and established old-school media pertaining to the Internet and what can be found there, especially regarding abusive and addictive content (Pujazon-Zazik & Park 2010; Young 2004).

The promotion of free dispersion of news and information should be seen as central in securing basic human rights such as freedom of speech and belief. The line between what is considered media and its connected technology is becoming increasingly blurred; so, to delineate between what is considered information technology and media in the contemporary sense is difficult. Therefore, possible engagement in media could be viewed through the lens of technology, and conversely, possible engagement in technology could be viewed through the lens of media. Contributing in media no matter the mode of information dispersal and connected technology would be included as beneficial, as this would be seen as supportive to upholding basic human rights. As the underlying infrastructure of the Internet is still connected to physical modes of delivery such as fibre optic cables, server parks and the like, it is the users and their technology that would be of particular interest to promote through financial participation, for the securing of a continued development of free and unencumbered dispersal of opinions and expressions of belief. The increasing number of social media operators, information providers and map services, to mention but a few well-known types of actors from the information technology sector, exemplify the kind of organisations that would possibly promote important human rights such as freedom of speech and belief. It is assumed that there are immense opportunities in this sector.

Involvement in information technology and media is well within Christian historical tradition and would fit in under a Christian banking strategy.

Technology manufacturing and distribution

Technology hardware and software plays an ever more important role in all levels of human interaction, whether in business, education or for recreational use, for the days when pen and paper, blackboard and chalk were at the centre of human non-verbal professional activity, communication and educational activity are long gone. I have already touched upon the software side, my main focus here is on the hardware, and how to participate in the production and distribution of technology-driven products useful in business, education and recreation. Any forward-leaning Christian banking strategy will consider such opportunities with care.

Chinn and Fairlie (2010) conducted a study focusing on differences in computer and Internet penetration between developed and developing countries. Their findings are not surprising and revealed that in the period from 1999 to 2004, computer penetration in the developed nations was approximately five times higher than in the developing countries. As explained above, technology is becoming increasingly important in all realms of society, and the result of such gaps in computer prevalence amongst countries may lead to associated wealth and knowledge gaps in the global population. To participate, then, in the production and distribution of computers and adjacent technology could contribute positively to the advancement of business and education on a global scale. The sector offering computer hardware is substantial, and when attempting to assess this sector, it would be difficult to delineate clearly the software providers from the hardware ones, as frequently, one product spectrum supports the other, and computers are increasingly becoming integrated in telephones, cameras and other handheld devices. The term 'computer' is therefore used in its loosest and widest sense, and the kinds of devices that are currently available, or will be available in the future, will not be central for the purposes of this treatise. The industry distributing technological hardware is also substantial, both by way of traditional retail actors as well as online based ones. Many of the involved companies are publicly listed and are available for immediate involvement.

Involvement in manufacturers and retailers of computers and attendant technology is well within Christian historical tradition and would fit in under a Christian banking strategy.

☐ Equal opportunities

With most, if not all, possible banking activities there will be questions regarding equal opportunities for all involved actors in relation to race, gender, ethnicity, age, disability, political or religious affiliations, and more, that will appear as relevant for the ethically concerned practitioners.

It can be difficult to assess how an asset rates in regard to equal opportunities and diversity, but as the topic of inclusion and integration of all is a growing concern amongst the business community in the West, it will be increasingly possible to influence the development in a benign direction. For example, on matters or gender equality in organisations, there are currently several initiatives in place where focus is set on increasing female participation on all levels of organisation, such as for example the *SHE Index* as co-founded by EY, where actors from business life and academia cooperate in clearing the way for women in business (SHE Index n.d.). Also, there is an interest in the ethicality of gender equal participation in top level of business life, as for example is evidenced in the Gender Appreciative Recruitment Practice (GARP) format as developed by Bøsterud (C.E. 2019). Under the GARP paradigm, a framework for increasing the recruitment of women is given, where the aim is to even out the extant gender imbalance at the top level of management, all within a deontological Christian framework. Related to diversity and inclusion in general, in connection to the CSR/ESG movement, there is substantial interest, both within the business community as well as in the academic realm. The discourse there is as mentioned in Chapter 4 solely based on secular models of consequentialist ethics, but will nonetheless contribute interesting perspectives that may assist in financial activity. From this movement and adjacent initiatives, like that of the *SHE Index*, it will be more possible to assess assets and how they align to the ethical norms connected to equal opportunities and diversity as demonstrated in Chapter 6.

For the purpose of this treatise, the ethical norm pertaining to equal opportunities, race, gender, ethnicity, age, disability, political or religious affiliation is to actively protect the equal rights of all. It will of course not be possible to single out any particular bankable assets in this connection, as the qualities of equal opportunity and diversity are tenets that will have to be sought in all possible sectors.

Involvement where equal opportunities for all involved is supported as a core value, notwithstanding race, gender, ethnicity, age, disability, political or religious affiliations or more, is well within Christian historical tradition and would fit in under a Christian banking strategy.

☐ Dignified work life

In most of the conceivable bankable assets open for participation, there will be, or have been, people involved in their production, manufacturing or operating of the goods or services involved. As with equal opportunities and diversity, the question that arises for the ethically concerned banker is whether the involved people are reared with decency as aligned with the Christian norms set out in this treatise. In other words, are the workers fairly treated, and can they lead a decent work life and support themselves and their families to lead a life of dignity.

As with the topic of equal opportunities and diversity, also in connection to fairness in employment and work life, the UN Declaration of human rights (art. 23 and 24) and the CSR/ESG discourse will cast valuable light on what concerns that typically will be open for moral adjudication. Not least under the ESG paradigm will there be existing systems and tools in use for assessing whether targeted actors involve a morally viable treatment of workers and other stakeholders, and thus will be useful when adhering to the principles set out in Chapter 6 (e.g. Circular n.d.). For example, transparency vis-à-vis workforce makeup will be of importance so that it may be assessed whether child labour is in use and that fair wages and working conditions are observed.

For the purposes of this treatise, the norm is to actively promote a dignified work life through fair wages, where sufficient rest and leisure time is observed and children's right to childhood is protected.

Involvement where all involved workers receive fair wages, where sufficient rest and leisure time is observed and children's right to childhood is protected, is well within Christian historical tradition and would fit in under a Christian banking strategy.

■ Nature and ecology
Unacceptable practices
☐ Animal welfare

It is of importance to assess to what degree involvement in food production can be perceived as moral from the perspective of treating animals in ethically responsible ways. Furthermore, as humans we relate to animals also in connection to different recreational activities, which will bring to the fore ethical questions adjacent to those pertaining to directly to food production. Aspects of food production pertaining to pollution and other harmful practices such as fertilising and genetic modification of plants are covered under the sections pertaining to pollution ('Nature and ecology' and 'Pollution – Harmful products and practices'). The focus here is on how we treat animals in situations related to food production and recreation.

In modern-day farming practices, animal husbandry involves high concentrations of animals, effective breeds, transportation and high-efficiency feeding practices. From such husbandry, numerous new diseases have become increasingly problematic, and producers seek to counteract these by adding antibiotics and other medicine to the feed. Animal husbandry is then becoming a constant race between disease resistance and efficient product output (Gaggìa, Mattarelli & Biavati 2010). What is less discussed than the general problems of disease is that parts of the increasing disease challenges stem from the practice of breeding evermore fast-growing and meat-efficient animal breeds. This again leads to the situation in which the natural immune system of the animals is less and less capable of tackling disease, which will be counteracted by adding more medicine to the feed, in an ongoing escalating downward cycle. Other potentially harmful and sickness-inducing practices can involve genetically unhealthy breeding and over-feeding, to the extent that certain animals, like poultry, no longer possess the natural ability to freely move around and carry their own body weight, being crippled by design and prone to heart attacks and numerous other health problems (Mason & Finelly 2006).

Added to the problems related to health under production, animals are increasingly being transported over longer distances to abattoirs for slaughter, and this induces stress and disease in the animals, necessitating even more medication and artificial means of keeping them alive and in relative health (Ljungberg, Gebresenbet & Aradom 2007). It is possible to give numerous examples of modern farming practices, and how these may induce added and/or unnecessary suffering to the production animals, but for the purposes of this treatise, the few examples mentioned should suffice to illuminate the problems that are connected to financial engagement.

Animals are frequently being used in research and product testing as subjects of live experimentation. A central matter to identify in connection with the research use of animals is, as with food production, to assess whether the practice is painful, and/or if this pain is necessary. Examples of unnecessary experimentation could be those used for educational purposes when the experiments have been performed previously and the outcome is well known. In addition, some research projects may in themselves prove to be superfluous, as the result may be obvious, and thus, the inflicted pain is unnecessary (Ryder 2006).

In addition to being used as a source of food for human consumption, animals also serve as a source of other products, whether it be consumer objects such as leather goods or clothing, and in the supply chains of other productions such as for feed. In fact, the animals themselves may be bred for sale, so that the animal itself is the end product, such as in the pet industry, as when breeding test animals, when breeding for the sale of live agricultural animals for further rearing by others, and so on. Animals may also be used in services such as in entertainment and recreational industries, such as circuses, zoos and theme parks. As part of such entertainment and/or recreational use of animals, they may be used as prey in hunting and fishing, as well-being kept as pets or for fighting (e.g. in bullfights and cockfights), used in bull runs, et cetera. Regarding recreational hunting and fishing, this sector is catered to by a large industry, and pertaining to weapons, it has been established that such manufacturing and sales are immoral. Furthermore, the supplying of other kinds of equipment to this sector will also be considered unacceptable, such as for example fishing gear, traps, specialised tracking systems and more. That this sector is substantial can be understood based on the number of people involved, as for example, in the United States of America alone, the number of participants in recreational hunting and fishing activities for 2017 was staggering, at a total of more than 65 million (Statista n.d.). When it comes to financial engagement in bullfighting and other entertainment activities where the torture of animals is involved, it is clear that any such involvement is considered unacceptable. Finally, there are parts of the pet industry where unethical practices connected to unhealthy breeding, feeding and keeping animals are involved. For example. In the United Kingdom, more than 40% of all cats and dogs are overweight (McEachern & Cheetham 2013). Such practices involve inflicting harm on animals and/or depriving them of their natural needs, and to be involved in commercial activities promoting or including such practices will be deemed immoral.

For purposes of this treatise, it does not matter whether commercial activity based on animals relates to the direct use of the animal or through by-products of other animal-based activities. The theme here is how the animals are treated wherever they may contribute to the production of goods and/or services, as this is what bankers can influence through their practice.

The conclusion connected to animal welfare in production and testing would be that the 'best practice' banking strategy would be to avoid economic or scientific activities that contribute to inflict suffering in animals, or that deprive them of basic natural needs.

▢ Pollution – Harmful products and practices

The concept of sustainability can be useful to consider, as contributions that influence the natural environment in unsustainable ways should most likely not be seen as morally permissible under acceptable Christian norms (Wilson, Furniss & Kimbowa 2010). The Brundtland Commission, led by the former Norwegian prime minister Gro Harlem Brundtland under a United Nations mandate, introduced the concept of sustainability. The Commission concluded that sustainable development included the necessity for development to 'meet the needs of the present without compromising the ability of future generations to meet their needs' (Brundtland 1987). The Brundtland Commission is widely seen as a global starting point for using the term 'sustainable development', despite earlier use, and it reflects the UN's concern for the need for global thinking pertaining to the environment. In particular, the concept is of great importance in different efforts to alleviate poverty, as poor people have substantial physical needs that need to be met and will typically be lacking in the ability or capability to meet these needs in an environmentally friendly manner (Mulligan 2015). This guiding principle is in harmony with the Reformed position that has been explained in Chapter 6. To interpret it in practical terms may be challenging, but to determine what is unsustainable could prove simpler. A key aspect could be that of ecological diversity – to respect God's creation, and to uphold the extant biodiversity we enjoy on our planet, should be a natural way of interpreting the human obligation towards the creation, and our stewardship covenant with God (Gn 1:28, 2:15). This obligation surely includes a duty not to influence nature in a way that can permanently destroy it by way of eradicating species or risking permanent destruction of biodiversity, of which the lasting consequences under any circumstance cannot be known or knowable to us. This obligation is the main contention of Wilson (1992) who examines different modes of human destructive impact on ecological systems and strongly advocates that it is not within our stewardship role in nature to allow species and ecosystems to be destroyed so that they disappear for good.

The concepts of sustainability and biodiversity should guide thinking about the human impact on nature, and they could inform different modes and types of banking activity. For example, the topic of carbon emission and its possible effects on nature is contentious, but, since we do not know with certainty its effects, caution would be a prudent conclusion to draw from the sustainability thinking. That humans have a place in nature is given, but as we invent new modes of alleviation of our physical struggles, the impact of carbon emission increases steadily. For example, Berners-Lee (2010) explains that for every Internet search that is conducted, including, then, for this treatise, around 4.5 g of carbon dioxide is used. We do not know, of course, what this means exactly for nature, but it is certain that in earlier historical times this impact was not made, as we did not have computers. The obligation to care for nature, then, teaches us to be careful and diligent.

As most if not all human activity will affect our environment in some way, the pertinent question will then be what kind of financing practices can be seen as immoral. Many different industries and practices could be seen as immoral, but the practical baseline should be whether an activity promotes environmental destruction on a lasting level, by its participation in production, product use and/or disposal of the end product.

The conclusion connected to pollution, harmful products and practices would be that the 'best practice' banking strategy would be to avoid activities that directly or indirectly harm or alter the natural environment in a lasting manner, by destruction of species or causing irreparable damage to ecosystems.

Bioethical considerations

Bioethical concerns connected to modern-day scientific and commercial practices for the production of goods and services abound. The use of bio-scientific techniques is in use in numerous productions, and can be used in the manufacturing of food, feed, biomaterials, bioenergy, rare components such as biopharmaceuticals and enzymes (Twardowski 2010). For example, in connection to animal husbandry, there are many possibilities to alter and influence the genetic makeup of animals, and when this is done, we cannot know how it affects the animal in the now, its potential offspring or its surroundings. Such concerns are also relevant in the development of strains of agricultural plans where gene modification (GM) is used to enhance production output and disease resistance. Although there can be certain immediate production benefits by using GM in agricultural or other productions, there is no scientific evidence to support that such practice is safe; in fact, there are strong contentions within the natural science community as to whether we can even know the true effects of such bio-scientific practices (Domingo & Bordonaba 2011; Hilbeck et al. 2015).

Gene modification whether in the form of animals, plants or microorganism is frequently in use in many industrial productions, and for the concerned banking practitioner, it can be a difficult task to overview when a commercial activity is involved in such bio-scientific practice or not. However, even though it will be hard to assess, it will always be considered immoral to participate in any commercial activity where gene manipulation or other means of biological influencing is utilised in a degree where we as humans living today cannot overview the effects such manipulation has on the present or future environment.

The conclusion connected to bioethical considerations would be that the 'best practice' banking strategy would be to avoid activities that directly or indirectly alter natural organisms in a manner after which it is not known what will be the effects on nature, now or in the future.

Acceptable practices
Food and animals

Certain areas of the food production sector may be problematic because of the ecological concerns, but this should not induce any banking professional to refrain from partaking in the core human activity that is food production. The aim will then be how to participate in a manner that contributes constructively to added food output as compared to the utilised input, and that does not violate ecological principles of sustainability. Substantial progress has been made in food production over the years, and the feats of the Nobel Prize winner Norman Borlaug can exemplify what kind of progress can be made through constructive resource utilisation. Borlaug's contribution to increase the efficacy of agricultural output led to the so-called 'green revolution', and from 1950 to 2000 the global grain production was tripled, but the area under production increased by only 10% (Standage 2010). Within the sector of food production and attendant industries, it is difficult to point to specific financial opportunities that would qualify as acceptable, but it is assumed that there are many opportunities in this sector.

In addition to the agricultural sector, the pet industry is another industrial sector where animal welfare is a concern. This industry involves a host of products and services, which mostly can be matched by industries serving human needs. The sector will encompass live animals, feed, equipment, accommodation, kennel services, veterinary services, training and much more. To illustrate the size of this sector, the pet industry market in the United States of America alone stands at more than $5 billion in 2019 (American Pet Products Association n.d.).

A particular concern pertains to our scripturally founded obligation to exert stewardship over animals (Gn 1:28), and not to inflict suffering on them, or deprive them of their natural needs, and this is an added aspect to consider when contemplating involvement in the food production sector and in the pet industry, which is not directly linked to ecological sustainability. For the Christian, there is a scripturally based obligation to partake only in activities that honour this obligation. For banking practitioners, there are plentiful opportunities connected directly to the agricultural aspects of food production, in addition to opportunities to be found in attendant industries, such as food processing, distribution and retail, as well as in the pet industry.

Involvement in food and beverage production, the pet industry and attendant sectors, is well within Christian historical tradition and would fit in under a Christian banking strategy.

Sustainable production and technology

The norms of stewardship in our interaction with society and nature under our covenant with God in creation (Gn 1:28, 2:15) can be seen as aligned with the concept of sustainability, a concept connected to the findings and propositions of the Brundtland Report in 1987 (Brundtland 1987). The subsequent popularisation of the sustainability concept could be because of the ambiguity and lack of precision in the definition of sustainability. The sustainability concept in the original format allows for continued growth under sustainability, something that is criticised by those who see the world's resources as finite, and thus, adhere to the Scarcity Paradigm (Victor 2008). This discourse has lasted for decades and is part of and an extension of the CSR/ESG discourse that has gained traction in recent years within social sciences and management research (Grinde & Khare 2008).

Of interest for this part of the presentation is how private industries should take part in the promotion of sustainability. A pertinent stance was taken by Desrochers (2010), who explained that by way of efficient market mechanisms and competition throughout history, industrial production has generally become increasingly sustainable. His position is based on the fact that, in a competitive environment, waste of resources weakens the competitive edge, and that those who are best at utilising resources will lead in the free market. He builds on historical sources showing how, through a process of transmaterialisation, what has initially been deemed as waste in one production has been redefined to represent valuable input in others. He warns that if governments try to meddle in this natural market-driven process, we could end up with less sustainable production and resource utilisation than what the free market would ensure. His theories are based on the Sufficiency Paradigm, and he posits that, if the global resources are truly finite, the inevitable break down of our social order can only be postponed, and that we cannot influence in reality whether it will happen. He points to a soteriological understanding of human utility of creation, and through this explains the underlying eschatological tendencies amongst those arguing from a scarcity perspective. This cognition is in concert with the Sufficiency Paradigm that is adhered to in this treatise as a true representation of the global economic state, and this paradigm aligns well with Christian values. In other words, as humans, we are left to benefit from and care for creation in our covenant with God (Gn 1:28, 2:15), and in trusting God, we accept that the global resources are sufficient if we manage them diligently, as is our obligation (Dt 11:13–15).

Based on the market-based position of Desrochers (2010), bankers may engage in any acceptable industrial activity and attendant technologies, and their participation in a competitive market environment would then augment the global sustainability of our collective resource utilisation. However, it would also be conceivable to further contribute constructively in this process, and technologies ensuring increased resource utility would be a prudent locus of interest. It would be difficult to point to specific industries and opportunities here, but examples could be within the areas of waste management, alternative energy and facility management, to mention three sectors. The waste management market involves collecting, transporting, disposing, recycling and monitoring of waste. The global waste management market size in 2017 was estimated at $330.6 billion and is expected to reach $530 billion in 2025 (Statista n.d.). This is a sector where the concerned practitioner can contribute constructively to enhanced transmaterialisation, and the size of the sector would ensure ample financing possibilities. A market in strong growth is the solar energy market, which in 2003 stood at $4.7 billion in size, and at $91.3 billion in 2013, and which is expected to be at $158.4 billion in 2023 (Statista n.d.). This is also a market where there should be sufficient room for the concerned banker to participate. The facility management sector would be relevant in the sustainability perspective and in alignment with the Christian norms of stewardship. This is an industry that has as its core business maintaining and operating commercial and residential buildings, parks and infrastructure, and includes janitorial services, clearing, surface maintenance, pest control, landscaping and more, and where sustainability and resource utilisation would be assumed to be a central competitive factor. This is also a large global sector, and as it is difficult to fully define and delineate against other sectors, it is challenging to assess its global market size.

The above elaboration pertaining to sustainability as ideal in financial activity is a mere overview, and the main contentions are that we are obligated to utilise resources with diligence and that participation in free markets is acceptable to satisfy this expectation.

Involvement in assets aiming at diligent utilisation and maintenance of the environment and manmade resources is well within Christian historical tradition and would fit in under a Christian banking strategy.

Ecotourism

A way of constructively using nature in a sustainable commercial manner would be through different modes of ecotourism. This sector is witnessing substantial growth, and includes services such as whale safaris, volunteering in environmental protection initiatives, bird watching, witnessing a myriad of natural phenomena, such as volcanos, aurora borealis, and a many more.

The concept of ecotourism may not be set in stone, but the International Ecotourism Society (n.d.) offers the following definition: 'responsible travel to natural areas that conserves the environment, sustains the well-being of the local people, and involves interpretation and education'. Ecotourism is a substantial and growing sector open for engagement, and for example, in the United States of America alone, the figure for participants in wildlife and bird watching for 2017 was well in excess of 30 million (Statista n.d.). It will be the assumption here, that not only will such tourism produce income from nature without damaging it, but the educational ethos involved will in addition create an enhanced popular awareness of the intrinsic value of nature and creation amongst an increasingly alienated urban global population.

Involvement in ecotourism is well within Christian historical tradition and would fit in under a Christian banking strategy.

Societal morality
Unacceptable practices
Family

As demonstrated in Chapter 6, the traditional same-sex family with its privileged scriptural position deserves special protection, and, this will be of particular importance for the context here, as in these increasingly secular times in the Western world, the dismantling of family and family values happens at a breakneck speed. This is not least evidenced through high divorce rates, abortions, teenage drug abuse, the media's pushing of the LGBT agenda, materialism, and as well, an increasing interest in the LGBT customer demographic from central industrial actors, to mention but a few factors (Angelini & Bradley 2010; Douma 1996).

There will be a multitude of commercial opportunities where family values may be threatened, and at times, it may be difficult to assess when such values are at stake. This not least because of the family's foundational societal location which will mean that many, if not most, of the categories of immoral practices listed in this chapter will either directly or indirectly be harmful to the integrity of family and adjacent sound values. What then needs to be assessed here are practices directly damaging the traditional family structure as we know it. What will be of particular interest is how the consumer-driven economies of the Western world are increasingly being directed at the LGBT demographic, possibly because of the high disposable personal income (DPI), of this group. The LGBT community in the United States of America alone is estimated to represent a consumer market at $1 trillion per year, and when estimated on a nominal GDP basis, a global spending power of $3.6 trillion (Forbes n.d.; LGBT Capital n.d.). It is simple to understand the members of the LGBT community will have higher than average DPIs, as within this demographic, there will be no, or very few, children to bring up and pay for. As the LGBT community will be considered a high DPI customer base, several customer sector industries will target this community in their marketing. Such marketing may be hidden or evident, but in either case, it will be aimed not at the traditional heterosexual individuals or same-sex family structures but will rather be promoting values that are detrimental to the traditional family values (Cunningham & Melton 2014; Kostenberger 2010). In fact, it can be argued that marketing driven by free market opportunities in the predominantly capitalist Western societies in itself has promoted, and made possible the advent of the individual LGBT identity (Githens 2009). With the LGBT consumer demographic being perceived as such a valuable market, it will be of utmost importance to avoid any form of participation that involves marketing or other media influence that may be damaging to the traditional family. This will apply no matter what sector is involved, be it consumer goods, travel services, health services, leisure services, et cetera. The position here is clear: any banking practice that promotes any form of attack on, or dismantling of, the traditional family is immoral.

The conclusion connected to family would be that the 'best practice' banking strategy would be to avoid activities that promote the dismantling of the traditional family as society's foundational social and organisational structure.

☐ Pornography

With the advent of the Internet, the consumption, production and distribution of pornographic material have become increasingly prevalent. From the perspective of banking, pornography could typically appear in connection with various media and technology assets, and also by way of real estate connected to the operation of such businesses. It is clear that pornographic material today is being distributed on several different technological platforms, including 'apps', online services, film and picture databases, to mention but a few (Rea 2001). The Reformed ethical norm that pornography is immoral is of importance when contemplating a host of different opportunities, ranging from media houses, distribution providers, real estate, and technology and retail platforms. The position on pornography is clear, and it should be seen as immoral to engage in any activity that promotes the production, consumption or distribution of pornographic material.

The conclusion connected to pornography would be that the 'best practice' banking strategy would be to avoid activities that promote the production, consumption or distribution of pornographic material.

☐ Gambling

As with pornography, the development of Internet and attendant technological platforms has boosted the growth of the gambling industry, and thus opened up new realms of possibilities (Marshall 2003). From the perspective of financing then, gambling could typically appear in connection with various media and technology assets, and also by way of real estate connected to the operation of such businesses. The problems connected to this category are similar to those pertaining to pornography, as the consumption and distribution could be expected to follow similar paths. The position on the immorality of gambling is clear, and thus, to engage in any asset connected to gambling would be considered as immoral banking practice.

The conclusion connected to gambling would be that the 'best practice' banking strategy would be to avoid all activities connected to gambling.

☐ Drugs, alcohol and tobacco

The consumption, production and distribution of recreational drugs and tobacco are considered immoral from a Christian perspective. Thus, participating in assets connected to the consumption, production and distribution of recreational drugs and tobacco will always be immoral and cannot be an acceptable practice.

For the consumption, production and distribution of alcohol, the ethical position is that this is only immoral when the aim is abuse of the substances. This entails considering that financing related to alcohol will be problematic, and dependent on how the different products are marketed; the general rule would be that a close perusal of the underlying motivation of the asset would be necessary prior to involvement (Degenhardt et al. 2008). A typical question would be whether alcohol is being marketed to the underaged or other weak and vulnerable groups in society. For alcohol-related assets, these will be considered immoral to involve in if the aim is to target weak societal groups as consumers or to create an abusive state of product consumption.

The conclusion connected to drugs, alcohol and tobacco would be that the 'best practice' banking strategy would always be to avoid activities connected to the consumption, production and distribution of recreational drugs and tobacco, as well as activities connected to the consumption, production and distribution of alcohol aiming to target weak societal groups as consumers, or to create an abusive state of consumption.

Mass consumption

Extending from the above topics on societal morality, and also connected to stewardship of nature and all its gifts, an aspect to consider is that of human consumption of goods and services. Even if a financial participation cannot be directly or indirectly seen as promoting unsustainable environmental impact, it can contribute to unnecessary mass consumption. That is, activities that are otherwise morally acceptable may be harmful to individuals and the environment or ethically ambiguous because of marketing strategies of the organisation or gluttonous consumption on the part of end users. Thus, this problem sphere can connect to all manner of goods and services, ranging from the travel and entertainment sector to that of food and clothing. Such mass consumption can be harmful to individuals, the environment and societal interests and can lead to a diminished sense of psychological well-being amongst the consumers, and this effect may correlate with the rise of modern marketing (Abela 2006).

A further problematic side of mass consumerism can be connected to obesity and attendant health problems, which are on the rise in various parts of the world. For example, in the United States of America alone, obesity amongst youths had reached 20% by 2004 and could be expected to impose substantial societal costs by way of human suffering and monetary spending (Hill 2011). Added to these health and societal concerns are those pertaining to the environment. Even though humans have a certain place in nature, we have a responsibility to sustain ourselves within reason, and not to allow our consumer footprint in itself to be more destructive to nature than necessary, whether this is related to product types or otherwise healthy and/or environmentally friendly products or activities (Antweiler & Harrison 2003; Tanner & Wölfing Kast 2003).

The conclusion connected to mass consumption would be that the 'best practice' banking strategy would be to avoid activities aiming at unsustainable levels of consumption, also when this is related to product types or marketing of otherwise healthy and/or environmentally friendly products or activities.

Acceptable practices
Family

As the traditional family based on same-sex marriage is a core institution in society, which in Scripture is awarded the utmost repost and protection, it is clear that assets connected to the upholding of this foundational social and organisational institution are of interest here. Products and services undergirding family structure would be plentiful and difficult to comprehensively describe, but some thought on the subject can be presented.

Typically, financial participation aiming at supporting family and adjacent values would be expected to be found in the realms of services, but products of different kinds will also be invited. For example, a typical service category to be considered is that of third-party caregiving where artificial intelligence can provide care for individuals with special needs such as children, the elderly, or disabled family members. When a family member has a special care need, this could put substantial strain on the family, and not least, women will oftentimes be expected to take time to render such care. This could at times be more than what is possible to cope with within the resources of the family, and the purchasing of outside assistance will be of great value. That this is a substantial, and often silenced problem for families to cope with appears in the findings of the World Health Organization (2011), who estimates that well over 1 billion people worldwide suffer some forms of disability. In this connection, it will be useful to note that with old age, sometimes various forms of disabilities occur, and for example in the United States of America, more than 50% of people over the age of 65 are reported to experience disability (US Census Bureau 2008). It is difficult to assess the market possibilities, as it will encompass almost any realm of family life, including housing, care facilities, travel, information technology (IT), education, speciality equipment and much more. However, just to give a flavour of the size, the global market for child care services was in 2018 estimated at $339.1 billion, with a projected growth to $520 billion in 2022 (The Business Research Company n.d.). In the United States of America, only the market for special education of children was in 2015 estimated at $34 billion (Open Minds n.d.).

Involvement in activities involved in assets assisting in family-oriented needs is well within Christian historical tradition and would fit in under a Christian Banking strategy.

☐ Law and order

All the banking practices and categories mentioned above under the systematic 'acceptable practices' would be expected to benefit most parts of society, and at least indirectly benefit the social order and morality. To single out certain financing categories pertaining directly to the moral order of society could be challenging, but any activity supporting the moral and legal order of society would fall within accepted Christian norms (Rm 13:1-2). The question then is how to identify assets that will contribute constructively towards the promotion of scripturally based modes of upholding law and order.

Although the execution of law and order and the exertion of formal authority would be a typical task for extant civil authorities, some activities could be seen as directly promoting the aim of maintaining societal order and keeping crime and unwanted behaviour at bay. Typical activities that could satisfy this goal could be within prisons and correctional facilities and security-oriented assets. Related to prisons and correctional providers, there are possibilities both within private corporate operators, as well as through PPPs with civil governments. Public–private partnerships have been discussed in relation to emerging nations, but it should be pointed out that the PPP model has increasingly been utilised in developed nations as well, and then typically as part of privatisation programmes and financing measures (Savas 2000).

In addition to the prison and correctional industry, there would be opportunities in the private security industry, involving corporations rendering services to private individuals and organisations, both by way of traditional guard services as well as technology-focused and -aided operations, such as IT security, access control, alarms and surveillance systems. This is a substantial market, but, as this fragmented and divided market is ranging from lock and entry systems and armoured cars to IT security, it is difficult to estimate the total global market.

Involvement in the security industry, prisons, correctional facilities and attendant industries is well within Christian historical tradition and would fit in under a Christian banking strategy.

☐ Retail consumer sector

The retail consumer sector is yet another area where bankers will be able to contribute benign influence through their involvements in different markets. The topic here will not be connected to any special product range but will pertain to all manner of retail consumer goods.

The way that banking practitioners can contribute to the promotion of Christian values in the retail sector will be through the promotion of responsible consumption, and this may be connected both to how products are made, packaged, distributed, marketed and more. For example, when engaging in product manufacturing for the consumer sector, the onus will be on creating products that will last and be useful beyond the immediate season or scope of being the last new must-have, not meant to last. Related to packaging, responsible consumption will be promoted through using only the necessary packaging material, which also is sustainable. For instance, for food packaging, there are now new technologies where it is possible to eat both the packaged foodstuffs and its packaging, where it is non-stick so that all contents can be used, that is super-compressed or fully biodegradable (Albright 2015). The opportunities to participate in the sustainable packaging sector should be numerous, as the global market size of this industry is estimated at $224 billion in 2018 and projected to stand at $297 billion in 2024 (Mordor Intelligence n.d.). The packaging aspect of consumer goods is closely connected to its distribution, and also here, the focus will be on assuring the least possible impact on nature by way of energy use, pollution and more. This aspect of consumer retail sector is undergoing substantial interest, and efforts are allocated to its development amongst many of the distributors of major global consumer goods brands (Campos & Schoeder 2015). Finally, when marketing consumer goods, this needs to be performed in a manner where the impulse of thrift is promoted and instilled in the consumers, so as to establish a responsible level of non-gluttonous consumption.

Involvement in sustainable consumer goods and their responsible consumption and marketing, as well as in sustainable packaging and distribution industry is well within Christian historical tradition and would fit in under a Christian banking strategy.

Chapter 8

Operationalisation

Keywords: supervisory board; guidelines; training; recruitment; employees; indexing.

■ Introduction

In a general treatise like this, it is a near impossible task to render a description of how to operationalise Christian banking principles in any comprehensive manner. What I have explained in Chapter 5, Chapter 6 and Chapter 7 are some main principles for Christian banking and certain areas of possible application. They are necessarily general, not connected to specific realms of banking, and only to a limited degree exemplified as product-specific. As with other applications of Christian ethical and pastoral principles in practice, to operationalise them in a practical setting will include customising them to the specific practical realm in which they will be used. To ensure the practicability of Christian banking principles for use by banking practitioners, these principles will have to be translated into the specific area where the practitioner will use them and will have to be expressed in a strategic and product-based manner. Although how to formulate Christian banking guidelines in detail falls outside this treatise, it is nonetheless possible at this stage to point out that the creation of specific sets of rules for governance and banking conduct would benefit from a concrete and practical operationalisation amongst all involved practitioners. As true Christian banking is in its seminal stages, there may be some inspiration to draw on from the Islamic banking paradigm, where despite certain differences with the Christian banking paradigm, several of the organisational aspects in use there may be of use (Hosseini 2008; Jamaldeen 2012; Kettell 2011).

■ Organisation

The organisational technology

The principles of Christian banking as expressed herein, when applied in practice, will need organisational technologies to be put in place. This will in particular be the case in a banking activity that is established and/or existing in a traditional corporate format, but also when applied in smaller situations, as well as when individuals aim at adhering to the Christian banking norms. To be able to follow such norms, a number of organisational tasks need to be set out, but, this does not mean that there need be a number of new organisational positions and speciality functions, such as committees and boards. Already within the traditional organisational corporate model, there should be several extant capabilities embedded for practising banking in accordance with the Christian banking paradigm, as set forth here. This not least because the Christian banking paradigm will tend to display the same aspects of banking as any other modes of banking, but the difference lies in the consideration of the pastoral-ethical component. For many extant organisations, such as for example the Norwegian Sovereign Wealth Fund, there will already be in place a set of ethical rules with the attendant ethical board, where policies pertaining to human rights, CSR and ESG are integrated into the decision models throughout the organisation (NBIM n.d.). In such cases, given that the organisation is set up in a sufficiently competent manner, the existing organisational functions may be used to introduce a Christian banking methodology, at least in its most basic manner.

No matter how an organisation is set up or will be set up, in order to fully contribute to Christian banking practice, it is assumed here that there will be the need to establish an ethical code in compliance with the Christian banking principles, and that, connected to this, should be an ethical committee or board, containing members whose professional knowledge covers the fields necessary for the banking activities that are ongoing or contemplated. It is also expected that in order to ensure that the ethos of Christian banking permeates the organisation, specific learning initiatives and knowledge-sharing efforts must be established.

The establishment

No matter how competent an existing organisation may be, to create new banking structures may be more viable than trying to change existing ones, for example, as seen in the Visa example. In this well-known case, the banking industry in the 1960s did not agree to a joint common structure for new credit card and payment methodologies, but then, as a genuinely new effort and organisation, Visa was established as a solution all could accept. Famously, when Visa was established in 1970, the whole structure was put together in a few months, and the prototype of the whole and lasting payment system was established in only 90 days, and at a cost of less than $25 000 an impressive start for the mammoth global payment provider it would turn out to become (Hock 1995). For inspiration here, to use a start-up methodology to initiate Christian banking may be very possible, not least with the technologies now available at low cost, and the means of communication which wallows for real-time in-the-moment distribution of information and marketing. There is, of course, the case that the established actors may have certain advantages by way of capital and regulatory history, but change is the core of any field of commercial activity, and as we are scripturally reminded in Matthew 20:16, 'So the last will be first, and the first will be last'.

The personnel

When conducting Christian banking, it is of great importance to realise that it is the banking activity that is performed in accordance with Christian norms, and not, that those performing it may be considered 'Christians'. In other words, to be a confessed Christian is not a qualification to participate in such an organisation, and this pertains to all organisational levels, including the ethical board. In a successful and diverse Christian banking organisation, one will expect to find employees who are selected by virtue of their professional qualifications and merits, and not on their personal belief systems, which in itself represents alignment to the principles expounded in this treatise. In such organisations then, people of all cultural backgrounds and belief systems are welcomed, and the focus will solely be on how to perform the banking activity aligned with the Christian banking principles as set out in this treatise. This will be a manner of an organisation that aligns with the universalistic philosophy of the Christian faith and organising a Christian banking operation at odds with this principle would be impossible to conceive and accept.

Regarding the employees in Christian banking organisations, it is of importance to recognise that this is a banking paradigm that adheres to the traditional aims of profit making, and does not represent a charitable activity. Thus, it is expected that an organisation within the realm of Christian banking will be a place where the best and brightest actors of the banking community reside, and, where they will be rewarded by way of salaries and bonuses in accordance with the wider banking employment market. In fact, why should such organisations not be leaders in remunerating their staff? This goes against some of the assumptions found in certain extant organisations where

Christians are seen as the market, such as for example in the UK-based Salvation-Army-affiliated Reliance Bank, where it is stated on their webpage, that bonuses are capped at a maximum of GBP 2000 (Reliance n.d.).

■ Supervisory board
Organisational location

For overseeing and/or introducing Christian banking norms into a banking activity, it is recommended that an overriding supervisory board should be established or in place. Such a supervisory board should offer support to the banking professionals on all strata of organisation and practice, and not only on an overriding and executive level. It is worth emphasising here, that the core ethos of the Christian banking paradigm, is that of using a constructive methodology, where a proactive approach to general and specific banking activities is in use. Thus, to place a supervisory board in a purely executive and 'ivory tower'-like distant organisational position will not be sufficient here. Such a distant location will typically be found in the classic secular CSR/ESG paradigms, where an after-the-fact and negation-based methodology is in use. An example here would again be the Norwegian Sovereign Wealth Fund, whose ethical board operates on an after-the-fact basis, where the board only expresses which investments that are already made do not align with the ethical guidelines of the fund. This does not automatically mean that in this structure, the ethical board and their rulings are not considered in the day-to-day investment activity of the managers, but the onus will be on the ethical board and not the manager to forestall unwanted investments. Also, such a distant and after-the-fact based approach will only have any merit in the classical negation-based ethical management paradigms, where the interest is on what not to invest in rather than on how to actually invest (NBIM n.d.).

The transition from the typical, negation-based stance, whether based on secular consequentialism or religiously informed deontology, is to be considered when attempting to organise a banking activity to align with Christian banking norms. A main difference to be expected amongst the two different ethical vantage points would be that when aligning with a paradigm that is proactive and partaking in the ongoing and planned activities of the professional constituents, the level of organisational integration would need to be more thorough, as opposed to the negation-based model. Only when fully embedded in the organisational fabric will the pastoral-ethical norms connected to Christian banking permeate the minds and activities of all involved actors. Lest we forget, within Christian banking, there is a wide stakeholder group to be considered, and without organisation-wide actor agency, serving such a wider societal group may not be anticipated. To safeguard then, such alignment and state of mind, the supervisory board should advice, and be aware of, all organisational levels and their tasks, such as strategising, product development, human resources management, knowledge sharing and learning, indexing of investments, amongst other activities. The pastoral-ethical content of a Christian banking activity may be secured through such in-depth and participatory knowledge of the supervisory board. However, already at this point, it is worth noting that although participatory, the supervisory board and its members are not expected to partake practically in all organisational processes, nor would such level of involvement be considered conducive towards the aim that is alignment with Christian banking principles.

Composition

When establishing a supervisory board, the recommendation is that the members should have competencies in ethical and philosophical matters, as this would lend necessary knowledge and authority to the decisions made by the board. However, solely possessing these capabilities will not suffice, as the board would need to be able to fully understand what the underlying business activities involve and entail. Therefore, it will be necessary for members of the supervisory board also to possess knowledge about banking in its varied formats, and ideally, individuals who can combine such competencies would be the excellent choices. However, this may not be possible in all cases, as the most important factor will be the combined knowledge base of the supervisory board as a whole, as the board will be a collegial forum, where it is the collective that makes decisions. As the ethos under Christian banking paradigm will be that the pastoral-ethical principles will be embedded in all levels of organisation, it will be an advantage if banking professionals who have their daily work in the organisation are also represented on the board. It is of utmost importance as mentioned above, that the board does not distance itself from the organisation, and through participation from active intra-organisational banking professionals, there will be less likelihood of establishing group constituencies and loyalties such as in-group out-group cognition as detrimental organisational forces (Augoustinos, Walker & Donaghue 2006; Hogg & Terry 2001). If such unhealthy 'them and us' cognition is not staved off, it may lead to an intra-organisational bunker mentality and conflict, and in extreme conditions, intergroup animosity and counterproductive behaviour, which would counteract and possibly defeat the organisational goals (Arnold et al. 2010; Drummond 2001). It is, however, possible to use such intergroup perceptions in a constructive manner, and if all organisational actors perceive that the supervisory board is not just a group for 'them', but, a group in which all share allegiances and loyalties despite their perception of group belonging, then such a multi-group constituency may instil an added sense of team in the organisation.

Such an augmented team perception, where the individuals accept constituency in this added group, may allow the pastoral-ethical norms to permeate all levels of organisation and attendant activities (Heere & James 2007).

It is clear that to locate and appoint the perfect candidate to an supervisory board will be as difficult as appointing any other perfect candidate to any other position, and when recruiting for the board, it will, as ever, be important not to let the perfect be the worst enemy of the good. The Christian banking paradigm is in its inception, and it is expected that as the paradigm develops, more opportunities will emerge for learning about what it entails, and perhaps, in the future, there will be educational opportunities in formalised university settings like those found within the Islamic banking paradigm. However this may evolve, the more the Christian banking approach is applied, the more capable candidates will be found to choose from, both to take positions on ethical boards as well in other organisational roles.

Tasks
Formulating guidelines

A main task for the supervisory board will be the formulation of the rules or guidelines for the operation, as they need to be expressed within the context of the actual banking activity, to align with the Christian banking principles. If the business at hand is a broad and comprehensive operation, the guidelines may be more wide-reaching, as opposed to if the banking activity is one of mere asset management for example. However, it cannot be stressed enough how important it is for the supervisory board to be in close contact with the full scope of the organisation and its constituents, as if the rules are to be lived by, loyalty to the guidelines in all corners of the organisation will be crucial. Such loyalty and attendant practical adherence could be expected if the board that formulates the guidelines is seen to be in close touch with the practical users of the rules, and the more the users identify with the givers of the guidelines, the stronger the adherence to the rules will be (Augoustinos et al. 2006).

Product development

The supervisory board will also be involved in the development of new banking products, carried out in cooperation with the practicing banking professionals of the operation. This may be a merely consultative function, as when organisational actors seek the advice of the board, or, a supervisory role if new products follow from executive strategic decision-making. It will not be expected, however, that the board will initiate the creation of products, as this will be expected from the banking practitioners of the organisation who carry out the banking activities on a daily basis. It will typically be such hands-on professionals who have direct interaction with the market who will be the source of product innovation and development.

☐ Partaking in training programs

The supervisory board will have amongst its responsibilities to instigate and participate in different learning programmes connected to the foundations and use of the Christian banking principles, and their attendant Christian moral norms. This will entail initiating tutoring, mentoring and learning sessions, as well as overseeing the origination and issuance of manuals and other forms of communication to be used in the daily banking operations to ensure that the activities stay within the Christian banking paradigm. In this regard, it will be important to oversee that such educational efforts are practised continuously, and not that they become one-offs or periodical, in such a manner that they will create distance in the organisation between those who use and practice the rules, and those who initialise and market them.

☐ Supervising practicing guidelines

The supervisory board will partake on different levels of organisation to assist in the practical alignment with the established guidelines, and, this may again be in a consultancy or supervisory function, depending on where in the organisation the focus is needed. For example, when the theme is strategising, it is expected that a more supervisory executive role would be taken by the board, as it will be the organisational leadership who will be responsible for laying out the strategy for where the operation is going. If the matter is about how to implement the guidelines in specific business areas, the board may take on a consultancy role, as it will be expected that the matters at hand would be operational and fall within whatever strategy has already been decided. If the banking organisation makes investments, then indexing will be a vital part of it as explained in the section titled 'Indexing' and participating in – and advising on – how specific investments are to be indexed will be a typical supervisory activity connected with the daily investment operations.

☐ Deliberating specific cases

In addition to the continuous advisory and supervisions as mentioned above, there will be the need to adjudicate whether certain bank practises are viable under the Christian banking norms. This could be connected to existing or planned products as well as practises in place. For example, pressures from customers or competitors could be experienced which would induce a higher degree of risk-taking in products, or the acceptance of pledges for loans that could raise questions as to the morality of the pledge or pledger.

In such cases, the product or practice may be brought to the supervisory board for advice or decision, something that will assist the practitioners in their continuous decision-making, as well as contribute to easing the pressures they may experience to push their practice in an unwanted direction.

If a Christian banking activity includes investments in any mode, the role of the supervisory board will also be one of adjudicating on specific investments or investment opportunities, as to decide if such are suitable for inclusion under a Christian strategy. Investment activities under the Christian banking paradigm will typically be subject to an ongoing evaluation on whether an investment is acceptable or not, and such evaluations will most frequently take place amongst the investment professionals in their day-to-day activities. There will be cases where the investment professionals of the organisation find it problematic to evaluate a certain contemplated investment, or where the view on an investment already on the books may have developed since taken on. In the first category, the question may be whether an investment should be taken on because of its perceived fit with the Christian banking principles, and in the latter, whether new information related to the investment that has come to the knowledge of the practitioners would render the investment unfit for remaining included. It is important here to be reminded of the top-down approach that is the main approach of the Christian banking model, and that the more knowledge that the investment professionals receive about an investment, the more grounded will their assessments on its fit be. The supervisory board may be of assistance to the investment professionals when deciding on certain concrete investment opportunities, and the board may always decide that an investment already made may be discarded. Such exclusion of an investment, whether be it prior to taking it on or after the fact, should be considered for each individual investment, and how it would influence the composition of a wider portfolio will have to be raised as a separate matter.

▪ Guidelines

For banking organisations that seek to align with acceptable Christian banking norms, guidelines need to be created for the relevant practice, and a mission statement should be included where it is clearly stated that all involved banking activities are to be aligned with the Christian banking principles as outlined in this treatise. It should be further clarified that all banking activity should be seen in this light, and that this should be expressed in a positive manner, refraining from the traditional method of negation. Further, the mission statement should express the conviction that best banking practice in the Christian banking context aligns with constructive goals, and that merely abstaining from breaking moral codes will not qualify as moral. I accept that this could be perceived as problematic in some circles, but to express clear values would be an advantage in promoting morally viable banking practices.

The practical guidelines for operationalising Christian banking need to be developed in each organisation according to its business scope. When creating such rules, it would be of importance to attain a top-down and proactive approach, as this affirms the constructive foundations that support the espoused ethical-pastoral methodology as described in Chapter 5, as opposed to the approach of disqualification after the fact. As of today, many banking organisations with ethical guidelines operate on a basis where the ethical decisions regarding disqualification are taken after the fact, and even though the ethical guidelines may be regarded as important in the day-to-day decision-making, this methodology signals that staying ethical is the exception rather than the rule. To counteract such effects and possible influences on the attitudes of the professionals, it is recommended that the wording of the guidelines is clear and that room for individual interpretation is kept to a minimum. To this, it should be added that such clarity in wording would aid individual practitioners in their decision-making amidst the large amount of data that need to be interpreted in their day-to-day practical setting.

Guidelines need to be created with a top-down approach, so that the selected banking areas are viewed constructively, and not in a manner where the focus is on finding flaws. This needs to be seen in conjunction with the method of indexing, in particular with regard to investments. For instance, if an opportunity arrives within let housing, let us say in the form of a portfolio of properties, where some professional premises are included, of which one is occupied by an operator of an unwanted business, such as a pornographic activity, this should not preclude an otherwise benign banking opportunity. In such a case, it would be prudent to evaluate the opportunity on the basis of its beneficial qualities, among which housing would be under Christian banking norms, and either let the unwanted letting contract run till expiration without renewing, or, to buy out the unwanted tenant. In any case, the unwanted tenant should be treated fairly and in accordance with contract and law.

Any guidelines used in practice should be revised at regular intervals, to ensure their compliance with the actual practice as this evolves in the market situation wherein the practitioners reside.

■ Strategising

When starting a new business or planning ahead in an existing one, strategic planning is used as a means of defining the way forward; for example, to decide markets and customer groups of interest for the organisation. Part of such strategising will then be connected with market perceptions, and in the case of entering or staying within the Christian banking paradigm, this would be decided either on the basis of moral considerations amongst the owners, or for marketing reasons and purely pragmatic perceptions of economic viability of the banking operation. No matter which is it, strategising is a corporate activity often lauded in the corporate realm, but it is important to note that whatever level of prudence is put into it, strategising includes an element of anxiety reduction, something that may induce complacency in the involved actors. Thus, any corporate strategy, no matter how well devised and whoever is involved, may not always ensure that the goals it aims at are achieved (Stacey 2011). Therefore, to remain cognisant of the need to test and retest a Christian banking strategy and the connected guidelines against their practical applications and attendant effects is of utmost importance. Merely to design a strategy based on a set of theoretically created rules may not be sufficient to stay within the Christian banking paradigm.

■ Balance sheet

When assessing what would be a suitable composition of a balance sheet of a Christian banking activity, the scope of the business and its perceived stakeholders will determine what comes into consideration when modelling the ideal balance sheet. For a mere asset management activity, like for example within the sectors of alternative assets, or mutual funds under the Undertakings for the Collective Investment in Transferable Securities (UCITS) paradigm, it is assumed that most of the rules set out within this treatise would apply, as this could typically involve a wide range of societal stakeholders and a great variation of banking technologies. If, however, the operation is of a more specialised character where deposits are taken, and interbank instruments and other speciality banking technology is in use, more likely, support will have to be sought in a selection of the principles. Not least, the discussion on capital reserve requirements would be of interest in such cases, and although the Chicago Plan with its strict stipulations may not need to be followed to its letter, it will still render valuable inspiration to the concerned banking practitioner (Fisher 1935). However, as has been discussed and illustrated in several places in the treatise, the rule sets are general, and as a composite, they will define what Christian banking is. Thus, whatever banking activity is performed, to remain within the Christian banking paradigm, it is assumed that this will require a certain vigilance to ensure that all rule sets are observed. Based on this assumption, the Christian banking compliant balance sheet will have to be defined and maintained as part of ongoing and concrete vetting of the actual banking business, but the detailed depiction of how to compose such a balance sheet falls outside the scope of this treatise (Casu, Girardone & Molyneux 2015).

■ Product types – Financial instruments

In Christian banking, there are no financial product categories that are prohibited outright, and thus, it can be said that Christian banking is product-type agnostic. Bearing this in mind, the focus on the pastoral-ethical aspects is essential, rather than relying on simplifications as to the product types that would be allowed or forbidden. Such a holistic and concept-driven approach makes adhering to the paradigm when choosing or developing products more difficult in that the professionals need to focus on norms and principles, but also simpler, in that any product category in principle is open for utilisation. Not only does the Christian banking paradigm remain open for different products, but this open and non-dogmatic approach also applies to what kind of financial instruments may be used. With no forbidden financial instruments, it is the norm adherence that matters, and not mechanical reliance on taxonomic delineations.

The recommendation to practitioners who contemplate utilising Christian banking strategies in their practice is first to outline the product groups and the individual products and market segments they are aimed at, then to apply the Christian banking principles to each product and potential customer group in an easily understandable and practically useable manner and formulate a detailed set of regulations and guidelines for each product/consumer category. In this process, it would be helpful to include what kind of financial instruments would be used, such as third-party financing, derivatives or options, as a product will typically rely on the use of several different banking technologies when brought to market.

■ Indexing

For the field of Christian banking that involves investments, it would be useful to apply a framework where an investment is evaluated in a holistic manner, where all aspects are measured against the Christian banking methodology, and where a point system may give the final answer as to whether an investment is acceptable or not. It is of importance to remind ourselves of the constructive pastoral-ethical approach that is espoused in the Christian banking paradigm, and thus, that the main approach is a top-down one, where only assumed beneficial investments would be evaluated in the first place. Thus, as in the housing example mentioned above, the unacceptable pornographic activity would not prohibit the investment, but it need be noted, and considered in making the final decision. For example, if the maximum score is 100, it could be conceivable to subtract five points for the unwanted pornographic activity. Further, let us say the property needed massive upgrades to satisfy best practice for energy efficiency, this could perhaps mean the deduction of another 10 points, to reflect the property's negative influence on the environment prior to upgrading. Then, the score of this investment would be 85 on the 100 scale.

An advantage in using a points-based indexing system is that it allows for the constructive ethos of Christian banking to remain the main guiding principle, and smaller flaws, which could possibly be easily rectified, will not preclude an otherwise beneficial investment opportunity. In addition, a points-based indexing methodology also allows for building investment portfolios, where for example the rule is that the average score need be 75, but, no single investment may score lower than 60. Then even to accept a low score of 60 could perhaps only be accepted if it is expected that the investment will earn a higher score in a foreseeable future, for example, when the lease on the pornographic activity expires. Through such a model, banking professionals may construct portfolios that are easily understood and communicated from a pastoral-ethical point of view.

By using a points-based indexing model, banking practitioners can monitor their extant investments through ongoing vigilant evaluations against the Christian banking parameters, and if new information becomes known, this may contribute to an adjustment in the score in either direction, or, confirm how the already rated investment deserves the rating it enjoys.

When Christian banking becomes more widely known and accepted, it is the assumption here that we may see the emergence of rating agencies who rate according to the Christian banking principles, similar to those already found within the realm of Islamic banking (Jamaldeen 2012).

■ Learning initiatives

For a banking operation that wishes to adapt to the Christian banking paradigm, be it a newly established organisation or existing one, to merely create and publish a code for guiding the activity will not suffice. Therefore, in addition to producing such detailed and sector-specific rules of conduct, different knowledge sharing activities, such as learning sessions, should be held amongst the involved actors, where they will be taught the Christian banking principles in general, so as to be able to adapt the specific rules better to align with the general principles in each separate case. It will again be of paramount importance to attain an integrated perspective of knowledge generation and sharing, and traditional organisational methods of education and learning would be assumed to suffice for the establishment and practising of a Christian banking initiative. Based on this assumption, the Christian banking specific learning may well be fitted into ongoing initiatives on other training in the organisation, but the detailed description of such methodologies falls outside the scope of this treatise (Hislop 2013; Jashapara 2011).

■ Knowledge generation

Because of the limited scope of this treatise, it is expected that there will be room for substantial further inquiry into the possibilities for developing banking practices in a viable Christian direction. The construct of Christian banking is new, so it is assumed there is potential for continued exploration into this field. The intensified interrogation of the Christian banking norms would benefit from both academic and real-life organisational attention, and not least, in combination. Added proposals for the operationalisation of the Christian banking principles in a practical setting would be of interest, and it is assumed that different modes of in-practice action research or other real-life collaborative research methodologies would lend themselves well to such knowledge-generating endeavours (Coghlan & Brannick 2010; Swinton & Mowat 2006). Of particular interest for such practical real-world research might be the establishment of research projects based on the Appreciative Inquiry paradigm, as this methodology aims to mine out what is already perceived as positive in extant organisational practice, and to build new knowledge and practice on that (Cooperrider, Whitney & Stavros 2008). Such a constructive research ethos would fit well with the constructive ethical and pastoral principles that may spring out of a corporate understanding based on the Christian banking ethos.

■ Recommendation

For the reader who is part of the practical world of banking and financing in any capacity and on any level of organisation, it may be of interest how to set the Christian banking principles out in practice, and to include them in an ongoing process of corporate strategising. Although it is difficult if not impossible to render recommendations in a comprehensive manner for all to benefit from, I have in this chapter given some pointers as to how to operationalise Christian banking in real-life settings. To outline and articulate Christian banking guidelines in detail falls outside the scope of this treatise and would also not be possible in any comprehensive manner, even with vast resources available. This is because the practical application of the Christian banking principles in real-life settings needs to be related to the frame of business where they are to be used. However, relevant organisations should be urged to explore their current practice in light of the ethical and pastoral positions stated in this treatise, and appoint an individual, or if possible, establish a group, who would be designated to mine out concrete possibilities for improvement in the relevant organisation.

For the concerned individual practitioners, then, it would be advisable to attain a pastoral attitude and adopt a perspective of ministry, so as to allow for the Christian banking principles to permeate all levels of their practice.

Operationalisation

However, within the corporate constraints of the practical business world, this may be difficult to achieve. Thus, the recommendation, in general, is to seek out others connected to the practice, and attempt to anchor support for Christian banking strategising on as many levels of organisation as possible, for if an organisation becomes a venue for pastoral ministry in a holistic sense, then the realisation of Christian banking is possible.

References

Abdul-Rahman, Y., 2010, *The art of Islamic banking and finance*, John Wiley & Sons, Hoboken, NJ.

Abela, A.V., 2006, 'Marketing and consumerism: A response to O'Shaughnessy and O'Shaughnessy', *European Journal of Marketing* 40(1–2), 5–16. https://doi.org/10.1108/03090560610637284

Adams, J.E., 1986, *Competent to counsel: Introduction to nouthetic counseling*, Zondervan, Grand Rapids, MI.

Adrian, T. & Shin, H.S., 2010, 'The changing nature of financial intermediation and the financial crisis of 2007–2009', *Annual Review of Economics* 2(1), 603–618. https://doi.org/10.1146/annurev.economics.102308.124420

Agadjanian, V., 1998, '"Quasi-legal" abortion services in a sub-Saharan setting: Users' profiles and motivations', *International Family Planning Perspectives* 24(3), 111–116. https://doi.org/10.2307/3038207

Ahmad, A.U.F. & Hassan, M.K., 2007, 'Riba and Islamic banking', *Journal of Islamic Economics, Banking and Finance* 3(1), 1–33.

Akabayashi, H. & Psacharopoulos, G., 1999, 'The trade-off between child labour and human capital formation: A Tanzanian case study', *The Journal of Development Studies* 35(5), 120–140. https://doi.org/10.1080/00220389908422594

Albin, T.R., 1995, 'Wesley, John and Charles', in D.J. Atkinson, D.F. Field, A.F. Holmes & O. O'Donovan (eds.), *New dictionary of Christian ethics & pastoral theology*, p. 891, InterVarsity Press, Downers Grove, IL.

Albright, M.B., 2015, 'Food packaging: Have your cake and eat the wrapper, too', *National Geographic*, viewed 11 October 2018, from https://www.nationalgeographic.com/culture/article/food-packaging-have-your-cake-and-eat-the-wrapper-too.

Alesina, A. & Glaeser, E., 2004, *Fighting poverty in the US and Europe: A world of difference*, Oxford University Press, Oxford.

Alesina, A., Glaeser, E. & Sacerdote, B., 2001, *Why doesn't the US have a European-style welfare system? (No. w8524)*, viewed 17 November 2017, from https://scholar.harvard.edu/files/glaeser/files/why_doesnt_the_u.s._have_a_european-style_welfare_state.pdf.

Alexander, J.B., 1938, 'A Babylonian year of Jubilee?', *Journal of Biblical Literature* 57(1), 75–79. https://doi.org/10.2307/3259545

Allen, B., Chan, K.K., Milne, A. & Thomas, S., 2012, 'Basel III: Is the cure worse than the disease?', *International Review of Financial Analysis* 25(C), 159–166. https://doi.org/10.1016/j.irfa.2012.08.004

American Pet Products Association, n.d., *Official homepage*, viewed 12 September 2018, from https://www.americanpetproducts.org/.

Andreau, J., 1999, *Banking and business in the Roman world*, Cambridge University Press, Cambridge.

Angelini, J.R. & Bradley, S.D., 2010, 'Homosexual imagery in print advertisements: Attended, remembered, but disliked', *Journal of Homosexuality* 57(4), 485–502. https://doi.org/10.1080/00918361003608665

Angelini, P., Clerc, L., Cúrdia, V., Gambacorta, L., Gerali, A., Locarno, A. et al., 2015, 'Basel III: Long-term impact on economic performance and fluctuations', *The Manchester School* 83(2), 217–251. https://doi.org/10.1111/manc.12056

Anscombe, G.E.M., 1958, 'Modern moral philosophy', *Philosophy* 33(124), 1–19. https://doi.org/10.1017/S0031819100037943

Antić, R., 2010, 'The role of Christianity in the development of European and Serbian medieval medicine', *Archive of Oncology* 18(4), 111–114. https://doi.org/10.2298/AOO1004111A

References

Antommattei, O., Khanfar, N.M. & Mujtaba, B.G., 2011, 'Global abortion and marketing challenges for Misoprostol (Cytotec), the future of women's health', *International Business & Economics Research Journal (IBER)* 8(1), 105–112. https://doi.org/10.19030/iber.v8i1.3094

Antweiler, W. & Harrison, K., 2003, 'Toxic release inventories and green consumerism: Empirical evidence from Canada', *Canadian Journal of Economics/Revue Canadienne D'économique* 36(2), 495–520. https://doi.org/10.1111/1540-5982.t01-1-00011

Aquinas, T., 1993, *Commentary on Aristotle's Nicomachean ethics*, Dumb Ox Books, Notre Dame, IN.

Aquinas, T., 1998, *Thomas Aquinas: Selected writings*, Penguin Books, London.

Aquinas, T., 2003, *On evil (De Malo)*, transl. R. Regan, Oxford University Press, Oxford.

Aquinas, T., 2010, *Summa Theologica*, Kindle edition, Coyote Canyon Press, s.l.

Ariff, M., 1988. 'Islamic banking', *Asian-Pacific Economic Literature* 2(2), 48–64. https://doi.org/10.1111/j.1467-8411.1988.tb00200.x

Aristotle., 1992, *The politics*, Penguin Books, London.

Aristotle., 2009, *The Nicomachean ethics*, Oxford University Press, Oxford.

Arnold, J., Randall, R., Silvester, J., Patterson, F., Robertson, I. & Cooper, C., 2010, *Work psychology, understanding human behaviour in the workplace*, 5th edn., Pearson Education, Harlow.

Atkinson, D.J., 1995a, 'Eduard Thurneysen', in D.J. Atkinson, D.F. Field, A.F. Holmes & O. O'Donovan (eds.), *New dictionary of Christian ethics & pastoral theology*, pp. 849–850, InterVarsity Press, Downers Grove, IL.

Atkinson, S.E., 1995b, 'Education', in D.J. Atkinson, D.F. Field, A.F. Holmes & O. O'Donovan (eds.), *New dictionary of Christian ethics & pastoral theology*, pp. 334–336, InterVarsity Press, Downers Grove, IL.

Augoustinos, M., Walker, I. & Donaghue, N., 2006, *Social cognition: An integrated introduction*, 2nd edn., Sage, London.

Augustine, 1887a, 'Retractions', in P. Schaff (ed.), *Nicene and post-Nicene fathers. First series*, vol. 3, viewed 12 May 2017, from http://www.newadvent.org/fathers/1312.htm.

Augustine, 1887b, 'To consentius, against lying', in P. Schaff (ed.), *Nicene and post-Nicene fathers. First series*, vol. 3, viewed 15 October 2018, from http://www.newadvent.org/fathers/1313.htm.

Augustine, 1887c, 'Enchiridion', in P. Schaff (ed.), *Nicene and post-Nicene fathers. First series*, vol. 3, viewed n.d., from http://www.newadvent.org/fathers/1302.htm.

Augustine, 2003, *City of God*, Penguin Books, London.

Augustine, 2015, *On Christian doctrine*, viewed 07 April 2017, from http://www.ccel.org/ccel/augustine/doctrine.pdf.

Ave Maria Mutual Funds, n.d., *Official homepage*, viewed 14 June 2017, from https://avemariafunds.com.

Ayres, J.M., 2004, 'Framing collective action against neoliberalism: The case of the "anti-globalization" movement', *Journal of World-Systems Research* 10(1), 11–34. https://doi.org/10.5195/jwsr.2004.311

Badaracco, J.L., 1998, 'The discipline of building character', *Harvard Business Review* 76(2), 114–124. https://doi.org/10.1007/978-1-349-14665-9_9

Bainton, R.H., 1946, 'The early church and war', *Harvard Theological Review* 39(3), 189–212. https://doi.org/10.1017/S0017816000023191

Baldwin, J.W., 1959, 'The medieval theories of the just price: Romanists, canonists, and theologians in the twelfth and thirteenth centuries', *Transactions of the American Philosophical Society* 49(4), 1–92. https://doi.org/10.2307/1005819

Banerjee, A.V. & Duflo, E., 2012, *Poor economics: A radical rethinking of the way to fight global poverty*, Public Affairs, New York, NY.

Banner, M., 1998, 'Christian anthropology at the beginning and end of life', *Scottish Journal of Theology* 51(1), 22–60. https://doi.org/10.1017/S0036930600050006

Barber, S., Boyen, X., Shi, E. & Uzun, E., 2012, 'Bitter to better – How to make bitcoin a better currency', in A.D. Keromytis (ed.), *International conference on financial cryptography and data security. Conference proceedings,* pp. 399–414, Springer, Cham.

Barkai, H., 1989, 'The old historical school: Roscher on money and monetary issues', *History of Political Economy* 21(2), 179–200. https://doi.org/10.1215/00182702-21-2-179

Barnwell, P.S., 2000, 'Emperors, jurists and kings: Law and custom in the late Roman and early medieval west', *Past and Present* 168(1), 6–29. https://doi.org/10.1093/past/168.1.6

Barofsky, N.M., 2011, 'Where the bailout went wrong', *New York Times,* 30 March, p. A27, viewed 12 October 2016, from https://www.nytimes.com/2011/03/30/opinion/30barofsky.html.

Barth, K., 1968, *The epistle to the Romans,* transl. E.C. Hoskyns, Oxford University Press, Oxford.

Barton, J., 1996, *Reading the Old Testament: Method in biblical study,* Darton, Longman and Todd, London.

Battle, J.A., 2008, 'Property rights and responsibilities in the Old Testament', *WRS Journal* 15(1), 14–27.

Baumol, W.J., 1983, 'Marx and the iron law of wages', *The American Economic Review* 73(2), 303–308.

Baumol, W.J., 1990, 'Entrepreneurship: Productive, unproductive, and destructive', *Journal of Political Economy* 98(5, part 1), 893–921. https://doi.org/10.1086/261712

Benes, J. & Kumhof, M., 2012, 'The Chicago plan revisited', *IMF Working Paper,* WP/12/220, Research Department, s.l.

Bennett, C., 2010, *What is this thing called ethics?,* Routledge, Abingdon.

Bentham, J., 1907, *An introduction to the principles of morals and legislation,* viewed 02 July 2018, from http://www.econlib.org/library/Bentham/bnthPML.html.

Berkhof, L., 1958, *Systematic theology,* Versa Press, East Peoria, IL.

Berners-Lee, M., 2010, *How bad are bananas? The carbon footprint of everything,* CPI Group, Croydon.

Bernier, P., 2015, *Ministry in the church: A historical and pastoral approach,* 2nd edn., Orbis, Ossining, NY.

Bhattacharya, S. & Nyborg, K.G., 2013, 'Bank bailout menus', *The Review of Corporate Finance Studies* 2(1), 29–61. https://doi.org/10.1093/rcfs/cft001

Billings, J.T., 2005, 'Calvin, participation and the gift: The activity of believers in union with Christ', Doctoral dissertation, Harvard University.

Birch, B.C. & Rasmussen, L., 1989, *Bible and ethics in the Christian life,* Augsburg Fortress, Minneapolis, MN.

Bloesch, D.G., 1995, 'Karl Barth', in D.J. Atkinson, D.F. Field, A.F. Holmes & O. O'Donovan (eds.), *New dictionary of Christian ethics and pastoral theology,* pp. 184–185, InterVarsity Press, Downers Grove, IL.

Boczar, G.E., 1978, 'Competition between banks and finance companies: A cross section study of personal loan debtors', *The Journal of Finance* 33(1), 245–258. https://doi.org/10.1111/j.1540-6261.1978.tb03402.x

Bonta, J. & Gendreau, P., 1990, 'Reexamining the cruel and unusual punishment of prison life', *Law and Human Behavior* 14(4), 347. https://doi.org/10.1007/BF01068161

Bordo, M.D., 1986, 'Money, deflation and seigniorage in the fifteenth century: A review essay', *Journal of Monetary Economics* 18(3), 337–346. https://doi.org/10.1016/0304-3932(86)90046-2

Bordo, M.D., 1993, 'The gold standard, Bretton Woods and other monetary regimes: An historical appraisal', *NBER Working Papers 4310,* National Bureau of Economic Research, Cambridge.

Börzel, T.A. & Risse, T., 2005, 'Public-private partnerships: Effective and legitimate tools of international governance', in *Reconstituting political authority. Complex sovereignty and the foundations of global governance,* Toronto, pp. 195–216, viewed 12 February 2018, from http://userpage.fu-berlin.de/~atasp/texte/021015_ppp_risse_boerzel.pdf.

References

Bøsterud, C.E., 2019a, 'Gender equality in top management (C-suite): A Christian-ethical perspective', Doctoral dissertation, North-West University.

Bøsterud, M., 2016, 'Public ownership and morality: Proposed investment guidelines of the Norwegian Sovereign Wealth Fund: A Christian ethical perspective', PhD thesis, Faculty of Theology, North-West University.

Bøsterud, M., 2017, 'Inter-professional intra-clinic knowledge sharing and management as means to increased intra-clinic patient referrals', Doctoral dissertation, University of Liverpool.

Bøsterud, M., 2018, 'Financing, credit, moneylending and charging of interest. A Christian-ethical and pastoral perspective', PhD thesis, Faculty of Theology, North-West University.

Bøsterud, M., 2019b, 'Animal welfare: A human right?', *In Die Skriflig* 53(1), a2439. https://doi.org/10.4102/ids.v53i1.2439

Bøsterud, M., 2020, 'A reformed epistemology for praxis', *Christianity in the Middle East* 4, 66–98. https://doi.org/10.24411/2587-9316-2020-10028

Bøsterud, M. & Vorster, J.M., 2017, 'Reoriented Investment Protocol – a Christian-ethical perspective on investments', *In die Skriflig* 51(1), a2202. https://doi.org/10.4102/ids.v51i1.2202

Bøsterud, M. & Vorster, J.M., 2019, 'Pastoral banking practice – A Christian-ethical and pastoral perspective on financing, credit and moneylending', *In die Skriflig* 53(1), a2409. https://doi.org/10.4102/ids.v53i1.2409

Bottero, W., 2005, *Stratification: Social division and inequality*, Routledge, New York, NY.

Boughton, J.M., 2004, 'The IMF and the force of history: Ten events and ten ideas that have shaped the institution', *International Monetary Fund working paper 04/75,* IMF, Washington, DC.

Bridge, C. & Fedorowich, K., 2003, 'Mapping the British world', *The Journal of Imperial and Commonwealth History* 31(2), 1–15. https://doi.org/10.1080/03086530310001705576

Bromberg, B., 1957, 'Temple banking in Rome', *The Economic History Review* 10(2), 128–131. https://doi.org/10.1111/j.1468-0289.1957.tb01901.x

Brown, C., 2007, 'Financial engineering, consumer credit, and the stability of effective demand', *Journal of Post-Keynesian Economics* 29(3), 427–450. https://doi.org/10.2753/PKE0160-3477290304

Brundtland, G., 1987, *Report of the world commission on environment and development: Our common future*, Document A/42/427, United Nations General Assembly, New York, NY.

Brunner, E. & Barth, K., 2002, *Natural theology,* Wipf and Stock, Eugene, OR.

Bucer, M., 2009, *Concerning the true care of souls*, transl. P. Beale, Banner of Truth Trust, Edinburgh.

Buckley, R. & Nixon, J., 2009, 'The role of reputation in banking', *Journal of Banking and Finance Law and Practice* 20, 37–50.

Buckley, S.L., 1998, *Usury friendly? The ethics of money-lending. Grove ethical studies,* Grove Books, Cambridge.

Bunkowske, E.W., 1985, 'Was Luther a missionary?', in K.E. Marquart, J.R. Stephenson & B.W. Teigen (eds.), *A lively legacy: Essays in honor of Robert Preus*, pp. 15–32, Graphic Publishing, Lake Mills, WI.

Burnes, B. & By, R.T., 2012, 'Leadership and change: The case for greater ethical clarity', *Journal of Business Ethics* 108(2), 239–252. https://doi.org/10.1007/s10551-011-1088-2

Butler, R.N., 1969, 'Age-ism: Another form of bigotry', *The Gerontologist* 9(4), 243. https://doi.org/10.1093/geront/9.4_Part_1.243

Buvinić, M. & Gupta, G.R., 1997, 'Female-headed households and female-maintained families: Are they worth targeting to reduce poverty in developing countries?', *Economic Development and Cultural Change* 45(2), 259–280. https://doi.org/10.1086/452273

Cain, J.W., 1994, 'Extraterritorial application of the United States' trade embargo against Cuba: The United Nations General Assembly's call for an end to the US trade embargo', *The Georgia Journal of International and Comparative Law* 24(2), 379.

Cain, P.J. & Hopkins, A.G., 1987, 'Gentlemanly capitalism and British expansion overseas II: New imperialism, 1850–1945', *The Economic History Review* 40(1), 1–26. https://doi.org/10.2307/2596293

Calàs, M.B. & Smircich, L., 1999, 'Past postmodernism? Reflections and tentative directions', *Academy of Management Review* 24(4), 649–671. https://doi.org/10.5465/amr.1999.2553246

Calvert, S.J., 2008, '"Ours is the food that Eden knew": Themes in the theology and practice of modern Christian vegetarians', in D. Grumett & R. Muers (eds.), *Eating and believing: Interdisciplinary perspectives on vegetarianism and theology*, pp. 3186–3460, A&C Black, London.

Calvin, J., 1542, 'To Viret. Geneva, 19th August 1542', in J. Bonnet (ed.), *Letters, Part I: 1528–1545*, Project Gutenberg, Salt Lake City, UT.

Calvin, J., 1545, 'De Usuris Responsum. Calvin's letter on usury', in C. Elliott (ed.), *Usury: A scriptural, ethical and economic view*, viewed 20 September 2017, from http://www.readcentral.com/chapters/Calvin-Elliott/Usury-A-Scriptural-Ethical-and-Economic-View/012.

Calvin, J., 1845, *Commentary on Matthew, Mark, Luke,* Christian Classics Ethereal Library, vol., 1, Grand Rapids, MI.

Calvin, J., 1847, *Commentary on Genesis*, Christian Classics Ethereal Library, vol. 1, Grand Rapids, MI.

Calvin, J., 1849a, *Commentary on the prophet Ezekiel*, Christian Classics Ethereal Library, vol. 1, Grand Rapids, MI.

Calvin, J., 1849b, *Commentary on Psalms*, Christian Classics Ethereal Library, vol. 5, Grand Rapids, MI.

Calvin, J., 1849c, *Commentary on Romans*, Christian Classics Ethereal Library, Grand Rapids, MI.

Calvin, J., 1849d, *Commentary on Zechariah, Malachi,* Christian Classics Ethereal Library, Grand Rapids, MI.

Calvin, J., 1850, *Commentary on Jeremiah and lamentations,* Christian Classics Ethereal Library, vol. 5, Grand Rapids, MI.

Calvin, J., 1852a, *Harmony of the law,* Christian Classics Ethereal Library, vol. 1, Grand Rapids, MI.

Calvin, J., 1852b, *Harmony of the law,* Christian Classics Ethereal Library, vol. 3., Grand Rapids, MI.

Calvin, J., 1969, *Commentary on Seneca's de Clementia,* E.J. Brill, Leiden.

Calvin, J., 2006, *Theological treatises*, Westminster John Knox Press, Louisville, KY.

Calvin, J., 2012, *Institutes of the Christian religion*, Hendrickson, Boston, MA.

Campos, J.K. & Schoeder, D., 2015, 'Sustainable distribution in the consumer goods supply chain', in W. Kersten, T. Blecker, M. Christian & C.M. Ringle (eds.), *Sustainability in logistics and supply chain management*, pp. 185–207, epubli GmbH, Berlin.

Carroll, A.B., 1991, 'The pyramid of corporate social responsibility: Toward the moral management of organizational stakeholders', *Business Horizons* 34(4), 39–48. https://doi.org/10.1016/0007-6813(91)90005-G

Case, K., Fair, M., Gärtner, M. & Heather, K., 1999, *Economics*, Prentice Hall, London.

Casu, B., Girardone, C. & Molyneux, P., 2015, *Introduction to banking,* Pearson Education, London.

Cataldo, L.M., 2007, 'Religious experience and the transformation of narcissism: Kohutian theory and the life of St. Francis of Assisi', *Journal of Religion and Health* 46(4), 527–540. https://doi.org/10.1007/s10943-007-9116-3

Circular, n.d., *Official homepage*, viewed 14 July 2018, from https://www.circularsolutions.is/.

Chachi, A., 2005, 'Origin and development of commercial and Islamic banking operations', *Islamic Economics* 18(2), 3–25. https://doi.org/10.4197/islec.18-2.1

Chadwick, W.E., 1907, *The pastoral teaching of St. Paul: His ministerial ideals*, T&T Clark, London.

Chewning, R.C., 1995, 'Debt', in D.J. Atkinson, D.F. Field, A.F. Holmes & O. O'Donovan (eds.), *New dictionary of Christian ethics and pastoral theology,* pp. 286–287, InterVarsity Press, Downers Grove, IL.

Chinn, M.D. & Fairlie, R.W., 2010, 'ICT use in the developing world: An analysis of differences in computer and internet penetration', *Review of International Economics* 18(1), 153–167. https://doi.org/10.1111/j.1467-9396.2009.00861.x

Chong, B.S. & Liu, M.H., 2009, 'Islamic banking: Interest-free or interest-based?', *Pacific-Basin Finance Journal* 17(1), 125–144. https://doi.org/10.1016/j.pacfin.2007.12.003

Christian, D., 2000, 'Silk roads or steppe roads? The silk roads in world history', *Journal of World History* 11(1), 1–26. https://doi.org/10.1353/jwh.2000.0004

Christian Finance Observatory, n.d., *Official homepage*, viewed 05 March 2019, from http://www.christianfinanceobservatory.org/en/.

Chrysostom, S., 2017, *On the priesthood: Ascetic treatises; select homilies and letters; homilies on the statutes*, Devoted Publishing, Woodstock.

Clark, M.T., 2001, 'De Trinitate', in E. Stump & N. Kretzmann (eds.), *The Cambridge companion to Augustine*, pp. 91–102, Cambridge University Press, Cambridge.

Coghlan, D. & Brannick, T., 2010, *Doing action research in your own organisation*, 3rd edn., Sage, London.

Cohen, E., 1997, *Athenian economy and society: A banking perspective*, Princeton University Press, Princeton, NJ.

Collier, P., 2008, *The bottom billion: Why the poorest countries are failing and what can be done about it*, Oxford University Press, Oxford.

Collins, J.J., 2014, *Introduction to the Hebrew Bible*, 2nd edn., Augsburg Fortress, Minneapolis, MN.

Compton, W.M. & Volkow, N.D., 2006, 'Abuse of prescription drugs and the risk of addiction', *Drug and Alcohol Dependence* 83(Suppl. 1), S4–S7. https://doi.org/10.1016/j.drugalcdep.2005.10.020

Confucius, 1979, *The analects*, Penguin Books, London.

Constitution, 1814, *Norwegian constitution as laid down on 17 May 1814 by the Constituent Assembly at Eidsvoll and subsequently amended*, viewed 11 June 2016, from https://www.stortinget.no/In-English/About-the-Storting/The-Constitution/The-Constitution.

Cook, E.D., 1995, 'Health and healthcare', in D.J. Atkinson, D.F. Field, A.F. Holmes & O. O'Donovan (eds.), *New dictionary of Christian ethics and pastoral theology*, pp. 435–437, InterVarsity Press, Downers Grove, IL.

Cooperrider, D.L., Whitney, D.K. & Stavros, J.M., 2008, *Appreciative inquiry handbook*, 2nd edn., Berrett-Koehler, Oakland, CA.

Coulibaly, B., 2009, 'Effects of financial autarky and integration: The case of the South Africa embargo', *Journal of International Money and Finance* 28(3), 454–478. https://doi.org/10.1016/j.jimonfin.2008.11.003

Court, J.H., 1995, 'Pornography', in D.J. Atkinson, D.F. Field, A.F. Holmes & O. O'Donovan (eds.), *New dictionary of Christian ethics and pastoral theology*, pp. 675–677, InterVarsity Press, Downers Grove, IL.

Cowdrey, H.E., 1970, 'Pope urban II's preaching of the first crusade', *History* 55(184), 177–188. https://doi.org/10.1111/j.1468-229X.1970.tb02491.x

Cramp, A.B., 1995, 'Economic ethics', in D.J. Atkinson, D.F. Field, A.F. Holmes & O. O'Donovan (eds.), *New dictionary of Christian ethics and pastoral theology*, pp. 115–121, InterVarsity Press, Downers Grove, IL.

Crisp, R., 1998, 'Modern virtue theory, in virtue ethics', in *The Routledge encyclopaedia of philosophy*, Taylor and Francis, s.l. https://doi.org/10.4324/9780415249126-L111-1

Crouch, C., 2008, 'What will follow the demise of privatised Keynesianism?', *The Political Quarterly* 79(4), 476–487. https://doi.org/10.1111/j.1467-923X.2008.00970.x

Crowe, C. & Meade, E.E., 2007, 'The evolution of central bank governance around the world', *The Journal of Economic Perspectives* 21(4), 69–90. https://doi.org/10.1257/jep.21.4.69

Cumberland, R., 2005, *A treatise of the laws of nature*, transl. J. Maxwell, R. Phillips, London.

Cunningham, G.B. & Melton, E.N., 2014, 'Signals and cues: LGBT inclusive advertising and consumer attraction', *Sport Marketing Quarterly* 23(1), 37.

Dale, C.A., 2007, 'Matthew', in J. Barton & J. Muddiman (eds.), *The Oxford Bible commentary*, pp. 844–886, Oxford University Press, Oxford.

Dalton, G., 1982, 'Barter', *Journal of Economic Issues* 16(1), 181–190. https://doi.org/10.1080/00213624.1982.11503968

Daly, H.E. & Farley, J., 2011, *Ecological economics: Principles and applications*, Island Press, Washington, DC.

Danielsson, J., Taylor, A. & Zigrand, J.P., 2005, 'Highwaymen or heroes: Should hedge funds be regulated? A survey', *Journal of Financial Stability* 1(4), 522–543. https://doi.org/10.1016/j.jfs.2005.09.003

Deane-Drummond, C., 2008, *Eco-theology*, Saint Mary's Press, Winona, MN.

Degenhardt, L., Chiu, W.T., Sampson, N., Kessler, R.C., Anthony, J.C., Angermeyer, M. & Wells, J.E., 2008, 'Toward a global view of alcohol, tobacco, cannabis, and cocaine use: Findings, from the WHO World Mental Health Surveys', *PLoS Medicine* 5(7), e141. https://doi.org/10.1371/journal.pmed.0050141

Deigh, J., 2010, *An introduction to ethics*, Cambridge University Press, Cambridge.

De la Torre, I., 2008, 'The London and Paris temples: A comparative analysis of their financial services for the kings during the thirteenth century', in J. Upton Ward (ed.), *The military orders, vol. 4: On land and by sea*, pp. 121–128, Ashgate, Aldershot.

Demyanyk, Y. & Van Hemert, O., 2009, 'Understanding the subprime mortgage crisis', *The Review of Financial Studies* 24(6), 1848–1880. https://doi.org/10.1093/rfs/hhp033

De Roover, R., 1944. 'What is dry exchange? A contribution to the study of English mercantilism', *Journal of Political Economy* 52(3), 250–266. https://doi.org/10.1086/256185

Derrida, J., 1997, *Of grammatology*, Corrected edn., John Hopkins University Press, Baltimore, MD.

Desrochers, P., 2010, 'The environmental responsibility of business is to increase its profits (by creating value within the bounds of private property rights)', *Industrial and Corporate Change* 19(1), 161–204. https://doi.org/10.1093/icc/dtp046

De Vries, J., 1994, 'The industrial revolution and the industrious revolution', *The Journal of Economic History* 54(2), 249–270. https://doi.org/10.1017/S0022050700014467

Dhiman, S., 2008, 'Products, people, and planet: The triple bottom line sustainability imperative', *Journal of Global Business Issues* 2(2), 51–57.

Dietz, R. & O'Neill, D., 2013, *Enough is enough. Building a sustainable economy in a world of finite resources*, Routledge, Taylor and Francis, San Francisco, CA.

Dignitas, n.d., *Official homepage*, viewed 15 May 2020, from http://dignitas.ch/index.php?lang=en.

Dimitrov, V., Palia, D. & Tang, L., 2015, 'Impact of the Dodd-Frank act on credit ratings', *Journal of Financial Economics* 115(3), 505–520. https://doi.org/10.1016/j.jfineco.2014.10.012

Domingo, J.L. & Bordonaba, J.G., 2011, 'A literature review on the safety assessment of genetically modified plants', *Environment International* 37(4), 734–742. https://doi.org/10.1016/j.envint.2011.01.003

Donlan, W., 1985, 'The social groups of dark age Greece', *Classical Philology* 80(4), 293–308. https://doi.org/10.1086/366938

Dorn, J.H., 1993, 'The social gospel and socialism: A comparison of the thought of Francis Greenwood Peabody, Washington Gladden, and Walter Rauschenbusch', *Church History* 62(1), 82–100. https://doi.org/10.2307/3168417

Douma, J., 1996, *The ten commandments*, P&R, Phillipsburg, NJ.

Downes, J. & Goodman, J., 2014, *Dictionary of finance and investment terms*, Barron's Educational Series, Hauppauge, NY

Driver, J., 2007, *Ethics, the fundamentals*, Blackwell, Malden, MA.

Drummond, H., 2001, *The art of decision-making: Mirrors of imagination, masks of fate*, Wiley, Chichester.

Easterly, W., 2002, 'How did heavily indebted poor countries become heavily indebted? Reviewing two decades of debt relief', *World Development* 30(10), 1677–1696. https://doi.org/10.1016/S0305-750X(02)00073-6

Economou, E.M.L., Kyriazis, N.C. & Metaxas, T., 2015, 'The institutional and economic foundations of regional proto-federations', *Economics of Governance* 16(3), 251–271. https://doi.org/10.1007/s10101-014-0155-4

References

Edwards, F.R., 1999, 'Hedge funds and the collapse of long-term capital management', *The Journal of Economic Perspectives* 13(2), 189–210. https://doi.org/10.1257/jep.13.2.189

Ekelund, R.B., Hébert, R.F. & Tollison, R.D., 2005, 'Adam Smith on religion and market structure', *History of Political Economy* 37(4), 647–660. https://doi.org/10.1215/00182702-37-4-647

Elshtain, J.B., 2004, 'Foreword', in E. Owens, J.D. Carlson & E.P. Elshtain (eds.), *Religion and the death penalty: A call for reckoning*, pp. 43–81, Wm. B. Eerdmans Publishing, Grand Rapids, MI.

Engel, E., Fischer, R. & Galetovic, A., 2013, 'The basic public finance of public–private partnerships', *Journal of the European Economic Association* 11(1), 83–111. https://doi.org/10.1111/j.1542-4774.2012.01105.x

Evangelical Christian Credit Union, n.d., *Official homepage*, viewed 08 April 2019, from https://www.eccu.org/.

EY, 2016, *EY world Islamic Banking competitiveness report 2016*, viewed 01 February 2018, from https://ceif.iba.edu.pk/pdf/EY-WorldIslamicBankingCompetitivenessReport2016.pdf

Fein, M.L., 2013, *The shadow banking charade*, viewed 25 May 2016, from http://feinlawoffices.com/images/2013--Shadow_banking_March_4.pdf.

Feinberg, C.L. 1972, 'The image of God', *Bibliotheca Sacra* 129(515), 235–246.

Ferreira, J., Perry, M. & Subramanian, S., 2015, 'Spending time with money: From shared values to social connectivity', in *Proceedings of the 18th ACM Conference on Computer Supported Cooperative Work & Social Computing*, March 14–18, 2015, pp. 1222–1234.

Field, D.H., 1995, 'Gambling', in D.J. Atkinson, D.F. Field, A.F. Holmes & O. O'Donovan (eds.), *New dictionary of Christian ethics and pastoral theology*, pp. 401–402, InterVarsity Press, Downers Grove, IL.

Fisher, I., 1935, *100% money*, Adelphi Publication, New York, NY.

Flandreau, M., 1996, 'The French crime of 1873: An essay on the emergence of the international gold standard, 1870–1880', *The Journal of Economic History* 56(4), 862–897. https://doi.org/10.1017/S0022050700017502

Flandreau, M., 2002, '"Water seeks a level": Modeling bimetallic exchange rates and the bimetallic band', *Journal of Money, Credit, and Banking* 34(2), 491–519.

Fletcher, J., 1966, *Situation ethics: The new morality*, Westminster John Knox Press, Louisville, KY.

Forbes, n.d., *Official homepage*, viewed 19 November 2019, from https://www.forbes.com.

Forster, G.S., 1995, 'Property', in D.J. Atkinson, D.F. Field, A.F. Holmes & O. O'Donovan (eds.), *New dictionary of Christian ethics & pastoral theology*, pp. 696–697, InterVarsity Press, Downers Grove, IL.

Foster, B.R., 1977, 'Commercial activity in Sargonic Mesopotamia', *Iraq* 39(1), 31–43. https://doi.org/10.2307/4200046

Foster, H.D., 1908, 'Calvin's programme for a puritan state in Geneva, 1536–1541', *Harvard Theological Review* 1(4), 391–434. https://doi.org/10.1017/S0017816000006672

Frank, T., 1935, 'The financial crisis of 33 AD', *The American Journal of Philology* 56(4), 336–341. https://doi.org/10.2307/289972

Franklin, E., 2007, 'Luke', in J. Barton & J. Muddiman (eds.), *The Oxford Bible commentary*, pp. 922–959, Oxford University Press, Oxford.

Freeman, I. & Hasnaoui, A., 2011, 'The meaning of corporate social responsibility: The vision of four nations', *Journal of Business Ethics* 100(3), 419–443. https://doi.org/10.1007/s10551-010-0688-6

Friedman, D.D., 1980, 'In defense of Thomas Aquinas and the just price', *History of Political Economy* 12(2), 234–242. https://doi.org/10.1215/00182702-12-2-234

Friedman, M., 1970, 'The social responsibility of business is to increase its profits', *The New York Times Magazine*, viewed 12 January 2018, from http://umich.edu/~thecore/doc/Friedman.pdf.

Friedman, M., 1991, *The island of stone money*, Hoover Institution Press, Stanford, CA.

Friedman, M., 2002, *Capitalism and freedom*, The University of Chicago Press, Chicago, IL.

Fritschy, W., 2003, 'A "financial revolution" revisited: Public finance in Holland during the Dutch Revolt, 1568-1648', *The Economic History Review* 56(1), 57-89. https://doi.org/10.1111/1468-0289.00242

Furness, W.H., 1910, *The island of stone money: Uap of the Carolines,* J.B. Lippincott, Philadelphia, PA.

Gaggìa, F., Mattarelli, P. & Biavati, B., 2010, 'Probiotics and prebiotics in animal feeding for safe food production', *International Journal of Food Microbiology* 141(Suppl. 1), S15-S28. https://doi.org/10.1016/j.ijfoodmicro.2010.02.031

Gamblers Anonymous, n.d., *Official homepage*, viewed 04 August 2020, from http://www.gamblersanonymous.org/ga/.

Gandhi, M.K., 1959, *Gandhi's life in his own words: My life is my message,* Navajivan Publishing House, Ahmedabad.

Galbraith, J.K., 1989, *A history of economics,* Penguin Books, London.

Galbraith, J.K., 1998, *The affluent society,* Penguin Books, London.

Galbraith, J.K., 2009, *The great crash 1929,* Penguin Books, London.

Galbreath, J., 2009, 'Building corporate social responsibility into strategy', *European Business Review* 21(2), 109-127. https://doi.org/10.1108/09555340910940123

Gandal, N. & Sussman, N., 1997, 'Asymmetric information and commodity money: Tickling the tolerance in medieval France', *Journal of Money, Credit and Banking* 29(4), 440-457. https://doi.org/10.2307/2953707

Gavin, M. & Rodrik, D., 1995, 'The World Bank in historical perspective', *The American Economic Review* 85(2), 329-334.

Gay, J., 1731, 'A dissertation concerning the fundamental principle and immediate criterion of virtue', in W. King (ed.), *An essay on the origin of evil*, pp. 298-319, W. Thurlbourn, Cambridge.

Geisler, N.L., 2010, *Christian ethics, contemporary ethics & options,* 2nd edn., Baker, Grand Rapids, MI.

Geljon, P. & De Graaf, T., 2013, 'Dutch Banking in Overseas Territories: Different Ways of Entry and Exit', in *2013 EABH Annual Conference*, Warsaw, Poland, June 07-08, 2013, pp. 251-284.

Gick, E., 2003, 'Cognitive theory and moral behavior: The contribution of F.A. Hayek to business ethics', *Journal of Business Ethics* 45(1-2), 149-165. https://doi.org/10.1023/A:1024141017104

Githens, R.P., 2009, 'Capitalism, identity politics, and queerness converge: LGBT employee resource groups', *New Horizons in Adult Education & Human Resource Development* 23(3), 18-31. https://doi.org/10.1002/nha3.10347

Gladden, W., 1916, *The Christian pastor and the working church*, Scribners, New York, NY.

Glander, S.S., Moore, M.L., Michielutte, R. & Parsons, L.H., 1998, 'The prevalence of domestic violence among women seeking abortion', *Obstetrics & Gynecology* 91(6), 1002-1006. https://doi.org/10.1097/00006250-199806000-00025

Global Islamic Finance Report, 2019, *Home*, viewed 22 December 2020, from http://www.gifr.net/.

Globenewswire, n.d., *Official homepage*, viewed 11 April 2019, from https://www.globenewswire.com/Index.

Gnuse, R., 1985, 'Jubilee legislation in Leviticus: Israel's vision of social reform', *Biblical Theology Bulletin* 15(2), 43-48. https://doi.org/10.1177/014610798501500202

Goetzmann, W.N., 2016, *Money changes everything: How finance made civilisation possible,* Princeton University Press, Princeton, NJ.

Goitein, S.D., 1967, *A Mediterranean society: The Jewish communities of the Arab world as portrayed in the documents of the Cairo Geniza*, vol. 1, University of California Press, Berkeley, CA.

Goodhart, C.A.E., 1999, 'Myths about the lender of last resort', *International Finance* 2(3), 339-360. https://doi.org/10.1111/1468-2362.00033

Goodpaster, K.E., 1991, 'Business ethics and stakeholder analysis', *Business Ethics Quarterly* 1(1), 53-73. https://doi.org/10.2307/3857592

Goody, J., 2003, 'Religion and development: Some comparative considerations', *Development* 46(4), 64-67. https://doi.org/10.1177/1011637003046004010

References

Gordon, B., 2011, *Calvin*, Yale University Press, Newhaven, CT.

Gotham, K.F., 2009, 'Creating liquidity out of spatial fixity: The secondary circuit of capital and the subprime mortgage crisis', *International Journal of Urban and Regional Research* 33(2), 355–371. https://doi.org/10.1111/j.1468-2427.2009.00874.x

Graafland, J., 2009, 'Calvin's restrictions on interest: Guidelines for the credit crisis', *Journal of Business Ethics* 96(2), 233–248. https://doi.org/10.1007/s10551-010-0462-9

Graeber, D., 2012, *Debt: The first 5000 years*, Melville House Publishing, New York, NY.

Graham, E.L., 2002, *Transforming practice: Pastoral theology in an age of uncertainty*, Wipf and Stock, Eugene, OR.

Greene, T.A., 1923, 'Ecclesiastical organization of Geneva in the time of Calvin', *Journal of the Presbyterian Historical Society (1901–1930)* 11(8), 305–367.

Gregory, 1890, 'The book of the pastoral rule and selected epistles', in P. Schaff (ed.), *A select library of the Nicene and post-Nicene fathers of the Christian Church*, vol. 12, pp. 575–724, WM. B. Eerdmans Publishing Company, Grand Rapids, MI.

Griffin, J., 2008, *On human rights*, Oxford University Press, Oxford.

Grinde, J. & Khare, A., 2008, 'The ant, the grasshopper or Schrödinger's cat: An exploration of concepts of sustainability', *Journal of Environmental Assessment Policy & Management* 10(2), 115–141. https://doi.org/10.1142/S1464333208003007

Groenhout, R., 2006, 'Not without hope: A reformed analysis of sickness and sin', *Christian Bioethics* 12(2), 133–150. https://doi.org/10.1080/13803600600805278

Gros, D. & Schoenmaker, D., 2014, 'European deposit insurance and resolution in the banking union', *Journal of Common Market Studies* 52(3), 529–546. https://doi.org/10.1111/jcms.12124

Grudem, W., 1994, *Systematic theology*, Inter Varsity Press, Nottingham.

Gushee, D.P. & Stassen, G.H., 2016, *Kingdom ethics: Following Jesus in contemporary context,* 2nd edn., Eerdmans, Grand Rapids, MI.

Gustafson, J.M., 1989, 'Roman Catholic and Protestant interaction in ethics: An interpretation', *Theological Studies* 50(1), 44–69. https://doi.org/10.1177/004056398905000103

Gutiérrez, G. & Muller, C.G.L., 2015, *On the side of the poor: The theology of liberation*, Orbis Books, New York, NY.

Haaugaard, W.P., 1979, 'Renaissance patristic scholarship and theology in sixteenth-century England', in R.B. Waddington & M. Wiesner-Hanks (eds.), *The sixteenth century journal*, pp. 37–60, Truman State University, Kirksville, MO.

Habib, I., 1985, 'Studying a colonial economy – Without perceiving colonialism', *Modern Asian Studies* 19(3), 355–381. https://doi.org/10.1017/S0026749X00007654

Hadders, H., 2009, 'The adaptive quadruple bottom line scorecard: Measuring organizational sustainability performance', *Canadian Sustainability Indicators Network*, viewed 22 June 2017, from http://www.csin-rcid.ca/downloads/csin_conf_henk_hadders.pdf.

Hall, D., 2008, *The legacy of John Calvin: His influence on the modern world*, P & R Publishing, Phillipsburg, NJ.

Hall, T. & Barrett, H., 2012, *Urban geography*, 4th edn., Routledge, Abingdon.

Harcourt, G.C. & Kerr, P., 2003, 'Keynes and the Cambridge School', in J.S. Samuels, J.E. Biddle & J.B. Davis (eds.), *A companion to the history of economic thought*, pp. 343–359, Blackwell, Malden, MA.

Hardin, R., 1991, 'Hobbesian political order', *Political Theory* 19(2), 156–180. https://doi.org/10.1177/0090591791019002002

Harris, W.V., 2006, 'A revisionist view of Roman money', *Journal of Roman Studies,* 96, 1–24. https://doi.org/10.3815/000000006784016215

Harris, W.V., 2008, *The monetary systems of the Greeks and Romans*, Oxford University Press, Oxford.

Hayek, F.A., 1967, *Studies in philosophy, politics and economics*, viewed 14 August 2018, from http://direitasja.files.wordpress.com/2012/05/studies-in-philosophy-and-economics-friedrich-a-hayek.pdf.

Hayek, F.A., 2001, *The road to serfdom*, Routledge, Abingdon.

Heckscher, E.F., 2013, *Mercantilism*, Routledge, Abingdon.

Heere, B. & James, J.D., 2007, 'Stepping outside the lines: Developing a multi-dimensional team identity scale based on social identity theory', *Sport Management Review* 10(1), 65–91. https://doi.org/10.1016/S1441-3523(07)70004-9

Heitink, G., 1999, *Practical theology: History, theory, action domains: Manual for practical theology*, Wm. B. Eerdmans, Grand Rapids, MI.

Hertz, N., 2002, *The silent takeover, global capitalism and the death of democracy*, The Random House Group, London.

Higginson, R.A., 1994, 'The world of business', in D.J. Atkinson (ed.), *Pastoral ethics: A guide to the key issues of daily living*, pp. 153–164, Lynx Communications, London.

Higginson, R.A., 1995, 'Ethics of medical care', in D.J. Atkinson, D.F. Field, A.F. Holmes & O. O'Donovan (eds.), *New dictionary of Christian ethics and pastoral theology*, pp. 93–99, InterVarsity Press, Downers Grove, IL.

Hilbeck, A., Binimelis, R., Defarge, N., Steinbrecher, R., Székács, A., Wickson, F. et al., 2015, 'No scientific consensus on GMO safety', *Environmental Sciences Europe* 27(1), 4. https://doi.org/10.1186/s12302-014-0034-1

Hill, J.A., 2011, 'Endangered childhoods: How consumerism is impacting child and youth identity', *Media, Culture & Society* 33(3), 347–362. https://doi.org/10.1177/0163443710393387

Hiltner, S., 1949, *Pastoral counseling*, Abingdon Cokesbury Press, New York, NY.

Hiltner, S., 1969, *Ferment in the ministry*, Abingdon Press, Nashville, TN.

Hiltner, S., 2000, 'The meaning and importance of pastoral theology', in J. Woodward, S. Pattison & J. Patton (eds.), *The Blackwell reader in pastoral and practical theology*, pp. 27–48, Wiley-Blackwell, Oxford.

Hislop, D., 2013, *Knowledge management in organizations, a critical introduction*, 3rd edn., Oxford University Press, Oxford.

Hitchcock, J., 2012, *History of the Catholic Church, from the apostolic age to the third millennium*, Ignatius Press, San Francisco, CA.

Hobbes, T., 2008, *Leviathan*, Oxford University Press, Oxford.

Hock, D.W., 1995, 'The chaordic organization: Out of control and into order', *World Business Academy Perspectives* 9(1), 5–18.

Hodge, C., 1873, *Systematic theology*, Christian Classics Ethereal Library, Grand Rapids, MI, viewed 12 May 2020, from http://www.ccel.org/ccel/hodge/theology3.pdf.

Hoekema, D.A., 1986, 'A practical Christian pacifism', *Christian Century* 22, 917–919.

Hoffmann, J.P., 2000, 'Religion and problem gambling in the US', *Review of Religious Research* 41(4), 488–509. https://doi.org/10.2307/3512317

Hogg, M.A. & Terry, D.J., 2001, 'Social identity theory and organizational processes', in M.A. Hogg & D.J. Terry (eds.), *Social identity processes in organizational contexts*, pp. 31–48, Psychology Press, Hove.

Holder, R., 2001, 'Karl Barth and the legitimacy of natural theology', *Themelios* 26(3), 22–37.

Holmes, A.F., 1995, 'Just-war theory', in D.J. Atkinson, D.F. Field, A.F. Holmes & O. O'Donovan (eds.), *New dictionary of Christian ethics & pastoral theology*, pp. 521–523, InterVarsity Press, Downers Grove, IL.

Homer, S., 1991, *The Iliad*, Penguin Books, London.

Homer, S., 2003, *The odyssey*, Penguin Books, London.

References

Homer, S. & Sylla, R.E., 1996, *A history of interest rates*, Rutgers University Press, New Brunswick.

Horne, C.F. & Johns, C.H.W., 2007, *The code of Hammurabi*, Forgotten Books, Charleston, SC.

Horrell, D.G., 2008, 'Biblical vegetarianism? A critical and constructive assessment', in D. Grumett & R. Muers (eds.), *Eating and believing: Interdisciplinary perspectives on vegetarianism and theology*, Location 1101–1512, A&C Black, London.

Hosseini, H.S., 2008, 'Contributions of medieval Muslim scholars to the history of economics and their impact: A refutation of the Schumpeterian great gap', in W.J. Samuels, J.E. Biddle & J.B. Davis (eds.), *A companion to the history of economic thought*, pp. 28–45, Blackwell, Malden, MA.

Houston, W., 2007, 'Exodus', in J. Barton & J. Muddiman (eds.), *The Oxford Bible commentary*, pp. 67–91, Oxford University Press, Oxford.

Howard-Hassmann, R.E. & Donnelly, J., 1986, 'Human dignity, human rights, and political regimes', *American Political Science Review* 80(3), 801–817. https://doi.org/10.2307/1960539

Huff, P.A., 1999, 'Calvin and the beasts: Animals in John Calvin's theological discourse', *Journal of the Evangelical Theological Society* 42(1), 67.

Hughes, J.A, Sharrock, W. & Martin, P.J., 2010, *Understanding classical sociology*, 2nd edn., Sage, London.

Hurding, R.F., 1995a, 'Biblical counselling', in D.J. Atkinson, D.F. Field, A.F. Holmes & O. O'Donovan (eds.), *New dictionary of Christian ethics and pastoral theology*, pp. 192–193, InterVarsity Press, Downers Grove, IL.

Hurding, R.F., 1995b, 'Seward Hiltner', in D.J. Atkinson, D.F. Field, A.F. Holmes & O. O'Donovan (eds.), *New dictionary of Christian ethics and pastoral theology*, pp. 440–441, InterVarsity Press, Downers Grove, IL.

Hursthouse, R. & Glen Pettigrove, G., 2018, 'Virtue ethics', in E.N. Zalta (ed.), *The Stanford encyclopaedia of philosophy* (Winter 2018 Edition), viewed 14 December 2020, from https://plato.stanford.edu/archives/win2018/entries/ethics-virtue/.

Hyman, L., 2008, 'Debtor nation: How consumer credit built postwar America', *Enterprise and Society* 9(4), 614–618. https://doi.org/10.1017/S1467222700007552

International Committee of the Red Cross, n.d, *Official homepage*, viewed 05 October 2020, from https://www.icrc.org/en.

International Conference of Reformed Churches, 2017, *Press release, International conference of reformed churches*, viewed 07 May 2020, from https://cdn.website-editor.net/aad80025ed07433d8325aaff6b4572f3/files/uploaded/Press%20Release%20ICRC%2012-19%20July%202017.pdf.

International Finance, n.d., *Official homepage*, viewed 24 February 2019, from https://internationalfinance.com/islamic-financial-assets-grow-over-2-tn-globally-imf/.

International Labour Office, 2017, *World social protection report 2017–19: Universal social protection to achieve the sustainable development goals*, Geneva, viewed 03 August 2020, from https://www.ilo.org/wcmsp5/groups/public/---dgreports/---dcomm/---publ/documents/publication/wcms_604882.pdf.

Investopedia, n.d., *Official homepage*, viewed 17 February 2020, from https://www.investopedia.com/.

IOR (Istituto per le Opere di Religione), n.d., *Official homepage,* viewed from http://www.ior.va/content/ior/en.html.

Islamic Finance, n.d., *Official homepage*, viewed 05 July 2019, from https://www.islamicfinance.com/#.

Jaffe, J.F., 1989, 'Gold and gold stocks as investments for institutional portfolios', *Financial Analysts Journal* 45(2), 53–59. https://doi.org/10.2469/faj.v45.n2.53

Jamaldeen, F., 2012, *Islamic finance for dummies*, John Wiley & Sons, Hoboken, NJ.

James, S., Lahti, T. & Zettelmeyer, F., 2006, '$1,000 cash back: The pass-through of auto manufacturer promotions', *The American Economic Review* 96(4), 1253–1270. https://doi.org/10.1257/aer.96.4.1253

Jashapara, A., 2011, *Knowledge management, an integrated approach*, 2nd edn., Pearson Education, Harlow.

Jenson, R.W., 1997, *Systematic theology: Vol. 1: The triune god,* Oxford University Press, Oxford.

Jones, G., Cardinal, D. & Hayward, J., 2006, *Moral philosophy: A guide to ethical theory,* Hodder Education, London.

Jordanova, L.J., 1987, 'Conceptualizing childhood in the eighteenth century: The problem of child labour', *Journal for Eighteenth-Century Studies* 10(2), 189–199. https://doi.org/10.1111/j.1754-0208.1987.tb00015.x

Jursa, M. (ed.), 2010, *Aspects of the economic history of Babylonia in the first millennium BC. Economic geography, economic mentalities, agriculture, the use of money and the problem of economic growth,* Ugarit-Verlag, Münster.

Kaiser Jr., W.C., 2012, 'Ownership and property in the old testament economy', *Journal of Markets & Morality* 15(1), 227–237.

Kant, I., 1947, *The critique of practical reason,* eBook prepared by Matthew Stapleton, viewed 18 November 2019, from http://www.lacanianworks.net/?p=315.

Kant, I., 2007, *Critique of pure reason,* Penguin Books, London.

Karlan, D. & Zinman, J., 2009, 'Observing unobservables: Identifying information asymmetries with a consumer credit field experiment', *Econometrica* 77(6), 1993–2008. https://doi.org/10.3982/ECTA5781

Kavus, K., 1951, *Qabus Nameh* [A mirror for princes], transl. from the Persian by R. Levy, Dutton, New York, NY.

Kay, J., 2016, *Other people's money: Masters of the universe or servants of the people?,* Profile Books, London.

Kearns, L., 1996, 'Saving the creation: Christian environmentalism in the United States', *Sociology of Religion* 57(1), 55–70. https://doi.org/10.2307/3712004

Keister, O.R., 1963, 'Commercial record-keeping in ancient Mesopotamia', *The Accounting Review* 38(2), 371–376.

Kerkhofs, J., 1994, 'Catholics and protestants in Europe: Different ethical views?', *Ethical Perspectives* 1(1), 123. https://doi.org/10.2143/EP.1.3.630088

Kettell, B., 2011, *Introduction to Islamic banking and finance*, vol. 1, John Wiley & Sons, Hoboken, NJ.

Keynes, J.M., 1915, 'The island of stone money', *Economic Journal* 25(98), 281–283. https://doi.org/10.2307/2222196

Keynes, J.M., 1930, *A treatise on money,* Macmillan & Co Ltd, London.

Keynes, J.M., 1933, 'Economic possibilities for our grandchildren', in *Essays in persuasion*, pp. 358–373, Macmillan & Co Ltd, London.

Keynes, J.M., 2012, *General theory of employment, interest and money*, Snowball Publishing, Dallas, TX.

Khandker, S.R., 2005, 'Microfinance and poverty: Evidence using panel data, from Bangladesh', *The World Bank Economic Review* 19(2), 263–286. https://doi.org/10.1093/wber/lhi008

Kieser, A., 1989, 'Organizational, institutional, and societal evolution: Medieval craft guilds and the genesis of formal organizations', *Administrative Science Quarterly* 34(4), 540–564. https://doi.org/10.2307/2393566

Kim, J., 2011, 'How modern banking originated: The London goldsmith-bankers' institutionalisation of trust', *Business History* 53(6), 939–959. https://doi.org/10.1080/00076791.2011.578132

Kim, Y. & Short, J.R., 2008, *Cities and economies,* Routledge, Abingdon.

Kim, Y.S., 2009, '*Lex talionis* in Exod 21: 22–25: Its origin and context', *Journal of Hebrew Scriptures* 6(3), 1–11. https://doi.org/10.5508/jhs.2006.v6.a3

References

King, J., 2013, *David Ricardo*, Springer, Berlin.

King, J.E., 2003, 'Non-Marxian socialism', in J.S. Samuels, J.E. Biddle & J.B. Davis (eds.), *A companion to the history of economic thought*, pp. 184–200, Blackwell, Malden, MA.

Kingdom Bank, n.d., *Official homepage*, viewed 12 December 2020, from https://www.kingdom.bank/.

Klein, N., 2001, *No logo*, HarperCollins, London.

Klijn, E. H., & Teisman, G. R., 2003, Institutional and strategic barriers to public—private partnership: An analysis of Dutch cases, *Public Money and Management*, *23*(3), 137-146.

Korthals, M., 2008, 'Ethical rooms for maneuver and their prospects vis-à-vis the current ethical food policies in Europe', *Journal of Agricultural and Environmental Ethics* 21(3), 249–273. https://doi.org/10.1007/s10806-007-9078-1

Kostenberger, A.J., 2010, *God, marriage and family: Rebuilding the biblical foundation*, 2nd edn., Crossway, Wheaton, IL.

Krugman, P.R., 2008, *The return of depression economics,* Penguin Books, London.

Kurtz, P. & Wilson, E.H., 1973, 'Humanist manifesto II', *The Humanist* 33(8), 4–9.

Kurz, H.D., 2016, *Economic thought: A brief history*, Columbia University Press, New York, NY.

Kymlicka, W., 1995, *Multicultural citizenship*, Oxford University Press, New York, NY.

Labib, S.Y., 1969, 'Capitalism in medieval Islam', *The Journal of Economic History* 29(1), 79–96. https://doi.org/10.1017/S0022050700097837

Langholm, O.I., 1984, *The Aristotelian analysis of usury,* Scandinavian University Press, Oslo.

Langholm, O.I., 2009, 'Martin Luther's doctrine on trade and price in its literary context', *History of Political Economy* 41(1), 89-107. https://doi.org/10.1215/00182702-2008-038

Lawrence, N., 1948, 'Benevolence and self-interest', *The Journal of Philosophy* 45(17), 457–463. https://doi.org/10.2307/2019212

Lazenby, H.F., 1987, 'The image of God: Masculine, feminine, or neuter?', *Journal of the Evangelical Theological Society* 30(1), 63-70.

Lee, M.K. & Turban, E., 2001, 'A trust model for consumer internet shopping', *International Journal of Electronic Commerce* 6(1), 75–91. https://doi.org/10.1080/10864415.2001.11044227

Lee, S.P., 2012, *Ethics and war: An introduction*, Cambridge University Press, Cambridge.

LGBT Capital, n.d., *Official homepage*, viewed 19 November 2019, from http://www.lgbt-capital.com/.

Lieber, A.E., 1968, 'Eastern business practices and Medieval European Commerce, 1', *The Economic History Review* 21(2), 230-243. https://doi.org/10.2307/2592433

Ljungberg, D., Gebresenbet, G. & Aradom, S., 2007, 'Logistics chain of animal transport and abattoir operations', *Biosystems Engineering* 96(2), 267–277. https://doi.org/10.1016/j.biosystemseng.2006.11.003

Lo Cascio, E., 1994, 'The size of the Roman population: Beloch and the meaning of the Augustan census figures', *Journal of Roman Studies* 84, 23–40. https://doi.org/10.2307/300868

Locke, J., 1695, *Further considerations concerning raising the value of money wherein Mr. Lowndes's arguments for it in his late report concerning an essay for the amendment of silver coins are particularly examined*, viewed 14 April 2020, from http://avalon.law.yale.edu/17th_century/locke01.asp.

Long, R.T., 1994, 'A university built by the invisible hand', Formulations, 1 (3), FNF Publications, viewed 05 March 2018, from http://www.freenation.org/a/index.html#f13

Lowry, S.T., 2003, 'Ancient and medieval economics', in J.S. Samuels, J.E. Biddle & J.B. Davis (eds.), *A companion to the history of economic thought,* pp. 11–27, Blackwell, Malden, MA.

Luther, M., 1521, *Letter, from Luther to Melanchthon, Letter no. 99, 1 August 1521, from the Wartburg (segment)*, transl. E.B. Flores, viewed 03 March 2019, from http://www.iclnet.org/pub/resources/text/wittenberg/luther/letsinsbe.txt.

Luther, M., 1824, 'Trade and usury', in T.G. Tappert (ed.), *Selected writings of Martin Luther*, n.p., Fortress Press, Minneapolis, MN.

Luther, M., 2018, *The premium collection*, e-artnow, s.l.

Maali, B., Casson, P. & Napier, C., 2006, 'Social reporting by Islamic banks', *Abacus* 42(2), 266–289. https://doi.org/10.1111/j.1467-6281.2006.00200.x

MacCulloch, D., 2004, *Reformation: Europe's house divided 1490–1700,* Penguin, London.

MacCulloch, D., 2010, *A history of Christianity*, Penguin Books, London.

Machiavelli, N., 2009, *The prince,* Penguin Books, London.

Macintyre, A.G., Christopher, G.W., Eitzen Jr, E., Gum, R., Weir, S., DeAtley, C. et al., 2000, 'Weapons of mass destruction events with contaminated casualties: Effective planning for health care facilities', *Journal of the American Medical Association* 283(2), 242–249. https://doi.org/10.1001/jama.283.2.242

MacMillan, K., 2006, *Sovereignty and possession in the English new world: The legal foundations of empire, 1576–1640,* Cambridge University Press, Cambridge.

Mallaby, S., 2010, *More money than God: Hedge funds and the making of the new elite,* A&C Black, London.

Malthus, T.R., 2013, *An essay on the principle of population*, vol. 1, viewed 22 August 2020, from http://129.237.201.53/books/malthus/population/malthus.pdf.

Marginson, S., 2006, 'Dynamics of national and global competition in higher education', *Higher Education* 52(1), 1–39. https://doi.org/10.1007/s10734-004-7649-x

Markussen, T., 2008, 'Property rights, productivity, and common property resources: Insights from rural Cambodia', *World Development* 36(11), 2277–2296. https://doi.org/10.1016/j.worlddev.2008.04.008

Marrero, J.A., Fontana, R.J., Fu, S., Conjeevaram, H.S., Su, G.L. & Lok, A.S., 2005, 'Alcohol, tobacco and obesity are synergistic risk factors for hepatocellular carcinoma', *Journal of Hepatology* 42(2), 218–224. https://doi.org/10.1016/j.jhep.2004.10.005

Marshall, K., 2003, 'Fact-sheet on gambling', *Perspectives on Labour and Income* 15(1), 1–5.

Martin, F., 2014, *Money: The unauthorised biography*, Random House, London

Martin, N., 2010, '1,000% interest – Good while supplies last: A study of payday loan practices and solutions', *Arizona Law Review* 52(3), 563–622.

Martin, S., 2011, *The knights templar,* Oldcastle Books, Harpenden.

Marx, K., 2013, *Capital*, Wordsworth Editions, Hertfordshire.

Marx, K. & Engels, F., 2002, *The communist manifesto*, Penguin Books, London.

Mason, J. & Finelly, M., 2006, 'Brave new farm?', in P. Singer (ed.), *In defense of animals, the second wave,* pp. 104–122, Blackwell, Malden, MA.

Maunder, P., Meyers, D., Wall, N. & Miller, R.L., 1991, *Economics explained,* 3rd edn., HarperCollins, New York, NY.

Mayhew, N., 1999, *Sterling: The rise and fall of a currency,* Allen Lane, London.

Mayoux, L., 2001, 'Tackling the down side: Social capital, women's empowerment and microfinance in Cameroon', *Development and Change* 32(3), 435–464. https://doi.org/10.1111/1467-7660.00212

Mayr-Harting, H., 1996, 'Charlemagne, the Saxons, and the imperial coronation of 800', *English Historical Review* 111(444), 1113–1133. https://doi.org/10.1093/ehr/CXI.444.1113

Mazzucato, M., 2014, *The entrepreneurial state,* Anthem Press, London.

McCabe, S.E., Teter, C.J. & Boyd, C.J., 2006, 'Medical use, illicit use, and diversion of abusable prescription drugs', *Journal of American College Health* 54(5), 269–278. https://doi.org/10.3200/JACH.54.5.269-278

McDonald, G., 2010, 'Ethical relativism vs absolutism: Research implications', *European Business Review* 22(4), 446–464. https://doi.org/10.1108/09555341011056203

McEachern, M.G., & Cheetham, F., 2013, 'A conception of moral sensitivity and everyday consumption practices: Insights from the moralizing discourses of pet owners', *International Journal of Consumer Studies* 37(3), 337–343. https://doi.org/10.1111/ijcs.12005

References

McGrath, A.E., 2011, *Christian theology: An introduction,* 5th edn., John Wiley & Sons, Chichester.

McGrath, A.E., 2012, *Historical theology: An introduction to the history of Christian thought,* John Wiley & Sons, Chichester.

McManus, J., 2011, 'Revisiting ethics in strategic management', *Corporate Governance* 11(2), 214–223. https://doi.org/10.1108/14720701111121074

McNally, R.E., 1967, 'The ninety-five theses of Martin Luther 1517–1967', *Theological Studies* 28(3), 439–480. https://doi.org/10.1177/004056396702800301

Merriam-Webster, n.d., *Official homepage,* viewed 06 August 2020, from https://www.merriam-webster.com/.

Mian, A. & Sufi, A., 2015, *House of debt: How they (and you) caused the great recession, and how we can prevent it, from happening again,* University of Chicago Press, Chicago, IL.

Micklethwait, J. & Woolridge, A., 2005, *The company: A short history of a revolutionary idea,* vol. 12, Random House Digital, New York, NY.

Middleton, J.R., 2006, 'A new heaven and a new earth: The case for a holistic reading of the biblical story of redemption', *Journal for Christian Theological Research* 6(4), 73–97.

Mill, J.S., 2001, *Utilitarianism and the 1868 speech on capital punishment,* 2nd edn., Hackett, Indianapolis, IN.

Mill, J.S., 2005, *On liberty,* Cosimo, New York, NY.

Millett, P., 2002, *Lending and borrowing in ancient Athens,* Cambridge University Press, Cambridge.

Moffitt, R.A., 2003, 'The negative income tax and the evolution of US welfare policy', *Journal of Economic Perspectives* 17(3), 119–140. https://doi.org/10.1257/089533003769204380

Moore, G.E., 1903, *Principia ethica,* viewed 12 September 2019, from https://archive.org/details/principiaethica00mooruoft.

Moore, M., Gould, P. & Keary, B.S., 2003, 'Global urbanization and impact on health', *International Journal of Hygiene and Environmental Health* 206(4), 269–278. https://doi.org/10.1078/1438-4639-00223

Mordor Intelligence, n.d., *Official homepage,* viewed 04 November 2020, from https://mordorintelligence.com/.

Morduch, J., 1999, 'The microfinance promise', *Journal of Economic Literature* 37(4), 1569–1614. https://doi.org/10.1257/jel.37.4.1569

Morgan, M.L. (ed.), 2011, *Classics of moral and political theory,* 5th edn., Hackett, Indianapolis, IN.

Moseley, C.A.E., 2016, 'Healing', in M. Davie, T. Grass, S.R. Holmes, J. McDowell & T.A. Noble (eds.), *New dictionary of theology: Historical and systematic,* pp. 389–391, InterVarsity Press, Downers Grove, IL.

Moss M.J., 1995, 'Ageing', in D.J. Atkinson, D.F. Field, A.F. Holmes & O. O'Donovan (eds.), *New dictionary of Christian ethics & pastoral theology,* pp. 148–149, InterVarsity Press, Downers Grove, IL.

Mulgan, G., Reeder, N., Aylott, M. & Bo'sher, L., 2011, *Social impact investment: The challenge and opportunity of social impact bonds,* The Young Foundation, London.

Mulligan, M., 2015, *An introduction to sustainability. Environmental, social and personal perspectives,* Routledge, Abingdon.

Munro, J.H., 2003, 'The medieval origins of the financial revolution: Usury, rents, and negotiability', *The International History Review* 25(3), 505–562. https://doi.org/10.1080/07075332.2003.9641005

National Rifle Association, n.d., *Official homepage,* viewed 12 July 2020, from https://home.nra.org/.

Neal, L., 2015, *A concise history of international finance: From Babylon to Bernanke,* Cambridge University Press, Cambridge.

Norges Bank Investment Management (NBIM), n.d., *Official homepage,* viewed 17 December 2020, from https://www.nbim.no/en/.

Neal, L. & Quinn, S., 2001, 'Networks of information, markets, and institutions in the rise of London as a financial centre, 1660–1720', *Financial History Review* 8(1), 7–26. https://doi.org/10.1017/S0968565001000130

Negus, D.P., 1995, 'Common ownership', in D.J. Atkinson, D.F. Field, A.F. Holmes & O. O'Donovan (eds.), *New dictionary of Christian ethics & pastoral theology*, pp. 241–242, InterVarsity Press, Downers Grove, IL.

Niczyporuk, P., 2011, 'Mensarii, bankers acting for public and private benefit', *Studies in Logic, Grammar and Rhetoric* 24(37), 105–115.

NIV, 2011, *The Holy Bible, New International Version*, Biblica, London.

Nord, C., 2001, 'Loyalty revisited: Bible translation as a case in point', *The Translator* 7(2), 185–202. https://doi.org/10.1080/13556509.2001.10799100

Norman, R., 1998, *The moral philosophers: An introduction to ethics*, 2nd edn., Oxford University Press, Oxford.

Norwegian Government, n.d., *Official homepage*, viewed 17 December 2020, from https://www.regjeringen.no/en/id4/.

Novak, M., 1990, *The spirit of democratic capitalism*, Madison Books, Lanham, MD.

O'Collins, G., 2009, *Christology: A biblical, historical, and systematic study of Jesus*, Oxford University Press, Oxford.

Oden, T.C., 1978, *Kerygma and counseling: Toward a covenant ontology for secular psychotherapy*, Harper & Row, San Francisco, CA.

Oden, T.C., 1983, *Pastoral theology: Essentials of ministry*, Harper Collins, San Francisco, CA.

Office of the High Commissioner for Human Rights, n.d., *Official Homepage*, viewed 22 May 2020, from https://www.ohchr.org/EN/pages/home.aspx.

O'Mathuna, D.P.O., 2003, 'Bodily injuries, murder, manslaughter', in T.D. Alexander & D.W. Baker (eds.), *Dictionary of the Old Testament, Pentateuch*, pp. 90–94, InterVarsity Press, Leicester.

Onwuteaka-Philipsen, B.D., Van der Heide, A., Koper, D., Keij-Deerenberg, I., Rietjens, J.A., Rurup, M.L. et al., 2003, 'Euthanasia and other end-of-life decisions in the Netherlands in 1990, 1995, and 2001', *The Lancet* 362(9381), 395–399. https://doi.org/10.1016/S0140-6736(03)14029-9

Open Minds, n.d., *Official homepage*, viewed 17 August 2020, from https://www.openminds.com/.

Osborne, S., 2000, *Public-private partnerships: Theory and practice in international perspective*, Routledge, London.

Osmer, R.R., 2008, *Practical theology: An introduction*, Eerdmans, Grand Rapids, MI.

Parker, T.H.L., 2006, *John Calvin: A biography*, Lion Hudson plc., Oxford.

Parmar, B.L., Freeman, R.E., Harrison, J.S., Wicks, A.C., Purnell, L. & De Colle, S., 2010, 'Stakeholder theory: The state of the art', *The Academy of Management Annals* 4(1), 403–445. https://doi.org/10.5465/19416520.2010.495581

Parson, A., 2006, 'The long journey, from stem cells to medical product', *Cell* 125(1), 9–11. https://doi.org/10.1016/j.cell.2006.03.024

Partee, C., 1995, 'John Calvin', in D.J. Atkinson, D.F. Field, A.F. Holmes & O. O'Donovan (eds.), *New dictionary of Christian ethics and pastoral theology*, pp. 209–211, InterVarsity Press, Downers Grove, IL.

Pattison, S. & Woodward, J., 2000, 'An introduction to an evaluation in pastoral theology and pastoral care', in J. Woodward, S. Pattison & J. Patton (eds.), *The Blackwell reader in pastoral and practical theology*, pp. 300–310, Wiley-Blackwell, Oxford.

Pava, M.L., 2008, 'Why corporations should not abandon social responsibility', *Journal of Business Ethics* 83(4), 805–812. https://doi.org/10.1007/s10551-008-9666-7

Peck, J., 2004, 'Geography and public policy: Constructions of neoliberalism', *Progress in Human Geography* 28(3), 392–405. https://doi.org/10.1191/0309132504ph492pr

References

Peck, J., 2008, 'Remaking laissez-faire', *Progress in Human Geography* 32(1), 3–43. https://doi.org/10.1177/0309132507084816

Peck, J. & Tickell, A., 2002, 'Neoliberalizing space', *Antipode* 34(3), 380–404. https://doi.org/10.1111/1467-8330.00247

Pigott, G.J., 1995, 'Covetousness', in D.J. Atkinson, D.F. Field, A.F. Holmes & O. O'Donovan (eds.), *New dictionary of Christian ethics and pastoral theology*, pp. 267–268, InterVarsity Press, Downers Grove, IL.

Piketty, T., 2014, *Capital in the twenty-first century*, The Belknap Press of Harvard University Press, Cambridge, MA.

Plato, 1977, 'The republic', in S. Buchanan (ed.), *The portable Plato*, pp. 281–696, Penguin Books, London.

Popkin, R.H., 1950, 'A note on the "proof" of utility, in J.S. Mill', *Ethics* 61(1), 66–68. https://doi.org/10.1086/290751

Popper, K., 1947, *The open society and its enemies*, Routledge, London.

Posner, G., 2015, *God's bankers: A history of money and power at the Vatican,* Simon and Schuster, New York, NY.

Powell, M.A., 1996, 'Money in Mesopotamia', *Journal of the Economic and Social History of the Orient* 39(3), 224–242. https://doi.org/10.1163/1568520962601225

Pujazon-Zazik, M. & Park, M.J., 2010, 'To tweet, or not to tweet: Gender differences and potential positive and negative health outcomes of adolescents' social internet use', *American Journal of Men's Health* 4(1), 77–85. https://doi.org/10.1177/1557988309360819

Purnanandam, A., 2010, 'Originate-to-distribute model and the subprime mortgage crisis', *The Review of Financial Studies* 24(6), 1881–1915. https://doi.org/10.1093/rfs/hhq106

Purves, A., 2001, *Pastoral theology in the classical tradition,* Westminster John Knox Press, Louisville, KY.

Quinn, S., 1996, 'Gold, silver, and the glorious revolution: Arbitrage between bills of exchange and bullion', *The Economic History Review* 49(3), 473–490. https://doi.org/10.1111/j.1468-0289.1996.tb00578.x

Quinn, S., 2001, 'The glorious revolution's effect on English private finance: A microhistory, 1680–1705', *The Journal of Economic History* 61(3), 593–615.

Quinn, S. & Roberds, W., 2006, 'An economic explanation of the early Bank of Amsterdam, debasement, bills of exchange, and the emergence of the first central bank', Working Paper, Federal Reserve Bank of Atlanta, No. 2006-13.

Rachels, J., 1975, 'Active and passive euthanasia', *New England Journal of Medicine* 292(2), 78–80. https://doi.org/10.1056/NEJM197501092920206

Raelin, J.A., 2003, *Creating leaderful organisations: How to bring out leadership in everyone*, Berrett-Koehler, San Francisco, CA.

Raelin, J.A., 2010, *The leaderful fieldbook: Strategies and activities for developing leadership in everyone*, Nicholas Brealey, London.

Ravenhill, J., 2014, *Global political economy*, Oxford University Press, Oxford.

Rawls, J., 1971, *A theory of justice*, The Belknap Press of Harvard University Press, Cambridge, MA.

Rea, M.C., 2001, 'What is pornography?', *Nous* 35(1), 118–145. https://doi.org/10.1111/0029-4624.00290

Read, P.P., 2001, *The Templars: The dramatic history of the Knights Templar, the most powerful military order of the crusades*, Da Capo Press, Boston, MA.

Regan, T., 1985, 'The case for animal rights', in P. Singer (ed.), *In Defense of Animals*, pp. 13–26, Blackwell, New York, NY.

Reichberg, M., Syse, H. & Begby, E., 2006, *The ethics of war, classic and contemporary readings*, Blackwell, Hoboken, NJ.

Reinhart, C.M. & Rogoff, K.S., 2002, 'The modern history of exchange rate arrangements: A reinterpretation', *Working paper 8963*, National Bureau of Economic Research, Cambridge.

Reliance Bank, n.d., *Official homepage*, viewed 03 December 2020, from http://www.reliancebankltd.com/.

Rempel, J., 2005, 'Peace churches', in J. Bowden (ed.), *Christianity: The complete guide*, pp. 907–909, Continuum, London.

Repullo, R. & Saurina, J., 2011, 'The countercyclical capital buffer of Basel III: A critical assessment', *CEPR discussion paper 8304*, Centre for Economic Policy Research, London.

Ricardo, D., 1891, 'The principles of political economy', in E.C.K. Gonner (ed.), *Bohn's economic library*, G. Bells & Sons, London, viewed 12 April 2017, from http://www.fordham.edu/halsall/mod/ricardo-summary.asp.

Ricardo, D., 2001, *On the principles of political economy and taxation*, Batoche Books, Kitchener.

Ridderbos, H., 1997, *Paul: An outline of his theology*, Eerdmans, Grand Rapids, MI.

Roberts, R. & Kynaston, D., 1995, *The Bank of England: Money, power, and influence 1694–1994*, Oxford University Press, Oxford.

Robertson, C.J. & Athanassiou, N., 2009, 'Exploring business ethics research in the context of international business', *Management Research News* 32(12), 1130–1146. https://doi.org/10.1108/01409170911006894

Robertson, G., 2012, *Crimes against humanity: The struggle for global justice*, 4th edn., Penguin, London.

Robertson, J.A., 1975, 'Involuntary euthanasia of defective newborns: A legal analysis', *Stanford Law Review* 27(2), 213–269. https://doi.org/10.2307/1228265

Rogaly, B., 1996, 'Micro-finance evangelism, "destitute women", and the hard selling of a new anti-poverty formula', *Development in Practice* 6(2), 100–112. https://doi.org/10.1080/0961452961000157654

Rogers, R.M., 2005, *Gambling: Don't bet on it*, Kregel Publications, Grand Rapids, MI.

Rogerson, J. & Davies, P.R., 2005, *The Old Testament world*, T&T Clark, London.

Rolnick, A.J., Velde, F.R. & Weber, W.E., 1996, 'The debasement puzzle: An essay on medieval monetary history', *The Journal of Economic History* 56(4), 789–808. https://doi.org/10.1017/S0022050700017472

Roniger, L., 1983, 'Modern patron-client relations and historical clientelism: Some clues, from ancient republican Rome', *European Journal of Sociology/Archives Européennes de Sociologie* 24(1), 63–95. https://doi.org/10.1017/S0003975600003969

Roseveare, H.G., 2014, *The financial revolution 1660–1750*, Routledge, Abingdon.

Ruffin, R., 2002, 'David Ricardo's discovery of comparative advantage', *History of Political Economy* 34(4), 727–748. https://doi.org/10.1215/00182702-34-4-727

Ryan, A., Trumbull, G. & Tufano, P., 2011, 'A brief postwar history of US consumer finance', *Business History Review* 85(3), 461–498. https://doi.org/10.1017/S0007680511000778

Ryder, R.D., 2006, 'Speciesism in the laboratory', in P. Singer (ed.), *In defense of animals, the second wave*, pp. 87–103, Blackwell, Malden, MA.

Saltuk, Y., Bouri, A. & Leung, G., 2011, *Insight into the impact investment market*, J.P. Morgan, London.

Santana, A., 2012, 'Three elements of stakeholder legitimacy', *Journal of Business Ethics* 105(2), 257–265. https://doi.org/10.1007/s10551-011-0966-y

Savas, E.S., 2000, *Privatization and public-private partnerships*, viewed 08 November 2020, from http://hum.ttu.ee/failid/oppematerjalid/PPP/Savas_PPP_privat_seletav.pdf.

Scheidel, W., 2008, 'The divergent evolution of coinage in eastern and western Eurasia', in W.V. Harris (ed.), *The monetary systems of the Greeks and Romans*, pp. 267–286, Oxford University Press, Oxford.

Schein, E.H., 1999, 'Kurt Lewin's change theory in the field and in the classroom: Notes toward a model of managed learning', *Reflections* 1(1), 59–74. https://doi.org/10.1162/152417399570287

Schleiermacher, F., 1966, *Brief outline on the study of theology*, Westminster John Knox Press, Louisville, KY.

Schleiermacher, F., 1998, *Schleiermacher: Hermeneutics and criticism, and other writings*, Cambridge University Press, Cambridge.

Schleiermacher, F., 2011, *The Christian faith*, Apocryphile Press, Berkeley, CA.

Schlosser, E., 2003, *Reefer madness*, Penguin, London.

Schumpeter, J.A., 2009, *History of economic analysis*, Routledge, New York, NY.

Schwab, K., 2008, 'Global corporate citizenship: Working with governments and civil society', *Foreign Affairs* 87(1), 107–118.

Scott, B., 2015, 'Visions of a techno-leviathan: The politics of the bitcoin blockchain', viewed 27 February 2019, from http://www.e-ir.info/2014/06/01/visions-of-a-techno-leviathan-the-politics-of-the-bitcoin-blockchain/.

Seaford, R., 1994, *Reciprocity and ritual in tragedy: Homer and tragedy in the developing city-state*, Clarendon Press, Oxford.

Selby, A.M., 2012, 'Bishops, elders, and deacons in the Philippian church: Evidence of plurality, from Paul and Polycarp', *Perspectives in Religious Studies* 39(1), 79–94.

Seneca, 2008, *Dialogues and essays*, Oxford University Press, Oxford.

Seneca, 2010, *Selected letters*, Oxford University Press, Oxford.

Shane, S. & Hubbard, B., 2014, 'ISIS displaying a deft command of varied media', *New York Times*, p. 31, viewed 12 November 2019, from http://www.garyvollbracht.com/wp-content/uploads/14.08.31NYT-ISIS-Displaying-a-Deft-Command-of-Varied-Media.pdf.

SHE Index, n.d., *Official homage*, viewed 09 December 2020, from https://shecommunity.no/.

Sidgwick, H., 1874, *The methods of ethics*, viewed 21 August 2019, from http://www.earlymoderntexts.com/pdfs/sidgwick1874.pdf.

Singer, P., 1995, *Animal liberation*, Pimlico, London.

Singer, P., 2011, *Practical ethics*, 3rd edn., Cambridge University Press, Cambridge.

Skidelsky, R., 2010, *Keynes, the return of the master*, Penguin, London.

Smith, A., 2009, *The theory of moral sentiments*, Penguin, London.

Smith A., 2012, *An inquiry into the nature and causes of the wealth of nations*, Wordsworth Classics of World Literature, London.

Smithies, A., 1951, 'Schumpeter and Keynes', *The Review of Economics and Statistics* 33(2), 163–169. https://doi.org/10.2307/1925880

Spufford, P., 2002, *Power and profit: The merchant in medieval Europe*, Thames & Hudson, London.

Stacey, R.D., 2011, *Strategic management and organizational dynamics, the challenge of complexity*, 6th edn., Pearson Education, Edinburgh.

Standage, T., 2010, *An edible history of humanity*, Atlantic Books, London.

Stango, V., 2012, 'Are payday lending markets competitive?', *Regulation* 35(3), 26.

Statista, n.d., *Official homepage*, viewed 02 December 2020, from http://www.statista.com/.

Stiastny, T., 2014, *Dictionary of finance and banking*, Oxford University Press, Oxford.

Stiglitz, J.E. & Charlton, A., 2005, *Fair trade for all. How trade can promote development*, Oxford University Press, Oxford.

Stone, A., 2009, 'John Calvin, the work ethic, and vocation', *Western Reformed Seminary Journal* 16(2), 24–30.

Strathern, P., 2005, *The Medici: Godfathers of the Renaissance*, Random House, New York, NY.

Stringham, E., 2002, 'The emergence of the London Stock Exchange as a self-policing club', *Journal of Private Enterprise* 17(2), 1–19.

Sutton, A., 2008, *Christian bioethics, a guide for the perplexed*, T & T Clark, London.

Swinton, J. & Mowat, H., 2006, *Practical theology and qualitative research*, SCM, London.

Takahashi, C., Yamagishi, T., Liu, J.H., Wang, F., Lin, Y. & Yu, S., 2008, 'The intercultural trust paradigm: Studying joint cultural interaction and social exchange in real time over the Internet', *International Journal of Intercultural Relations* 32(3), 215-228. https://doi.org/10.1016/j.ijintrel.2007.11.003

Tanner, C. & Wölfing Kast, S., 2003, 'Promoting sustainable consumption: Determinants of green purchases by Swiss consumers', *Psychology & Marketing* 20(10), 883-902. https://doi.org/10.1002/mar.10101

Tappert, T.G. (ed.), 2007, *Selected writings of Martin Luther*, Fortress Press, Minneapolis, MN.

Taylor, M., 2014, '"Being useful" after the ivory tower: Combining research and activism with the Brixton pound', *Area* 46(3), 305-312. https://doi.org/10.1111/area.12117

Temin, P., 2004, 'Financial intermediation in the early Roman Empire', *The Journal of Economic History* 64(3), 705-733. https://doi.org/10.1017/S0022050704002943

The Business Research Company, n.d., *Official homepage*, viewed 19 November 2020, from https://www.thebusinessresearchcompany.com/.

The International Ecotourism Society, n.d., *Official homepage*, viewed 15 June 2020, from https://ecotourism.org/.

Thompson, J.G.S.S., 1996, 'Desire', in I.H. Marshall, A.R. Millard, J.I. Packer & D.J. Wiseman (eds.), *New Bible dictionary*, 3rd edn., p. 272, Inter Varsity Press, Nottingham.

Thornton, M.K. & Thornton, R.L., 1990, 'The financial crisis of AD 33: A Keynesian depression?', *The Journal of Economic History* 50(3), 655-662. https://doi.org/10.1017/S0022050700037207

Thurneysen, E., 2010, *A theology of pastoral care*, Wipf and Stock, Eugene, OR.

Tidball, D., 1997, *Skilful shepherds: Explorations in pastoral theology*, Apollos, Nottingham.

Tonry, M., 2001, 'Symbol, substance, and severity in western penal policies', *Punishment & Society* 3(4), 517-536. https://doi.org/10.1177/14624740122228401

Trapido, S., 1978, 'Landlord and tenant in a colonial economy: The Transvaal 1880-1910', *Journal of Southern African Studies* 5(1), 26-58. https://doi.org/10.1080/03057077808707993

Treggiari, S., 1979, 'Lower class women in the Roman economy', *Florilegium* 1, 65-86. https://doi.org/10.3138/flor.1.006

Trentmann, F., 2004, 'Beyond consumerism: New historical perspectives on consumption', *Journal of Contemporary History* 39(3), 373-401. https://doi.org/10.1177/0022009404044446

Trianosky, G., 1990, 'What is virtue ethics all about?', *American Philosophical Quarterly* 27(4), 335-344.

Triodos Bank, n.d., *Official homepage*, viewed 12 April 2019, from https://www.triodos.com/.

Twardowski, T., 2010, 'Chances, perspectives and dangers of GMO in agriculture', *Journal of Fruit and Ornamental Plant Research* 18(2), 63-69.

UNEP Finance Initiative, n.d., *Official homepage*, viewed 09 August 2020, from https://www.unepfi.org/.

United Nations, n.d., *Official homepage*, viewed 22 March 2019, from https://www.un.org/en/.

United Nations Food and Agriculture Organization (UNFAO), 2012, *Statistical yearbook 2012*, viewed 06 September 2019, from http://www.fao.org/docrep/015/i2490e/i2490e00.htm.

Università di Bologna, n.d., *Official homepage*, viewed 14 January 2020, from https://www.unibo.it/en.

Université de Genève, n.d., *Official homepage*, viewed 14 January 2020, from https://www.unige.ch/.

University of Malaya, n.d., *Official homepage*, 14 January 2020, viewed from https://www.um.edu.my/.

University of Salford, n.d., *Official homepage*, 14 January 2020, viewed from http://www.salford.ac.uk/.

References

US Census Bureau, 2008, *Americans with disabilities: 2005*, viewed 17 April 2019, from https://www.census.gov/en.html.

Valeri, M., 1997, 'Religion, discipline, and the economy in Calvin's Geneva', *The Sixteenth Century Journal* 28(1), 123-142. https://doi.org/10.2307/2543226

Van Aelst, P. & Walgrave, S., 2002, 'New media, new movements? The role of the internet in shaping the "anti-globalization" movement', *Information, Communication & Society* 5(4), 465-493. https://doi.org/10.1080/13691180208538801

Vanclay, F., 2004, 'The triple bottom line and impact assessment: How do TBL, EIA, SIA, SEA and EMS relate to each other?', *Journal of Environmental Assessment Policy and Management* 6(3), 265-288. https://doi.org/10.1142/S1464333204001729

Van de Mieroop, M., 1992, 'Society and enterprise in Old Babylonian Ur', *Berliner Beiträge zum Vorderen Orient*, vol. 12, D. Reimer, Berlin.

VanDrunen, L.D., 2012, 'The two kingdoms and the social order: Political and legal theory in light of God's covenant with Noah', *Journal of Markets and Morality* 14(2), 445-462.

VanDrunen, L.D., 2015, 'Debt, risk, and grace', *Journal of Markets and Morality* 18(1), 61-80.

Van Ness, D.W., 1995, 'Capital punishment', in D.J. Atkinson, D.F. Field, A.F. Holmes & O. O'Donovan (eds.), *New dictionary of Christian ethics & pastoral theology*, pp. 214-215, InterVarsity Press, Downers Grove, IL.

Van Oosterzee, J.J., 1878, *Practical theology: A manual for theological students*, Hodder and Stoughton, London.

Var, T., Brayley, R. & Korsay, M., 1989, 'Tourism and world peace: Case of Turkey', *Annals of Tourism Research* 16(2), 282-286. https://doi.org/10.1016/0160-7383(89)90078-9

Varoufakis, Y., 2016, *And the weak suffer what they must? Europe, austerity and the threat to global stability*, Penguin Random House, London.

Veblen, T., 2007, *The theory of the leisure class*, Oxford University Press, Oxford.

Veenhof, K.R., 2010, 'Ancient Assur: The city, its traders, and its commercial network', *Journal of the Economic and Social History of the Orient* 53(1), 39. https://doi.org/10.1163/002249910X12573963244205

Velde, F.R. & Weber, W.E., 2000, 'A model of bimetallism', *Journal of Political Economy* 108(6), 1210-1234. https://doi.org/10.1086/317687

Verhagen, E. & Sauer, P.J., 2005, 'The Groningen protocol - Euthanasia in severely ill newborns', *New England Journal of Medicine* 352(10), 959-962. https://doi.org/10.1056/NEJMp058026

Victor, P.A., 2008, *Managing without growth, slower by design, not disaster*, Edgar Elgar, Cheltenham.

Von Reden, S., 2010, *Money in classical antiquity*, Cambridge University Press, Cambridge.

Vorster, J.M., 2007, *Christian attitude in the South African liberal democracy*, Potchefstroom Theological Publications, Potchefstroom.

Vorster, J.M., 2017a, *Ethical perspectives on human rights*, Potchefstroom Theological Publications, Potchefstroom.

Vorster, J.M., 2017b, 'Hermeneutic and ethics: The quest for a "biblical ethic"', in S.P. Van der Walt & N. Vorster (eds.), *Reformed theology today: Practical-theological, missiological and ethical perspectives*, pp. 139-154, AOSIS, Cape Town.

Vorster, J.M., 2019, 'The theological-ethical implications of Galatians 3:28 for a Christian perspective on equality as a foundational value in the human rights discourse', *In die Skriflig* 53(1), 1-9. https://doi.org/10.4102/ids.v53i1.2494

Waldau, P., 2006, 'Religion and animals', in P. Singer (ed.), *In defense of animals, the second wave*, pp. 69-83, Blackwell, Malden, MA.

Walsh, A., 2004, 'The morality of the market and the medieval schoolmen', *Politics, Philosophy and Economics*, 3(2), 241-259. https://doi.org/10.1177/1470594X04042967

Weatherford, J., 1997, *The history of money*, Three Rivers Press, New York, NY.

Weber, M., 1978, *Economy and society.*, 2 vols., University of California Press, Berkeley, CA.

Weber, M., 2012, *The protestant ethic and the spirit of capitalism [1905]*, Renaissance Classics, Provo, UT.

Wesley, J., 2018, *The ministerial office*, viewed 06 August 2020, from http://www.umcmission.org/Find-Resources/John-Wesley-Sermons/Sermon-115-The-Ministerial-Office.

Westminster, 2015, *The Westminster larger catechism*, Christian Classics Ethereal Library, Grand Rapids, MI, viewed 19 May 2019, from http://www.ccel.org/ccel/anonymous/westminster2.

Whipp, M., 2013, *SCM study guide: Pastoral theology*, SCM Press, London.

Wikström, P., 2010, 'Sustainability and organizational activities – Three approaches', *Sustainable Development* 18(2), 99–107. https://doi.org/10.1002/sd.449

Wilken, R.L., 2019, *Liberty in the things of God: The Christian origins of religious freedom*, Yale University Press, Newhaven, CT.

Wilmarth, A.E., 2004, 'OCC's preemption rules exceed the agency's authority and present a serious threat to the dual banking system and consumer protection', *Annual Review of Banking and Financial Law* 23, 225–364.

Wilson, E.O., 1992, *The diversity of life*, The Belknap Press of Harvard University Press, Cambridge, MA.

Wilson, G., Furniss, P. & Kimbowa, R. (eds.), 2010, *Environment, development and sustainability. Perspectives and cases, from around the world*, Oxford University Press, New York, NY.

Wirzba, N., 2019, *Food and faith: A theology of eating*, 2nd edn., Cambridge University Press, Cambridge.

Witte, J., 2007, *The reformation of rights,* Cambridge University Press, Cambridge.

Wolter, M. & Brawley, R.L., 2015, *Paul: An outline of his theology*, Baylor University Press, Waco, TX.

Woods, T.E., 2005, *The church and the market*, Lexington Books, Lanham, MD.

Woods, T.E., 2012, *How the Catholic church built the western civilization*, Regnery, Washington, DC.

World Bank Group, n.d., *Official homepage*, viewed 22 April 2020, from http://www.worldbank.org/.

World Health Organization, 2011, *World report on disability 2011*, viewed 17 September 2020, from www.who.int.

Wright, C.J.H., 1995, 'Jubilee', in D.J. Atkinson, D.F. Field, A.F. Holmes & O. O'Donovan (eds.), *New dictionary of Christian ethics and pastoral theology*, pp. 512–513, InterVarsity Press, Downers Grove, IL.

Wright, D.P., 2009a, *Inventing God's law: How the covenant code of the Bible used and revised the laws of Hammurabi*, Oxford University Press, New York, NY.

Wright, J.L., 2009b, 'The commemoration of defeat and the formation of a nation in the Hebrew Bible', *Prooftexts* 29(3), 433–472. https://doi.org/10.2979/pft.2009.29.3.433

Wykes, M., 2003, 'Devaluing the scholastics: Calvin's ethics of usury', *Calvin Theological Journal* 38(1), 27–51.

Young, K.S., 2004, 'Internet addiction: A new clinical phenomenon and its consequences', *American Behavioral Scientist* 48(4), 402–415. https://doi.org/10.1177/0002764204270278

Zeller, M. & Sharma, M., 2000, 'Many borrow, more save, and all insure: Implications for food and micro-finance policy', *Food Policy* 25(2), 143–167. https://doi.org/10.1016/S0306-9192(99)00065-2

Zinman, J., 2009, 'Debit or credit?', *Journal of Banking & Finance* 33(2), 358–366. https://doi.org/10.1016/j.jbankfin.2008.08.009

Ziskind, J.R., 1974, 'Sea loans at Ugarit', *Journal of the American Oriental Society* 94(1), 134–137. https://doi.org/10.2307/599741

Zou, H.F., 1994, '"The spirit of capitalism" and long-run growth', *European Journal of Political Economy* 10(2), 279–293. https://doi.org/10.1016/0176-2680(94)90020-5

Index

A

accept, 2-3, 12-13, 23, 31, 76, 80, 83, 87, 89, 108, 116, 125, 130, 133, 144, 162, 165, 168, 170, 200-201, 205, 215, 229-230, 240, 251, 254, 256, 260

acceptance, 8, 11-13, 21, 23, 26, 32, 62, 78, 92, 107, 125, 132, 136, 150, 157, 188, 202, 226, 255

Acts, 7, 72, 82, 85, 94, 102-103, 109, 113, 146, 156, 174, 178-179, 183

Africa, 29-30, 53, 94, 167, 169, 179, 229

age, 16, 18, 25, 36, 49-51, 107-108, 112, 169, 171, 174, 228, 232-233, 245

animal welfare, 119, 182-183, 186-187, 195, 236, 238

attitude, 11-12, 93-95, 104, 116, 118, 201, 212-213, 217, 261

awareness, 4-5, 112, 241

B

banking practices, 5, 47, 63-65, 68, 118-119, 139, 194-195, 197, 199, 201, 206, 211-214, 216, 230, 246, 257, 261

behaviour, 60, 78, 89, 131, 194, 246, 253

borrowing, 33, 46, 50, 59, 119-123, 125, 195, 197-199, 202-203, 208-209, 212, 214-217

business, 1, 4, 11, 14, 48, 55, 60-61, 118, 121-122, 126-129, 132-134, 140, 190, 198, 201, 206, 213, 226-227, 231-233, 240, 245, 253-255, 257-258, 261-262

C

care, 21, 47, 62, 71-73, 97-98, 100, 103, 105, 108-111, 113, 123-125, 127, 133-134, 138, 140, 144, 146, 157, 173, 175, 182-187, 194, 199, 211, 231, 237, 240, 245

challenges, 23, 66, 76, 112, 145, 161, 186-187, 234

change, 17-18, 28, 37, 83, 94, 168, 187, 189, 196, 218, 230, 250-251

character, 10, 72, 76, 83, 87, 90, 92, 102, 110, 128, 142, 148, 163, 177, 180, 187, 196, 201, 220, 258

characteristics, 60, 67, 78, 141, 169, 171, 203, 228

child, 97, 104, 160, 163, 172-174, 227, 233, 245

children, 8, 24, 97, 99-101, 160-161, 165-166, 169-170, 172-174, 223, 227, 234, 242, 245

Christian banking, 1, 5-7, 33, 47, 68-71, 118-119, 163, 195-196, 202-204, 206, 212-213, 215, 217, 223, 225-226, 229-234, 239, 241, 245-247, 249-262

church, 11-12, 24, 53, 68, 73, 100-103, 105-113, 116, 128, 131, 151, 156-157, 164-166, 178, 181, 188, 222, 224, 228

citizenship, 61

community, 5, 27, 48, 57, 61, 67, 93, 95, 105-106, 110-115, 128, 132, 168, 232-233, 238, 242, 251

concept, 2, 9-10, 21, 34, 36-37, 39, 42, 44-45, 49, 51, 64-65, 70, 79-80, 85, 92, 117, 120-122, 129, 142, 148, 151, 156, 164, 175-177, 188, 206, 220, 236, 239, 241, 259

constructive ethics, 71

context, 9, 34, 51, 72, 78, 84, 95-96, 100, 105-108, 116-118, 120-121, 127, 129, 134-138, 140, 144, 146-147, 149, 151, 154, 159, 161, 163-164, 167, 169, 182, 187, 194, 220, 230, 241, 254, 256

contextual, 116, 188, 226

covenant, 99, 130, 146, 188, 222, 236, 239-240

create, 10, 15, 21, 33, 35, 44, 49, 61, 63, 79, 87, 140, 175, 207, 210, 215, 217, 241, 244, 250, 255, 260

creating, 4, 18, 21-22, 29, 37, 57-59, 64-65, 67, 86, 108, 169, 171, 213, 247, 257

creation, 3, 11, 14, 18, 23, 26, 29, 44, 54, 56-57, 60, 92, 94, 111, 118, 137, 141-143, 145-146, 155, 158-160, 162, 164, 169, 175, 182-187, 210, 222, 226, 236, 239-241, 249, 254

crypto currency, 33

CSR, 4, 47, 61, 67-69, 233, 239, 250, 252

culture, 24, 36, 48-49, 62, 72

D

defined, 1, 8, 49, 76, 78, 125-126, 129, 152-153, 190, 226, 258

deontology, 71-75, 82-85, 95-96, 252

develop, 10, 40, 56, 63, 66, 96, 131, 195, 226

developing, 3, 19, 34-35, 37, 50, 54-56, 59, 67, 69, 92, 107-108, 111, 113, 123, 128, 167, 174-175, 186, 196-197, 223, 226, 231-232, 259, 261

development, 8-10, 12-14, 16-17, 19, 21, 28, 30, 33, 35, 47, 49, 54-58, 63, 66-67, 69, 73, 78, 94, 105-112, 115, 118, 120, 132-133, 161-162, 165, 167, 169, 174, 178, 182, 198, 203, 207, 223-224, 227, 229-232, 236-237, 243, 247, 253-255

dignity, 18, 95, 142, 164, 169, 171-172, 174, 201, 228, 233

diversity, 232-233, 236

Index

E

economic, 1-2, 4, 7-36, 38-39, 43, 45-46, 48, 50, 52, 56, 58-59, 61-63, 112, 120, 123-125, 128-132, 137, 139, 163, 174, 177, 200-201, 210-211, 223, 227, 236, 240, 258
education, 1, 24-26, 58, 70, 108, 110, 123, 141, 164-166, 173-174, 185, 222-223, 227-232, 241, 245, 260
employees, 60, 249, 251
environment, 3, 29, 69, 182, 185-187, 223, 228, 236-241, 244, 260
equal opportunities, 119, 169, 195, 223, 232-233
ethical banking, 47, 67
ethical, 3-6, 11, 13, 47, 61, 64, 67-69, 71-73, 75-78, 81-86, 88-89, 91-95, 116-121, 123, 125, 135, 140, 143-146, 150, 154-155, 161-162, 172, 181-182, 195, 219, 226-228, 233-234, 243, 249-254, 257, 259-261
ethics, 1, 6, 9, 63, 65, 67-69, 71-77, 80-81, 84-86, 88-89, 91, 94-96, 116, 128, 131, 141, 163, 191, 226, 233
Europe, 13, 21, 24, 26, 28, 38-40, 51-56, 62-63, 67, 107-108, 128, 166-167, 175, 198, 224
exploitation, 14, 28, 128, 136, 172, 182, 189, 227

F

families, 2, 4, 14, 36, 53-54, 90, 123-124, 133, 180, 188, 190, 219, 223, 233, 245
family, 11, 23-24, 45, 74, 97-98, 100, 124-126, 134, 141, 155-156, 164-165, 171, 182, 187-189, 191, 200, 222-223, 241-242, 245
father, 95, 97, 101, 104, 166, 173-175, 187-188, 190
fiat money, 33, 42-43
formation, 19, 41, 98, 112

G

Galatians, 105, 170-171, 190
globalisation, 7, 27-29
gold standard, 21, 33, 42-43, 45-46, 57
government investors, 7
government, 5, 7, 21-22, 24-27, 40-46, 51, 53, 56, 62, 90, 147, 150-153, 168-169, 179-181, 197, 202, 209, 218-219, 221, 227
growth, 19, 21, 25, 28, 30, 40, 48, 57-58, 66, 107, 110, 155, 223, 239-241, 243, 245
guidelines, 5-6, 90, 95, 103, 249, 252, 254-259, 261

H

holistic, 15, 116, 118, 259, 262
human rights, 119, 160, 163-164, 166-167, 169, 171-173, 175-176, 179, 183-185, 195, 226-227, 229-231, 233, 250
human, 1, 8-9, 12, 15, 17, 20, 23, 25, 27, 29-31, 33-35, 47, 58, 63, 73-80, 83, 86, 88, 91-92, 95-98, 102, 113, 118-120, 130, 132, 136, 138, 140-146, 148, 155-156, 158-164, 166-167, 169-179, 182-188, 193, 195, 211, 218, 221-224, 226-227, 229-231, 233, 235-238, 240, 244, 250, 253
humanity, 7, 15, 30-31, 34, 78, 90, 94, 102, 141-144, 150, 155-156, 158, 162, 164-165, 168-169, 173, 175, 179, 182, 184-185, 188

I

imago Dei, 119, 141-147, 159, 162, 188, 192, 195, 218-219, 221
importance, 4, 8, 21, 34, 45, 58-59, 62, 64, 88, 102-103, 106, 108-110, 116-118, 120, 125, 134, 139, 142, 149-150, 154, 163, 165, 174-175, 177-178, 183, 187-188, 192, 196, 200, 211, 213, 218, 233-234, 236, 241-243, 251, 253, 257-260
inclusion, 86, 113, 117, 125, 175, 232-233, 256
inclusive, 94-95, 106, 114, 117-118
independent currency, 33, 44
indexing, 249, 253, 255, 257, 259-260
inequality, 8, 20, 30-32, 171, 228
influence, 4, 7-8, 24, 26-27, 30, 46, 49, 52, 54, 57, 62, 78, 107, 109, 112-113, 132-133, 140, 156, 160, 180, 182, 187, 232, 236-237, 240, 242, 246, 256, 260
instruction, 98, 100-101, 103-105, 110-111, 124, 130, 134, 137, 139, 148, 150, 153, 156, 165, 167, 171, 181, 184, 189, 205
integrity, 124, 137, 142, 186, 242
Interest, 1-5, 9-14, 16, 21, 24, 34, 40, 50-53, 56-57, 59-61, 63-64, 66, 68-69, 71-72, 75, 77-79, 96, 103, 105, 114-115, 119-121, 123, 125-132, 134-136, 144, 148, 152, 154, 161, 163-164, 167-168, 171-173, 186, 189-190, 192-193, 195, 198, 200-201, 203-208, 210, 212-215, 220, 224, 226, 231-233, 239-242, 245, 247, 252, 257-258, 261
interests, 14, 40-41, 48, 54-55, 60, 80-81, 161, 200, 211-212, 218, 244
interpret, 115, 128, 216, 236
interpretation, 76, 78, 86, 95, 98, 120-121, 124-125, 127-128, 140-145, 149-150, 167, 169, 172-173, 177-178, 184, 188, 190, 193, 197, 199, 201, 206, 211, 213-214, 216, 219, 229, 241, 257
investment management, 1, 3, 5
Islam, 2, 65-66
Israel, 97-99, 124, 154-155, 176, 181

J

justice, 10, 12, 74, 78, 80-81, 95, 123, 129, 144, 146, 153, 170, 228

L

language, 25, 48, 109, 116, 159, 177, 229
laws, 20, 25, 48, 78, 87, 89, 92-93, 120, 126, 158, 165, 168, 180-181, 184, 189
leadership, 96, 98-100, 103, 105-106, 110, 115, 117-118, 201-202, 214, 255
legislation, 10, 25, 79, 204
lending, 9, 46, 50-51, 59, 65, 119-123, 125-127, 195-197, 199-202, 204, 208, 210-213, 216-217
Leviticus, 48, 124, 126, 135, 143-144, 171, 176

M

maturity gap, 47, 59-60
media, 22, 138, 167, 169, 187-190, 230-231, 241-243
mission, 105, 156, 256
money, 9-10, 12, 21, 33-54, 58-59, 64, 82, 117, 120-121, 125-129, 133, 135-137, 172-173, 177, 191, 193, 198-199, 201-204, 206-210, 212, 214-216
Moneylending, 1-2, 5, 9, 13, 33, 47, 59, 120, 123, 125, 127, 140, 196
moral, 1-5, 12-14, 47, 68, 72, 74-75, 78-83, 85-93, 95-96, 116-118, 121-122, 128-129, 136, 146, 152, 154, 161-162, 164-165, 169, 171, 176, 178, 180, 187, 192-193, 195-199, 205, 215, 217, 219-221, 226-227, 233-234, 246, 255-256, 258
motivation, 40, 69, 88, 243

N

narrative, 8-9, 16, 24, 90, 98, 102, 118, 124, 128, 151, 156, 159, 180-181, 188
need, 1-2, 14, 19, 30-31, 36-37, 45-47, 52, 57, 60, 62-63, 65, 68, 70, 72, 75, 80-82, 85, 87, 94-95, 97, 101, 103, 107, 110-111, 117, 119-122, 126-127, 134, 136-137, 139, 143, 145, 150, 154, 162, 167-168, 174, 176, 178-179, 185-187, 192, 196-198, 201, 203-206, 208, 212-214, 216, 223, 229, 236, 245, 250, 252-260
needs, 7, 10, 19, 22-23, 25-27, 31, 33-34, 36, 54, 58, 64-65, 68, 74, 92-93, 110-111, 116-117, 121, 123, 126, 131, 138, 141, 143, 147, 151, 159, 162, 166, 172, 175, 179, 183, 185-186, 188, 191, 196-198, 201, 203, 206, 213, 216-217, 222-223, 229, 236, 238-239, 242, 245, 247, 257, 261

P

paradigm, 2, 6-9, 11, 13, 15, 17-20, 22-26, 28, 30-32, 38, 42-44, 63-64, 66, 69, 72-73, 76, 78, 81, 85-89, 91, 93-95, 114, 116-117, 129, 133-134, 136, 147, 150, 153, 161, 172, 181, 184, 189, 196, 204-206, 218, 220, 230, 232-233, 239-240, 250-261
parents, 90, 166, 173, 176
participation, 24-26, 30, 56, 66, 75, 80, 92-93, 96, 111-112, 118, 147, 150, 154-155, 163, 182, 192, 198, 218-219, 221, 223, 228, 231-233, 237, 240-242, 244-245, 253
pastoral principles, 1, 5, 103, 111, 113, 118, 195, 208, 249, 261
Paul, 85, 91-92, 102-105, 144, 190-192
peace, 94-95, 152, 154, 191, 224
people, 14, 16, 18, 22, 25, 30, 35, 45-46, 49, 78-80, 85-86, 89, 91-93, 97-99, 102, 106, 108, 110, 115, 117-118, 120-121, 127, 129, 132, 136-137, 139, 144, 152, 158, 160, 167, 170, 179-180, 191, 193, 197, 200, 216, 218, 224, 229, 233, 235-236, 241, 245, 251
philosophy, 2, 8-9, 14-15, 17, 19, 21, 23, 29, 31-32, 45, 47, 61-62, 64, 71-76, 79-80, 85, 87-88, 147-148, 151, 165, 169, 251
politics, 9, 35, 42, 229-230
poor, 11, 15-16, 18-19, 22-23, 25-26, 30, 41, 67, 82, 111, 120-121, 123, 130, 133, 135-136, 170, 172-173, 177, 181, 186, 196, 205, 223, 236
poverty, 8, 11, 13, 18, 25, 28, 30-31, 51, 63, 67, 130-131, 136, 172, 174, 177, 222-223, 236
power, 2, 8, 14, 24, 26, 37, 50, 52, 54, 62, 92, 102, 116, 144, 152, 180, 227, 242
practical theology, 1, 6, 73, 112, 116, 118
process, 18, 105, 167, 210, 229, 239-240, 259, 261
protection, 30, 55, 65, 108, 123, 170, 174, 198, 204, 212, 241, 245
purpose, 4, 11-12, 19, 74, 80, 82-84, 86-87, 89, 95, 124, 140, 143, 166, 191, 197, 211, 218, 220, 233

R

recognition, 14, 169
recruitment, 232, 249
relation, 25, 77, 90, 147, 157, 159, 168, 185, 200, 204, 213, 232, 246
relationship, 54-55, 92, 96-98, 101, 115, 124, 143, 171, 178, 188, 192
research, 68-69, 161, 174, 182-183, 193, 202, 221, 235, 239, 245, 261
resources, 7-10, 16, 19-20, 23, 28, 30-31, 139, 174, 194, 239-241, 245, 253, 261
responsibilities, 101, 103, 105, 109, 142, 188, 255
responsibility, 4, 14, 18, 31-32, 61, 90, 97-98, 104-105, 110-111, 124, 144-146, 151, 183-184, 202, 244
rights, 10-11, 55, 101, 112, 119, 142, 160, 163-164, 166-167, 169-173, 175-179, 182-185, 195, 209-210, 226-231, 233, 250

Index

risk, 2, 14, 16, 40, 51, 55, 59, 64, 66, 124, 129-134, 167, 198-201, 203-204, 206-215, 223-224, 255

S

salvation, 68, 78, 92-93, 98, 103, 152, 252
scarcity paradigm, 7-9, 11, 15, 17-18, 20, 24-25, 28, 30-31, 239
school, 20, 22, 72, 76, 113, 164, 166, 202, 231
schools, 71, 75, 84, 164-165, 230
services, 7-8, 10-11, 20, 25-26, 28-29, 44, 46, 52-53, 108, 128, 132, 140, 172, 215-217, 225-226, 228-231, 233, 235-246
sharia banking, 2, 47, 62-64, 66
social technology, 33-34, 42, 45-46, 58, 211
societies, 1-3, 8, 13, 15-16, 19, 25, 31-32, 35-36, 38-39, 45, 49, 56-57, 59, 67, 98, 107, 120, 138, 148-149, 151, 164, 174, 178, 197, 210, 228, 242
society, 3, 8-16, 18-20, 22, 24-26, 31, 33-37, 39-41, 45, 47, 50-51, 57-60, 62-63, 65, 68, 72-73, 75, 79-83, 91, 94, 99-102, 107-109, 113, 118, 120, 122, 125, 127-128, 131, 133, 137, 139-140, 145, 148, 151, 162, 166, 168-170, 173-176, 178, 181, 187-188, 190, 192, 198-199, 206-207, 209, 211-213, 223, 228-229, 232, 239, 241-242, 244-246
South Africa, 94, 167, 169, 179, 229
space, 75, 91, 169
stakeholder construct, 47, 60-61
status, 18, 23, 92, 124, 164, 198
sufficiency paradigm, 7-8, 18-20, 22-23, 26, 31-32, 240
supervisory board, 66, 249, 252-256

T

teach, 101, 165-166
theology, 1, 6, 18, 73, 88-89, 92, 96, 100-101, 104, 106-118, 128, 132-133, 142, 150-151, 155, 157, 166, 171, 181-183, 187, 228
training, 92, 239, 249, 255, 260

U

utilitarianism, 71-72, 74-83, 96

V

value, 4-6, 9, 15, 34, 36, 38-39, 41-46, 49-50, 59-60, 64-65, 72, 76, 78-82, 84-85, 102-103, 126, 132-133, 141, 145-146, 157-158, 160-161, 163-164, 166-168, 170-171, 173-174, 176, 179, 188, 190, 198-199, 201, 203, 206-209, 215, 217, 223, 233, 241, 245
values, 35, 39, 49, 61, 63, 65, 67-69, 75, 79-80, 85-86, 108, 114, 125, 133, 140, 145, 152, 160, 162, 164, 167, 173, 175-176, 187-189, 191, 195, 198, 210, 219-220, 222, 226-228, 230, 240-242, 245-246, 257
violence, 144, 151, 153-154, 181, 218, 222
virtue ethics, 71-77, 94

W

welfare state, 7, 13, 25
well-being, 16, 18, 74, 78, 125, 155-156, 174, 190-191, 200-201, 209-210, 235, 241, 244
worship, 50, 100, 106, 168-169
written, 34, 91, 93, 103, 127, 130, 134, 137-138, 190, 194

www.ingramcontent.com/pod-product-compliance
Lightning Source LLC
Chambersburg PA
CBHW081145230426
43664CB00018B/2802